Capitalism and modern social theory

An analysis of the writings of Marx, Durkheim and Max Weber

Capitalism and modern social theory

An analysis of the writings of Marx, Durkheim and Max Weber

ANTHONY GIDDENS
Fellow of King's College Cambridge

Cambridge at the University Press 1971

Published by the Syndics of the Cambridge University Press
Bentley House, 200 Euston Road, London NW1 2DB
American Branch: 32 East 57th Street, New York, N.Y.10022

Library of Congress Catalogue Card Number: 70-161291

ISBN: 0 521 08293 5

Printed in Great Britain by
The Eastern Press Limited
London and Reading

Contents

Acknowledgements

I wish to express my indebtedness to the following persons, all of whom have either read or commented verbally upon papers which I have drawn upon for parts of this book: John Barnes, Basil Bernstein, John Carroll, Percy Cohen, Norbert Elias, Geoffrey Ingham, Terry Johnson, Gavin Mackenzie, Ilya Neustadt and Irving Zeitlin. I should like to thank in particular those who have looked at the manuscript as a whole: Martin Albrow, Tom Bottomore, David Lockwood, Steven Lukes, and John Rex. My gratitude is also due to Barbara Leonard, Laurette Mackenzie and Brigitte Prentice; and to my wife, Jane Giddens.

Preface

Die Vernunft hat immer existiert, nur
nicht immer in der vernünftigen Form

Marx

This book is written in the belief that there is a widespread feeling among sociologists that contemporary social theory stands in need of a radical revision. Such a revision must begin from a reconsideration of the works of those writers who established the principal frames of reference of modern sociology. In this connection, three names rank above all others: Marx, Durkheim and Max Weber. My objectives in this work are twofold: firstly, to set out a precise, yet comprehensive, analysis of the sociological ideas of each of these three authors; and secondly, to examine some of the main points of divergence between Marx's characteristic views on the one hand, and those of the two later writers on the other. I do not pretend to provide any sort of overall evaluation of the relationship between 'Marxist' and 'bourgeois' sociology, but I hope that this book may help to accomplish the preparatory task of clearing a way through the profuse tangle of assertions and counter-assertions which have surrounded the debate on this issue. I have, inevitably, covered a great deal of familiar ground. However, recent scholarship has illuminated basic aspects of the writings of all three authors, and I believe that my analysis departs considerably from some of the established works in the field.

I do not, of course, wish to argue that the writings of the authors discussed in this book represent the only significant streams of social thought which have become embodied into sociology. On the contrary, the most striking characteristic of social thought over the hundred years from 1820 to 1920 is the very plethora of diverse forms of theory which were developed over that period. The works of Marx's contemporaries, such as Tocqueville, Comte and Spencer, continue to have a definite relevance to the problems of modern sociology, and it would perhaps have been more logical to have included these authors as the subject of detailed discussion in this volume. I decided against this, partly from reasons of space, and partly because the influence of Marx today is so much greater than any of these writers (and rightly so, in terms of the more profound intellectual content of Marx's works). Moreover, most of the dominant branches of modern social theory can be traced, although with numerous intermediate modifications and extensions, to the three authors upon whom I have concentrated in this book. Marx's works, obviously, are the primary source of the various forms of contemporary neo-Marxism; Durkheim's writings may be identified as the dominant inspiration lying behind 'structural-functionalism'; and at least some of the modern variants of phenomenology derive, directly or indirectly, from the writings of Max Weber. Moreover, within more specific fields of sociology, such as in the study of social stratification, religion, and so on, the influence of Marx, Durkheim and Weber has been fundamental.

As Durkheim himself pointed out in a preface to a book on Kant by his friend and colleague Hamelin, anyone who wishes to portray the thought of men of a different time to his own, faces a certain dilemma. Either he preserves the original terminology in which the author couched his works, in which case he runs the risk that his exposition appears outdated, and hence irrelevant to modern times; or he consciously modernises his terms, and faces the danger that his analysis will be untrue to the ideas of the writer concerned. It says much for the contemporary relevance of the social thought of the three authors discussed in this book that, in analysing their work, this dilemma does not offer difficulties of an acute kind. Where there are problems of this sort, I have opted to preserve the original phraseology. But in the case of the writers whose works are analysed in this volume, the main difficulties which are posed concern the rendition of culturally specific German or French terms into English. Terms such as *Geist* or *représentation collective* have no satisfactory English equivalents, and themselves express some of the differences in social development between Britain, Germany and France which are touched upon in the book. I have attempted to meet such problems, as far as is possible, by paying attention to the particular shades of meaning contained in the original texts, and in making quotations I have frequently modified the existing English translations.

This is not a critical, but an expository and comparative work. By using the present tense wherever possible, I have tried to emphasise the *contemporary* relevance of these authors. I have not sought to identify the weaknesses or ambiguities in the works of Marx, Durkheim or Weber, but rather have attempted to demonstrate the internal coherence which can be discerned in the writings of each author. I have also avoided, as far as possible, the scholarly travail of identifying the sources of the ideas comprised in the writings of the three figures. But inevitably, because all three wrote in a polemical vein, reference to other authors and traditions of thought cannot be eschewed altogether. I have given some degree of prominence to the social and historical 'rooting' of the three writers whose work is analysed here, since this is essential to the adequate interpretation of their writings. In various ways, of course, the personalities of the three men present dramatic contrasts, and are also no doubt relevant to the explication of the social theories which they formulated. I have ignored this, because it is not my objective to analyse in any amount of detail the 'causal' origins of the writings examined in the book. My concern is directed at disentangling some of the complex intellectual relationships among the three.

I have not attempted, in the concluding chapters, to compare the works of Durkheim and Weber directly, but instead have used Marx's writings as the point of reference. Assessment of the convergences and discrepancies between the writings of Marx on the one hand, and Durkheim and Weber on the other, is complicated by the fact of the retarded publication of Marx's early works. It is only relatively recently, since something like a decade after the death of Durkheim (1917) and Weber (1920), that it has become possible to assess the intellectual content of Marx's writings in the light of these works which, while they are of extreme importance to the evaluation of Marx's thought, were published for the first time almost a century after they were originally written. In my account of Marx's writings, I have tried to break away from the dichotomy between the works of the ' young ' and the ' mature ' Marx which has tyrannised most Marxist scholarship since the last war. Close scrutiny of the notes which Marx originally wrote as the basis of *Capital* in 1857–8 (*Grundrisse der Kritik der politischen Ökonomie*), leaves no doubt that Marx did not abandon the perspective which guided him in his early writings. But, in practice, those who have granted the truth of this, in analysing Marx's thought, have still tended to concentrate upon one part of Marx's writings to the exclusion of the other. I have attempted to provide a more balanced and integrated analysis, which preserves the basic place of *Capital* in Marx's life's work.

Apart from Marx himself, there can be few social thinkers whose fate it has been to be so persistently misunderstood as Durkheim. In his own day, Durkheim's theoretical writings were regarded by most critics as embodying an unacceptable metaphysical notion of the ' group mind '. More recent sympathetic accounts have largely dispelled this sort of misinterpretation, but have supplanted it with one which places virtually the whole emphasis upon Durkheim's functionalism. In this book, I have sought to rescue Durkheim as an historical thinker. Durkheim always emphasised the crucial significance of the historical dimension in sociology, and I believe that an appreciation of this leads to quite a different assessment of Durkheim's thought from that which is ordinarily given. Durkheim was *not* primarily concerned with ' the problem of order ', but with the problem of ' the *changing* nature of order ' in the context of a definite conception of social development.

Weber's writings are perhaps the most complex of those analysed in this book, and they defy easy treatment upon a general level. This fact has led, I think, to a failure in some secondary accounts to grasp the essential consistency in Weber's work. It is only an apparent paradox to say that the very *diversity* of Weber's contributions expresses the epistemological principles which unify them as a single corpus of writings. Weber's radical neo-Kantianism constitutes the underlying standpoint which combines his various essays in different fields within a coherent framework. It is this which, in certain important respects, creates irremediable divergences, some of which

I have analysed in the concluding chapters, between Weber's social theory and that of both Durkheim and Marx.

One final point should perhaps be made. I believe that sociologists must always be conscious of the social context within which theories are formulated. But to stress this does not entail acceptance of a wholly relativistic position, according to which the 'validity' of a given conception is only limited to the circumstances which gave rise to it. The fortunes of Marx's writings bear witness to this. I have argued that Marx's theory was formulated at an early stage of capitalist development, and that the subsequent experience of the leading countries of western Europe helped to fashion a version of 'Marxism' which differed substantially from that originally framed by Marx. Every form of practical theory has its Saint Paul, and within certain limits this may be regarded as inevitable. But to admit this is not to accept the stock view that the subsequent development of capitalism has 'falsified' Marx. Marx's writings today still offer a conception of society and history which it is valuable to contrast with those of other, later, authors. I do not believe that these divergences can be settled in the conventional sense in which scientific theories are 'confirmed' or 'invalidated' by empirical test. But neither are they refractory to empirical reference in the sense in which philosophical theories are. If the borderline between sociology and social philosophy is difficult to draw, it exists nonetheless. It is mistaken, I am certain, for sociologists to seek to restrict the scope of their discipline to those areas in which the empirical testing of propositions is easily applied. This is the way to a sterile formalism in which sociology becomes *Lebensfremd*, and thus irrelevant to the very issues to which the sociological perspective has most of all to contribute.

Anthony Giddens

3 March 1971

Introduction

In his inaugural lecture, delivered at Cambridge in 1895, Lord Acton expressed the conviction that there is 'an evident and intelligible line' which marks off the modern age in Europe from that which preceded it. The modern epoch did not succeed the mediaeval era 'by normal succession, with outward tokens of legitimate descent':

Unheralded, it founded a new order of things, under a law of innovation, sapping the ancient reign of continuity. In those days Columbus subverted the notions of the world, and reversed the conditions of production, wealth, and power; in those days Machiavelli released government from the restraint of law; Erasmus diverted the current of ancient learning from profane into Christian channels; Luther broke the chain of authority and tradition at the strongest link; and Copernicus erected an invincible power that set for ever the mark of progress upon the time that was to come... It was an awakening of new life; the world revolved in a different orbit, determined by influences unknown before.[1]

This shattering of the traditional order in Europe, Acton goes on to say, was the source of the development of historical science. Traditional society, by definition, continually looks back into the past, and the past is its present. But it is exactly because this is the case that there is no concern with 'history' as such; the continuity of yesterday and today minimises the clarity with which distinctions are drawn between what 'was' and what 'is'. The existence of a science of history, therefore, presupposes a world in which change is ubiquitous, and, more especially, one in which the past has become, in some degree, a burden from which men seek to be freed. In the modern era, men no longer accept the conditions of life into which they are born as necessarily given for all time, but attempt to impose their will upon reality in order to bend the future into a shape which conforms to their desires.

If Renaissance Europe gave rise to a concern with history, it was industrial Europe which provided the conditions for the emergence of sociology. It could be said that the French Revolution of 1789 was the catalyst between these two enormously complex sets of events. Britain was, according to the usual measures, the first country to acquire some degree of democratic government; but, in spite of the fact that this was not obtained without political revolution, the process of social and economic change which transformed society in Britain from the seventeenth century onwards was relatively progressive in character. The Revolution in France, by contrast, dramatically set off the privileged, aristocratic order of the *ancien régime*

---

[1] Lord Acton: *Lectures on Modern History* (London, 1960), p. 19.

against the vision of a new society which would realise general principles of justice and freedom. The Declaration of Human Rights, adopted in 1789, proposed that 'ignorance, disregard or contempt of the rights of man is the sole cause of public misfortune'. Thus the French Revolution, or so it seemed, finally extended the secular rationalism of the sixteenth and seventeenth centuries into the sphere of human society itself. But the political changes instituted by the 1789 Revolution in fact both expressed and signalled the occurrence of a more deeply-rooted reorganisation of society, and in this Britain again assumed the leading role. The transition from agrarian, handicraft production to an industrial economy founded upon the factory and the machine was one which began in Britain towards the end of the eighteenth century. The full effects of these changes were felt in the nineteenth century, both in Britain and in the other major countries of western Europe.

It has often been pointed out, of course, that the conjunction of events linking the political climate of the French Revolution and the economic changes wrought by the Industrial Revolution provided the context from within which sociology was formed. It is necessary to remember, however, how divergent were the experiences of the various countries in western Europe from the late eighteenth century onwards, because it is in the framework of these differences that the main traditions of social thought were created in the nineteenth century. Sociologists today talk blandly of the emergence of 'industrial society' in nineteenth-century Europe, ignoring the complexities which this process involved.

For each of the three major countries of western Europe – Britain, France and Germany – the closing decades of the eighteenth century were years of advancing economic prosperity. The pace of economic development in Britain in the late eighteenth century far outstripped that of the others; and during these years a number of profound technological innovations effected a metamorphosis in the organisation of cotton manufacture and thereby initiated the rapid spread of mechanisation and factory production. But at the turn of the nineteenth century, only a relatively confined sector of the British economy had been directly affected by the Industrial Revolution. Even two decades later, the picture was little different, save that cotton – fifty years before of minor significance in the economy as a whole – had assumed the role of Britain's leading manufacturing industry.[2] Not until the mid-point of the nineteenth century could Britain adequately be described as an 'industrial society'. The situation in France and Germany was very different from this. It would be quite wrong to call these countries, as in the common parlance of today, 'under-developed'.[3] In some respects, as for instance in standards of cultural achievement, especially in literature, art,

---

[2] Phyllis Deane and W. A. Cole: *British Economic Growth* (Cambridge, 1969), pp. 182–92.

[3] cf. David S. Landes: *The Unbound Prometheus* (Cambridge, 1969), p. 125.

and philosophy, both continental countries could lay claim to outstripping comparable British attainments. But, from the middle of the eighteenth century, each country clearly lagged behind Britain in its level of economic development, and it was not until well over a century later that either France or Germany succeeded in recapturing in substantial degree the lead which had been ceded to the former country.[4]

Moreover, regarding Britain as the measure, neither Germany nor France in the early part of the nineteenth century could match the internal political stability of a state in which the liberal bourgeoisie had achieved a strong position in government. The Restoration in France gave material expression to the heavy retrenchment of reactionary interests which dispelled the extravagant progressive hopes that had guided the Jacobins twenty-five years earlier. The social and political cleavages which had been exposed by the Revolution were aggravated rather than resolved by the events of 1789 and their immediate aftermath; in fact, not until after 1870 did any regime in France manage to continue in power for more than two decades. Germany, as Marx noted early in his intellectual career, ' shared in the restorations of modern nations without ever sharing in their revolutions '.[5] The country, in fact, was not a nation at all, in the modern sense, at the opening of the nineteenth century, but was composed of a loose aggregate of sovereign states; this situation was not remedied until, under Bismarck, Prussia was able to use her dominant position to secure the full political unification of Germany.

The problem of the ' backwardness ' of Germany stands at the root of Marx's early formulations of historical materialism. As a ' Young Hegelian ' Marx initially shared the view that the rational criticism of existing institutions was sufficient to provoke the radical changes necessary to allow Germany to match, and to overtake, the two other leading western European countries. But, as Marx soon perceived, this radical—critical posture merely preserved the typical German concern with ' theory ' to the exclusion of ' practice '. ' In politics ', Marx wrote, ' the Germans have *thought* what other nations have *done*.' [6] Hegel's system represented the most perfect philosophical example of this, transforming the whole of human history into the history of the mind or spirit. If Germany was to advance further, Marx concluded, philosophical criticism would have to be complemented by knowledge of the material forces which are always at work in change which does not remain merely on the level of ideas.

Many writers have laid great stress, quite correctly, upon the threefold

[4] Differences in level of economic advancement between Britain and the other two countries can, of course, be traced back well beyond the eighteenth century. cf., for example, F. Cronzet: ' England and France in the eighteenth century: a comparative analysis of two economic growths ', in R. M. Hartwell: *The Causes of the Industrial Revolution in England* (London, 1967), pp. 139–74.

[5] *EW*, p. 45.

[6] *EW*, p. 51.

set of influences which were combined in Marx's writings.[7] Marx effected a powerful synthesis of the streams of thought which had developed in conjunction with the social, economic and political differences between the three leading western European countries. Political economy, closely interconnected with the philosophy of utilitarianism, remained effectively the only significant form of social theory in Britain throughout most of the nineteenth century. Marx accepted several of the key propositions developed by Adam Smith and Ricardo, but merged them with certain of the perspectives upon the finite character of bourgeois society contained in the various currents of French socialism. The latter were the proximate source of the society of the future first envisaged by Marx in the *Economic and Philosophical Manuscripts* of 1844, written in Paris. The historical dimension integrating political economy and socialism was provided by the Hegelian dialectic. In this way, Marx's works reunited, in a coherent fashion, the intellectual consciousness of the diverse experience of Britain, France and Germany, and yet at the same time offered a basis for the theoretical interpretation of these differences in social, economic, and political structure.

When Marx died, in 1883, Durkheim and Weber were young men standing at the threshold of their academic careers. But already by this date, the social structures of all of the three major countries of western Europe had changed considerably from the time at which Marx had developed his basic views. In both France and Germany – in contrast to Britain – working-class movements of a potentially revolutionary nature came to play a leading role in the political system. However, the influence of these movements was counterbalanced by a growing surge of nationalism: and, especially in Germany, which did not experience a successful bourgeois revolution, the bourgeoisie was kept subordinate to a powerful autocratic order, operating through control of the state bureaucracy, the army, and the established hierarchy. Inside Germany, in spite of the anti-socialist laws, the Social Democratic Party – an explicitly 'Marxist' party after 1875 – swelled in size, but towards the end of the century found its revolutionary posture increasingly out of alignment with its real position in a society which had largely become transformed into an industrial society 'from the top'.

It was in this context, beginning shortly before Marx's death, that Engels began to publish a set of writings furnishing a defence and an exposition of Marxism as a systematic doctrine – the most important and influential of these being *Anti-Dühring*. In emphasising the 'scientific' character of Marxist socialism as against utopian and voluntarist forms of socialist theory, *Anti-Dühring* prepared the ground for the positivistic interpretation of Marxism which ruled in Marxist circles until after the First World War, and

---

[7] cf. Lenin: 'The three sources and three component parts of Marxism', *V. I. Lenin, Selected Works* (London, 1969), pp. 20–32.

which has become the official philosophy in the Soviet Union.[8] The decade following Marx's death – that is, the time at which both Durkheim and Weber were each consolidating the views which informed their life's work – was the crucial period during which Marxism became a really important force, both politically and intellectually. The philosophical materialism that, under the influence of Engels, came to be universally identified as ' Marxism ', offered a theoretical framework for Social Democracy which allowed a substantial divergence between theory and practice: the Social Democrats became more and more a reformist party in substance, while remaining a revolutionary party in name. But by this very token, their leading spokesmen failed to appreciate the significance of the changes which had made it possible to rapidly cut back the lead in industrialisation which Britain had previously enjoyed.

The problem of the influence of ' ideas ' in social development, which so dominated the polemical interchanges between Marxists and their critics at around the turn of the present century, has to be understood against this backdrop. Both Durkheim and Weber accepted the philosophical materialism disseminated by Engels, Kautsky, Labriola, and others as the object of their critical evaluations of the claims of Marxism. Liberals and Marxists alike thus structured their debate around the classical dichotomy between idealism and materialism. The controversy over the validity of Marx's writings, then, became concerned primarily with the question of whether or not ideas are mere ' epiphenomena ' which have no ' independent ' part to play in social development. One of my concerns in this book is to demonstrate the essential irrelevance of this debate, in so far as Marx's writings may be compared with those of Durkheim and Weber as contrasting forms of social theory. Marx, no less than the latter two writers, sought to break through the traditional philosophical division between idealism and materialism, and it is the confusion between this time-honoured dichotomy and Marx's own ' materialistic ' critique of idealism which has obscured the sources of the real divergences between Marx and ' academic ' or ' bourgeois ' sociology.

This is a matter which has only fairly recently become apparent, in the course of the tremendous revival of western Marxist scholarship since the last World War. The appearance, in Rjazanov's *Marx–Engels Gesamtausgabe*, of various previously unpublished writings of Marx and Engels, has, of course, played a major role in stimulating this revival. The publication of such works as the 1844 *Economic and Philosophical Manuscripts*, however, has given rise to as many new interpretative problems as it has helped to resolve. These concern both the ' internal ' nature and coherence of Marx's own writings, and the intellectual connections between Marx's theoretical position and that of other social thinkers. The intricate difficulties which are posed by this

[8] George Lichtheim: *Marxism, an Historical and Critical Study* (London, 1964), pp. 238–43.

situation have largely dictated the structure of this book. In evaluating some
of the sources of the contemporary debate between Marxism and ' academic '
sociology it seemed necessary, as a prior task, to reconstruct the principal
themes in the writings of the major thinkers whose works are at the origins
of modern social theory. The first two-thirds of the book, therefore, are taken
up with separate treatments of the forms of social theory established by Marx,
Durkheim and Weber respectively (Chapters 1–12). The need to formulate,
in as precise and coherent a manner, the leading themes in the writings of
each author has precluded any attempt at the critical analysis of either the
' logic ' or the factual ' validity ' of their thought.

The first of the three concluding chapters (Chapter 13) sets out an analysis
of the principal ways in which Durkheim and Weber themselves sought to
separate their views from those they attributed to Marx. But these views cannot simply be accepted at their ' face value '. Chapters 14 and 15 abstract
from the stated positions of Durkheim and Weber in this respect, and provide
a new assessment of some of the main parallels and divergencies between
their writings and those of Marx. It should also be stressed that there are
several important lines of comparison between Marx, Durkheim and Weber
which have been neglected, or ignored altogether, in the three concluding
chapters. The most obvious omission here concerns the question of the divergent methodological views espoused by the three writers: *prima facie*, the
most basic comparative issues might seem to lie here. In some senses this is
indeed the case; but it is a basic contention of this book that the overwhelming interest of each of these authors was in the delineation of the characteristic
structure of modern ' capitalism ' as contrasted with prior forms of society.
The typical emphasis in sociology over the past few decades has been directed towards the search for a formal ' general theory '. Laudable as such an
objective may be, it diverges from the main focus of the works of the men
who established the foundations of modern social thought, and has had important consequences in obscuring the significance of problems which they
placed at the forefront of social theory. I do not believe that any of the three
authors discussed in this book sought to create all-embracing ' systems ' of
thought in the sense in which such an intention is ordinarily attributed to
them: indeed, each categorically denied this. Thus while I have accentuated
the integral unity of the works of each writer, I have at the same time endea-
voured to convey the partial and incomplete character which each stressed
as qualifying the perspectives which he established and the conclusions which
he reached.

List of abbreviations used

Abbreviations, as listed below, have been used for titles which are frequently cited in the references. The particular editions of these works which have been employed are given in the bibliography, at the end of the book. Where a double reference is given, this indicates that a quotation in the text is my own translation, or that I have in some way amended the existing English translation. The first reference always relates to the English edition, the second to the original.

Works by Marx and Engels

Cap	*Capital*
CM	*The Communist Manifesto*
EW	*Karl Marx, Early Writings*
GI	*The German Ideology*
Gru	*Grundrisse der Kritik der politischen Ökonomie*
SW	*Selected Works*
We	*Werke*
WYM	*Writings of the Young Marx on Philosophy and Society*

Works by Durkheim

DL	*The Division of Labour in Society*
DTS	*De la division du travail social*
EF	*The Elementary Forms of the Religious Life*
FE	*Les formes élémentaires de la vie religieuse*
PECM	*Professional Ethics and Civic Morals*
RMS	*Les règles de la méthode sociologique*
RSM	*The Rules of Sociological Method*
Soc	*Socialism*
Su	*Suicide*
LS	*Le Suicide*

Journals

AS	*Année sociologique*
RP	*Revue philosophique*

Works by Max Weber

ES	*Economy and Society*
FMW	*From Max Weber : Essays in Sociology*
GAR	*Gesammelte Aufsätze zur Religionssoziologie*
GASS	*Gesammelte Aufsätze zur Soziologie und Sozialpolitik*
GAW	*Gesammelte Aufsätze zur Wissenschaftslehre*
GPS	*Gesammelte politische Schriften*
MSS	*Methodology of the Social Sciences*
PE	*The Protestant Ethic and the Spirit of Capitalism*
RC	*The Religion of China*
RI	*Religion of India*
WuG	*Wirtschaft und Gesellschaft*

For M. C. G.

Part 1: Marx

1. Marx's early writings

There is a sense in which Marx's writings span three centuries. Although Marx was born nearly two decades after the opening of the nineteenth century, and died well before the end of it, his writings have had their greatest influence – certainly in the political sphere, and possibly even in the intellectual world – in the twentieth century. But they have their roots in the late eighteenth century, in the outburst of social and political changes stemming from the Revolution of 1789 in France. Marx's works thus draw the shattering effects of the French Revolution into the modern age, and express a line of direct continuity between 1789 and the October Revolution in Russia of almost one hundred and thirty years later.

While rather little is known of Marx's early childhood, various fragments and letters survive from his adolescent pen. The earliest of these are three short essays which Marx wrote during the course of his final school examinations. Inevitably enough, these are of little intrinsic interest or originality, but they do give an indication of the enthusiastic grandiosity which inspired many of Marx's subsequent adult works.[1] The most novel of the three is called ' Reflections of a young man on choosing a career ', and discusses the moral obligations and the range of freedoms open to an individual who is choosing which vocation to follow in his life. ' The main principle ', Marx concludes,

> ... which must guide us in the selection of a vocation is the welfare of humanity, our own perfection. One should not think that these two interests combat each other, that one must destroy the other. Rather, man's nature makes it possible for him to reach his fulfilment only by working for the perfection and welfare of his society... History calls those the greatest men who ennobled themselves by working for the universal.[2]

Such an outlook eventually led Marx, as a university student, to close study of Hegel, in whose philosophy we find precisely this: a theory of the self-fulfilment, of the culmination of ' our own perfection '. A letter which Marx wrote to his father in 1837 describes how, finding the philosophy of Kant and Fichte unsatisfactory, and finally rejecting his youthful love of lyrical poetry, Marx ' dived into the ocean ' of Hegel.[3] But even while he was first under the

---

[1] It might be noted that some commentators have attempted to discern in these essays a number of themes which were fundamental to Marx's later writings (cf. A. Cornu: *Karl Marx et Friedrich Engels* (Paris, 1955), vol. 1, pp. 65–6). But the most striking characteristic of the essays is their conventional adolescent idealism.

[2] *WYM*, p. 39.

[3] *WYM*, pp. 40–50.

spell of Hegel's philosophical system as a student, it is clear that Marx was at no point a blindly orthodox Hegelian. The genesis of Marx's initial attraction to Hegelianism is revealed in his description of the notes which, as a student in Berlin, he made of his readings in philosophy and law.[4] The Kantian dualism of what ' is ' and what ' ought to be ', seems to Marx – and this view he continued to maintain throughout the rest of his life – totally irreconcilable with the demands of the individual who wishes to apply philosophy to the pursuit of his objectives. The philosophy of Fichte is subject to the same objection: it separates the properties of logic and truth (such as is involved in mathematics and empirical science respectively) from the intervention of the human subject in a continuously developing world. This standpoint, therefore, has to be supplanted by one which recognises that ' the object itself must be studied in its development; there must be no arbitrary divisions; the rationale (*Vernunft*) of the thing itself must be disclosed in its contradictoriness and find its unity in itself '.[5]

Marx discovered himself unable to resolve these issues alone, and was thus unavoidably led to pursue in his own thought the process of evolution followed by German idealist philosophy as a whole – moving from Kant to Fichte and thence on to Hegel.[6] However, what first drew Marx to Hegel was neither the impressive comprehensiveness of the latter's philosophy, nor the specific content of his philosophical premises as such, but the closure which Hegel effected between the dichotomous strands of classical German philosophy which formed the principal legacy of Kant. The impact of Hegel upon Marx was mediated by two partially separate sources, each of which involved the conjunction of Hegelianism to political standpoints at variance with the conservatism of Hegel.[7] One of these influences is to be found in the teachings of Eduard Gans, whose lectures at Berlin made some considerable impression upon Marx. Gans seasoned Hegel with a strong element of Saint-Simonianism.[8] However, Marx had almost certainly been exposed to contact with Saint-Simonian ideas earlier on in his youth, and a case can be made for the view that the influence on Saint-Simon's writings over Marx in his formative years was in some respects almost as great as that of Hegel.[9]

The second factor conditioning Marx's acceptance of Hegel was Marx's membership of the ' Doctor's Club ' in Berlin University. In this circle, Marx

[4] *WYM*, pp. 42–7.
[5] *WYM*, p. 43; *We, Ergänzungsband (Ergd)*, vol. 1, p. 5.
[6] cf. Robert C. Tucker: *Philosophy and Myth in Karl Marx* (Cambridge, 1965), pp. 31–69.
[7] On the views of the ' young Hegel ', cf. the analysis given in Georg Lukács: *Der junge Hegel* (Zurich and Vienna, 1948), pp. 27–130.
[8] See Hanns Günther Reissner: *Eduard Gans* (Tübingen, 1965).
[9] This view is stated forcefully in Georges Gurvitch: ' La sociologie du jeune Marx ', in *La Vocation actuelle de la sociologie* (Paris, 1950), pp. 568–80. This chapter is replaced in the second edition (1963) by a more general discussion entitled ' La sociologie de Karl Marx '.

made the acquaintance of a heterogeneous assortment of young followers of Hegel, of whom Bruno Bauer was the outstanding figure.[10] The immediate problems which concerned Bauer, and the group of ' Young Hegelians ' which formed around him, preserved the concern with Christian theology which was intrinsic to Hegel's own writings. Marx's doctoral dissertation, which is concerned with a comparative discussion of the philosophies of Democritus and Epicurus, shows the strong imprint of Bauer's ideas. But at about the same time as Marx submitted his doctoral thesis, Feuerbach's *The Essence of Christianity* (1841) was published.[11] Engels later wrote of the impact of the book upon the Young Hegelians: ' The spell was broken: the " system " was shattered and thrown aside... Enthusiasm was general: we all became at once " Feuerbachians ".' [12] The immediate influence of the work upon Marx's developing thought was almost certainly, in fact, more diffuse and less immediate than is described in Engels' account, written over forty years later.[13] Marx no more adopted Feuerbach's position in a wholesale fashion than he had that of Hegel.[14] Nevertheless, it cannot be doubted that the influence of Feuerbach among the Young Hegelians was dominant by the end of 1842. Marx's critical discussion of Hegel's philosophy of the state, written in 1843, is heavily influenced by Feuerbach: and the standpoint of the latter is basic to the *Economic and Philosophical Manuscripts* of 1844.

In *The Essence of Christianity*, and other subsequent publications, Feuerbach seeks to reverse the idealistic premises of Hegel's philosophy, stating bluntly that the starting-point of the study of humanity must be ' real man ', living in ' the real, material world '. Whereas Hegel sees the ' real ' as emanating from the ' divine ', Feuerbach argues that the divine is an illusory product of the real; being, existence, precede thought in the sense in that men do not reflect upon the world prior to acting in it: ' thought proceeds from being, not being from thought.' [15] Hegel viewed the development of mankind in terms of God having been divided against himself. In Feuerbach's philosophy, God can only exist in so far as man is divided against himself, in so far as man is alienated from himself. God is a fantasied being upon whom man has pro-

---

[10] For a recent discussion of the influence of Bauer upon Marx, see David McClellan: *The Young Hegelians and Karl Marx* (London, 1969), pp. 48ff and *passim*; see also the same author's *Marx before Marxism* (London, 1970).

[11] Ludwig Feuerbach: *The Essence of Christianity* (New York, 1957).

[12] *SW*, vol. 2, p. 368.

[13] cf. McClellan: *The Young Hegelians and Karl Marx*, pp. 92–7. McClellan's claim that ' Engels' description of the effect of the book is completely at variance with the facts ' (p. 93), however, is exaggerated. cf. Marx's well-known statement, written in the early part of 1842, that ' there is no other way to truth and freedom but through the " river of fire " ' (Feuer-Bach: lit., ' brook of fire '). *WYM*, p. 95.

[14] It might be remarked that Feuerbach's own views were characterised by a number of deep-rooted ambiguities, and underwent some definite changes, over the period from 1834 to 1843. cf. Feuerbach: *Sämmtliche Werke*, vols. 1–3. (There are some errors, however, in the allocation of writings to particular years in this collection.)

[15] *Ibid.* vol. 2, p. 239.

jected his own highest powers and faculties, who thus is seen as perfect and all-powerful, and in contrast to whom man himself appears as limited and imperfect.

But at the same time, according to Feuerbach, the depth of the comparison between God and man can be a positive source of inspiration to the realisation of human capabilities. The task of philosophy is to enable man to recover his alienated self through transformative criticism, by reversing the Hegelian perspective, and thus asserting the primacy of the material world. Religion must be replaced by humanism, whereby the love formerly directed towards God will become focused upon man, leading to a recovery of the unity of mankind, man for himself. 'Whereas the old philosophy said: what is not thought, has no existence, so the new philosophy says, on the contrary: that which is not loved, which cannot be loved, has no existence.'[16]

The effect of assimilating the ideas of Feuerbach was to turn Marx back to Hegel, in an attempt to draw out the implications of the new perspective, and especially to apply it to the sphere of politics. The aspects of Feuerbach's philosophy which attracted Marx were essentially the same as those which originally drew him to Hegel: the possibilities which seemed to be offered of fusing analysis and criticism, and thereby of 'realising' philosophy. It is usually held that Marx's early writings on alienation in politics and industry represent little more than an extension of Feuerbach's 'materialism' to spheres of society not dealt with by the latter. This is misleading, however: Marx does not accept, at any point, what Feuerbach considers to be the primary significance of his philosophy – that it provides an 'alternative' to, and thereby a *replacement of*, Hegel. Even when most imbibed with enthusiasm for Feuerbach, Marx seeks to juxtapose him to Hegel. Marx thus succeeds in retaining the historical perspective which, while central to Hegel's philosophy, is, in effect if not in intention, largely abandoned by Feuerbach.[17]

The state and ' true democracy '

Marx's critique of Hegel's philosophy of the state, written in 1843, is the first publication in which Marx's nascent conception of historical materialism [18] can be discerned, and forms the starting-point of the treatment of alienation which Marx set out at greater length in *Economic and Philosophical Manuscripts* one year later. Marx proceeds via a close textual analysis of Hegel, 'inverting' Hegel in the manner of Feuerbach. 'Hegel', Marx says, 'subjectifies the predicates, the objects, but he subjectifies them in separation from

---

16 *Sämmtliche Werke*, vol. 2, p. 299.
17 In a letter to Ruge of 1843, Marx also states that Feuerbach 'concerns himself too much with nature and too little with politics. But the latter is the only means whereby contemporary philosophy can be realised'. *We*, vol. 27, p. 417.
18 As is well known, the phrase 'historical materialism' is not used by Marx, but first appears in the writings of Engels. It is used here with the qualification that the term perhaps suggests a greater degree of theoretical closure than Marx would be willing to admit of his studies of history.

their true subjectivity, the subject '.[19] The point of Marx's analysis, therefore, is to reidentify the true subject (the acting individual, living in the ' real ', ' material ' world), and to trace the process of his ' objectification ' in the political institutions of the state.[20] The real world is not to be inferred from the study of the ideal; on the contrary, it is the ideal which has to be understood as a historical outcome of the real. For Hegel, civil society (*bürgerliche Gesellschaft*), which includes all those economic and familial relationships which are outside the political and juridical structure of the state, is intrinsically a sphere of unrestrained egoism, where each man is pitted against every other. Men are rational, orderly beings to the degree that they accept the order inherent in the state, which is a universal sphere cutting across the egoistic interests of human actions in civil society. In Hegel's account, therefore, the state is not only presented as severed from the lives of individuals in civil society, but as logically prior to the individual. The acting individual, the real creator of history, is subordinated to the ideals of political participation embodied in the state, which thus appear as the motive-power of social development.

Feuerbach has shown, Marx continues, that in religion men participate vicariously in an unreal, fantasy world of harmony, beauty and contentment, while living in a practical everyday world of pain and misery. The state is, similarly, an alienated form of political activity, embodying universal ' rights ' which are as ephemeral as is the idealised world of religion. The basis of Hegel's view is that political rights of representation mediate between the egoistic individualism of civil society and the universalism of the state. But, Marx emphasises, there is no existing form of political constitution where this connection exists in actuality; in extant states, general participation in political life is the ideal, but the pursuance of sectional interests is the reality. Thus what appears in Hegel's account to be separate from and superordinate to the particular interests of individuals in civil society is, in fact, derivative of them. ' Up to now the *political constitution* has been the *religious sphere*, the *religion* of the people's life, the heaven of their universality in contrast to the particular *mundane existence* of their actuality.' [21]

In the Greek *polis* every man – that is, every free citizen – was a *zoon politikon*: the social and political were inextricably fused, and there was no separate sphere of the ' political '. Private and public life was not distinct, and the only ' private individuals ' were those who, as slaves, lacked public status as citizens altogether. Mediaeval Europe contrasts with this. In the Middle Ages, the various strata of civil society themselves became political agencies: political power was directly contingent upon and expressive of the division

---

[19] *WYM*, p. 166; *We*, vol. 1, p. 224.

[20] For a perceptive discussion of the ' Critique ', see Jean Hyppolite: ' La conception hégélienne de l'Etat et sa critique par Karl Marx ', in *Etudes sur Marx et Hegel* (Paris, 1955), pp. 120–41.

[21] *WYM*, p. 176.

of society into stable socio-economic orders.[22] 'Each private sphere has a political character, is a political sphere...'[23] In this form of society, the various strata become politicised, but there is still no separation between the 'private' or the 'individual', and the 'political'. The very notion of the 'state' as separable from civil society is a modern one because it is only in the post-mediaeval period that the sphere of interests in civil society, especially economic interests, have become part of the 'private rights' of the individual, and as such separable from the 'public' sphere of politics. The distribution of property is now presumed to lie outside the constitution of political power. In reality, however, the ownership of property still largely determines political power – no longer in the legalised manner of mediaeval society, however, but under the cloak of universal participation in government.[24]

The realisation of what Marx calls 'true democracy' entails, according to his analysis, overcoming the alienation between the individual and the political community, through resolving the dichotomy between the 'egoistic' interests of individuals in civil society and the 'social' character of political life. This can only be achieved by effecting concrete changes in the relations between state and society, such that what is at present only ideal (universal political participation) becomes actual. 'Hegel proceeds from the state and makes man into the state subjectivised. Democracy proceeds from man and makes the state into man objectivised... In democracy the *formal* principle is at the same time the *material* principle.'[25] The attainment of universal suffrage, Marx says, is the means whereby this can be brought about. Universal suffrage gives all the members of civil society a political existence and, therefore, *ipso facto* eliminates the 'political' as a separate category. 'In *universal franchise*, active as well as passive, does civil society first raise itself *in reality* to an abstraction of itself, to *political* existence as its true universal and essential existence.'[26]

Revolutionary *Praxis*

There has been some considerable dispute concerning the relevance of the views set out by Marx in the 'Critique', to the writings which he produced subsequently in 1844.[27] It is evident that the 'Critique' represents only a prefatory analysis of the state and politics; the manuscript is not complete, and Marx states his intention to develop certain points without in fact doing so. Moreover, the tenor of Marx's analysis is in the direction of a radical

---

[22] cf. Marx's discussion of the transformation of the feudal *Stände*. *We*, vol. 1, pp. 273ff.
[23] *WYM*, p. 176; *We*, vol. 1, p. 232.
[24] *WYM*, pp. 187–8.
[25] *WYM*, pp. 173–4.
[26] *WYM*, p. 202; *We*, vol. 1, p. 326.
[27] For divergent views on this question, see Lichtheim, pp. 38–40; Shlomo Avineri: *The Social and Political Thought of Karl Marx* (Cambridge, 1968), pp. 33–40.

Jacobinism; what is needed in order to progress beyond the contemporary form of the state is to realise the abstract ideals embodied in the 1789 Revolution. But it cannot be doubted that the ' Critique ' embodies notions which Marx did not subsequently relinquish. Indeed, it supplies the key to the understanding of the theory of the state, and of the possibility of its abolition, and thus the conceptions contained within it underlie the whole of Marx's mature writings. But at this stage Marx was, in common with the other Young Hegelians, still thinking in terms of the necessity for the 'reform of consciousness ', as posited by Feuerbach. Immediately prior to leaving Germany for France in September 1843, Marx wrote to Ruge expressing his conviction that all ' dogmas ' must be questioned, whether they be religious or political :

Our slogan, therefore, must be: Reform of consciousness, not through dogmas, but through analysis of the mystical consciousness that is unclear about itself, whether in religion or politics. It will be evident, then, that the world has long dreamed of something of which it only has to become conscious in order to possess it in actuality... To have its sins forgiven, mankind has only to declare them for what they are.[28]

The effects of Marx's direct contact with French socialism in Paris are evident in ' An introduction to the Critique of Hegel's Philosophy of Law ', written at the end of 1843.[29] Most of the points in the article are elaborations of themes already established in Marx's previous ' Critique ', but Marx abandons the stress upon ' demystification ', such as urged by Bauer, which informs his earlier critical analysis of Hegel. ' The criticism of religion ', Marx admits, ' is the premise of all criticism '; but this is a task which has been largely accomplished, and the immediate and necessary task is to move directly to the field of politics.

The abolition of religion as the *illusory* happiness of the people is the demand for their *real* happiness. The demand to abandon illusions about their real condition is a *demand to abandon a condition which requires illusions*. The criticism of religion is thus the *germ* of the *criticism of the vale of tears* of which religion is the *halo*.[30]

But ' criticism ' in itself, Marx now goes on to say, is not enough. This is nowhere more obvious, he asserts, than in Germany, which is so retarded in its development. The abstract, philosophical ' negation ' of the German political structure is irrelevant to the real demands which have to be met if Germany is to be transformed: ' Even the negation of our political present is already a

---

[28] *WYM*, pp. 214–15.

[29] Originally published in Ruge's *Deutsch-französische Jahrbücher*, in February 1844. *WYM*, pp. 249–64. Similar ideas are also developed in Marx's other contribution to the same issue, ' On the Jewish Question ', *WYM*, pp. 216–48. An alternative translation of the latter article is available in *EW*, pp. 3–31.

[30] *EW*, p. 44; *We*, vol. 1, p. 379. All of Marx's statements, throughout his writings, upon the ' abolition ' (*Aufhebung*) of religion, the state, alienation, or capitalism as a whole, have to be understood in the light of the threefold connotation of the verb *aufheben* (to abolish, to preserve, to raise up). Thus the ' abolition ' of religion involves, not its eradication in any simple sense, but its dialectical transcendence.

dusty fact in the historical lumber room of modern nations.'[31] The contributions of Germany to the social advancement of the European nations are limited to the realm of ideas. The Germans are 'philosophical contemporaries of the present' in lieu of being its 'historical contemporaries'. To seek, therefore, to abolish this state of affairs through philosophical criticism is futile, since this merely preserves the existing dislocation between ideas and reality. The exposure of contradictions on the intellectual level does not thereby remove them. It is necessary to proceed 'to *tasks* the solution of which admits of only one means – *practice (Praxis)* '.[32]

If Germany is to experience reform, it cannot be brought about by slow progressive advancement, but must take the form of a radical revolution: in this way, Germany can attain 'not only to the *official level* of modern nations, but to the *human level* which will be the immediate future of those nations'.[33] The very backwardness of the social composition of Germany can provide the circumstances whereby the country can leap ahead of the other European states. This cannot be attained, however, unless the 'theoretical' criticism of politics is conjoined to the experience of a definite social grouping whose position in society renders them revolutionary. It is here that Marx first makes mention of the proletariat. As yet, the low level of economic development of Germany, Marx points out, means that the industrial proletariat is only beginning to appear. But its further expansion, in combination with the peculiarly retarded form of social and political structure extant in Germany, will provide the requisite combination of circumstances which can propel Germany beyond the other European countries.[34]

Marx finds in the proletariat the 'universal character' which Hegel sought in the ideals embodied in the rational state. The proletariat is 'a class which has radical chains'; it is 'a sphere of society having a universal character because of its universal suffering and claiming no particular right because no particular wrong, but unqualified wrong, is perpetrated upon it'. The proletariat localises within itself all of the worst evils of society. It lives in conditions of poverty which is not the natural poverty resulting from lack of material resources, but is the 'artificial' outcome of the contemporary organisation of industrial production. Since the proletariat is the recipient of the concentrated irrationality of society, it follows that its emancipation is at the same time the emancipation of society as a whole:

total loss of humanity ... can only redeem itself by a *total redemption of humanity*... When the proletariat announces the *dissolution of the hitherto existing order of things*, it merely announces the *secret of its own existence* because it *is* the *effective (faktisch)* dissolution of this order... As philosophy finds its material weapons in the proletariat, the proletariat finds its intellectual weapons in philosophy.[35]

---

[31] *EW*, p. 45.
[32] *EW*, p. 52; *We*, vol. 1, p. 385.
[33] *EW*, p. 52.
[34] *EW*, pp. 57–9.
[35] *EW*, pp. 58–9; *We*, vol. 1, p. 391.

During the early part of 1844, Marx began an intensive study of political economy, the preliminary results of which are recorded in a set of fragments which were first published only in 1932, under the title *Economic and Philosophical Manuscripts*. The direction of movement of Marx's thought which this stimulated led to a further divergence from the other Young Hegelians, with the notable exception of Engels, whose influence was important in directing Marx's energies towards economics. There are several reasons why the *Manuscripts* are of decisive importance for the whole of Marx's work. They form, in substance, the earliest of several drafts of *Capital* which Marx made prior to the publication of the latter work itself. The preface which Marx prepared for the *Manuscripts* outlines the framework of an ambitious project which he originally planned, but which he was never destined to complete. These plans which Marx sketched out at this relatively early stage of his intellectual career show beyond any question that *Capital*, lengthy and detailed as it eventually turned out to be, forms only one element in what Marx conceived as a much broader critique of capitalism. Marx originally intended to publish 'a number of independent brochures' covering the 'critique of law, morals, politics' separately. These diverse treatments were then to be connected together in a concluding work of synthesis.[36] In the *Manuscripts*, Marx set out only to cover these institutional spheres in so far as they are directly influenced by economic relationships. The work is, therefore, Marx's earliest attempt at a critique of that discipline which claims to deal with this field: political economy.

The *Manuscripts* are also of great intrinsic interest in that in them Marx deals explicitly with problems which, for varying reasons, occupied his attention less directly in his subsequent writings. Some of these issues dropped out of Marx's later works because he considered them to have been satisfactorily dealt with, given his over-riding aim of providing a theoretical critique of modern capitalism. The analysis of religion is one of these. The *Manuscripts* is the last place where Marx still devotes some considerable attention to religion. But certain of the topics which are prominent in the *Manuscripts* disappear from Marx's ensuing writings for other reasons. The most significant of these is that of the analysis of alienation, which occupies a central place in the *Manuscripts*. There can be no doubt at all that the notion of alienation continues to be at the root of Marx's mature works in spite of the fact that the term itself appears only rarely in his writings after 1844. In his subsequent writings, Marx disentangles the various threads comprised generically within the concept of alienation as used in the *Manuscripts*. Thus the term itself, which possesses an abstract, philosophical character from which Marx wished to dissociate himself, became redundant. But the explicit discussion of alienation which appears in the *Manuscripts* offers an invalu-

[36] *EW*, p. 63.

able source of insight into the principal underlying themes of Marx's later thought.

Alienation and the theory of political economy

The main suppositions informing the critique of political economy which Marx develops in the *Manuscripts* are the following. There are two principal criticisms which have to be made of the writings of the political economists. The first is in reference to their assumption that the conditions of production characteristic of capitalism can be attributed to all forms of economy. The economists begin from the premise of the exchange economy and the existence of private property. Self-seeking and the pursuit of profit are seen as the natural characteristics of man. In fact, Marx points out, the formation of an exchange economy is the outcome of a historical process, and capitalism is an historically specific system of production. It is only one type of productive system amongst others which have preceded it in history, and it is no more the final form than the others which went before it. The second fallacious assumption of the economists is that purely ' economic ' relations can be treated *in abstracto*. Economists speak of ' capital ', ' commodities ', ' prices ', and so on, as if these had life independently of the mediation of human beings. This is plainly not so. While for example, a coin is a physical object which in this sense has an existence independent of men, it is only ' money ' in so far as it forms an element within a definite set of social relationships. The economists, however, attempt to reduce everything to the ' economic ', and eschew whatever cannot be treated in these terms.

Political economy thus does not recognise the unemployed worker, the working man so far as he is outside this work relationship. Thieves, tricksters, beggars, the unemployed, the starving, wretched and criminal working-man, are *forms* which do not exist *for political economy*, but only for other eyes, for doctors, judges, grave-diggers and beadles, etc.; they are ghostly figures outside its domain.[37]

Any and every ' economic ' phenomenon is at the same time always a social phenomenon, and the existence of a particular kind of ' economy ' presupposes a definite kind of society.[38]

It is symptomatic of these misconceptions that the economists treat workers as ' costs ' to the capitalist, and hence as equivalent to any other sort of capital expenditure. Political economy declares it to be irrelevant that the real ' objects ' of analysis are men in society. It is for this reason that the economists are able to obscure what is in fact intrinsic to their interpretation of the capitalist mode of production: that capitalism is founded upon a class division between proletariat, or working class, on the one hand, and bourgeoisie, or capitalist class, on the other. These classes are in endemic conflict as regards the distribution of the fruits of industrial production. Wages on the

[37] *EW*, pp. 137–8; *We, Ergd*, vol. 1, pp. 523–4.
[38] *EW*, pp. 120–1.

one side, and profits on the other, are determined ' by the bitter struggle between capitalist and worker ', a relation in which those who own capital are
easily dominant.[39]

Marx's analysis of alienation in capitalist production starts from a ' contemporary economic fact ', which is again an early statement of a theme later
developed in detail in *Capital*: the fact that the more capitalism advances,
the more impoverished the workers become. The enormous wealth which
the capitalist mode of production makes possible is appropriated by the
owners of land and capital. This separation between the worker and the
product of his labour is not, however, simply a matter of the expropriation
of goods which rightfully belong to the worker. The main point of Marx's
discussion is that, in capitalism, the material objects which are produced become treated on a par with the worker himself – just as they are, on a purely
theoretical level, in the discipline of political economy. ' The worker becomes
an ever cheaper commodity the more goods he creates. The *devaluation* of the
human world increases in direct relation with the *increase in value* of the
world of things.' [40] This involves a distortion of what Marx calls ' objectification ' (*Vergegenständlichung*).   Through his labour, the worker acts to
modify the world of nature; his production is the result of this interaction
with the external world, in so far as he fashions it. But under capitalism, the
worker (the subject, the creator) has become assimilated to his product (the
object).[41]

The process of production, objectification, thus takes the form of ' a *loss*
and *servitude to the object* '; the worker ' becomes a slave of the object. . .'.[42]
The alienation of the worker in the capitalist economy is founded upon this
disparity between the productive power of labour, which becomes increasingly great with the expansion of capitalism, and the lack of control which
the worker is able to exert over the objects which he produces. As in the case
of alienation in the sphere of politics, this offers a parallel to alienation in
religion. The qualities which are attributed to God in the Christian ethic are
thereby removed from the control of men, and become as if imposed by an
external agency. In a similar fashion, the product of the worker is ' alien to
him, and . . . stands opposed to him as an autonomous power. The life which
he has given to the object sets itself against him as an alien and hostile

---

[39] *EW*, p. 69.
[40] *EW*, p. 121.
[41] *EW*, p. 123. On a broader epistemological level, Marx criticises Hegel for having
    mistaken the nature of the connection between objectification and alienation. Funda-
    mental to Hegel's idealism, Marx points out, is the premise that ' thinghood ' is the
    same as ' alienated self-consciousness ', and consequently that objectification is only
    made possible by human self-alienation. The truth of the matter, Marx avers, is the
    other way around: the existence of alienation presupposes objectification, and is
    (in Marx's use of the concept) consequent upon the specific distorted form of
    objectification characteristic of capitalism. Many secondary writers have, unfortu-
    nately, failed to grasp this essential distinction between objectification and alienation.
[42] *EW*, pp. 122 & 123.

force.' [43] Objectification, therefore, which is a necessary characteristic of *all* labour (involving the transference of labour power to the object which is created by it) becomes, in capitalism, identical with alienation. The product of labour is, in other words, ' external ' to the worker not only in an ontological sense but also in the much more profound yet more specific sense that ' What is embodied in the product of his labour is no longer his own.' [44]

The alienation of the worker from his product takes a number of distinct forms. In discussing these, Marx uses terminology which draws heavily upon Feuerbach; but it is clear that he is thinking in concrete terms of the effects of capitalism as a particular, historical mode of production. The main dimensions of Marx's discussion of alienation are as follows:

1. The worker lacks control over the disposal of his products, since what he produces is appropriated by others, so that he does not benefit from it. It is the core principle of the market economy that goods are produced for exchange; in capitalist production, the exchange and distribution of goods are controlled by the operations of the free market. The worker himself, who is treated as a commodity to be bought and sold on the market, thus has no power to determine the fate of what he produces. The workings of the market act in such a way as to promote the interests of the capitalist at the expense of those of the worker. Thus ' the more the worker produces the less he has to consume; the more value he creates the more worthless he becomes '.

2. The worker is alienated in the work task itself: ' if the product of labour is alienation, production itself must be active alienation – the alienation of activity and the activity of alienation.' [45] The work task does not offer intrinsic satisfactions which make it possible for the worker ' to develop freely his mental and physical energies ', since it is labour which is imposed by force of external circumstances alone. Work becomes a means to an end rather than an end in itself: this is shown by the fact that ' as soon as there is no physical or other compulsion, men flee from labour like the plague '.[46]

3. Since all economic relationships are also social relationships, it follows that the alienation of labour has directly social ramifications. This takes Marx back to his starting-point: human relations, in capitalism, tend to become reduced to operations of the market. This is directly manifest in the significance of money in human relationships. Money promotes the rationalisation of social relationships, since it provides an abstract standard in terms of which the most heterogeneous qualities can be compared, and re-

---

[43] *EW*, p. 123. In discussing alienation in this context, Marx uses two terms: *Entfremdung* (estrangement) and *Entäusserung* (externalisation). The two are used more or less interchangeably in Marx's analysis.

[44] *EW*, p. 122.

[45] *EW*, pp. 123–4.   [46] *EW*, p. 125; *We, Ergd*, vol. 1, p. 514.

duced, to one another. ' He who can purchase bravery is brave, though a coward ... Thus, from the standpoint of its possessor, it exchanges every quality and object for every other, even though they are contradictory.' [47]

4. Men live in an active inter-relationship with the natural world. Technology and culture are both the expression and the outcome of this inter-relationship, and are the chief qualities distinguishing man from the animals. Some animals do produce, of course, but only in a mechanical, adaptive fashion. Alienated labour reduces human productive activity to the level of adaptation to, rather than active mastery of, nature. This detaches the human individual from his ' species-being ' (*Gattungswesen*), from what makes the life of the human species distinct from that of the animals.[48] Marx's discussion at this point closely echoes Feuerbach. But the import of what Marx says is quite different. Many secondary accounts of Marx's analysis of alienation in the 1844 *Manuscripts*, through assimilating Marx's position to that of Feuerbach, give Marx's discussion a more ' utopian ' connotation than in fact it has.[49] Marx uses Feuerbachian terms in holding that man is a ' universal producer ', in contrast to the animals, who only produce ' partially ' and in limited contexts established by the instinctual components of their biological makeup: but his analysis is far more concrete and specific than this terminology suggests.

What distinguishes human life from that of the animals, according to Marx, is that human faculties, capacities and tastes are shaped by society. The ' isolated individual ' is a fiction of utilitarian theory: no human being exists who has not been born into, and thus shaped by, an on-going society. Each individual is thus the recipient of the accumulated culture of the generations which have preceded him and, in his own interaction with the natural and social world in which he lives, is a contributor to the further modification of that world as experienced by others. ' Individual human life and species-life are not *different things* ', Marx asserts ' ... Though a man is a unique individual ... he is equally the *whole*, the ideal whole, the subjective existence of society as thought and experienced.' [50] It is, then, man's membership of society, together with the technological and cultural apparatus which supports that society and which makes it possible, which serves to differentiate the human individual from the animal, which confers his ' humanity ' upon him. Some animals have similar sense-organs to man; but the perception of beauty in sight or sound, in art or music, is a human faculty, a creation of society. Sexual activity, or eating and drinking, are not for men the simple satisfaction of biological drives, but have become

---

[47] *EW*, p. 193.

[48] Feuerbach: *Essence of Christianity*, pp. 1–12. Marx also makes liberal use of the term *Gattungsleben*, literally meaning ' species-life '.

[49] For two different instances of this, see H. Popitz: *Der entfremdete Mensch* (Frankfurt, 1967); also Tucker.

[50] *EW*, p. 158; *We, Ergd*, vol. 1, p. 539.

transformed, during the course of the development of society, in creative interplay with the natural world, into actions which provide manifold satisfactions.[51] 'The cultivation of the five senses is the work of all previous history'; but ' it is not simply the five senses, but also the so-called spiritual senses, the practical senses (desiring, loving, etc.), in brief, *human* sensibility and the human character of the senses, which can only come into being through the existence of *its* object, through *humanised* nature.' [52]

In bourgeois society, men are estranged, in specifiable ways, from the ties to society which alone confer their ' humanity ' upon them. Firstly, alienated labour ' alienates species-life and individual life ', and, secondly, ' it turns the latter, as an abstraction, into the purpose of the former, also in its abstract and alienated form '.[53] In capitalism, both in theory and in practice, the life and the needs of the individual appear as ' given ' independently of his membership of society. This finds clear theoretical expression in political economy (and, in a somewhat different way, in the Hegelian theory of civil society which Marx previously criticised), which founds its theory of society upon the self-seeking of the isolated individual. Political economy in this way ' incorporates private property into the very essence of man '.[54] But not only does the ' individual ' become separated from the ' social ', the latter becomes *subordinated* to the former. The productive resources of the community are applied – in the case of the majority of the population who live in penury – to support the minimal conditions necessary for the survival of the organism. The mass of wage-labourers exist in conditions where their productive activity is governed solely by the most rudimentary needs of physical existence:

man is regressing to the *cave dwelling*, but in an alienated malignant form. The savage in his cave (a natural element which is freely offered for his use and protection) does not feel himself a stranger ; on the contrary he feels as much at home as a *fish* in water. But the cellar dwelling of the poor man is a hostile dwelling, ' an alien, constricting power which only surrenders itself to him in exchange for blood and sweat '.[55]

As Marx presents it, therefore, the alienation of man from his ' species-being ' is couched in terms of his analysis of capitalism, and is, in considerable degree, *assymetrical*: in other words, the effects of alienation are focused through the class structure, and are experienced in concentrated fashion by the proletariat. The transfer of the notion of alienation from a general ontological category, which is how it is used both by Hegel and by Feuerbach, to a specific social and historical context, is the main theme of Marx's approach in the *Manuscripts*. Marx does not hold, however, that alienation is wholly confined to the position of the wage-labourer. The

---

51 cf. below, pp. 21–2.
52 *EW*, p. 161; *We, Ergd*, vol. 1, p. 541. For further discussion of this point, in relation to Durkheim, see below, pp. 224–8.
54 *EW*, p. 148.
53 *EW*, p. 127.
55 *EW*, p. 177.

capitalist is himself subservient to capital in the sense that the rule of private property and of money dominates his own existence. The industrialist has to be ' *hard-working, sober, economical, prosaic* ':

his enjoyment is only a secondary matter; it is recreation subordinated to production and thus a *calculated, economic* enjoyment, for he charges his pleasures as an expense of capital and what he squanders must not be more than can be replaced with profit by the reduction of capital. Thus enjoyment is subordinated to capital and the pleasure-loving individual is subordinated to the capital-accumulating individual, whereas formerly (in feudal society) the contrary was the case.[56]

The *Manuscripts* are a set of preliminary notes rather than a finished work. The discussion of alienated labour which they contain gives ample evidence of the fact that Marx was still, in 1844, groping towards the clear formulation of a distinctive perspective of his own. While the main themes of his treatment of alienation are not difficult to identify, Marx's account of them is frequently cryptic and elliptical. Where Marx is analysing the works of the economists, he writes in the language of political economy; where he discusses alienation directly, he uses the terminology of Feuerbach. It is unquestionably true that, at this stage, Marx had not successfully integrated the conceptions which he derived from these two diverse sources, and in the *Manuscripts* the two rest in uneasy relationship with each other. Nonetheless, the *Manuscripts* provide the framework of a general critical analysis of capitalism, and these fragmentary notes contain the germ of virtually all of the important ideas which Marx developed with greater precision at later writings.

It is usually assumed that, in speaking, in the 1844 *Manuscripts*, of man's ' being reduced to the level of the animals ', and of man's alienation from his ' species-being ' under the conditions of capitalist production, Marx is thinking in terms of an abstract conception of ' man ' as being alienated from his biological characteristics as a species. So, it is presumed, at this initial stage in the evolution of his thought, Marx believed that man is essentially a creative being whose ' natural ' propensities are denied by the restrictive character of capitalism. Actually, Marx holds, on the contrary, that the enormous productive power of capitalism generates possibilities for the future development of man which could not have been possible under prior forms of productive system. The organisation of social relationships within which capitalist production is carried on in fact leads to the failure to realise these historically generated possibilities. The character of alienated labour does not express a tension between ' man in nature ' (non-alienated) and ' man in society ' (alienated), but between the potential generated by *a*

[56] *EW*, p. 179. My parenthesis. Elsewhere Marx echoes Moses Hess, remarking: ' Private property has made us so stupid and partial that an object is only *ours* when we have it, when it exists for us as capital or when it is directly eaten, drunk, worn, inhabited, etc., in short, *utilised* in some way ' (p. 159).

specific form of society – capitalism – and the frustrated realisation of that potential. What separates man from the animals is not the mere existence of biological differences between mankind and other species, but the cultural achievements of men, which are the outcome of a very long process of social development. While the biological attributes of man are a necessary condition of these achievements, the sufficient condition is the evolution of society itself. The alienation of men from their ' species-being' is a social separation from socially generated characteristics and propensities.[57]

Early conception of communism

The *Manuscripts* also contain Marx's first extensive discussion of communism. The continuity is evident between this exposition and the earlier analysis of ' true democracy ' in Marx's critique of Hegel's philosophy of the state. But in the discussion in the *Manuscripts*, the influence of French socialism is unmistakable, and Marx drops the term ' democracy ' in favour of ' communism '.[58] The overcoming of alienation, Marx declares, hinges upon the supersession of private property. It follows from the fact that alienation in production is basic to other forms of alienation, such as in religion or the state, that the establishment of ' true democracy ' is not enough; what is demanded is a more thorough-going reorganisation of society, based upon the eradication of the contemporary relationship between private property and wage-labour.

Marx separates his own conception of communism from that of ' crude communism '.[59] The main form of crude communism is based upon emotional antipathy towards private property, and asserts that all men should be reduced to a similar level, so that everyone has an equal share of property. This is not genuine communism, Marx asserts, since it rests upon the same sort of distorted objectification of labour as is found in the theory of political economy. Crude communism of this sort becomes impelled towards a primitive asceticism, in which the community has become the capitalist instead of the individual. In crude communism, the rule of property is still dominant, but negatively;

Universal *envy* setting itself up as a power is only a camouflaged form of *cupidity* which re-establishes itself and satisfies itself in a *different* way... How

---

[57] Statements such as Meyer's that Marx ' posited a noble and intelligent human species, whose goodness and intelligence are frustrated by the process of civilisation ' (Alfred G. Meyer: *Marxism, the Unity of Theory and Practice* (Ann Arbor, 1963), p. 57) are plainly inadequate. As Mészáros remarks: ' There is no trace of a sentimental or romantic nostalgia for nature in (Marx's) conception. His programme... does not advocate a return to " nature ", to a " natural " set of primitive, or " simple " needs...' István Mészáros: *Marx's Theory of Alienation* (London, 1970).

[58] Marx mentions the influence of the German socialists; but argues that ' the *original* and important German works on this subject ' are limited to certain of the writings of Hess, Weitling and Engels. *EW*, p. 64.

[59] It is not wholly clear whom Marx has in mind here, but the reference is probably to the followers of Babeuf and Cabet. Engels discusses these groups in his ' The progress of social reform on the Continent ', *We*, vol. 1, pp. 480–96.

little this abolition of private property represents a genuine appropriation is shown by the abstract negation of the whole world of culture and civilisation, and the regression to the *unnatural* simplicity of the *poor*, crude and wantless individual who has not only surpassed private property but has not yet even attained to it.[60]

Crude communism, Marx continues, has not grasped the possibility of the positive transcendence of private property. The destruction of private property is certainly a necessary condition for the transition to a new form of society. But the organising principle of the future socialist society must be centred upon ' the *positive* abolition of *private property*, of *human self-alienation*, and thus the real *appropriation* of *human* nature through and for man '; it will involve ' the return of man himself as a *social*, i.e., really human, being (*als eines gesellschaftlichen, d.h. menschlichen Menschen*) a complete and conscious return which assimilates all the wealth of previous development.' [61] The recovery of the social character of human existence is integral to Marx's conception of communism, as stated in the *Manuscripts*. Communist society will be based, not upon the egoistic self-seeking which the economists assume to be characteristic of human nature in general, but upon the conscious awareness of the reciprocal dependence of the individual and the social community. The social nature of man, Marx stresses, penetrates to the roots of his being, and is by no means simply manifest in those activities which are conducted in direct association with others. Communism will not, however, deny the individuality of each person. On the contrary, the whole import of Marx's discussion is that communist society will allow, in a way which is impossible under prior systems of production, the expansion of the particular potentialities and capabilities of individuals. For Marx, there is no paradox in this. It is only through the social community that man becomes individualised, via the utilisation of the resources which are collective products.

This exciting and brilliant formula is integrated with a reiteration of the limitations of the ' critical philosophy ' of the Young Hegelians. It is not enough to supersede private property in theory, to replace the ' idea ' of private property with the ' idea ' of communism. The actual attainment of communism ' will in reality involve a very severe and protracted process '.[62]

[60] *EW*, p. 154; *We, Ergd*, vol. 1, pp. 534–5.
[61] *EW*, p. 155; *We, Ergd*, vol. 1, p. 536.
[62] *EW*, p. 176; *We, Ergd*, vol. 1, p. 553.

2. Historical materialism

The first fruit of Marx's association with Engels was the heavily polemical *The Holy Family*, which was begun in the latter part of 1844, and was published towards the end of 1845. The bulk of the book is the work of Marx, and it documents Marx's final break with the rest of the Young Hegelians. It was followed shortly afterwards by *The German Ideology*, written in 1845–6, also primarily a critical work, but one in which Marx for the first time outlines a general statement of the tenets of historical materialism. From this time onwards, Marx's general outlook changed little, and the rest of his life was devoted to the theoretical exploration and the practical application of the views set out in this latter work.

The full text of *The German Ideology* was not published in the lifetime of Marx or Engels. In 1859, looking back to the period at which *The German Ideology* was written, Marx wrote that he and Engels were not disappointed that they could not get the work published: they 'abandoned the work to the gnawing criticism of the mice all the more willingly ', since the main purpose – ' self-clarification ' – had been achieved.[1] Nonetheless, Marx explicitly refers to his ' Critique ' of Hegel, and to the year 1844, as marking the most significant line of demarcation in his intellectual career. It was the analysis of Hegel's philosophy of the state, Marx wrote in his preface to *A Contribution to the Critique of Political Economy*, which led him to the conclusion ' that legal relations as well as forms of State are to be grasped neither from themselves nor from the so-called general development of the human mind (*Geist*), but rather are rooted in the material conditions of life '.[2]

Engels later remarked of *The German Ideology* that the exposition of the materialistic conception of history presented therein ' proves only how incomplete our knowledge of economic history still was at that time '.[3] But, although Marx's knowledge of economic history was indeed thin at this period – the scheme of ' stages ' of the development of productive systems set out there was subsequently considerably overhauled – the account of historical materialism which is given in the work accords closely with that later portrayed by Marx on other occasions. All precise dividing lines are arbitrary; but while *The German Ideology* is sometimes regarded as part of Marx's

---

[1] *SW*, vol. 1, p. 364. For Engels' subsequent appraisal of the significance of the early writings, up to and including *The German Ideology*, see A. Voden: ' Talks with Engels ', in *Reminiscences of Marx and Engels* (Moscow, n.d.), pp. 330ff.

[2] *SW*, vol. 1, p. 362; *We*, vol. 13, p. 8.

[3] *SW*, vol. 2, p. 359.

' early ' period, it is more appropriate to regard it as the first important work representing Marx's mature position.

Debate over the relevance of Marx's writings of 1843 and 1844 to his mature conception of historical materialism has simmered continuously since their publication in 1929–32. The controversy has obvious ramifications of a directly political nature, and it is difficult to suppose that the points at issue are likely to be resolved to the satisfaction of all parties involved. But in fact the main lines of continuity between the ' Critique ' of Hegel, the 1844 *Manuscripts*, and Marx's mature thought, are evident enough. The most important themes which Marx developed in the early writings and embodied within his later works, are the following:

1. The conception, for which Marx was heavily indebted to Hegel, of the progressive ' self-creation ' of man. As Marx expresses it in the 1844 *Manuscripts*, ' the *whole of what is called world history* is nothing but the creation of man by human labour. . . '.[4]

2. The notion of alienation. One reason why Marx largely dropped the term ' alienation ' from his writings after 1844 was certainly his desire to separate his own position decisively from abstract philosophy. Thus in *The Communist Manifesto* (1848), Marx writes derisively of the ' philosophical nonsense ' of the German philosophers who write of the ' alienation of the human essence '.[5] The main implication of the views which, although they were substantially present in the *Manuscripts*, were not fully worked out until the writing of *The German Ideology*, is that alienation must be studied as an historical phenomenon, which can only be understood in terms of the development of specific social formations. Marx's studies of the stages of historical development trace the growth of the division of labour and the emergence of private property, culminating in the process of the alienation of the peasantry from control of their means of production with the disintegration of European feudalism. This latter process, the creation of a large mass of propertyless wage-labourers, is portrayed in *Capital* as a necessary precondition for the rise of capitalism.[6]

3. The kernel of the theory of the state, and its supersession in the future form of society, as set out in Marx's ' Critique ' of Hegel's philosophy of the state. While Marx had, at the time of the writing of the ' Critique ', only a rudimentary conception of the sort of social order which he hoped and

---

[4] *EW*, p. 166. On Marx's concept of ' labour ', see Helmut Klages: *Technischer Humanismus* (Stuttgart, 1964), pp. 11–128.

[5] *CM*, p. 168; *We*, vol. 4, p. 486.

[6] The view that Marx eliminated the concept of ' alienation ' from his later writings, and therefore that there is a major break in continuity between Marx's early and later works, is expressed by Louis Feuer: ' What is alienation? The career of a concept ', *New Politics*, 1962, pp. 116–34; and by Daniel Bell: ' The debate on alienation ', in Leopold Labedz: *Revisionism* (London, 1963), pp. 195–211. For a comparable statement, but from an opposed political perspective, cf. Louis Althusser: *For Marx* (London, 1969), pp. 51–86 and *passim*.

expected would replace capitalism, the thesis that the abolition of the state can be achieved through the elimination of the separate sphere of the ' political' remains intrinsic to his later views upon this issue.

4. The main rudiments of historical materialism as a perspective for the analysis of social development. In spite of the fact that Marx frequently writes in the language of Hegel and Feuerbach in his early works, it is very clear that Marx's emergent standpoint constitutes a decisive epistemological break with these writers, and especially with Hegel. It is not a new philosophy which Marx seeks to substitute for the older views; Marx repudiates philosophy in favour of an approach which is social and historical. Thus Marx already stresses in the 1844 *Manuscripts* that capitalism is rooted in a definite form of society, the main structural characteristic of which is a dichotomous class relation between capital and wage-labour.

5. A summary conception of the theory of revolutionary *Praxis*. Marx's comments on Strauss and Bauer (that they substitute ' the " self-consciousness " of abstract man for the substance of " abstract nature " ') [7] anticipate the views stated at length in *The Holy Family* and *The German Ideology*, that critical philosophy is irrelevant to anything but the very early stages of a revolutionary movement. Only by the union of theory and practice, by the conjunction of theoretical understanding and practical political activity, can social change be effected. This means integrating the study of the emergent transformations potential in history with a programme of practical action which can actualise these changes.

The crux of the transition between the 1844 *Manuscripts* and *The German Ideology* is to be found in the short set of critical propositions on Feuerbach which Marx wrote in March 1845, and which have since become famous as the *Theses on Feuerbach*.[8] Marx makes several criticisms of Feuerbach. In the first place, Feuerbach's approach is unhistorical. Feuerbach conceives of an abstract ' man ' prior to society : he not only reduces man to religious man, but fails to see ' that " religious feeling " is itself a social product and that the abstract individual he analyses belongs to a particular form of society '.[9] Secondly, Feuerbach's materialism remains at the level of a philosophical doctrine, which simply regards ideas as ' reflections ' of material reality. There is, in fact, a constant reciprocity between the consciousness and human *Praxis*. Feuerbach, in common with all previous materialist philosophers, treats ' material reality ' as the determinant of human activity, and does not analyse the modification of the ' objective ' world by the ' subject ', i.e., by the activity of men. Marx also makes this extremely important point

---

[7] *EW*, p. 195.

[8] The *Theses on Feuerbach* were first published in 1888 by Engels, who remarks that they contain ' the brilliant germ of a new world outlook ' (*SW*, vol. 2, p. 359). Here I quote from the translation in *WYM*, pp. 400–2.

[9] *WYM*, p. 402.

in another way. Feuerbach's materialistic doctrine, he states, is unable to deal with the fact that revolutionary activity is the outcome of the conscious, willed acts of men, but instead portrays the world in terms of the ' one-way ' influence of material reality over ideas. However, Marx points out, ' circumstances are changed by men and ... the educator must himself be educated ...'.[10]

In Marx's eyes, Feuerbach has made a contribution of decisive importance in showing that ' philosophy [i.e., Hegel's philosophy] is nothing more than religion brought into thought and developed by thought, and that it is equally to be condemned as another form and mode of existence of human alienation '.[11] But, in so doing, Feuerbach sets out a ' contemplative ' or passive materialism, neglecting Hegel's emphasis upon ' the dialectic of negativity as the moving and creating principle ...'.[12] It is this dialectic between the subject (man in society) and object (the material world), in which men progressively subordinate the material world to their purposes, and thereby transform those purposes and generate new needs, which becomes focal to Marx's thought.

The materialist thesis

The general conception of historical materialism which is established in *The German Ideology* and subsequent writings is hence very different from that of Feuerbach, and from earlier traditions of philosophical materialism. As Marx employs it, ' materialism ' does not refer to the assumption of any logically argued ontological position.[13] Marx undoubtedly accepts a ' realist ' standpoint, according to which ideas are the product of the human brain in sensory transaction with a knowable material world; ideas are not founded in imminent categories given in the human mind independently of experience. But this definitely does not involve the application of a deterministic philosophical materialism to the interpretation of the development of society. Human consciousness is conditioned in dialectical interplay between subject and object, in which man actively shapes the world he lives in at the same time as it shapes him. This can be illustrated by Marx's observation, developing a point made in the *Theses on Feuerbach*, that even our perception of the material world is conditioned by society. Feuerbach does not see that sensory perception is not fixed and immutable for all time, but is integrated within a phenomenal world which is:

---

[10] *WYM*, p. 401. [11] *EW*, p. 197, my parenthesis.
[12] *EW*, p. 202. For an expanded treatment of the significance of this point, see below, pp. 403–6.
[13] Which is not to say, of course, that Marx's position does not imply definite ontological assumptions. cf. H. B. Acton: *The Illusion of the Epoch* (London, 1955). For a convincing refutation of the view that Marx is a ' materialist ' in the traditional sense, see Alfred Schmidt: *Der Begriff der Natur in der Lehre von Marx* (Frankfurt, 1962); also Z. A. Jordan: *The Evolution of Dialectical Materialism* (London, 1967).

an historical product, the result of the activity of a whole succession of generations, each standing on the shoulders of the preceding one, developing further its
industry and its intercourse, modifying its social order according to the changed
needs. Even the objects of the simplest ' sensuous certainty' are only given him
through social development, industry and commercial intercourse.[14]

For Marx, history is a process of the continuous creation, satisfaction and
re-creation of human needs. This is what distinguishes men from the animals,
whose needs are fixed and unchanging. This is why labour, the creative inter-
change between men and their natural environment, is the foundation of
human society. The relation of the individual to his material environment is
mediated by the particular characteristics of the society of which he is a
member. In studying the development of human society, we must start from
an empirical examination of the concrete processes of social life which are
the *sine qua non* of human existence. As Marx expresses it in a passage worth
quoting at length:

This method of approach is not devoid of premises. It starts out from the real
premises and does not abandon them for a moment. Its premises are men, not
in any fantastic isolation and rigidity, but in their actual, empirically perceptible
process of development under definite conditions. As soon as this active life-
process is described, history ceases to be a collection of dead facts as it is with
the materialists (themselves still abstract), or an imagined activity of imagined
subjects, as with the idealists.

Where speculation ends – in real life – there real, positive science begins: the
representation of the practical activity, of the practical process of development of
men. Talk about consciousness ceases, and real knowledge has to take its place.
When reality is depicted, philosophy as an independent branch of knowledge
loses its medium of existence. At most its place can be taken by a synthesis of the
most general results, that may be abstracted from observation of the historical
development of men. Separated from actual history, these abstractions have in
themselves no value whatsoever. They can only serve to facilitate the ordering of
historical materials, to indicate the sequence of its separate layers. But they by
no means provide a recipe or scheme, as does philosophy, for neatly trimming
the epochs of history. On the contrary, the difficulties only first begin when we
set about the observation and the arrangement – the real depiction – of the
materials, whether it be of a past epoch or of the present.[15]

In this resonant phraseology, Marx proclaims the need for an empirical
science of society which will be founded upon the study of the creative and
dynamic interaction between man and nature, the generative process whereby
man makes himself.

Marx's conception of the main ' stages' in the development of society, in
common with several other basic areas within his works, has to be recon-
structed from fragmentary materials. Apart from the scheme given in *The
German Ideology*, Marx nowhere makes an integrated exposition of the
main types of society which he distinguished. Nevertheless the general

[14] *GI*, p. 57; *We*, vol. 3, p. 43.
[15] *GI*, pp. 38–9; *We*, vol. 3, p. 27.

principles which inform Marx's interpretation of social development are clear. Each of the various types of society which Marx identifies has its own characteristic internal dynamics or 'logic' of development. But these can only be discovered and analysed by *ex post facto* empirical analysis. This is emphasised both as a broad theoretical principle and more specifically in tracing the process of development from one type of society to another. 'History is nothing', Marx affirms, 'but the succession of the separate generations, each of which exploits the materials, the capital funds, the productive forces handed down to it by all preceding generations, and thus, on the one hand, continues the traditional activity in completely changed circumstances and, on the other, modifies the old circumstances with a completely changed activity.' [16] It is simply a teleological distortion to attribute 'goals' to history, such that 'later history is made the goal of earlier history'.[17]

Marx expresses the same views when, commenting upon the assertion that a capitalist stage is a necessary prerequisite to the establishment of communism in every modern society, he rejects a unilinear standpoint. Taking an earlier period of history as illustrative, he cites the case of Rome. Certain of the conditions which were to play an essential role in the formation of capitalism in western Europe at a later period already existed in Rome, but instead giving rise to capitalist production, the Roman economy disintegrated internally. This shows 'that events of a striking similarity, but occurring in different historical contexts, produced quite different results'. This can be understood, Marx continues, if one studies these situations separately, 'but we shall never succeed in understanding them if we rely upon the *passe partout* of a historical–philosophical theory whose chief quality is that of being supra-historical'.[18]

Marx's typology of society is based upon tracing the progressive differentiation of the division of labour. As he states in the 1844 *Manuscripts*, the expansion of the division of labour is synonymous with the growth of alienation and private property. The formation of class society out of the original undifferentiated system of communal property is, of course, contingent upon specialisation in the division of labour; and it is the division of labour which by identifying men with their particular occupational specialisation (e.g.,

[16] *GI*, p. 60. cf. also *The Holy Family, or Critique of Critical Critique* (Moscow, 1956), p. 125.

[17] *GI*, p. 60. Marx makes the same criticism in reference to Proudhon's use of Hegel's dialectic. Proudhon simply substitutes economic categories for the Hegelian succession of ideas, and thus is absolved from studying historical development in detail. 'M. Proudhon considers economic relations as so many social phases engendering one another, resulting from one another like antithesis from thesis, and realising in their logical sequence the impersonal reason of humanity.' *The Poverty of Philosophy* (London, n.d.), p. 93.

[18] Letter to the editor of *Otyecestvenniye Zapisky*, translation after T. B. Bottomore and Maximilien Rubel: Karl Marx: *Selected Writings in Sociology and Social Philosophy* (London, 1963), p. 38.

'wage-labourer') negates their range of capacities as 'universal' producers. Thus: 'The various stages of development in the division of labour are just so many different forms of ownership; i.e., the existing stage in the division of labour determines also the relations of individuals to one another with reference to the material, instrument, and product of labour.'[19]

Pre-class systems

Every form of human society presupposes some rudimentary division of labour. But in the simplest type of society, tribal society, this is minimal, involving a broad division between the sexes: women, being largely occupied with the rearing of children, play a lesser productive role than men. Man is at first a wholly communal being; individualisation is a historical product, associated with an increasingly complex and specialised division of labour. A progressively more complicated division of labour goes hand in hand with the capacity to produce a surplus over and above what is necessary to satisfy basic wants. This in turn entails the exchange of goods; exchange in its turn produces the progressive individualisation of men – a process which reaches its apex under capitalism, with the development of a highly specialised division of labour, a money economy, and commodity production. Men thus only become individualised *through* the process of history: '[Man] originally appears as a *species-being*, a *tribal being, a herd animal*. . . Exchange itself is a major agent of this individualisation.'[20] Property is also at first communal; private property does not derive from a state of nature, but is the outcome of later social development. It is nonsense, Marx asserts, to conceive of human society as originally existing in conditions where separate individuals, each owning his little piece of private property, at some date came together to form a community through some kind of contractual agreement. 'An isolated individual could no more possess property in land than he could speak. At most he could live off it as a source of supply, like the animals.'[21] An individual's relation to the land he works, Marx emphasises, is mediated *through* the community. 'The producer exists as part of a family, a tribe, a grouping of his people, etc. – which assumes historically differing forms as the result of mixture with, and opposition to, others.'[22]

The simplest form of tribal society is that which follows a migratory existence, involving either hunting and gathering, or pastoralism. The tribe is not settled in any one fixed area, and exhausts the resources in one place before moving on to another. Men are not settled as part of their nature; they only become so when at a certain stage the nomadic group becomes a stable agricultural community. Once this transition has occurred, there are many

[19] *GI*, p. 33.
[20] *Pre-Capitalist Economic Formations* (London, 1964), p. 96; *Gru*, pp. 395–6.
[21] *Economic Formations*, p. 81.
[22] *Ibid*. p. 87; *Gru*, p. 389.

factors which influence how the community henceforth develops, including both the physical conditions of the environment, and the internal structure of the tribe, the ' tribal character '. Further differentiation in the division of labour develops through the related processes of population increase, conflicts between tribes thus forced into contact, and the subjugation of one tribe by another.[23] This tends to produce an ethnically-based slavery system, part of a differentiated stratification system involving ' patriarchal family chieftains; below them the members of the tribe; finally slaves'.[24] Contact between societies stimulates trade as well as war. Since ' different communities find different means of production, and different means of subsistence in their natural environment ',[25] exchange of products develops, stimulating further specialisation in the occupational sphere, and providing the first origin of the production of commodities: that is, products intended for sale on an exchange market. The first commodities include such things as slaves, cattle, metals, which are originally exchanged in direct barter. As such exchanges proliferate, and as they encompass a wider variety of commodities, the use of some form of money begins to occur. Exchange relations thus set up promote the interdependence of larger units, and thus make for societies of an expanded size.

While in Marx's earlier works a single line of development is portrayed, simply using historical materials from Europe, from tribal society to ancient society (Greece and Rome), Marx later distinguishes more than one line of development out of tribalism. This includes particularly oriental society (India and China), but Marx also distinguishes a specific type of tribal society, the Germanic, which in conjunction with the disintegrating Roman Empire formed the nexus out of which feudalism developed in western Europe.

Marx's views on the nature of the ' Asiatic mode of production ' (oriental society) underwent some change. In his articles in the *New York Daily Tribune*, beginning in 1853, Marx places considerable stress upon factors of climate and geography which made centralised irrigation important in agriculture, and thus led to strong central government, or ' oriental despotism '.[26] However, Marx's later view is that this is rooted in more integral characteristics of this type of society, generic to the local community itself. Oriental society is highly resistant to change; this tendency to stagnation does not derive solely from the rigid despotic control of the centralised agency of government, but also (and primarily) from the internally self-sufficient character of the village commune. The small village community is ' entirely self-sustaining and contains within itself all conditions of production and surplus production '.[27] The historical origins of this phenomenon are not at

---

[23] cf. *Cap*, vol. 1, pp. 87–9. The similarity to Durkheim may be noted.
[24] *Pre-Capitalist Economic Formations*, pp. 122–3.   [25] *Cap*, vol. 1, p. 351.
[26] *The American Journalism of Marx and Engels* (New York, 1966); *Articles on India* (Bombay, 1951); *Marx on China 1853–60* (London, 1968).
[27] *Pre-Capitalist Economic Formations*, p. 70.

all clear, but however this came about originally, the result is a ' self-sustaining unity of manufactures and agriculture ', which leads to no impetus to further differentiation.

Population increase in oriental society tends only to produce ' a new community . . . on the pattern of the old one, on unoccupied land '.[28] An essential factor in this is the lack of private property in land. Where private ownership of landed property does develop, as in parts of Europe and particularly in Rome, population growth leads to increasing pressure for proprietorship and consequently a constant tendency to expansion. However, in oriental society the individual ' never becomes an owner but only a possessor '. This type of society is not necessarily despotic; small village communes may exist as a segmentalised loosely associated grouping. However, the communities may devote part of their surplus product, often under the inspiration of religion, the ' imagined tribal entity of the god ', as tribute to a despot. But the unity of the ruler with his subjects is not based upon an integrated society bound together by extensive economic interdependence; it remains a society composed basically of segmental units connected by a religious affiliation to the person of the despot.

The self-sufficient character of the local village communities definitely limits the growth of cities, and the latter never came to play a dominant role in either India or China.[29] In the type of society represented by Greece and Rome, on the other hand, the city becomes of central importance. Marx lays considerable stress upon the growth of urbanisation generally as marking the clearest index of differentiation within the division of labour. ' The opposition between town and country begins with the transition from barbarism to civilisation, from tribe to state, from locality to nation, and runs through the whole history of civilisation up to the present day. . .'.[30] The division of city and country provides the historical conditions for the growth of capital, which first begins in the city, and its separation from landed property. In the cities we find the ' beginning of property having its basis only in labour and exchange '.[31]

Ancient society, a city-based civilisation, is the first definite form of class society. Although the Asiatic societies show a certain development of state organisation, they are not regarded by Marx as involving a developed class system, since property remains wholly communal at the local level.[32] Classes

---

[28] *Cap*, vol. 1, p. 358. The structure of the Asian mode of production is eventually undermined by the impact of western colonialism.

[29] This is a point later made by Weber, with reference to both India and China.

[30] *GI*, p. 65; *We*, vol. 3, p. 50.

[31] *GI*, p. 66.

[32] Wittfogel has argued that Marx ' failed to draw a conclusion, which from the standpoint of his own theory seemed inescapable—namely, that under conditions of the Asiatic mode of production the agro-managerial bureaucracy constituted the ruling class '. Karl A. Wittfogel: *Oriental Despotism* (New Haven, 1957), p. 6. Since Marx refers to Russia as a ' semi-Asiatic ' society, the class character of the ' Asian

only come into existence when the surplus of privately appropriated wealth
becomes sufficient for an internally self-recruiting grouping to be clearly set
off from the mass of the producers. Even in ancient society – and particularly
in Greece – private property is still overshadowed by ' communal and public
property'.

The ancient world

Ancient society results ' from the union of several tribes into a city,
either by agreement or conquest '.[33] Unlike in the East, the city is an
economic whole. The original tribes composing the city-states were
aggressive and warlike. The cities were first organised around the military,
and throughout their history both Greece and Rome preserved an expan-
sionist character. Marx's analysis of ancient society concentrates upon the
case of Rome. While Rome is an urban society, it is by no means completely
separated from the influence of landed property. The private landed proprietor is at the same time an urban citizen. Marx describes this as ' a form
in which the agriculturalist lives in a city '.[34] The ruling class is founded,
during all periods of Roman history, upon ownership of landed property.
Precisely because of this, population growth produces pressure for territorial
expansion; and this is the main source of change in Roman society, the main
' contradiction ' built into its structure: ' While . . . this is an essential part of
the economic conditions of the community itself, it breaks the real bond on
which the community rests.' [35] Population expansion, and the militaristic
adventures which this promotes, serve to produce an extension of slavery
and an increasing concentration of landed property. The wars of conquest
and colonisation lead to the emergence of more sharply drawn lines of social
differentiation, causing a swelling of the ranks of the slaves.[36] The slaves
come to bear the full brunt of the productive labour, while the patrician
landlords emerge as an increasingly separate ruling class monopolising public
funds and the organisation of warfare. ' The whole system . . . was founded
on certain limits of the numbers in the population, which could not be surpassed without endangering the conditions of antique civilisation itself.' This
caused the pressure to what Marx calls ' compulsory emigration ', in the
shape of the periodical setting-up of colonies, which ' formed a regular link
in the structure of society '.[37]

The pressure deriving from shortage of land is so strong because there is

mode of production' has considerable political ramifications. Wittfogel gives an
(unsympathetic) account of the debate on Asian society among Russian scholars
(*ibid*. chapter 9). cf. George Lichtheim: ' Marx and the " Asiatic mode of production " ', *St Anthony's Papers*, No. 14, 1963, pp. 86–112.

[33] *GI*, p. 33.
[34] *Pre-Capitalist Economic Formations*, pp. 79–80.
[35] *Ibid*. p. 83.
[36] *Ibid*. pp 92–3.   [37] *American Journalism of Marx and Engels*, p. 77.

no motivation to increase productivity from existing resources. There exists no ideology which would ' push ' toward an interest in maximising profits:

Wealth does not appear as the aim of production, although Cato may well investigate the most profitable cultivation of fields, or Brutus may even lend money at the most favourable rate of interest. The enquiry is always about what kind of property creates the best citizens. Wealth as an end in itself appears only among a few trading peoples. . .[38]

Wealth is not valued for its own sake, but the ' private enjoyment ' it brings; commerce and manufacture are thus looked upon by the ruling class with suspicion and even scorn. Moreover, labour in general is regarded with contempt, and as not worthy of free men.

By the end of the Republic, the Roman state is already founded on ' the ruthless exploitation of the conquered provinces ',[39] a process which is regularised openly under the emperors. Class conflict inside Roman society centres around a struggle between patricians and plebeians. The former exploit the plebeians shamelessly, primarily through usury, which reaches a high development in Rome although never forming part of a general process of capital accumulation. In discussing the role of usury, in the third volume of *Capital*, Marx indicates that while usurers' capital plays an important part in the development of capitalism in combination with other conditions, without these conditions it serves only as a debilitating influence in the economy. This is what happens in Rome; usury exerts an undermining influence upon the small peasantry, since, instead of replenishing the real needs of the plebeians who are continually facing ruin through being forced to serve in wars, the patricians lend money at exorbitant rates of interest. ' As soon as the usury of the Roman patricians had completely ruined the Roman plebeians, the small peasants, this form of exploitation came to an end and a pure slave economy replaced the small peasant economy.' [40]

Slavery as an institution passes through various stages in Roman history. Beginning as a patriarchal system where slaves assist the small producers, the increasing depression of the plebeians themselves into slavery leads to the growth of large estates, the *latifundiae*, where agricultural production for a market is practised on a large scale. But the failure of commerce and industry to develop beyond a certain point, combined with the exploitative depression

---

[38] *Pre-Capitalist Economic Formations*, p. 84. Marx notes that the outlook prevailing in the ancient world, although existing in alienated form – in terms of a ' narrowly national, religious, or political ' world-view – still places man very much at the centre of things as compared to *bourgeois* society, where human ends become subordinated to production and the accumulation of wealth. But Marx continues: ' In fact, however, when the narrow *bourgeois* form has been peeled away, what is wealth, if not the universality of needs, capacities, enjoyments, productive powers, etc., of individuals, produced in universal exchange? ' Thus while the ' childish world of the Ancients ' is in one aspect superior to the modern world, it is so only in terms of a relatively narrow range of human potentialities. *Ibid.* pp. 84–5.

[39] The phrase is Engels', *SW*, vol. 2, p. 299.

[40] *Cap*, vol. 3, p. 582.

of the majority of the population into poverty, means that the *latifundiae* eventually themselves become uneconomical. A further decline in trade sets in, together with the decay of the towns. What commerce survives is reduced to ruin by the taxation imposed by state officials seeking to prop up a disintegrating state. Slavery itself begins to be abolished, and the large plantations are broken up and leased to hereditary tenants in small farms. Small-scale farming against becomes predominant.

Thus Rome, at its height a great empire producing a concentration of enormous wealth, eventually decays; while a considerable development of productive forces is attained, the internal composition of the society prevents growth beyond a certain point. The expropriation of large numbers of peasants from their means of production – a process upon which Marx lays great stress in discussing the origins of capitalism – does not lead to the development of capitalist production, but instead to a system based on slavery, which eventually disintegrates from within.

Feudalism and the origins of capitalist development
The barbarian onslaught upon Rome, therefore, was only the precipitating condition of the fall of the ancient world: the real causes derive from the internal development of Rome itself. Marx apparently does not regard ancient society as a *necessary* stage in the development of feudalism;[41] but in western Europe at any rate the disintegration of the Roman Empire forms the basis for the emergence of feudal society. Marx nowhere discusses the early phases of feudalism in any detail. But it is probable that he would accept the substance of the views set out by Engels in his *Origin of the Family, Private Property and the State*, according to which the barbarians, faced with the task of administering the territories they have acquired, are forced to modify their own system of government and adopt elements of the Roman legacy. This new social order centres upon the dominant position of the military commander, and eventuates in the transformation of military leadership into monarchy.[42] A new nobility thus forms itself around a personal retinue of military retainers, and supplemented by an educated elite drawn from Romanised officials and scholars. Several centuries of continual warfare and civil disorder in western Europe lead to the permanent impoverishment of the free peasant farmers, who make up the core of the barbarian armies, and to their consequent enserfment to local noble landlords. By the ninth century selfdom becomes predominant. Marx does say in one place, however, that throughout the feudal period a substructure of the old barbarian (Germanic) form of social organisation remains, evinced

---

[41] *Pre-Capitalist Economic Formations*, p. 70.
[42] Marx does in one place refer briefly to the system following Rome in Europe as a 'synthesis' in which 'two systems mutually modified each other'. *A Contribution to the Critique of Political Economy* (Chicago, 1904), p. 288.

concretely in the survival of communal property on the local level. This substructure 'remained throughout the Middle Ages the unique stronghold of popular liberty and popular life '.[43]

Marx has no great interest in delineating the characteristics of feudal society, concentrating more of his attention upon the process of transition from feudalism to capitalism – although even here there are large gaps and obscurities in his treatment. What can be gleaned of Marx's view of the mature period of feudal society in Europe follows the standard conceptions in the economic history of his day. The basis of feudal economy consists in small-scale peasant agriculture involving the bonded serf; this is supplemented by domestic industry and by handicraft production in the towns. But the feudal system is basically a rural one: ' If Antiquity started out from the *town* and its little territory, the Middle Ages started out from the *country*.' [44] In serfdom, although the worker must surrender a certain amount of his produce to the lord, there is only a low degree of alienation between the producer and his product. The serf is his own proprietor, by and large producing for the needs of himself and his family. ' The lord does not try to extract the maximum profit from his estate. He rather consumes what is there, and tranquilly leaves the care of producing it to the serfs and tenant farmers.' [45] The history of the early stages of capitalism is, for Marx, very largely a history of the progressively increasing alienation of the small producer from control of his product: in other words, of his expropriation from his means of production, and his consequent dependence upon the sale of his labour on the market.

The disintegration of feudalism, and the early development of capitalism, is bound up with the growth of towns. Marx emphasises the importance of the emergence of the municipal movements in the twelfth century, which had a ' revolutionary character ', and as a result of which the urban communities eventually secure a high degree of administrative autonomy.[46] As in Antiquity, the development of urban centres goes hand in hand with the formation of mercantile and usurers' capital, and a monetary system in terms of which they operate, which act as a force undermining the system based upon agricultural production.[47] While a few towns probably did persist from the period of the Roman Empire, the development of urban centres into wealthy

---

[43] *Pre-Capitalist Economic Formations*, pp. 144–5. (From the third draft of Marx's letter to Zasulich.)

[44] *GI*, p. 35.

[45] *EW*, p. 115.

[46] Marx quotes Thierry to the effect that the word *capitalia* first appears with the rise of the autonomous urban communes. Letter from Marx to Engels, July 1854, *Selected Correspondence* (London, 1934), p. 72.

[47] Dobb has argued that the primary factor producing the decay of feudalism ' was the inefficiency of feudalism as a system of production, coupled with the growing needs of the ruling class for revenue . . .'. Maurice Dobb: *Studies in the Development of Capitalism* (London, 1963), p. 42. For a discussion of Dobb's book, see Paul M. Sweezy: *The Transition from Feudalism to Capitalism* (London, 1954).

commercial and manufacturing centres only really begins in the twelfth century; these are populated mainly by freed serfs. The growth of commerce stimulates an ever-widening extension of the use of money, and consequently of commodity exchange, into the formerly self-sufficient rural feudal economy. This facilitates the growth of usury in the towns, stimulates a decline in the fortunes of the land-owning aristocracy and allows the more prosperous peasant to discharge his obligations to the lord in monetary form, or to free himself from the latter's control altogether. In England, by the conclusion of the fourteenth century, serfdom has virtually disappeared. Whatever their feudal title, the vast mass of the labouring population in that country are by that date free peasant proprietors. The fate of serfdom, of course, varies greatly in different parts of Europe, and in some areas serfdom undergoes periods of ' revival '.[48]

Although as early as the fourteenth century we find ' the beginnings of capitalist production ' in Italy,[49] and in the fifteenth century in England, these are very restricted in scope. The towns are dominated by strong guild organisations which strictly limit the number of journeymen and apprentices whom a master may employ, and the guilds keep themselves separate from mercantile capital, ' the only form of free capital with which they came into contact '.[50] Moreover, there is no possibility of capitalism developing while the majority of the labouring population consists of independent peasantry. The process of ' primary accumulation '[51] – that is, the initial formation of the capitalist mode of production – involves, as Marx stresses many times, the expropriation of the peasant from his means of production, a set of events which ' is written in the annals of mankind in letters of blood and fire '.

This process occurs at divergent periods, and in various ways, in different countries, and Marx concentrates upon the example of England, where it appears in ' classic form '. In England, the transformation of independent peasant into wage-labourer begins in earnest in the late fifteenth century.[52] By this time, the great feudal wars have sapped the resources of the nobility. The first ' mass of free proletarians ' is thrown onto the market through the disbanding of retainers by the impoverished aristocracy, and the declining position of the feudal aristocracy is hastened by the growing power of the monarchy. The land-owning aristocracy is increasingly drawn into an ex-

---

[48] A phenomenon to which Engels gives some attention, speaking of the rise of a ' second serfdom ' in eastern parts of Europe in the fifteenth century. Letter to Marx, December 1882, *Selected Correspondence*, pp. 407–8.

[49] Marx mentions that, in Italy, where the earliest development of capitalist production occurs, ' the dissolution of serfdom also took place earlier than elsewhere '. *Cap*, vol. 1, p. 716.

[50] *Cap*, vol. 1, p. 358.

[51] The phrase is usually rendered ' primitive accumulation '. Here I follow Sweezy (p. 17) and others in translating *ursprünglich* as ' primary ', which avoids the potentially misleading implications of the usual rendering.

[52] *Cap*, vol. 1, pp. 718ff.

change economy. The result is the enclosure movement, to which the rise of Flemish wool manufacture, leading to a sharp rise in the price of wool in England, gives a further impetus. In 'defiant opposition to King and Parliament' the feudal lords uproot large numbers of the peasantry, forcibly driving them from their land. Arable land is turned into pasture, which only requires a few herdsmen. This whole process of expropriation receives in the sixteenth century 'a new and frightening impulse' from the Reformation; the extensive church lands are handed out to royal favourites or sold cheaply to speculators who drive out the hereditary tenants and consolidate their holdings into large units. The expropriated peasantry are 'turned *en masse* into beggars, vagabonds, partly from inclination, in most cases from stress of circumstances'.[53] This is met with fierce legislation against vagrancy, by which means the vagabond population is subjected to 'the discipline necessary for the wage system'.[54]

By the early period of the sixteenth century then, there exists in England the beginnings of a proletariat – a stratum of dispossessed peasants who are a 'floating', mobile group, separated from their means of production, and thrown onto the market as 'free' wage-labourers. Marx notes scornfully that political economists interpret this in a purely positive light, speaking of the liberation of men from feudal ties and restrictions, neglecting altogether the fact that this freedom entails 'the most shameless violation of the " sacred rights of property " and the grossest acts of violence to persons '.[55]

In themselves, however, these events cannot, Marx indicates, be regarded as sufficient conditions for the rise of capitalism. At the turn of the sixteenth century, the decaying remnants of feudalism are poised between further disintegration and a movement into a more advanced productive form: capitalism. A factor of some importance in stimulating the latter development is the rapid and vast expansion of overseas commerce which develops as a result of the startling geographical discoveries made in the last part of the fifteenth century. These include principally the discovery of America and the rounding of the Cape, which 'gave to commerce, to navigation, to industry, an impulse never before known, and thereby, to the revolutionary element in the tottering feudal society, a rapid development'.[56] The rapid influx of capital deriving from this mushrooming trade, plus the flood of precious metals coming into the country following the discovery of gold and silver in America, cuts through the existing social and economic arrangements in England. New manufacturers become established at the sea-ports, and at inland centres outside the control of the older corporate towns and their guild organisations. The former undergo rapid growth, in spite of 'an embittered struggle of the corporate towns against these new industrial nur-

[53] *Cap*, vol. 1, pp. 718, 721 & 734; *We*, vol. 23, pp. 746, 748 & 762.
[54] *Cap*, vol. 1, p. 737.
[55] *Cap*, vol. 1, p. 727.
[56] *CM*, p. 133; *GI*, p. 73.

series '.[57] Modern capitalism thus begins away from the older centres of manufacture, ' on the basis of large-scale maritime and overland trade '.[58] Organised manufacture does not originate in the craft industries controlled by the guilds, but in what Marx calls the ' rural subsidiary operations ' of spinning and weaving, which need little technical training. While rural society is the last place where capitalism develops in its ' purest and most logical form ', the initial impetus is located there.[59] Not before this stage is reached is capital a revolutionary force. While the previous development of mercantilism beginning in the eleventh century acts as a major factor in dissolving feudal structures, the towns which develop are essentially dependent upon the old system, and play an essentially conservative role once they attain a certain level of power.

The ascendency of those who control capital, the emergent bourgeoisie, develops progressively from the opening of the sixteenth century onwards. The influx of gold and silver produces a sharp increase in prices. This acts to offer large profits in trade and manufacturing, but is a source of ruination to the great landlords, and swells the number of wage-labourers. The fruit of all this in the political sphere is the first English revolution, which is one moment in a rapid extension of state power. The developing mechanisms of centralised administration and consolidated political power are used ' to hasten, hothouse fashion, the process of transformation of the feudal mode of production into the capitalist mode, and to shorten the transition '.[60]

Not a great deal is known, even today, of the specific origins of the first capitalists, and Marx has little in the way of concrete historical material to offer on this matter. He does indicate, however, that there are two contrasting historical modes of progression into capitalist production. The first is where a segment of the merchant class moves over from purely trading operations to take a direct hand in production. This occurred in the early development of capitalism in Italy, and is the main source of recruitment of capitalists in England in the late fifteenth and early sixteenth centuries. However, this form of capitalist formation soon becomes ' an obstacle to a real capitalist mode of production and declines with the development of the latter '.[61] The second avenue of capitalist development is, according to Marx, ' the really revolutionary way '. Here individual producers themselves accumulate capital, and move from production to expand the sphere of their activities to include trade. They therefore from the very beginning operate outside the guilds and in conflict with them. While Marx gives only a few hints of how this second mode of development occurs in manufacture, he

---

[57] *Cap*, vol. 1, p. 751.
[58] *Pre-Capitalist Economic Formations*, p. 116.
[59] *Ibid.* p. 116. Marx adds: ' Hence the ancients, who never advanced beyond specifically urban craft skill and application, were never able to achieve large-scale industry' (p. 117).
[60] *Cap*, vol. 1, p. 751.   [61] *Cap*, vol. 3, p. 329.

does specify some aspects of the process as it occurs in farming in England. By the middle of the seventeenth century much of the land is owned by capitalist farmers employing wage-labour and producing for a commodity market. Their property is considerably augmented by their forcible usurpation of those common lands which still survive from the feudal period. But this latter process is an extended one, not completed until the second half of the eighteenth century. Its completion is contemporaneous with the final disappearance of the independent peasantry, ' incorporating land as capital ' and creating for the industries of the town ' the necessary supply of an outlawed proletariat '.[62]

Marx distinguishes two broad stages of productive organisation in the capitalist period. The first stage is dominated by manufacture. The distinctive characteristic of this form is that it involves the breaking-down of craft skills into various specialised tasks carried out by a number of workers, who accomplish collectively what one skilled man would do under the guild system. Manufacture is more efficient than handicraft production, not because of any technical advances, but because the division of labour it involves makes it possible to produce more units per man-hour. This form of production, which is predominant from the sixteenth century until the concluding part of the eighteenth in England, has definite limitations. The expansion of markets by the end of the eighteenth century is so great that manufacture is insufficiently productive to meet the demands placed upon it. As a consequence, a strong pressure builds up to create technically more efficient means of production; ' the development of machinery was a necessary consequence of the needs of the market '.[63] The result is the ' industrial revolution '.[64] Mechanisation henceforth dominates the capitalist mode of production. There is set in motion the constant impetus towards technological modification which becomes a hallmark of capitalism. The development of increasingly more complicated and expensive machinery is a primary factor in the centralisation of the capitalist economy upon which Marx lays so much stress in *Capital* in discussing the predicted dissolution of capitalism.

[62] *Cap*, vol. 1, p. 733; *We*, vol. 23, p. 761.
[63] Letter to Annenkov, quoted in *Poverty of Philosophy*, p. 156.
[64] Engels used this term before Marx. See the former's *Condition of the Working Class in England in 1844* (Oxford, 1968), pp. 9–26. There is some dispute over the origin of the term ' industrial revolution '. cf. Dobb, p. 258.

3. The relations of production and class structure

1618907

According to Marx, the development of society is the result of the continual productive interaction between men and nature. Men ' begin to distinguish themselves from animals as soon as they begin to *produce* their means of subsistence. . .'.[1] The ' production and reproduction of life ' is both an exigency dictated by the biological needs of the human organism and, more importantly, the creative source of new needs and capabilities. Thus productive activity is at the root of society in both an historical and an analytical sense. Production is ' the first historical act '; and ' the production of material life . . . is . . . a fundamental condition of all history, which today, as thousands of years ago, must daily and hourly be fulfilled merely in order to sustain human life '.[2] Every individual, in his day-to-day actions, recreates and reproduces society at every moment: this is both the source of what is stable in social organisation and the origin of endless modification.

Every kind of production system entails a definite set of social relationships existing between individuals involved in the productive process. This is at the root of one of Marx's most important criticisms of political economy and of utilitarianism generally. The conception of the ' isolated individual ' is a construction of the bourgeois philosophy of individualism, and serves to conceal the social character which production always manifests. Marx refers to Adam Smith as the ' Luther of political economy ' because he, and after him the other economists, have correctly identified labour as the source of man's own self-creation.[3] But what the economists have obscured is that the self-creation of man through production entails a process of *social* development. Human beings never produce simply as individuals, but only as members of a definite form of society. There is no type of society, therefore, which is not founded upon a definite set of relations of production.[4]

In production, men not only act on nature but also on one another. They produce only by cooperating in a certain way and mutually exchanging their activities. In order to produce, they enter into definite connections and relations with one another and only within these social connections and relations does their action on nature, does production, take place.[5]

---

[1] *GI*, p. 31. [2] *GI*, p. 39.
[3] *EW*, p. 147.
[4] The term usually employed by Marx (*Produktionsverhältnisse*) has, in fact, a double meaning in English, and can refer both to ' conditions ' and to ' relations ' of production. On the use of the term ' relations of production ' in Marx's writings, see Louis Althusser *et al.*: *Lire le Capital* (Paris, 1967), vol. 2, pp. 149–59.
[5] *SW*, vol. 1, p. 89.

In every form of society there exists ' a sum of productive forces, an historically created relation of individuals to nature and to one another, which is handed down to each generation from its predecessor. . .'.[6] Marx does not attempt to construct any sort of general theory of what brings about expansion in the forces of production (*Produktionskräfte*). This can only be explained by concrete social and historical analysis. Thus the modifications of the productive forces involved in the transition from feudalism to capitalism can be explained in terms of a convergent set of historical events. Moreover, there are cases of societies where the forces of production become quite highly evolved, but where other elements of the social organisation retard any further advance. Marx quotes the instance of Peru, which in certain respects had a developed economy, but was held back by the lack of a monetary system. The failure to develop a monetary system was largely contingent upon the isolated geographical position of the country, which inhibited the expansion of trade.[7]

Class domination

According to Marx, classes emerge where the relations of production involve a differentiated division of labour which allows for the accumulation of surplus production that can be appropriated by a minority grouping, which thus stands in an exploitative relationship to the mass of producers. In discussing the relationships between classes in society, Marx usually employs the terms *Herrschaft* and *Klassenherrschaft*. In English versions of Marx's writings, it is customary to translate these as ' rule ' and ' class rule '. But these terms suggest rather more of a deliberate imposition of power than is necessarily implied in the German terminology. Consequently it is more appropriate to use the term ' domination ' rather than ' rule '.[8]

Marx's various analyses of class domination are all primarily directed towards the end of explicating the characteristic structure and dynamics of bourgeois society, and conceptual precision is secondary in importance to this overriding focus of attention. Consequently, Marx often uses the term *Klasse* in a somewhat cavalier fashion, and he did not feel compelled, until quite near the end of his intellectual career, to confront the problem of spelling out the concept of class in a precise fashion.[9] As with the concept of ' rationalisation ' in Max Weber's thought, the notion of class is so fundamental to Marx's writings that, in his most important works, he takes its

---

[6] *Gl*, p. 51.

[7] *Gru*, p. 22.

[8] cf. W. Wesolowski: ' Marx's theory of class domination: an attempt at systematisation ', in Nicholas Lobkowicz: *Marx and the Western World* (Notre Dame, 1967), pp. 54–5. On the problem of *Herrschaft* in Weber's writings, see below, p. 156.

[9] ' no credit is due to me for discovering the existence of classes in modern society, nor yet the struggle between them.' Letter to Weydemeyer, March 1852, *Selected Correspondence*, p. 57. cf. Stanislaw Ossowski: *Class and Class Structure in the Social Consciousness*. London, 1963, pp. 69–88 and *passim*.

meaning for granted. It is an irony which has frequently been noted that the manuscripts which Marx left at his death should have broken off at the point at which he was entering upon a systematic analysis of the concept of class.[10] Here, for the first time in his writings, he explicitly poses the question, ' what constitutes a class? ' But what Marx says, before the manuscript ends, is mainly negative. Class must not be identified with either source of income or functional position in the division of labour. These criteria would yield a large plurality of classes: doctors, who receive their income from treatment of the sick, would be a separate class from farmers, who derive theirs from cultivation of land, etc. Moreover, use of such criteria would cut across the position of groupings of individuals in the productive process: two men may, for instance, both be builders, but one may be the propertyless employee of a large firm, while the other owns a small business of his own.

Marx's emphasis that classes are not income groups is a particular aspect of his general premise, stated in *Capital*, that the distribution of economic goods is not a sphere separate to and independent of production, but is determined by the mode of production. Marx rejects as ' absurd ' the contention made by John Stuart Mill, and many of the political economists, that while production is governed by definite laws, distribution is controlled by (malleable) human institutions.[11] Such a view underlies the assumption that classes are merely inequalities in the distribution of income, and therefore that class conflict can be alleviated or even eliminated altogether by the introduction of measures which minimise discrepancies between incomes. For Marx, then, classes are an aspect of the relations of production. The substance of Marx's conception of class is, in spite of the variability of his terminology, relatively easy to infer from the many scattered references which Marx makes in the course of different works. Classes are constituted by the relationship of groupings of individuals to the ownership of private property in the means of production: This yields a model of class relations which is basically dichotomous: all class societies are built around a primary line of division between two antagonistic classes, one dominant and the other subordinate.[12] In Marx's usage, class of necessity involves a conflict relation. On more than one occasion, Marx makes this point by linguistic emphasis. Thus, discussing the position of the peasantry in nineteenth-century France, Marx comments:

The small-holding peasants form a vast mass, the members of which live in similar conditions but without entering into manifold relations with one another. Their mode of production isolates them from one another instead of bringing them into mutual intercourse... In so far as millions of families live under economic conditions of existence that separate their mode of life, their interests and their

[10] The section on ' The classes ', placed at the end of the third volume of *Capital* (edited by Engels) (*Cap*, vol. 3, pp. 862–3), is a mere fragment.

[11] *Gru*, p. 717.

[12] cf. Ralf Dahrendorf: *Class and Class Conflict in an Industrial Society* (Stanford, 1965), pp. 18–27.

culture from those of the other classes, and put them in hostile opposition to the latter, they form a class. In so far as there is merely a local interconnection among these small-holding peasants, and the identity of their interests begets no community, no national bond and no political organisation among them, they do not form a class.[13]

In another context, Marx makes a similar point with reference to the bourgeoisie: capitalists form a class only to the degree that they are forced to carry on a struggle against another class. Otherwise capitalists are in economic competition with each other in the pursuit of profit in the market.[14]

Class structure and market relationships

It is important to emphasise that the dichotomous class conception appears in Marx's writings as a theoretical construct. Only bourgeois society – as Marx projects its future development – approximates closely to this picture. All historical class societies show a more complicated system of relationships which overlaps with the dichotomous axis of class structure. Thus in bourgeois society, these complicating groupings are of three sorts:

1. Classes which, although they play an important economic and political role in the extant form of society, are marginal in the sense that they derive from a set of relations of production which are either being superseded or, conversely, are in the ascendant.[15] An instance of the first is the case of the free peasantry, which although still strong in France and Germany, is becoming drawn into dependence upon capitalistic farmers, or is being forced to join the urban proletariat.[16]

2. Strata which stand in a relationship of functional dependence upon one of the classes, and which consequently tend to identify politically with that class. Those whom Marx calls the 'officers' among administrative workers in industry – the higher managerial staff – fall into this category.[17]

3. Finally, there are heterogeneous clusters of individuals in the *Lumpenproletariat* who stand on the margins of the class system because they are not wholly integrated into the division of labour. These are composed of 'thieves and criminals of all kinds, living on the crumbs of society, people without a definite trade, vagabonds, people without a hearth or home'.[18]

The degree to which a class constitutes a homogeneous entity is historically variable: 'subordinate gradations' exist in all classes.[19] In *The Class Struggles in France* Marx analyses the conflict between financial and in-

---

[13] *SW*, vol. 1, p. 334.
[14] *GI*, p. 69.
[15] cf. Donald Hodges: 'The "intermediate classes" in Marxian theory', *Social Research*, vol. 28, 1961, pp. 241–52.
[16] *SW*, vol. 1, p. 217.
[17] cf. *Cap*, vol. 3, pp. 376ff. Marx also refers to 'savants, lawyers, doctors, etc.', as the '*ideological* representatives and spokesmen' of classes. *SW*, vol. 1, p. 140.
[18] *SW*, vol. 1, p. 155.
[19] *CM*, p. 132.

dustrial capitalists between 1848 and 1850. This is an empirical example of a persistent subdivision within the bourgeoisie as a whole; like other sub-divisions of the same sort, it is founded upon divergent interests of a definite kind: 'it is because profit can be divided into two sorts of revenue. These two sorts of capitalists express nothing other than this fact.' [20] According to Marx, the ordering of classes and the nature of class conflict change considerably with the emergence of successive forms of society. Pre-capitalist societies are overwhelmingly localised in their organisation. To generalise from a metaphor Marx applies to the French peasantry, it can be said that every pre-capitalist society 'is formed by the simple admixture of homologous magnitudes, much as potatoes in a sack form a sack of potatoes'.[21] Economic relationships do not, in such forms of society, manifest themselves as purely market relationships; economic domination or subordination is fused with personal ties between individuals. Thus the domination of the feudal landowner operates through personal connections of bondage and the direct payment of tithes. Moreover, the serf preserves a large measure of control over his means of production in spite of the fact that he has to cede a part of his product as tribute to a master. It is only with the advent of capitalism, which depends upon the expropriation of a mass of labourers who have nothing save their labour-power to offer in exchange for the means of obtaining a livelihood, that naked market relationships appear as the determinant of human productive activity. Bourgeois society 'has pitilessly torn asunder the motley feudal ties that bound man to his "natural superiors", and has left no other nexus between man and man than naked self-interest, than callous "cash payment"' ... In one word, for exploitation, veiled by religious and political illusions, it has substituted naked, shameless, direct, brutal exploitation.' [22] In bourgeois society, therefore, class relationships become simplified and universalised. The progressive development of capitalism, once it is established, more and more tends toward the creation of two great classes in direct opposition on the market: bourgeoisie and proletariat. The other classes – landowners, petty bourgeoisie, and peasantry – are transitional classes, which are increasingly swallowed up by one or other of these two major class groupings.

In Marx's conception, classes form the main linkage between the relations of production and the rest of society, or social 'superstructure' (*Überbau*). Class relationships are the main axis around which political power is distributed, and upon which political organisation depends. For Marx, economic and political power are closely, although not inseparably, linked. Again, however, this theorem has to be placed in an historical dimension. The form of the political agency is closely related to the mode of production, and hence to the degree to which market relationships are of primary significance in

[20] *Gru*, p. 735.
[21] *SW*, vol. 1, p. 334.
[22] *CM*, p. 135.

the economy. Private property as such first emerges in the ancient world, but remains confined to restricted segments of economic life. In the Middle Ages, property moves through several stages, from feudal landed property, to corporative moveable property, eventually giving rise to capital invested in manufacture in the towns. In both ancient society and in the Middle Ages, property continues to be bound largely to the community, and thus so also do relationships of class domination. This means that the operations of political power are still primarily conducted in a diffuse fashion in the *communitas*. Modern capitalism, however, is 'determined by big industry and universal competition, which has cast off all semblance of a communal institution'.[23]

The modern state emerges in conjunction with the struggle of the bourgeoisie against the remnants of feudalism, but is also stimulated by the demands of the capitalist economy.

To this modern private property corresponds the modern state, which, purchased gradually by the owners of property by means of taxation, has fallen entirely into their hands through the national debt, and its existence has become wholly dependent on the commercial credit which the owners of property, the bourgeois, extend to it, as reflected in the rise and fall of state funds on the stock exchange.[24]

The particular form of the state in bourgeois society varies according to the circumstances in which the bourgeoisie has gained the ascendancy. In France, for example, the alliance of the bourgeoisie with the absolute monarchy has stimulated the development of a strongly established official-dom. In Britain, by contrast, the state represents 'an archaic, timeworn and antiquated compromise between the landed aristocracy, which *rules officially*, and the bourgeoisie, which in fact *dominates* in all the various spheres of civil society, but *not officially*'.[25] The specific process which has given rise to this political order in Britain has minimised the importance of bureaucratic elements in the state.

Ideology and consciousness

The dissipation of the community, and the expansion of private property which brings this about, underlies the origins of civil law. The codification of such a body of law occurs for the first time in Rome, but has no lasting consequences because of the internal disintegration of manufacture and commerce in Roman society. With the emergence of modern capitalism, a new phase in the formation of law occurs: Roman law was taken over in the early centres of capitalism in Italy and elsewhere, and made the source of civil law. In civil law, authority is based upon rationalised norms rather than upon the religious prescriptions which are predominant in traditional communities.[26] The modern legal system and judiciary is a principal ideological

[23] *GI*, p. 79.   [24] *GI*, p. 79.
[25] *We*, vol. 11, p. 95.
[26] For Weber's treatment of this issue, see *ES*, vol. 2; cf. also Durkheim: *DL*, pp. 142ff.

support of the bourgeois state. But it is only the contemporary expression of the fact that, in all class societies, the dominant class develops or takes over ideological forms which legitimise its domination. ' The class which has the means of *material* production at its disposal, has control at the same time over the means of *intellectual* (*geistig*) production, so that thereby, generally speaking, the ideas of those who lack the means of intellectual production are subject to it.' [27]

According to Marx, consciousness is rooted in human *Praxis*, which is in turn social. This is the sense of the statement that ' It is not the consciousness of men that determines their being, but, on the contrary, their social being that determines their consciousness '.[28] Much calumny has been heaped upon Marx for this observation. But the operative term here is *social* being, and there can be little objection to the generalisation that consciousness is governed by human activity in society. The case of language, Marx points out, gives a concrete example of this. Language, Marx says, ' is as old as consciousness, language *is* practical consciousness that exists also for other men, and for that reason alone it really exists for me personally as well. . .'.[29] The expression of ideas, and indeed the very existence of anything beyond mere sensation, is conditional upon the existence of language. But language is a social product, and it is only in virtue of his membership of society that the individual acquires the linguistic categories which constitute the parameters of his consciousness.

Marx's conception of the role of particular forms of ideology in class societies follows directly from these more general considerations. The main defect of idealism in philosophy and history is that it attempts to analyse the properties of societies by inference from the content of the dominant systems of ideas in those societies. But this neglects altogether the fact that there is not a unilateral relationship between values and power: the dominant class is able to disseminate ideas which are the legitimations of its position of dominance. Thus the ideas of freedom and equality which come to the fore in bourgeois society cannot be taken at their ' face value ', as directly summing up social reality; on the contrary, the legal freedoms which exist in bourgeois society actually serve to legitimise the reality of contractual obligations in which propertyless wage-labour is heavily disadvantaged as compared to the owners of capital. The import of this is that ideology must be studied in relation to the social relationships in which it is embedded: we must study both the concrete processes which give rise to various types of ideas, together with the factors which determine which ideas come into prominence within a given society. While ideologies obviously show continuity over time, neither this continuity, nor any changes which occur, can

---

[27] *GI*, p. 61; *We*, vol. 3, p. 46.
[28] *SW*, vol. 1, p. 363. See below, pp. 208–223ff, for further treatment of this matter, in relation to Weber and Durkheim.
[29] *GI*, p. 42.

be explained purely in terms of their internal content. Ideas do not evolve on their own account; they do so as elements of the consciousness of men living in society, following a definite *Praxis*: 'Whilst in ordinary life every shopkeeper is very well able to distinguish between what somebody professes to be and what he really is, our historians have not yet won even this trivial insight. They take every epoch at its word concerning what it says and imagines about itself.' [30]

There are two related emphases in Marx's treatment of ideology which it is important to distinguish: both have already been mentioned above. The first is that the social circumstances in which the activity of individuals occurs condition their perception of the world in which they live. This is the sense in which language forms the 'practical consciousness' of men. The second theorem concerns the *diffusion*, as well as the creation, of ideas: this is Marx's generalisation that, in class societies, the ruling ideas of any epoch are the ideas of the ruling class. It follows from this latter proposition that the dissemination of ideas is heavily dependent upon the distribution of economic power in society. It is in this latter sense that ideology constitutes part of the social 'superstructure': the prevalent ethos at any given time is one which provides legitimation of the interests of the dominant class. Thus the relations of production, via the mediation of the class system, compose 'the real foundation, on which rises a legal and political superstructure and to which correspond definite forms of social consciousness'.[31] Marx does not postulate an unvarying connection between these two modes in which consciousness is moulded by social *Praxis*. An individual or group may develop ideas which are partially at variance with the prevalent views of his age: but these ideas will not come into prominence unless they articulate with interests held by the dominant class, or with those of a class which comes in a position to challenge the existing authority structure.[32] Thus many of the ideas which were used in constructing machines in the late eighteenth and early nineteenth centuries had been known for many years: but their rapid application and spread only occurred when the expansion of capitalism generated the need for capitalists to augment production over and beyond what was possible through handcraft manufacture.

Acceptance of the role of class domination against the background of a dialectical conception of the relationship between social activity and consciousness resolves some of the apparent dilemmas concerning the connections between the relations of production and the ideological 'superstructure' in any given society.[33] The productive activity of individuals, in inter-relationship with one another and with nature, involves a continual

---

[30] *GI*, p. 64; *We*, vol. 3, p. 49.

[31] *SW*, vol. 1, p. 363.

[32] cf. *GI*, pp. 472–3.

[33] cf., for example, John Plamenatz: *Man and Society* (London, 1968), vol. 2, pp. 279–93.

and reciprocal interaction between social behaviour and consciousness: the ideas which are thus generated are conditioned in their diffusion or acceptance by the structure of class domination. Hence the dominant ideology always comprises ' partly . . . an elaboration or consciousness of domination, partly . . . a moral means for this domination '.[34] The ' real foundation ' of society, upon which the ' superstructure ' arises, is always constituted of the relationships of active, willing individuals, and thus always involves both the creation and application of ideas. The main point about the ' superstructure ' is not that it embodies ideas, whereas the relations of production do not, but that it is comprised of a system of social relationships (especially in the shape of politics, law and religion) which order and sanction a system of class domination.

The problem of the relativity of historical knowledge is disposed of by Marx without much difficulty. It is certainly the case that all forms of human consciousness, including the most highly complex kinds of ideologies, are rooted in definite sets of social conditions. But this does not preclude the retrospective understanding of history in terms of rational principles. Thus there are certain characteristics which are shared by all class societies: but these could not be until the advent of the conditions for the emergence of scientific knowledge of society, generated by capitalism. Marx illustrates this by analogy. The anatomy of man, the more developed creature, supplies us with the key to the understanding of the anatomy of the ape: similarly, understanding the structure and process of development of bourgeois society allows us to use the same categories to explain the social development of the ancient world. Using the concepts formulated by the political economists, it is possible to apply notions such as ' labour ' and ' production ' in a very general way, to apply to characteristics shared by societies at all levels of complexity. But these concepts have only emerged with the rise of capitalist production. ' *Production in general* is an abstraction, but a justified abstraction. . . .'[35]

The theories developed by the political economists contain very important elements of truth which can be applied to all societies; but the fact that the writings of the economists are heavily linked to the structure of bourgeois class domination means that they are unable to discern the limited and one-sided character of their formulations. Like the German historians and philosophers, they share the ' illusion of the epoch ';[36] but this in no way implies that the whole of their ideas are ' illusory ' in an epistemological sense. The dominant modes of thought will not wholly shed their ideological character

[34] *GI*, p. 473; *We*, vol. 3, p. 405. See Karl Korsch: *Marxismus und Philosophie* (Leipzig, 1930), pp. 55–67.
[35] *Gru*, p. 7. This, of course, is basically a transmuted Hegelian standpoint. As Lukács remarks, for Marx ' the present must be correctly understood in order for the history of previous times to be adequately grasped . . .', *Der junge Hegel*, p. 130.
[36] *GI*, p. 52.

until ' class domination in general ceases to be the form in which the social order is organised, that is to say, as soon as it is no longer necessary to represent a particular interest as general or the " general interest " as ruling '.[37]

Every dominant class lays claim to the universality of the ideology which legitimates its position of domination. But, according to Marx, this does not entail that the social changes effected by the rise of a new revolutionary class to dominance are equivalent in different types of society. While Marx does set out an overall schema in terms of which every process of revolutionary changes shares common characteristics, he also holds that the forms of revolutionary transformation found in history differ in certain crucially important respects. The overall schema which Marx employs in the analysis of revolutionary social change runs as follows. In any relatively stable society, there exists an equilibrium between the mode of production, the social relations which are integral to that mode of production, and the ' superstructure ' which, through the medium of class domination, is tied in with it. When progressive changes occur in the sphere of productive activity – such as happened in Rome with the emergence of manufacture and commerce within a predominantly agrarian economy – a tension is set up between these new productive forces and the existing relations of production. The existing relations of production then increasingly form barriers to the emergent forces of production. These ' contradictions ' become expressed as overt class conflicts, terminating in revolutionary struggles fought out in the political sphere, and manifest ideologically as a clash between competing ' principles '. The outcome of these struggles is either ' the common ruin of the contending classes ', as in Rome, or ' a revolutionary reconstitution of society at large ', as occurred in the supersession of feudalism by capitalism.[38] The class engaging in a revolutionary struggle for power fights in the name of absolute human rights, presenting its ideas as ' the only rational, universally valid ones '.[39] While only one subordinate class stands to gain from the revolutionary overthrow of the existing dominant class, it may invoke the aid of others to assist its movement to power: the French bourgeoisie, for instance, made its revolution in 1789 with the aid of the peasantry. Once the revolutionary class has acceded to power, its erstwhile revolutionary character becomes transposed into a defence of the existing order, i.e., of its own hegemony:

it is in the interest of the ruling section of society to sanction the existing order as law and to perpetuate its habitually and traditionally fixed limits as legal ones. Aside from all other matters, this comes about of itself in proportion as the continuous reproduction of the foundation of the existing order of the relations corresponding to it gradually assumes a regulated and orderly form. And such regulation and order are themselves indispensable elements of any mode of pro-

[37] *GI*, p. 63; *We*, vol. 3, p. 48.
[38] *CM*, p. 132.
[39] *GI*, p. 62.

duction, provided that it is to assume social firmness and an independence from mere accident and arbitrariness.[40]

Thus the ascendance of the new class to power inaugurates another period of relative stability, eventually generating a repetition of the same pattern of change.

This general conception would be a wholly positivistic one were it not for the fact that Marx relates the occurrence of revolutionary change to the historical process as a whole. 'Every new class', Marx states, 'achieves its domination only on a broader basis than that of the previously dominant class, whereas the opposition of the non-dominant class against the new ruling class later develops all the more sharply and profoundly.' [41] The effect of the rise to power of the bourgeoisie is to introduce profound changes in the character of class relationships as compared to those extant in feudalism. Bourgeois society makes for a far broader realisation of human productive capacities than was feasible in previous periods of history. But this is only rendered possible by the formation of an increasingly numerous class of propertyless wage-labourers: bourgeois society universalises class relationships around a single class division, between bourgeoisie and proletariat. It is this which, in fact, provides for the fundamental difference between bourgeois society and the other forms of class society which have preceded it. Whereas previous revolutionary classes, once they have acquired power, have 'sought to protect the position they have acquired by subjecting society at large to their conditions of appropriation', the proletariat cannot come to a position of domination 'except by abolishing [its] own previous mode of appropriation, and thereby also every other previous mode of appropriation'.[42]

According to Marx, the rise to power of the working-class culminates the historical changes wrought by bourgeois society. The development of bourgeois society fosters an extreme dislocation between the accomplishments of human productive powers and the alienation of the mass of the population from the control of the wealth which they have thus created. The supersession of capitalism, on the other hand, provides the circumstances in which it will be possible for man to recover his alienated self within a rational order which has freed itself from class domination. The economic presuppositions of this process are detailed in *Capital*.

[40] *Cap*, vol. 3, pp. 773–4; *We*, vol. 25, p. 801.
[41] *GI*, p. 63; *We*, vol. 3, p. 48.
[42] *CM*, p. 147.

4. The theory of capitalist development

The theory of surplus value

Although much of *Capital* is concerned with economic analysis, Marx's over-riding interest in the work is always in the dynamics of bourgeois *society*: the primary object of *Capital* is to disclose the ' economic law of motion ' of this society, through an examination of the dynamics of the productive foundation upon which it rests.[1]

Capitalism, as Marx emphasises on the first page of *Capital*, is a system of *commodity* production. In the capitalist system producers do not simply produce for their own needs, or for the needs of individuals with whom they are in personal contact; capitalism involves a nation-wide, and often an international, exchange-market. Every commodity, Marx states, has a ' two-fold ' aspect: its ' use-value ', on the one hand, and its ' exchange-value ' on the other. Use-value, which ' is realised only in the process of consumption ', has reference to the needs which the properties of a commodity as a physical artifact can be employed to cater to.[2] An object can have use-value whether or not it is a commodity; while to be a commodity a product must have use-value, the reverse does not hold. ' Exchange-value ' refers to the value a product has when offered in exchange for other products.[3] In contrast to use-value, exchange-value presupposes ' a definite economic relation ', and is inseparable from a market on which goods are exchanged; it only has meaning in reference to commodities.

Now any object, whether it is a commodity or not, can only have value in so far as human labour power has been expanded to produce it: this is the core proposition of the labour theory of value which Marx takes over from Adam Smith and Ricardo.[4] It follows from this that both exchange-value and use-value must be directly related to the amount of labour embodied in the production of a commodity. It is clear, Marx says, that exchange-value cannot be

---

[1] Only the first volume of *Capital* was published in Marx's life-time, but Marx worked on all three volumes simultaneously. Volumes 2 and 3 were edited and published by Engels in 1885 and 1894 respectively. In the preface to the first volume, Marx speaks of a projected fourth volume, to deal with ' the history of theory '. Notes for this work were published by Kautsky between 1905 and 1910, as *Theorien über den Mehrwert*. Sections from this have been translated into English as *Theories of Surplus Value*, ed. Bonner & Burns (London, 1951). Two volumes of a full English translation have appeared (London, vol. 1, 1964; vol. 2, 1969).

[2] *Contribution to the Critique of Political Economy*, p. 20.

[3] Whenever Marx speaks of ' value ' without qualification, he means ' exchange-value '.

[4] For an account of the development of the labour theory of value, see Ronald L. Meek: *Studies in the Labour Theory of Value* (London, 1956).

derived from use-value. This can be shown by the example of the exchange-value of two commodities such as corn and iron. A given quantity of corn is worth a specifiable quantity of iron. The fact that we can express the worth of these two products in terms of each other, and in quantified form, shows that we are using some common standard which is applicable to both. This common measure of value has nothing to do with the physical properties of corn or iron, which are incommensurate. Exchange-value must then rest upon some quantifiable characteristic of labour. There are obviously many differences between specific kinds of labour: the actual tasks involved in the work of growing corn are very different from those involved in manufacturing iron. Just as exchange-value abstracts from the specific characteristics of commodities, and treats them in abstract quantitative ratio, in the derivation of exchange-value we have to consider only 'abstract general labour', which can be measured in terms of the amount of time expended by the worker in the production of a commodity.

Abstract labour is the basis of exchange-value, while 'useful labour' is the basis of use-value. The two aspects of commodities are simply an expression of the dual character of labour itself – as labour *power*, the physical expenditure of the energy of the human organism, something common to all forms of productive activity; and as a definite kind of labour, a specific set of operations into which this energy is channelled, something peculiar to the production of particular commodities for specific uses.

On the one hand all labour is, speaking physiologically, an expenditure of human labour power, and in its character as similar or as abstract human labour it creates the value of commodities. On the other hand, all labour is the expenditure of human labour power in a special form and with a definite aim, and in this, its character of concrete useful labour, it produces use-value.[5]

'Abstract labour' is an historical category, since it is only applicable to commodity production. Its existence is predicated upon what are, for Marx, some of the intrinsic characteristics of capitalism. Capitalism is a far more fluid system than any which preceded it, demanding that the labour force should be highly mobile, and adaptable to different kinds of work; as Marx puts it, '"labour in general", labour *sans phrase*, the starting-point of modern political economy, becomes realised in practice'.[6]

There is an obvious problem which presents itself if abstract labour is to be measured in terms of units of time as the mode of calculating exchange-value. It would appear to follow from this that an idle worker, who takes a long while to produce a given item, would produce a more valuable commodity than an industrious man completing the same task in a shorter time.[7]

---

[5] *Cap*, vol. 1, p. 47; *We*, vol. 23, p. 61.
[6] *Contribution to the Critique of Political Economy*, p. 299.
[7] Skilled labour also offers a source of difficulty. Marx holds, however, that all skilled labour can be reduced to time units of unskilled or 'simple' labour. A skill normally represents the results of a certain period of training; to convert skilled labour

Marx stresses, however, that the concept applies not to any particular individual worker, but to the ' socially necessary ' labour time. This is the amount of time required for the production of a commodity under the normal conditions of production, and with the ' average degree of skill and intensity ' prevalent at a given time in a particular industry. The socially necessary labour time can be fairly readily determined, according to Marx, through empirical study. A sudden technological improvement can reduce the amount of socially necessary labour time required to produce a particular commodity, and will therefore lead to a corresponding diminution in its value.[8]

This whole analysis, including Marx's discussion of surplus value described below, is set out in the first volume of *Capital*.[9] It should be emphasised that Marx's treatment of value and surplus value at this point is deliberately phrased on a highly abstract level. Marx sets out to ' disregard all phenomena that hide the play ' of the ' inner mechanism ' of capitalism. Failure to appreciate this has given rise to numerous misconceptions, including the one that Marx allows no role at all to demand. For most of his discussion in volume 1 Marx assumes a situation in which supply and demand are in equilibrium. Marx does not ignore the importance of demand; but it follows from the labour theory of value that demand does not determine value, although it can affect prices.[10] For Marx, demand is most significant in relation to the allocation of the labour force to different sectors of the economy. If the demand for a certain commodity becomes particularly high, then producers of other goods will be stimulated to move into the production of that commodity. The increase in price following the heightened demand will then become reduced in the direction of its value.[11] But demand is not the independent variable some economists make of it : ' supply and demand presuppose the existence of different classes and sections of classes which divide the total revenue of a society and consume it among themselves as revenue, and, therefore, make up the demand created by revenue.'[12]

It follows from the analysis of exchange-value discussed above that products exchange at their values : that is, according to the amount of socially

---

into simple labour, it is necessary to assess the amount of labour (expended on his own part and by those who train him) which goes into the training procedure. But, in Marx's view, capitalism eventually tends to do away with skilled labour in any case, through progressive mechanisation. cf. Paul M. Sweezy: *The Theory of Capitalist Development* (New York, 1954), pp. 42–4.

[8] As an example of the impact of technological change in this direction, Marx cites the case of the English clothing industry. Here the introduction of power looms reduced by something like fifty per cent the labour time necessary to weave yarn into cloth. Of course a hand weaver still needed the same amount of time as before, ' but the product of one hour of his individual labour represented after the change only one-half an hour's social labour, and consequently fell to one-half its former value '. *Cap*, vol. 1, p. 39; *We*, vol. 23, p. 53.

[9] *Cap*, vol. 1, pp. 508ff.

[10] *SW*, vol. 1, pp. 84ff.

[11] *Cap*, vol. 3, pp. 181–95. cf. Meek, p. 178.   [12] *Cap*, vol. 3, p. 191.

necessary labour time embodied in them.[13] Marx rejects the notion that capitalists derive their profits from any sort of dishonesty or deliberate underhand dealing. Although in actual buying or selling transactions a particular capitalist might make money by taking advantage of the vagaries of the market, such as a sudden increase in demand for his product, the existence of profit in the economy as a whole cannot be explained in this way. On the average, Marx holds, the capitalist buys labour, and sells commodities, at their real value. As he puts it, the capitalist ' must buy his commodities at their value, must sell them at their value, and yet at the end of the process must withdraw more value from circulation than he threw into it at starting '.[14]

This apparent paradox is resolved by Marx with reference to that historical condition which is the necessary basis of capitalism, the fact that workers are ' free ' to sell their labour on the open market. What this signifies is that labour power is itself a commodity, which is bought and sold on the market. Thus its value is determined like that of any other commodity, by the labour time socially necessary for its production. Human labour power involves the expenditure of physical energy, which must be replenished. To renew the energy expended in labour, the worker must be provided with the requirements of his existence as a functioning organism – food, clothing, and shelter for himself and his family. The labour time socially necessary to produce the necessities of life of the worker is the value of the worker's labour power. The latter's value is, therefore, reducible to a specifiable quantity of commodities : those which the worker requires to be able to subsist and reproduce. ' The worker exchanges with capital his labour itself ... he *alienates* it. The price he receives is the value of this alienation.' [15]

The conditions of modern manufacturing and industrial production allow the worker to produce considerably more, in an average working day, than is necessary to cover the cost of his subsistence. Only a proportion of the working day, that is, needs to be expended to produce the equivalent of the worker's own value. Whatever the worker produces over and above this is surplus value. If, say, the length of the working day is ten hours, and if the worker produces the equivalent of his own value in half that time, then the remaining five hours' work is surplus production, which may be appropriated by the capitalist. Marx calls the ratio between necessary and surplus labour the ' rate of surplus value ' or the ' rate of exploitation '. The rate of surplus value, as with all of Marx's concepts, has a social rather than a biological reference. The labour time necessary to ' produce labour power ' cannot be defined in purely physical terms, but has to be ascertained by reference to culturally expected standards of living in a society. ' Climatic and physical conditions ' have an

[13] This statement is only true given the simplified model Marx employs in volume 1 of *Capital*; in the real world there is often considerable divergence between values and prices.
[14] *Cap*, vol. 1, p. 166.
[15] *Gru*, pp. 270–1.

influence, but only in conjunction with ' the conditions under which, and consequently on the habits and degree of comfort in which, the class of free labourers has been formed '.[16]

Surplus value is the source of profit. Profit is, so to speak, the visible ' surface ' manifestation of surplus value; it is ' a converted form of surplus value, a form in which its origin and the secret of its existence are observed and extinguished '.[17] The analysis which Marx offers in the first volume of *Capital* sets out to remove this disguise, and does not discuss the actual relationship between surplus value and profit, which in the empirical world is a complicated one. The amount the capitalist has to spend on hiring labour is only one part of the capital outlay he has to make in the productive process. The other part consists in the machinery, raw materials, maintenance of factory fittings, etc., necessary for production. That segment of capital laid out on such matters is ' constant capital ', while that spent on wages is ' variable capital '. Only variable capital creates value; constant capital ' does not, in the process of production, undergo any quantitative alteration of value '.[18] In contrast to the rate of surplus value, which is the ratio of surplus value to variable capital (s/v), the rate of *profit* can only be calculated with reference to both variable and constant capital. The ratio of constant to variable capital constitutes the ' organic composition ' of capital; since the rate of profit depends upon the organic composition of capital, it is lower than the rate of surplus value. The rate of profit is given by the formula $p = s/c + v$: the lower the ratio of expenditure on constant capital to that on variable capital, the higher the rate of profit.[19]

In the third volume of *Capital*, Marx relates the simplified theory of surplus value presented in volume 1 to actual prices. It is clear that, in the real world, the organic composition of capital varies widely from industry to industry. In some sectors of production, the amount of constant capital involved is far higher in relation to variable capital than in other sectors: for example, annual capital outlay on machinery and plant equipment in the iron and steel industry is much greater than it is in the clothing industry. Following the simplified model advanced in the first volume of *Capital*, this would lead to widely divergent rates of surplus value, and if profit were directly correlative to surplus value, would lead to marked variations in profits between different sectors of the economy. But such a state of affairs, except on a short-term basis, would be incompatible with the organisation of the capitalist economy in which capital always tends to flow into those channels which offer the highest levels of profit.

---

[16] *Cap*, vol. 1, p. 171.

[17] *Cap*, vol. 3, p. 47.

[18] *Cap*, vol. 1, p. 209.

[19] Marx assumes here that no rent is being paid by the capitalist to a landlord. As Marx puts it: ' landed property is taken as $=0$.' Marx moves on to the problem of ground-rent in the third volume of *Capital*.

Setting aside the assumptions made for analytic purposes in volume 1, therefore, Marx concludes that commodities do not generally sell at their values, but according to what he calls their ' prices of production '.[20] The *total* amount of profit in the economy is determined by the amount of surplus value created within it, but the share which each individual capitalist takes from this total is not proportionate to the rate of surplus value realised within his own enterprise. Capitalists share the total surplus value in proportion to their capital invested, not in ratio to the organic composition of that capital. ' Prices of production ', in other words, the real prices of commodities, can be calculated on the basis of a division of the total social capital into the total surplus value. The price of production is equal to the ' cost price ', or sum of expenditure actually incurred in production (the amount of constant capital used up in producing a commodity, together with capital expended on wages), plus the average rate of profit on the capital employed.

What are the influences which make commodities sell at their prices of production, and not at their values? Marx devotes a substantial part of volume 3 of *Capital* to discussion of this problem. Before the advent of capitalism, commodities do tend to sell at their values, but the competitive structure of capitalism breaks this down. ' Average profit' develops historically with the development of capitalism itself. If one sector of production, having a higher rate of variable to constant capital, creates a very high rate of surplus value and profit, then

... capital withdraws from spheres with low rates of profit and invades others which yield a higher profit. By means of this incessant outflow and inflow, in short, by its distribution among the various spheres in relation to a rise of the rate of profit here, and its fall there, it brings about a ratio of supply to demand such that the average profit in the various spheres of production becomes the same; values are converted into prices of production. This equilibration is accomplished by capital more or less perfectly to the degree that capitalist development is advanced in a certain nation: in other words, to the extent that conditions in the respective countries are adapted to the capitalist mode of production.[21]

There are two conditions which facilitate this process: fluidity of capital, and labour mobility. The first demands ' complete freedom of trade in the interior of society ', and the eradication of feudal monopolistic privilege. It is further stimulated by the development of the credit system, which serves to concentrate capital instead of allowing it to remain in the hands of individual capitalists. The second condition, involving mobility of labour, rests upon a familiar set of circumstances: the ' freeing' of labour from proprietory and localised relations to the means of production, and the reduction of craft

---

[20] It is upon the relationship between values and prices that most criticism of Marx's economics has centred. cf. Paul Sweezy: *Böhm-Bawerk's Criticism of Marx* (New York, 1949). Two recent discussions of Marx's economics are Murray Wolfson: *A Reappraisal of Marxian Economics* (New York, 1964); and Fred M. Gottheil: *Marx's Economic Predictions* (Evanston, 1966).

[21] *Cap*, vol. 3, p. 192; *We*, vol. 25, p. 206.

skills to unskilled work which allows workers to move from job to job without difficulty. The development of the average rate of profit is thus intrinsically bound up with the economic structure of capitalist production.

Marx continues to stress that the theory of surplus value presented in the first volume of *Capital* underlies the analysis given in volume 3. However complicated the relationship between prices and value may be, the former nevertheless rest upon the latter, and any increase or decrease in the total surplus value will affect prices of production. Most of the subsequent criticism of Marx's position offered by economists has centred upon the fact that prediction of prices is extremely difficult using Marx's theory, since the connection between values and prices is so convoluted. But it must be emphasised that, from Marx's standpoint, such prediction is of secondary importance: the whole weight of his theory is towards setting out the principles which underlie the operation of the capitalist economy. Marx's analysis moves upon the level of an attempt to undercut the influence which physical categories such as prices, rents, or rates of interest have in the theory of political economy, in order to expose the social relationships which lie at the root of them. As he expresses it,

The social character of activity, the social form of the product, and of the participation of the individual in production, appear as alienated, reified (*sachlich*) in relation to the individual... Universal exchange of activities and products, which has become the condition of existence of, and the mutual connection between, particular individuals, take the form of a thing, alienated from and independent of themselves.[22]

Marx's theory of capitalist development is founded upon the nature of capitalist expropriation as set out in the theory of surplus value. The general tenor of Marx's argument is that, while capitalism is originally structured around a free-market system in which commodities are allowed to ' find their own values ' on the basis of individual entrepreneurial initiative, the immanent tendency of capitalist production undermines the empirical conditions upon which the capitalist economy is based.

The economic ' contradictions ' of capitalist production

In Marx's view, the search for profit is intrinsic to capitalism; ' the aim of capital is not to minister to certain wants, but to produce profit...'.[23] But at the same time there is rooted in the capitalist economy a structural tendency for the rate of profit to decline. Most of the classical economists accepted this notion; Marx's contribution, as expressed in his formulation of the ' law of the falling tendency of the rate of profit ', derives from the integration of this theory with his analysis of the organic composition of capital, and the relation of the latter to surplus value. The total amount of profit in the capitalist

---

[22] *Gru*, p. 75. See below, pp. 228–9.
[23] *Cap*, vol. 3, p. 251.

economy depends upon the surplus value created within it: the ratio of constant to variable capital in the economy as a whole determines the average rate of profit. The rate of profit thus stands in inverse proportion to the organic composition of capital.

Since capitalism is founded upon the competitive search for profit, technological improvement, including above all the increasing mechanisation of production, is a major weapon of each capitalist in the battle for survival on the market, whereby an individual entrepreneur can increase his share of the available profit by producing at a cheaper rate than his competitors. But his success in obtaining increased profits leads other capitalists to follow suit by introducing similar technical improvements, thus producing a new (although equally temporary) equilibrium where, however, each capitalist has a higher ratio of capital expenditure on constant capital than before. Hence the overall consequence is a rise in the organic composition of capital, and a fall in the average rate of profit.

Of course, this does not necessarily entail a decline in the absolute total of profit in the economy; this may increase even though the *rate* of return falls. Moreover, there are various factors which Marx distinguishes as countering the tendency of the rate of profit to decline. These are those which either retard the relative increase of constant capital or, what is the other side of the coin, increase the rate of surplus value. A rise in expenditure on constant capital frequently goes along with an increase in the productivity of labour, which therefore effectively reduces the proportionate unit value of the constant capital, and thereby may keep the rate of profit stable or even raise it: ' with respect to the total capital, the value of the constant capital does not increase in the same proportion as its material volume. . .'.[24] Another mode of offsetting the declining rate of profit is via the feeding in of cheap materials through foreign trade, the result of which is to increase the rate of surplus value if these are used to supply the subsistence needs of workers, and to lower the value of constant capital. But Marx lays most stress upon those countervailing forces to the falling rate of profit which involve the intensified exploitation of labour. These include the expansion of the working-day, and the depression of wages below their value. Other things being equal the lengthening of the working-day, which was a definite empirical phenomenon during the early years of the nineteenth century, raises the rate of surplus value. The productivity of labour relative to constant capital can also be augmented, and the rate of surplus value increased, through making more intensive use of existing machinery – by, for example, speeding up its operation, or by utilising it for twenty-four hours a day through some kind of shift-work system. Enforced depreciation of wages is normally only a temporary expedient, and has no long-term effects upon the rate of profit. While employers treat wages as part of their costs, and will tend to pare them whenever pos-

[24] *Cap*, vol. 3, p. 230. cf. also Sweezy: *Theory of Capitalist Development*, pp. 98ff.

sible, it follows from Marx's general analysis that wages are basically determined by marked forces, not by coercive restrictions on the part of capitalists.

The periodic crises which regularly occur in capitalism are, for Marx, the most evident manifestation of the internal ' contradictions ' of the capitalist system. Marx did not, however, write a systematic discussion of the nature of crises, taking the view that crises are the end-result of various possible combinations of factors, and are not to be explained in terms of any simple causative process. He makes no attempt to trace the multiple chains of causation which actually precipitate crises: such a task could only be accomplished against the background of the general movements of capitalist production,[25] Marx's analysis is thus limited to an account of the basic factors in the capitalist economy which underlie its propensity to regular crises.

Where commodity production exists in forms of society prior to capitalism, particularly before the widespread use of money, it involves fairly direct bartering between individuals or groups who were generally aware of each other's needs, and who produced for those needs. In primitive forms of commodity production, in other words, exchange is controlled in the interests of use-values, and knowledge of wants furnishes a source of regulation connecting supply and demand. But as commodity production becomes more and more widespread, that is, as capitalism develops, this regulative tie is broken. The use of money plays an important part in this, allowing the parties to exchange transactions to act autonomously to a far greater degree than is possible in barter. Capitalism is thus in an important sense an ' anarchic ' system,[26] because the market is not regulated by any definite agency relating production to consumption. It is also an intrinsically expanding system, the basic motor of which is the restless search for profit. Since the profit motive is dominant, any state of affairs involving a pronounced imbalance between the volume of commodities produced and their saleability at the average rate of profit, constitutes a crisis for the system. Capitalism is the first system in human history where a large volume of overproduction is possible. This is, of course, only overproduction in terms of the requisites of the capitalist economy, overproduction in terms of exchange-values and not use-values: the commodities which are ' unsaleable ' could normally be made use of. But whenever a sufficient level of return on investment is not made, the *modus operandi* of capitalism is undermined. Production becomes restricted to a fraction of its potential in spite of the fact that ' not enough is produced to satisfy, in a decent and humane fashion, the wants of the great mass '.[27]

---

[25] *Theories of Surplus Value*, ed. Bonner & Burns, pp. 376–91.

[26] This does not mean there is not ' order ' in the operations of the market, but simply that the principles which govern the market operate outside of men's own conscious control, as if regulated by, in Adam Smith's famous phrase, ' an invisible hand '.

[27] *Cap*, vol. 3, p. 252; see also Marx's note on the ' contradictions ' between the worker's position as producer, and his position as consumer. *Cap*, vol. 2, p. 316. Marx rejects the more naïve ' underconsumptionist' theories of his day. See his remarks on Rodbertus, *cap*, vol. 2, pp. 410–11.

A crisis is simply an expansion of production beyond what the market can absorb and still return an adequate rate of profit. Once overproduction occurs, even only in one segment of the economy, it can set into motion a vicious circle of reactions. As the rate of profit falls, investment declines, part of the labour force has to be laid off, which further diminishes consumer purchasing power, producing another decline in the rate of profit, and so on. The spiral continues until unemployment has increased to such a degree, and the wages of those still in work has been forced down to such a level, that there exist new conditions for the creation of an increased rate of surplus value, and thereby a stimulus to the resumption of investment. During the crisis, some of the less efficient enterprises will have gone out of business; those remaining can therefore take over their share of the market, and are in a position to begin a new period of expansion. Thus the cycle is renewed, and another upward phase gets under way.

Crises therefore do not represent a ' break-down ' of the capitalist system, but on the contrary form the regulating mechanism which enables the system to survive the periodic fluctuations to which capitalism is subject. The effect of a crisis is to restore equilibrium, and make further growth possible. As Marx expresses it, crises are ' momentary and forcible solutions of the existing contradictions. They are violent eruptions which for a time restore the disturbed equilibrium.' [28] Since the tendency of the rate of profit to decline is ever present, there is in any case a pressure upon profits at all stages of capitalist development. The effect of a crisis is to further the centralisation of capital, temporarily consolidating the system.[29] Crises are endemic in capitalism, because while the whole impetus of capitalist production is towards ' an unconditioned development of the productive forces of society ', the relations of production, founded upon an exploitative class relationship, are organised around the expansion of capital alone. Thus Marx reaches his famous conclusion:

The *real barrier* of capitalist production is *capital itself*. It is that capital and its self-extension appear as the starting and closing point, as the motive and the purpose of production ; that production is merely production for *capital*, and not vice versa, the means of production the means for a constant expansion of the life-process of the *society* of producers.[30]

The ' pauperisation ' thesis

It has sometimes been assumed that Marx conceives the final dissolution of capitalism as taking the shape of an enormous crisis from which the system cannot recover. While Marx notes in *The Communist Manifesto* that crises ' in their periodic recurrence ever more threateningly place the existence of the whole of bourgeois society in question ', a final ruinous crisis is nowhere

[28] *Cap*, vol. 3, p. 244.
[29] *Cap*, vol. 2, pp. 75–7.
[30] *Cap*, vol. 3, p. 245; *We*, vol. 25, p. 260.

specifically predicted in his writings.[31] Moreover, such a prediction is difficult to reconcile with the conception of the re-equilibrating function of crises. While Marx certainly believed that capitalism could not perpetuate itself indefinitely, the nature of its dissolution depends both upon the laws which govern its development and upon specific historical circumstances which cannot themselves be known beforehand. Crises do, however, play an important role in fostering revolutionary consciousness, because they make dramatically evident the common class situation of the proletariat, the more so because they tend to occur as a sharp recession following a period of relative prosperity for the working class during which unemployment is low and wages are high.[32]

It is only rarely in the capitalist economy that conditions of near full employment prevail. The existence of a group of chronically unemployed, the industrial ' reserve army ', is necessary to capitalism. Marx has shown that it is an essential feature of capitalism that labour-power is itself a commodity; but labour-power clearly differs from other commodities in that there is no obvious factor which prevents a wide divergence of its price from its value. If the price of a commodity of the ordinary kind goes up, then capital will tend to flow into the production of that commodity, and will bring it down in the direction of its value.[33] But no one can ' produce ' more labour if its price goes up. It is here that Marx introduces the concept of the reserve army, or as he sometimes calls it, the ' relative surplus population '. The industrial reserve army, whose ranks are filled mainly by workers who become redundant through mechanisation, acts as a constant depressant upon wages. During periods of prosperity, when the demand for labour increases, part of the reserve army becomes absorbed into the labour force, and thus holds wages down; in other times, it provides a potential source of cheap labour which inhibits any attempt of the working class to improve their lot. The reserve army is ' the lever of capitalistic accumulation ', and is ' a condition of existence of the capitalist mode of production '.[34]

The analysis of the position of the reserve army of surplus labour is closely related to Marx's discussion of the physical poverty in which a considerable segment of the working class is condemned to exist in capitalism. Much controversy has centred round the so-called ' pauperisation ' or ' emiseration ' thesis, and this has formed the focus of many critical attacks upon Marx's prognosis of the future of capitalism.[35] In analysing this question, there are

---

[31] *CM*, p. 33; *We*, vol. 4, pp. 467–8. The nearest Marx comes to this is in *Gru*, p. 636.

[32] *Cap*, vol. 2, p. 411.

[33] This analysis, given in volume 1 of *Capital*, is in terms of the simplified model of value.

[34] *Cap*, vol. 1, p. 632.

[35] It is an undeniable fact that living standards for the great majority of the working population have risen in the capitalist societies of western Europe and the USA over the past one hundred years. There is a theoretical point here of some importance, which has been noted by various critics. According to Marx's own theory,

two themes in Marx's discussion which have to be distinguished, and it is the tendency to assimilate these into a single 'prediction' concerning the living standards of the working class which underlies the common misreading of Marx on this matter. One of these themes concerns the theory that the course of capitalist development is characterised by increasing relative disparity between the earnings of the working class and the income of the capitalist class; the second is that the development of capitalism produces a larger and larger reserve army, the majority of which are forced to live in extreme poverty. These two trends are bound up with one another, since it is the existence of the 'relative surplus population' which prevents wages from rising far above their value. But the confusion of the two has led to the quite unwarranted conclusion that Marx believed that the whole body of the working class would increasingly become depressed into increasingly severe physical poverty. Marx speaks of the 'increasing exploitation' of the worker as capitalism proceeds, but is it clear that the rate of exploitation (rate of surplus value) can increase without necessarily entailing any change in the real wages of the majority of the working class.[36] With regard to the increasing relative disparity between the earnings of labour and capital, Marx's main thesis is simply, in accord with the general theory of surplus value advanced in *Capital*, that while the capitalist class accumulates more and more wealth, the wages of the working class can never rise far above subsistence level.[37] What Marx does specify as the consequences of capitalism for the working class as a whole in *Capital* involves reference to the alienating effects of the division of labour, which serve to 'mutilate the worker into a fragment of a man, degrade him to the level of an appendage of a machine, destroy the content of work by his agony, and alienate (*entfremden*) him from the spiritual potentialities of the labour-process...'.[38]

It is, however, the increase in the 'relative mass of the industrial reserve army' which produces an extension of chronic pauperism; Marx calls this the 'absolute general law of capitalist accumulation', noting that 'like all other laws it is modified in its working by many circumstances'. Pauperism is the 'hospital of the active labour-army and the dead weight of the industrial re-

---

profits show a tendency to decline; now if it happens that the rate of surplus value remains the same, rising productivity must produce an increase in the real wages of labour. Robinson argues: 'Marx can only demonstrate a falling tendency in profits by abandoning his argument that real wages tend to be constant.' Joan Robinson: *An Essay on Marxian Economics* (London, 1966), p. 36.

[36] If productivity increases. But see note 35, above.

[37] Marx makes the point that, even under those conditions of rapid capitalist expansion which are most favourable to the working class, increases in wages never do more than *parallel* increased profits; thus even when standards of living of the working class rise during a period of boom in the economy, those of the capitalist class rise equally, maintaining the differential. *SW*, vol. 1, pp. 94–8.

[38] *Cap*, vol. 1, p. 645; *We*, vol. 23, p. 674.

serve army '.[39] Most of the worst forms of material exploitation are concentrated in this latter group, among whom there develops an ' accumulation of misery, agony of labour, slavery, ignorance, brutality, moral degradation. . .'.[40] Thus the contradictory character of capitalism manifests itself in the accumulation of wealth ' at one pole ', and of poverty and misery at the other.

Concentration and centralisation

The rising organic composition of capital which takes place as capitalism proceeds is intimately connected with a trend towards the centralisation and concentration of capital. ' Concentration ' refers to the process whereby, as capital accumulates, individual capitalists succeed in expending the amount of capital under their control. Centralisation, on the other hand, refers to the merging of existing capitals, ' a change in the distribution of capital already to hand '.[41] The effect of both is to lead to larger and larger productive units. The competitive character of capitalism entails that producers must constantly strive to undercut the prices of their rivals. Those capitalists controlling the larger organisations enjoy various advantages over the small producer which allow them, by and large, to triumph over the latter. The greater the resources at the command of an individual entrepreneur, the more efficiently he can produce, since he can introduce economies of scale, and can more easily withstand set-backs such as those which follow from temporary contractions of the market. Thus as a general rule, the larger units tend to drive smaller ones out of business and to absorb their capital.

Centralisation is further promoted by the credit system, the most important sector of which is banking. A bank both centralises the money-capital of the lenders and also makes for centralisation of the borrowers, while the banks themselves also tend to become linked to form a single financial system. This whole process ' is finally transformed into an enormous social mechanism for the centralisation of capitals '.[42] The expansion of the credit system, while forming ' one of the most effective vehicles of crises and swindle ' within the capitalist system, at the same time removes the distribution of capital from the hands of individual capitalists. The credit system ' does away with the private character of capital and thus contains in itself, but only in itself, the abolition of capital itself '. By introducing various forms of circulating credit which serve instead of money, the banking system shows that ' money is in reality nothing but a particular expression of the social character of labour and its products. . .'. As it exists, the credit system is itself a capitalistic enterprise, since it is organised on the basis of private profit, which comes from

---

[39] *Cap*, vol. 1, p. 644. Capitalism ' overworks a part of the labouring population and keeps the other part as a reserve army, half or entirely pauperised '. *Theories of Surplus Value*, ed. Bonner & Burns, p. 352.

[40] *Cap*, vol. 1, p. 645; *We*, vol. 23, p. 675.

[41] *Cap*, vol. 1, p. 625.

[42] *Cap*, vol. 1, p. 626.

interest levied on loans; but because it develops the ground for the centralised co-ordination of the economy, the credit system ' will serve as a powerful lever during the transition from the capitalist mode of production to the mode of production of associated labour. . .'.[43]

The expansion of the credit system goes hand in hand with a particular form of centralisation of corporate capital: that represented in the development of joint-stock companies. This is the type of industrial organisation, according to Marx, which is most compatible with large-scale centralisation, and it represents ' the ultimate development of capitalist production '. The joint-stock company, which serves to effect a separation between the individual capitalist and the productive organisation, represents ' the abolition of the capitalist mode of production within the capitalist mode of production itself '.[44] The separation between the owners of capital and the managers demonstrates the superfluousness of the former group, who now play no direct part in the productive process. In the joint-stock company, the social character of production has become apparent, and hence exposes as a ' contradiction ' the fact that a few individuals are able, through their own ownership of capital, to appropriate much of the wealth that is produced. Nevertheless, the joint-stock company is only a transitional form since, as it is still connected with interest-bearing capital, it continues to be ' ensnared in the boundaries of capitalism '. Moreover, the development of very large companies of this sort can lead to monopoly control of particular sectors of industry, creating a basis for various kinds of new exploitative relationships.[45]

Capital shows in detail that, as in the case of the society which preceded it in western European history, capitalism is an inherently unstable system, built upon antagonisms than can only be resolved through changes which eventually undermine it. These contradictions derive first of all from its class character: from the asymmetrical relationship between wage-labour and capital. The operation of the capitalist mode of production inevitably drives the system towards its dissolution. Here again Marx speaks of the *Aufhebung* of capitalism; the historical tendency towards the ' abolition ' of the capitalist mode of production must not be thought of as the wholesale destruction of capitalism, so that socialism has to ' start anew '. On the contrary, the imminent trend of movement of the capitalist system generates the social conditions which provide for its dialectical transcendence.

In these terms, the question of the ' inevitability ' of the revolution poses no ' epistemological ' (as opposed to ' practical ') problems. The process of

---

[43] The preceding four quotations are all from *Cap*, vol. 3, p. 593.

[44] *Cap*, vol. 3, p. 429.

[45] In the shape of ' a new financial aristocracy, a new variety of parasites in the shape of promoters, speculators and simply nominal directors; a whole system of swindling and cheating by means of corporation promotion, stock issuance, and stock speculation '. This is ' private production without the control of private property '. *Cap*, vol. 3, p. 429.

development of capitalism engenders the objective social changes which, in inter-relationship with the growing class-awareness of the proletariat, creates the active consciousness necessary to transform society through revolutionary *Praxis*.[46] The relative poverty of the mass of the working class, the physical misery of the ' reserve army ', and the rapid diminution in wages and upsurge of unemployment which occur in crises, all provide a growing reservoir of revolutionary potential. The industrial system itself provides a source of perception of community of interest, and a basis for collective organisation, since the factory concentrates large numbers of workers together in one place, Workers' organisations begin on a local level, but eventually merge to form national units. The self-consciousness of the proletariat expands progressively along with the undermining of the position of the entrepreneurial capitalist by the centralisation and concentration of capital. The conjunction of these circumstances makes possible the achievement of socialist society.

The whole corpus of Marx's writings contains no more than fragmentary or passing references to the nature of the society which will supplant capitalism. In separating his own position from that of ' utopian ' socialism, Marx refuses to offer a comprehensive plan for the society of the future. The new social order, as the dialectical transcendence of capitalism, will be organised according to principles which can only be vaguely glimpsed by those who live in the present form of society. The construction of detailed plans of the future society is an enterprise which relapses into philosophical idealism, because such schemes have no reality save in the mind of the thinker. Consequently, most of what Marx does have to say about the new society concerns the stage of its initial formation, in which it is ' still stamped with the birth marks of the old society from whose womb it emerges '.[47]

The transcendence of capitalism

The main sources from which insight into Marx's views on socialist society may be derived, embrace two widely separated points in his career. The first occurs in the 1844 *Manuscripts*, the second in the ' Critique of the Gotha Programme ', written in 1875. The terminology of the second is more direct and down to earth, but in outline the views expressed in the two writings are similar.[48] The first stage of socialism, Marx emphasises, is one in which the *latent* characteristics of bourgeois society are made *manifest*: in other words, in which the emergent properties of capitalism detailed in *Capital* are brought to their fullest development. Thus the socialisation of production, already

---

[46] See Georg Lukács: *Geschichte und Klassenbewusstsein* (Berlin, 1932), pp. 229ff.
[47] *SW*, vol. 2, p. 23.
[48] cf. Avineri, pp. 220–39. However, it is a mistake to identify too closely, as Avineri does, Marx's early discussion of ' crude communism ' with the later treatment of the transitional stage in the abolition of bourgeois society. Marx's discussion of the transitional stage is prospective, whereas ' crude communism ' is identified in a retrospective fashion as characteristic of the early stages of socialist *theory*. Crude communism is not the theory of the transitional stage.

implicit in capitalism in the shape of the growing centralisation of the market, is completed by putting an end to private property. In this phase, property becomes collectively owned, and wages are distributed according to a fixed principle. Out of the total social product, certain amounts are allocated to cover collective needs of the administration of production, the running of schools, health facilities, and so on; while each worker

receives back from society – after the deductions have been made – exactly what he gives to it . . . He receives a certificate from society that he has furnished such and such an amount of labour (after deducting from his labour for the common funds), and with this certificate he draws from the social stock of means of consumption as much as costs the same amount of labour.[49]

Such a social reorganisation, however, still preserves the underlying principles of bourgeois society, since it continues to assess human relationships in terms of an objective standard. In other words, it preserves the treatment of labour as an exchange value, but instead of this being confined to a class group (the proletariat), this now becomes universalised. At this stage, men are still ' regarded *only as workers* and nothing more is seen in them, everything else being ignored '[50]: ' The role of *worker* is not abolished, but is extended to all men. The relation of private property remains the relation of the community to the world of things.'[51] This stage preserves a society in which the subject is dominated by the object, in which alienation is still confused with objectification.

What is true of production also holds for the sphere of politics. Here again, Marx's most important discussions span the whole length of his career: the analysis given in the ' Critique of the Gotha Programme ' complements that developed in the early critical evaluation of Hegel's treatment of the state. That the substance of Marx's views is the same in both of these sources is indicated by his attack upon the call for the ' freeing of the basis of the State ' embodied in the Gotha Programme. Marx's criticism here takes the form of a repetition of the main point made over thirty years earlier in relation to Hegel. The state is already almost perfectly ' free ' in Germany, Marx points out: the objective of the workers' movement must not be to ' free ' the state from society, but on the contrary to convert the state ' from an organ superimposed upon society into one completely subordinate to it. . .'.[52] However, the transitional phase following the initial abolition of capitalism will again involve the full realisation of the principles only partially or imperfectly developed in bourgeois society itself. The ' dictatorship of the proletariat ' constitutes this intermediate stage, and represents a concentration of the political power which already exists in a more diffuse manner in bourgeois society. This makes possible the implementation of the programme of the centralisation of production and distribution outlined previously: ' The proletariat will use

---

[49] *SW*, vol. 2, p. 23.
[51] *EW*, p. 153.

[50] *SW*, vol. 2, p. 24.
[52] *SW*, vol. 2, p. 32.

its political domination to wrest, by degrees, all capital from the bourgeoisie, to centralise all instruments of production in the hands of the State, i.e., of the proletariat organised as the dominant class, and to increase the total of productive forces as rapidly as possible.' [53]

'Political' power only disappears when this stage has been completed. The abolition of the state, for Marx, does not, of course, involve a sudden ' reversal ' in social organisation whereby the concentrated form of the state described above is subsequently eradicated. Rather, the dialectical transformation of the state is accomplished by the subordination of state to society in such a way that the administration of public affairs is mediated through the organisation of society as a whole. Marx discerns a framework for this process in the optative structure of the Paris Commune. The relevant features are several: the Commune was to be composed of councillors selected on the basis of universal suffrage, and ' was to be a working, not a parliamentary body, executive and legislative at the same time '; police, judiciary and other officials were similarly ' to be elective, responsible, and revocable '.[54] Such a form of social organisation is predicated upon the disappearance of the class character of the state, which in turn makes possible the disappearance of the state itself as an entity separate to civil society. It should be evident how far removed this viewpoint is from anarchism, with which, *quid pro quo*, it is frequently identified. In anarchist theory, the state as such is evil, and is to be literally dismantled, since it expresses the coercive authority of some men over others. Marx's attitude towards the state is integrated with his views upon capitalist society generally; the bourgeois state, in spite of its coercive character, is a necessary element in providing the social foundation for the realisation of the form of society which will transcend capitalism. Nor is Marx's standpoint to be equated with the utilitarian theory of the state, according to which the state has no function except for the regulation of economic contracts.[55] According to Marx, such a conception simply perpetuates the ' war of all against all ' in civil society. For him, the abolition of the state is only one aspect of a broad, and extended, transformation of society.

The transitional phase of the new society, since it involves the universalisation of the inherent tendencies of bourgeois society, can be prospectively described in at least some degree of detail. The same does not apply to the society which has fully transcended capitalism, and consequently Marx only sketches in broad strokes the characteristics of the second stage of communism. In its transitional stage, the society which replaces the bourgeois form is already a classless society, since private property is eliminated. But the rule of material goods over human life as a whole, and thus the overcoming of alienation, can only be achieved by the abolition of the division of labour as

---

[53] *CM*, p. 160; *We*, vol. 4, p. 481.
[54] *SW*, vol. 1, pp. 519–20.
[55] cf. Durkheim's treatment of this matter in *Soc*, pp. 52ff.

it exists in bourgeois society. The society of the future, Marx says in *Capital*, will replace the worker of today ' by the fully developed individual, fit for a variety of labours '.[56] This will overcome the various dualities which, according to Marx, are the outcome of the differentiation entailed by the division of labour: between town and country, and between intellectual and manual labour. This is the background to the famous passage in *The German Ideology*:

for as soon as the division of labour begins to come into being, each man has a particular, exclusive sphere of activity, which is forced upon him and from which he cannot escape. He is a hunter, a fisherman, a shepherd, or a critical critic, and must remain so if he does not want to lose his means of livelihood; while in communist society, where nobody has one exclusive sphere of activity but each can be accomplished in any branch he wishes, society regulates the general production and thus makes it possible for one to do one thing today and another tomorrow, to hunt in the morning, fish in the afternoon, rear cattle in the evening, criticise after dinner, just as I have a mind, without ever becoming hunter, fisherman, shepherd or critic.[57]

The predominantly agrarian occupations which Marx uses by means of illustration appear to give this vision a wholly unrealistic connotation when juxtaposed with the facts of industrial production. But Marx retains the notion of the *Aufhebung* of the division of labour in all of his writings which mention the future society, and, in fact, conceives this to be possible through the *expansion* of mechanised production. Again, this represents a transposition of tendencies already extant in capitalism, in the shape of automated production, which releases men from the present requisites of the division of labour:

In proportion to the development of large-scale industry, the creation of real wealth depends less upon labour-time and the quantity of labour expended than upon the power of the technique employed during the labour-time. . . Human labour then no longer appears as circumscribed by the production process; rather, man relates himself to this process merely as a supervisor and controller.[58]

The abolition of the division of labour is both the prerequisite to and the expression of the transcendence of alienation. In socialist society, social relationships are no longer held under the sway of the objects which are the result of human creation. In its most fundamental aspect, communism is ' the real *appropriation* of *human* nature through and for man . . . the return of man to himself as a *social*, i.e., really human, being, a complete and conscious return which assimilates all the wealth of previous development '.[59]

---

[56] *Cap*, vol. 1, p. 488.
[57] *GI*, p. 45; *We*, vol. 3, p. 33.
[58] *Gru*, p. 592; cf. also *Poverty of Philosophy*, p. 121: ' What characterises the division of labour in the automatic workshop is that labour has there completely lost its specialised character. But the moment every special development stops, the need for universality, the tendency towards an integral development of the individual begins to be felt.'   [59] *EW*, p. 155.

In this most basic aspect as in others, socialist society is predicated upon the historical development of capitalism. This vital aspect of Marx's thought has often been obscured. The paeans which *The Communist Manifesto* offers to the bourgeoisie are well known: ' It has accomplished wonders far surpassing Egyptian pyramids, Roman aqueducts, and Gothic cathedrals. . .' [60] The point of this, however, is not the sheerly technological accomplishment of capitalism: rather, the technological expansion of capitalism is symptomatic of the ' universal tendency ' [61] of bourgeois society which distinguishes it from all previous social formations. Bourgeois society replaces the relatively autonomous local communities characteristic of prior types of society by a division of labour which draws the disparate cultural and even national groupings which formerly existed into the same social and economic system. At the same time as it expands the range of human interdependence, the spread of bourgeois society sweeps away the particular cultural myths and traditions under which men have lived from the beginning of time. Ultimately, bourgeois society brings the whole of mankind, for the first time in history, within the purview of a single social order, and is genuinely ' world-historical '.

But this is only achieved through the action of the market and the transformation of all personal ties of dependence (such as existed in feudal bonds of fealty) into exchange-value. Seen in this light, it is easy to understand why much of the controversy over the value-price problem between volumes 1 and 3 of *Capital* is essentially irrelevant to the objectives of the work as a whole, which are to document this metamorphosis of human relationships into phenomena of the market. The analysis given in the three volumes of *Capital* examines in detail the alienative effects of the progressive development of capitalism, and shows how the universalisation of social relationships achieved by bourgeois society is only accomplished by their transmutation into class relationships: ' The limitation of capital is that this whole development takes place in a contradictory manner, and that the elaboration of the productive forces, of universal wealth, science, etc., appears as the *alienation* of the individual worker from himself. . .' [62]

Since its very core is founded upon an antagonistic relationship, between capital and wage-labour, which by its very operation universalises the worker *only in a condition of alienation*, capitalism contains within it forces which both propel it towards its own demise and prepare the way for its transcendence.

[60] *CM*, p. 135.
[61] *Gru*, pp. 438–41. As Mandel remarks: 'The socialisation of production under the capitalist system is the most important and progressive effect of the generalisation of the capitalist mode of production.' Ernest Mandel: *Marxist Economic Theory* (London, 1968), vol. 1, p. 170.
[62] *Gru*, p. 440.

Part 2: Durkheim

5. Durkheim's early works

To move from Marx to Durkheim is not only to move from an earlier to a later generation of social thinkers; it is also to effect a major change in institutional context and intellectual tradition. Of the three writers discussed in this book, Durkheim was the least directly involved on a personal level in the great political events of his time: virtually all of his works are wholly academic in character, and consequently are far less scattered – and less propagandist – than many of those of Marx or Weber.[1] Moreover, the intellectual influences which were most important in contributing to Durkheim's theoretical outlook are more homogeneous and easy to specify than those moulding the work of the other two authors.

The significant influences over Durkheim's mature intellectual position come from within distinctly French intellectual traditions. The overlapping interpretations which Saint-Simon and Comte offered of the decline of feudalism and the emergence of the modern form of society constitute the principal foundation for the whole of Durkheim's writings. Indeed, it could be said that the main theme in Durkheim's life's work is concerned with the reconciliation of Comte's conception of the ' positive ' stage of society with Saint-Simon's partly variant exposition of the characteristics of ' industrialism '.[2] Other influences from an earlier generation are those of Montesquieu and Rousseau; to these, Durkheim conjoined the contemporary teachings of Renouvier, and at the *Ecole Normale* where Durkheim studied from 1879 to 1882, those of his professors Boutroux and Fustel de Coulanges.[3]

Durkheim's earliest writings, however, were concerned with the ideas of a group of contemporary German authors. There are some sorts of social theory which, although as recent in formulation as those which are very familiar in

---

[1] This judgement cannot be made too sweepingly, however. Durkheim's important article: ' L'Individualisme et les intellectuels ', *Revue bleue*, vol. 10, 1898, pp. 7–13, is directly related to the Dreyfus case, although it is hardly a wholly ' political ' statement. During the First World War, Durkheim worked on the preparation of various propaganda documents, including *Qui a voulu la guerre ?*, with E. Denis (Paris, 1915), and ' *L'Allemagne au-dessus de tout* ' (Paris, 1915).

[2] cf. Alvin W. Gouldner: ' Introduction ' to *Soc*, pp. 13–18.

[3] Further documentation of the sources of Durkheim's thought would be tedious and irrelevant to this work. The influence of German and English authors is obviously not completely absent. Renouvier mediated the interest which Durkheim maintained in Kant; as is indicated below in the text, Durkheim was marginally influenced by a number of contemporary German authors; the English influence is evident in Durkheim's early interest in Herbert Spencer and later in the writings of the English anthropologists (Frazer, Tylor and Robertson-Smith).

modern-day sociology, have rapidly become almost completely forgotten. One such type of theory is organicism, such as represented in the latter part of the nineteenth century by writings of Fouillée and Worms in France, and Schäffle and Lilienfeld in Germany. The notion that society forms an integrated unity which is in some sense comparable to that of a living organism is, of course, one which can be traced back to classical social philosophy. But the publication of Darwin's theory of biological evolution gave an entirely new stimulus to the elaboration of organicist theories.[4] It is difficult from the perspective of the modern age to recapture the extraordinary impact which Darwin's writings had upon social thought in the concluding decades of the nineteenth century. The century as a whole witnessed many considerable advances in biology: the properties of the cell were identified through microscopic analysis, and the thesis that all organisms are composed of combinations of similar cellular structures became a firmly established principle. In Darwin's work these notions are placed within the context of an empirically grounded dynamic theory; and nothing was more guaranteed to fire the imagination of his contemporaries than this powerful combination of positivism and a perspective of evolutionary progress. The writings of Schäffle and the others thus differ considerably from those of their many precursors who employed organic analogies, in that these later authors proceed from the premise that the established laws governing the functioning and evolution of animal organisms provide a model upon which the framework of a natural science of society may be based.

Sociology and the ' science of moral life '

Between 1885 and 1887, Durkheim published a number of critical discussions of the work of Schäffle, Lilienfeld and other German social thinkers. Durkheim's review of Schäffle's *Bau und Leben des Socialen Körpers* was his first publication, but it gives ample indication of the trend of Durkheim's early thought.[5] Durkheim's discussion of Schäffle's book makes it plain that he is sympathetic to some of the chief points of argument presented by that author. One of Schäffle's most important contributions, according to Durkheim, is to have outlined a useful morphological analysis of the principal structural components of different forms of society. In achieving this, Schäffle makes extensive use of organic analogies, comparing various parts of society to the organs and tissues of the body. This is not, in Durkheim's view, an illegitimate

---

[4] The publication of *The Origin of Species* was also regarded by Marx and Engels as an event of major significance, offering a direct parallel to their own interpretation of social development. Marx wrote to Darwin offering to dedicate the first volume of *Capital* to him. (Darwin declined the offer.)

[5] Durkheim: review of Albert Schäffle: *Bau und Leben des Socialen Körpers* (2nd. ed.); (the review covers only vol. 1 of Schäffle's work). *RP*, vol. 19, 1885, pp. 84–101. cf. my article: ' Durkheim as a review critic ', *Sociological Review*, vol. 18, 1970, pp. 171–96, which I have drawn upon for part of this chapter.

procedure, because Schäffle does not attempt in a direct sense to deduce the properties of social organisation from those of organic life. On the contrary, Schäffle insists that the use of biological concepts represents nothing more than a ' metaphor ' which can facilitate sociological analysis.

In fact, Durkheim points out approvingly, Schäffle insists that there exists a radical and highly significant discrepancy between the life of the organism and that of society. Whereas the life of the animal organism is governed ' mechanically ', society is bound together ' not by a material relation, but by the ties of ideas '.⁶ The notion of ' society as the ideal ', Durkheim stresses, occupies a focal place in Schäffle's thought, and is entirely consistent with the latter's emphasis that society has its own specific properties which are separable from those of its individual members. For Schäffle, ' Society is not simply an aggregate of individuals, but is a being which has existed prior to those who today compose it, and which will survive them; which influences them more than they influence it, and which has its own life, consciousness (*conscience*), its own interests and destiny '.⁷ Schäffle thus rejects the conception of the individual and society given primacy by Rousseau, in which the hypothetical ' isolated individual ' in a state of nature is freer and happier than when bonded to society. On the contrary, everything that makes human life higher than the level of animal existence is derived from the accumulated cultural and technological wealth of society. If this be removed from man, ' then you will have removed at the same time all that makes us truly human '. ⁸

The ideals and sentiments which constitute the cultural inheritance of the members of a society are ' impersonal ', that is, they are socially evolved, and are neither the product nor the property of any specific individuals. This is easily shown by reference to the example of language : ' each of us speaks a language which he did not create '.⁹ Schäffle shows, Durkheim continues, that to treat the *conscience collective* as having properties which are not the same as those of the individual consciousness does not imply anything metaphysical.¹⁰ The *conscience collective* is simply ' a composite, the elements of which are individual minds '.¹¹

Schäffle's work, together with that of other German authors, according to Durkheim, manifests the important advances being made in social thought in Germany – a state of affairs contrasting heavily with the retarded develop-

---

⁶ Review of Schäffle, p. 85. Quotations are from Durkheim. For Durkheim's views on the usefulness of organic analogies in sociology, see my article quoted above, pp. 179–80.

⁷ Review of Schäffle, p. 84.   ⁸ *Ibid.* p. 87.

⁹ *Ibid.* p. 87.

¹⁰ *Ibid.* pp. 99ff. I have followed the usual practice of leaving Durkheim's phrase *conscience collective* untranslated. There is a definite ambiguity in the term which overlaps with both the English words, ' consciousness ' and ' conscience '.

¹¹ Review of Schäffle, p. 92. Durkheim nevertheless criticises Schäffle for sometimes relapsing into idealism.

ment of sociology in France. 'Thus sociology, which is French by origin, is becoming more and more a German science.'[12]

In his long survey of 'positive moral science' in Germany, published in 1887, Durkheim reiterates some of these points.[13] But the main concern of this article is to examine the contributions which leading German authors have made towards founding a science of moral life.[14] In France, Durkheim asserts, only two broad forms of ethical theory are known – Kantian idealism on the one hand, and utilitarianism on the other. The recent works of the German social thinkers, however, have begun to establish – or rather, to re-establish, since some of their notions were previously stated by Comte – ethics on a scientific footing. This approach, Durkheim states, has been worked out primarily by economists and jurists, among whom the most important are Wagner and Schmoller.[15] The work of these two authors, as Durkheim describes it, differs considerably from that of orthodox economists. Orthodox economic theory is built upon individualistic utilitarianism, and is ahistorical: 'In other words, the major laws of economics would be exactly the same even if neither nations nor states had existed in the world; they suppose only the presence of individuals who exchange their products.'[16] But Wagner and Schmoller depart substantially from this standpoint. For them (as for Schäffle), society is a unity having its own specific characteristics which cannot be inferred from those of its individual members. It is false to suppose 'that a whole is equal to the sum of its parts': in so far as these parts are *organised* in a definite fashion, then this organisation of relationships has properties of its own.[17] This principle has to be applied also to the moral

---

12 Durkheim: review of Ludwig Gumplowicz: *Grundriss der Soziologie*, *RP*, vol. 20, 1885, p. 627.

13 'La science positive de la morale en Allemagne', *RP*, vol. 24, 1887, pp. 33–58, 113–42 & 275–84. cf. also 'Les études de science sociale', *RP*, vol. 22, 1886, pp. 61–80.

14 Durkheim usually employs the term 'la morale' which is ambiguous in English in that it can mean either 'morality' or 'ethics' (i.e. the study of morality). I have rendered the term variably according to context in quoting from Durkheim.

15 This establishes one of the few points of direct connection between the writings of Durkheim and Max Weber. Adolf Wagner and Gustav Schmoller were among the founders of the *Verein für Sozialpolitik*, of which Weber became a prominent member. But Weber never accepted that aspect of the views of Wagner and Schmoller which appealed most to Durkheim – their attempt to found a 'scientific' ethics. Weber also questioned the policy of state intervention in the economy, as advocated by Schmoller in particular.

16 'Science positive de la morale', part 1, p. 37.

17 This principle was already well known to Durkheim, through Renouvier. Durkheim applies it frequently in his writings. As he remarks in a review published much later, 'it is from Renouvier that we took the axiom that a whole is not equal to the sum of its parts' (Review of Simon Deploige: *Le conflit de la morale et de la sociologie*, *AS*, vol. 12, 1909–12, p. 326). Deploige's work is a scathing attack upon Durkheim's school from a Thomist standpoint. It has been translated into English as *The Conflict between Ethics and Sociology* (St Louis, 1938); see esp. pp. 15–185. Some of the more important reviews written by Durkheim in the *AS* have been collected together as *Journal sociologique* (Paris, 1969).

rules which men live by in society: morality is a collective property and must be studied as such. In the theory of orthodox political economy, on the other hand, ' the collective interest is only a form of personal interest ', and ' altruism is merely a concealed egoism '.[18]

Schmoller has shown, Durkheim states, that economic phenomena cannot be adequately studied in the manner of classical economic theory, as if these were separate from the moral norms and beliefs which govern the life of individuals in society. There is no society (nor could there conceivably be a society) where economic relationships are not subject to customary and legal regulation. That is to say, as Durkheim was later to express the matter in *The Division of Labour*, ' a contract is not sufficient unto itself '.[19] If it were not for the existence of social norms which provide the framework within which contracts are made, then ' incoherent chaos ' would reign in the economic world.[20] The regulations which control economic life cannot be explained purely in economic terms: ' One can understand nothing of the rules of morality which govern property, contract, work, etc., if one does not know the economic causes which underlie them; and, conversely, one would arrive at a completely false notion of economic development if one neglected the moral causes which influenced it.'[21]

It is a major achievement of the German thinkers to have shown that moral rules and actions can and must be studied scientifically, as properties of social organisation. Here Durkheim sets out a precept which was to form a main connecting thread of his subsequent writings. Up to the present, philosophers have assumed that ethics can be based upon a deductive system of abstract principles. But the work of the German authors has shown that it is fundamentally mistaken to proceed in this way, as if human social life could be reduced to a few intellectually formulated maxims. Rather, we must *begin* with reality, which means the study of concrete forms of moral rules comprised within definite societies. Here Durkheim again quotes Schäffle appreciatively: it is precisely Schäffle's major achievement to have shown that moral rules are shaped by society, under the pressure of collective needs. There can be no question, therefore, of assuming that such rules, as they really operate empirically, can be reduced to a few *a priori* principles of which all specific beliefs and actions are merely an expression. Moral facts are actually ' of prodigious complexity ': the empirical study of different societies shows that there exists a ' steadily increasing multitude of beliefs, customs and legal provisions '.[22] This diversity is not refractory to analysis; but only the sociologist, through observation and description, can hope to classify and to interpret it.

Durkheim devotes a large part of his article on the German thinkers to

[18] ' Science positive de la morale ', part 1, p. 38.
[20] ' Science positive de la morale ', part 1, p. 40.
[21] *Ibid*. p. 41.

[19] *DL*, p. 215.

[22] *Ibid*. part 3, p. 276.

analysing Wundt's *Ethik*, regarding this work as one of the most significant fruits of the perspectives outlined above. One of Wundt's primary contributions which Durkheim singles out, is to have shown the basic significance of religious institutions in society. Wundt has shown that primitive religions contain two sorts of interrelated phenomena: a set of ' metaphysical speculations on the nature and order of things ' on the one hand, and rules of conduct and moral discipline on the other.[23] Moreover, through providing ideals to be striven for, religion is a force making for social unity. Durkheim accepts this as a general postulate: these ideals may vary between different societies, ' but one can be confident that there have never been men who have completely lacked an ideal, however humble it may be; for this corresponds to a need which is deeply rooted in our nature '.[24] In primitive societies, religion is a strong source of altruism: religious beliefs and practices have the effect ' of restraining egoism, of inclining man towards sacrifice and disinterestedness '. Religious sentiments ' attach man to something other than himself, and make him dependent upon superior powers which symbolise the ideal '.[25] Individualism, Wundt has shown, is a product of social development: ' far from individuality being the primitive fact, and society the derived fact, the first only slowly emerges from the second.' [26]

One of Durkheim's criticisms of Wundt is that the latter does not fully perceive the dual character of the regulative effect of religious and other moral rules. All moral actions, Durkheim says, have two sides: the positive attraction, the attraction to an ideal or set of ideals, is one side. But moral rules also have characteristics of obligation or constraint, since the pursuit of moral ends is not always inevitably founded upon the positive valence of ideals. Both aspects of moral rules are essential to their functioning.

Durkheim's concerns in ' The Division of Labour '

Durkheim's early discussions of the works of the German social thinkers indicate that several of his characteristic views were established at the very outset of his career.[27] It is difficult to assess precisely how far Durkheim was

---

[23] *Ibid.* part 2, pp. 116–17. Weber's critical discussion of Wundt appears in *GAW*, pp. 52ff.

[24] *Ibid.* p. 117.

[25] *Ibid.* p. 120.

[26] *Ibid.* p. 129. For another source of information upon Durkheim's early views on religion, cf. his review of Guyau's *L'irréligion de l'avenir*, *RP*, vol. 23, 1887, pp. 299–311.

[27] It is important to emphasise this point, because most secondary interpreters have concentrated heavily upon the changes which are presumed to have occurred in Durkheim's thought over the course of his writings. The most influential analysis of this sort is given in Talcott Parsons: *The Structure of Social Action* (Glencoe, 1949), pp. 301–450. For a recent, more simplified statement of the same position, see Jean Duvignaud: *Durkheim, sa vie, son oeuvre* (Paris, 1965), pp. 39–50. A similar theme is reiterated by Nisbet: Robert A. Nisbet: *Emile Durkheim* (Englewood Cliffs, 1965), esp. p. 37. The effect of this is to minimise the importance of *The Division of*

directly influenced by their writings, and how far alternatively these simply reinforced conclusions which he had already reached from other sources. The latter is the most likely. When criticised, much later on in his life, for having 'imported his ideas wholesale from Germany', Durkheim bluntly denied the assertion, stating that the influence of Comte was much more profound, and formed the position from which he evaluated the contributions of the German authors.[28] The important point is that Durkheim's discussions in the early writings show that he was conscious, at the outset of his career, of notions which sometimes have been supposed to have appeared only much later.[29] Of course, these are only stated in a rudimentary way, or have to be inferred from Durkheim's presentation of the views of others. But they include a consciousness of the following elements: the importance of 'ideals' and moral unity in the continuity of society [30]; the significance of the individual as an active agent as well as a passive recipient of social influences [31]; the dual nature of the attachment of the individual to society, as involving both obligation and positive commitment to ideals; the conception that an organisation of units (i.e., individuals as the units of organised societies) has properties which cannot be directly inferred from the characteristics of the component units considered in isolation from one another; the essential foundations of what was to become the theory of anomie [32]; and the rudiments of the later theory of religion.

It is important to bear these considerations in mind when evaluating the

---

Labour in relation to Durkheim's later writings, and thereby to make Durkheim appear as much more of a 'conservative' theorist than is actually the case. cf. my 'Durkheim as a review critic', pp. 188–91.

[28] Review of Deploige, p. 326. It should be remembered, however, that Durkheim's comments were written in the shadow of the imminent World War. For an earlier exchange of critical letters between Durkheim and Deploige, see the *Revue néo-scolastique*, vol. 14, 1907, pp. 606–21.

[29] See esp. Parsons, pp. 303–7; also Alessandro Pizzorno: 'Lecture actuelle de Durkheim', *Archives européennes de sociologie*, vol. 4, 1963, pp. 3–4.

[30] In reviewing Tönnies' *Gemeinschaft und Gesellschaft*, Durkheim makes the point that, when primitive society is replaced by more modern forms, the moral basis of unity does not wholly disappear. Tönnies assumes, according to Durkheim, that in *Gesellschaft* all 'collective life resulting from internal spontaneity' has been lost. But we must recognise, Durkheim states, that the differentiated type of social order has not ceased to be a society: that is, it preserves a collective unity and identity. *RP*, vol. 27, 1889, p. 421.

[31] This emerges clearly in Durkheim's discussion of Gumplowicz's *Grundriss der Soziologie* (RP, vol. 20, 1885, pp. 627–34), where Durkheim says, in criticism of Gumplowicz's 'objectivism', that 'we are at the same time actors and acted upon, and each of us contributes to forming this irresistible current which sweeps him along' (p. 632).

[32] cf. Durkheim's early article on suicide, where the point is made that, contrary to the thesis of the utilitarians, there is no direct and universal relationship between increasing prosperity and the advance of human happiness. If the effect of satisfying wants is simply to stimulate further wants, then the disparity between desires and their satisfaction may become actually broadened. 'Suicide et natalité, étude de statistique morale', *RP*, vol. 26, 1888, pp. 446–7.

content of *The Division of Labour* (1893), which is a highly polemical work. Durkheim concentrates his critical attack in such a way that certain of the underlying themes of the work tend to become obscured. One main arm of the polemic in the book is directed against the utilitarian individualism of the political economists and English philosophers.[33] But there is also another, rather less evident, critical objective in the book. This concerns the stream of thought deriving from Comte, and adopted by such authors as Schäffle, which stresses the salience of strongly defined moral consensus to the perpetuation of social order.[34] Durkheim accepts this as appropriate to the analysis of traditional types of society. But the main proposition developed in *The Division of Labour* is that modern complex society is not, in spite of the declining significance of traditional moral beliefs, inevitably tending towards disintegration. Instead, the 'normal' state of the differentiated division of labour is one of organic stability. This does not mean, however (as Durkheim considers Tönnies's analysis in *Gemeinschaft und Gesellschaft* to imply), that the integrating effect of the specialised division of labour can be satisfactorily interpreted in the mode of utilitarianism, as the result of multifarious individual contracts. On the contrary, the existence of contract presupposes norms which are not themselves the outcome of contractual ties, but which constitute general moral commitments without which the formation of such ties could not proceed in an orderly fashion. The 'cult of the individual', a notion which Durkheim takes over from Renouvier – basic consensual beliefs concerning the dignity and worth of the human individual, such as were formulated by the *philosophes* of the eighteenth century and underlay the French Revolution – is the counterpart to the individualisation produced by the expansion of the division of labour, and is the main moral support upon which it rests.[35]

The standpoint from which Durkheim approaches his subject-matter in *The Division of Labour* is identical to that set out in his discussions of the German social thinkers. 'This book', Durkheim states at the outset, 'is above all an attempt to treat the facts of moral life according to the method of the positive sciences.'[36] Such a method has to be clearly separated from that of ethical philosophy: the moral philosophers begin either from some *a priori* postulate about the essential characteristics of human nature, or from propositions taken from psychology, and thence proceed by a process of logical deduction to work out a scheme of ethics. Durkheim sets out, on the other hand, not to 'extract ethics from science, but to establish a science of morality, which is quite different'.[37] Moral rules develop in society, and are integrally

---

[33] It is this which is given sole prominence by Parsons; see pp. 308–17.
[34] cf. Gouldner, pp. 28–9.
[35] *DL*, pp. 399–402.
[36] *DL*, p. 32. *DTS*, p. xxxvii. See J. A. Barnes: 'Durkheim's *Division of Labour in Society*', *Man* (New Series), vol. 1, 1966, pp. 158ff.
[37] *DL*, p. 32; *DTS*, p. xxxvii.

bound up with the conditions of social life pertaining in a given time and place. The science of moral phenomena thus sets out to analyse how changing forms of society effect transformations in the character of moral norms, and to ' observe, describe and classify ' these.

The main substantive problem which is at the root of Durkheim's concern in *The Division of Labour* stems from an apparent moral ambiguity concerning the relationship between the individual and society in the contemporary world. On the one hand, the development of the modern form of society is associated with the expansion of ' individualism '. This is a phenomenon clearly associated with the growth of the division of labour, which produces specialisation of occupational function, and therefore fosters the development of specific talents, capacities and attitudes which are not shared by everyone in society, but are possessed only by particular groups. It is not difficult, Durkheim states, to show that there are strong currents of moral ideals in the present age which express the viewpoint that the individual personality should be developed according to the specific qualities which the person has, and hence that not everyone should receive a uniform education.[38] On the other hand, there are other contradictory moral trends which are also strong, and which praise the ' universally developed individual '. ' In a general way, the precept (*maxime*) which commands us to specialise appears everywhere to be contradicted by the precept which commands us all to follow the same ideal.' [39]

An understanding of sources of these apparently contradictory moral ideals, according to Durkheim, can be achieved only through a historical and sociological analysis of the causes and effects of the expansion of the division of labour. The division of labour, Durkheim points out, is not wholly a modern phenomenon; but in the more traditional sorts of society, it is rudimentary, and usually confined to a sexual division. A high degree of specialisation in the division of labour is particularly consequent upon modern industrial production. It is fallacious, however, to suppose, as many economists are prone to do, that it is only in the strictly ' economic ' sphere that the division of labour is becoming more diversified, or that this diversification is the result of industrialism alone. The same process can be observed in all sectors of contemporary societies – in government, law, science and the arts. In all of these areas of social life, specialisation is becoming increasingly evident. This can be illustrated by the example of science : whereas once there existed a general discipline of ' philosophy ' which took as its subject-matter the whole of natural and social reality, it has long since become split into numerous separate disciplines.

The increase in social differentiation which is characteristic of the process

---

[38] Durkheim quotes Secrétant : ' To perfect oneself is to learn one's role, to become capable of fulfilling one's function ...' *DL*, pp. 42–3.

[39] *DL*, p. 44; *DTS*, p. 6.

of development from traditional to modern forms of society can be compared to certain biological principles. In the evolutionary scale, the first organisms to appear are simple in structure; but these cede place to organisms which show a higher degree of internal functional specialisation: 'the more specialised the functions of the organism, the higher its level on the evolutionary scale '.[40] This is paralleled in Durkheim's analysis of the development of the division of labour and its relationship to the moral order. In order to analyse the significance of differentiation in the division of labour, we have to compare and contrast the principles according to which the less developed societies are organised with those which govern the organisation of the ' advanced ' societies.

This entails attempting to measure changes in the nature of social solidarity.[41] Since social solidarity is, according to Durkheim – as in the case of every moral phenomenon – not directly measurable, it follows that in order to chart the changing form of moral solidarity ' we must substitute for the internal fact which escapes us an external index (*fait extérieur*) which symbolises it '.[42] Such an index can be found in legal codes. Whenever a stable form of social life exists, moral rules eventually come to be codified in the shape of laws. While on occasion there may be conflict between customary modes of behaviour and law, this is, according to Durkheim, exceptional, and occurs only when law ' no longer corresponds to the state of existing society, but maintains itself, without reason for so doing, by the force of habit '.[43]

A legal precept can be defined as a rule of conduct which is sanctioned; and sanctions can be divided into two major types. ' Repressive ' sanctions are characteristic of penal law, and consist in the imposition of some kind of suffering upon the individual as a punishment for his transgression. Such sanctions include the deprivation of liberty, the inflicting of pain, loss of honour, etc. ' Restitutive ' sanctions, on the other hand, involve restoration, the re-establishment of relationships as they were before the law was violated. Thus if one man claims damages from another, the object of the legal process is to recompense the claimant, if his claim is upheld, for some sort of loss which he has incurred as an individual. There is little or no social disgrace attaching to the individual who loses a case of this sort. This is typical of most areas of civil, commercial and constitutional law.

Repressive law is characteristic of that sort of transgression which is a ' crime '. A crime is an act which violates sentiments which are ' universally approved of ' by the members of society. The diffuse moral basis of penal law is evidenced by its generalised character. In the case of restitutive law,

[40] *DL*, p. 41; *DTS*, p. 3.
[41] See J. E. S. Hayward: ' Solidarist syndicalism: Durkheim and Duguit ', *Sociological Review*, vol. 8, 1960, parts 1 & 2, pp. 17–36 and 185–202.
[42] *DL*, p. 64.
[43] *DL*, p. 65.

both sides of the legal commitment are typically precisely defined – both the obligation, and the penalty for transgression.

Penal law, on the contrary, sets forth only sanctions, but says nothing of the obligations to which they correspond. It does not command respect for the life of another, but kills the assassin. It does not say to begin with, as does civil law: here is the duty; but rather, here is the punishment.[44]

The reason why the nature of the moral obligation does not have to be specified in repressive law, Durkheim says, is evident: because everyone knows of it and accepts it.

The predominance of penal law within the juridical system of a given society thus necessarily presupposes the existence of a strongly defined *conscience collective*, of beliefs and sentiments shared in common by the members of the society. Punishment consists above all in an emotive response to a transgression. This is shown by the fact that it is not always confined to the guilty: often those who are themselves entirely innocent, but closely connected to the guilty party – such as relatives or friends – also suffer, because they are 'tainted' by their association with the culpable agent. Especially in primitive societies, punishment tends to have a blind, reflexive character; but the principle underlying penal law remains the same in the more developed types of society. In contemporary societies, the rationale which is frequently offered for the continuance of repressive sanctions conceives of punishment only as a deterrent. But if this were really so, Durkheim argues, the law would not punish according to the gravity of the crime itself, but in relation to the strength of the *motivation* of the criminal to commit the crime. 'Robbers are as strongly inclined to rob as murderers are to murder...; but murder is nevertheless subject to more severe sanctions than robbery.'[45] Punishment thus retains its expiatory character (as regards the perpetrator of the criminal act), and remains an act of vengeance (on the part of society). 'What we avenge, what the criminal expiates, is the outrage to morality.'[46]

The primary function of punishment, therefore, is to protect and reaffirm the *conscience collective* in the face of acts which question its sanctity. In the simpler societies, there is a unitary religious system which is the prime embodiment of the common beliefs and sentiments of the *conscience collective*. Religion 'comprises all, extends to all', and contains an intermingled set of beliefs and practices regulating not only strictly religious phenomena, but also

---

[44] *DL*, p. 75; *DTS*, p. 41.
[45] *DL*, p. 89. Durkheim makes an important qualification, however, to the main trend of his argument. There are moral sentiments which, in certain societies, are as deeply rooted as those punished under penal law – Durkheim gives the example of filial piety. Thus it is not a wholly sufficient condition for the existence of 'crime' that collective sentiments should be strong; 'they must also be precise... relative to a very definite practice... penal laws are remarkable for their neatness and precision, while purely moral rules are generally somewhat nebulous' (p. 79).
[46] *DL*, p. 89.

' ethics, law, the principles of political organisation, and even science. . . .' [47]
All penal law is originally contained within a religious framework; conversely,
in the most primitive forms of society all law is repressive.[48]

Societies in which the principal bonds of cohesion are based upon ' mechanical solidarity' have an aggregate or segmental structure: that is, they
consist of juxtaposed politico-familial groups (clan groups) which are very
similar to each other in their internal organisation. The tribe as a whole forms
a ' society' because it is a cultural unity: because the members of the various
clan groups all adhere to the same set of common beliefs and sentiments.
Thus any part of such a society can break away without much loss to the
others – rather in the same way as simple biological organisms can split up
into several bodies which are nonetheless unitary and self-sufficient. In
primitive, segmental societies, property is communal, a phenomenon which is
only one specific aspect of the low level of individualisation generally. Since,
in mechanical solidarity, the society is dominated by the existence of a
strongly formed set of sentiments and beliefs shared by all members of the
community, it follows that there is little scope for differentiation between
individuals; each individual is a microcosm of the whole. ' Property is in fact
simply the extension of the person over things. Thus wherever the collective
personality is the only one which exists, property itself can be nothing other
than collective.' [49]

The growth of organic solidarity

The progressive displacement of repressive by restitutive law is an historical
trend which is correlated with the degree of development of a society: the
higher the level of social development, the greater the relative proportion of
restitutive laws within the juridical structure. Now the fundamental element
found in repressive law – the conception of expiation through punishment –
is absent in restitutive law. The form of social solidarity indexed by the
existence of the latter type of law consequently must be distinct from that
expressed by penal law. The very existence of restitutive law, in fact, presupposes the prevalence of a differentiated division of labour, since it covers
the rights of individuals either over private property, or over other individuals
who are in a different social position from themselves.

---

[47] *DL*, p. 135; *DTS*, p. 105.   [48] *DL*, p. 138.
[49] *DL*, p. 179; *DTS*, pp. 154–5. Durkheim stresses, in a subsequent publication, that
the development of the state is not necessarily parallel to the level of general
evolution of a given society. A relatively primitive society may have a fairly highly
developed state. Durkheim's analysis here is similar to Marx's discussion of ' oriental
despotism '. Durkheim says that in such societies: ' the right of property which the
community exercises over things in an undivided way passes intact into the superior
personality who finds himself thus constituted ' (*DL*, p. 180). This issue is analysed
in detail by Durkheim, and linked up with variations in intensity and quality of
penal sanctions, in ' Deux lois de l'évolution pénale ', *AS*, vol. 4, 1899–1900, pp.
65–95.

Society presents a different aspect in each case. In the first [mechanical solidarity] what we call by that name is a more or less organised totality of beliefs and sentiments common to all the members of the group: it is the collective type. On the other hand, the society which we are bound to [*dont nous sommes solidaires*] in the second case is a system of differentiated and special functions united in definite relationships.[50]

This second type of social cohesion is 'organic solidarity'. Here solidarity stems not simply from acceptance of a common set of beliefs and sentiments, but from functional interdependence in the division of labour. Where mechanical solidarity is the main basis of societal cohesion, the *conscience collective* 'completely envelops' the individual consciousness, and therefore presumes identity between individuals. Organic solidarity, by contrast, presupposes not identity but *difference* between individuals in their beliefs and actions. The growth of organic solidarity and the expansion of the division of labour are hence associated with increasing individualism.

The progression of organic solidarity is necessarily dependent upon the declining significance of the *conscience collective*. But commonly held beliefs and sentiments do not disappear altogether in complex societies; nor is it the case that the formation of contractual relations becomes amoral and simply the result of each individual following 'his best interest'. Here Durkheim reverts to the theme previously developed in his first writings, and applied specifically in criticism of Tönnies' conception of *Gesellschaft*. Herbert Spencer is Durkheim's target for critical attack in *The Division of Labour*, but the substance of his polemic is the same. A society in which each individual solely pursues his own interest would disintegrate within a short space of time. 'There is nothing less constant than interest. Today, it unites me to you; tomorrow, it will make me your enemy.'[51] It is true, Durkheim admits, that contractual relations generally multiply with the growth of the division of labour. But the expansion of contractual relations presupposes the development of norms which govern contract; all contracts are regulated by definite prescriptions. However complex the division of labour, society does not become reduced to a chaos of short-term contractual alliances. Durkheim here reiterates the point first made in reference to Tönnies: 'It is thus mistaken to oppose a society which derives from a community of beliefs to one based on co-operation, according a moral character only to the first and seeing in the second nothing more than an economic grouping. In reality, co-operation has its own intrinsic morality.'[52]

Utilitarian theory is unable to account for the basis of moral solidarity in contemporary societies; and it is also fallacious as a theory of the causes for the increase in the division of labour. In the latter form, it attributes the increase in specialisation to the increase in material wealth which is made

[50] *DL*, p. 129; *DTS*, p. 99. My parenthesis.
[51] *DL*, p. 204.
[52] *DL*, p. 228; *DTS*, p. 208.

possible through diversification and exchange. According to this conception, the more production increases, the more men's needs are met, and the greater the increase in human happiness. Durkheim puts forward various arguments against this position. The most important one, however, is that the thesis is simply fallacious on the empirical level. While it is true that there are a variety of pleasures open to modern man which were previously unknown, these are more than counterbalanced by sources of suffering which do not exist in previous forms of society.[53] The high incidence of suicide in contemporary societies is indicative of this. Melancholy suicide is almost wholly absent in the less developed societies; its importance in contemporary societies makes manifest that societal differentiation does not inevitably produce an increase in the general level of happiness.[54]

The explanation for the growth of the division of labour thus has to be sought elsewhere. We know that the development of the division of labour goes hand in hand with the disintegration of the segmental type of social structure. For this to occur, relationships must have formed where none previously existed, bringing erstwhile separate groups into contact. The differing modes of life and belief of such societies, once they are brought into contact with each other, breaks down the isolated homogeneity of each group, and stimulates economic and cultural exchange. Division of labour thus increases ' as there are more individuals sufficiently in contact to be able to act and react upon one-another'.[55] Durkheim calls the frequency of such contact moral or ' dynamic' density. The growth of diversified contacts between individuals obviously must derive from some sort of continuous physical relationships. In other words, the growth of dynamic density is mainly contingent upon an increase in the physical density of population. We can then formulate the general proposition that: ' The division of labour varies in direct ratio with the volume and density of societies, and, if it progresses in a continuous manner in the course of social development, it is because societies become regularly denser and generally greater in volume.'[56]

It has often been suggested that the interpretation offered by Durkheim here marks a relapse from the principle stated in *The Rules of Sociological Method*, that social phenomena must not be explained reductively. Durkheim himself seems to have felt uneasy about this point, and later amended some-

---

[53] Here Durkheim repeats the point made in his earlier article on suicide. See footnote 32, p. 71.

[54] *DL*, p. 249. In primitive societies, ' a man kills himself, not because he judges life bad, but because the ideal to which he is attached demands the sacrifice' (p. 246). This is, of course, the type which Durkheim later calls altruistic suicide.

[55] *DL*, p. 257.

[56] *DL*, p. 262; *DTS*, p. 244. Durkheim admits that there are partial exceptions to this: e.g., traditional China or Russia. Here ' the division of labour is not developed in proportion to the social volume. In fact, increase in volume is not necessarily a sign of superiority if density does not increase at the same time and in the same degree ...' (*DL*, p. 261; *DTS*, p. 243).

what his original assessment of the relation between physical and dynamic density.[57] But, in fact, it is clear in his statement of it in *The Division of Labour*, that the explanation Durkheim offers is a sociological one: physical density is important only in so far as it becomes transformed into moral or dynamic density, and it is the frequency of social contact which is the explanatory factor. A more convincing case could be made for the supposition that Durkheim employs a 'biological' explanation in the mode in which he seeks to analyse *conflict* as a mechanism, within a quasi-Darwinian framework, which accelerates the progression of the division of labour. Darwin and other biologists have demonstrated, according to Durkheim, that the struggle for existence is most acute between organisms of the same type. The existence of such conflict tends to generate complementary specialisation, such that organisms can exist side by side without the one hampering the survival of the other. Differentiation of function allows diverse types of organism to survive. A similar principle, Durkheim concludes, can be applied to human society:

Men submit to the same law. In the same city, different occupations can co-exist without being obliged mutually to destroy one another, for they pursue different objects. The soldier seeks military glory, the priest moral authority, the statesman power, the businessman riches, the scholar scientific renown.[58]

Individualism and anomie

Having set out both a functional and causal analysis of the division of labour, Durkheim is now in a position to answer the questions which formed the original stimulus to his work. We can be certain that the differentiation of the division of labour inevitably produces a decline in the pervasiveness of the *conscience collective* in society. The growth of individualism is an inevitable concomitant of the expansion of the division of labour: and individualism can only progress at the expense of the strength of common beliefs and sentiments. Thus the *conscience collective* ' comes increasingly to be made up of highly generalised and indeterminate modes of thought and sentiment, which leave room open for an increasing multitude of individual differences '.[59] Modern societies do not thereby collapse into disorder, as would follow from the standpoint of those who assume that a strongly defined moral consensus is requisite to social cohesion. In fact, in contemporary societies, this form of cohesion (mechanical solidarity) is increasingly supplanted by a new type of social cohesion (organic solidarity). But the functioning of organic solidarity cannot be interpreted in the matter of utilitarian theory; contemporary society is still a moral order. There is, indeed, one area where the *conscience collective* becomes ' strengthened and made more precise ':

[57] See *RSM*, p. 115.
[58] *DL*, p. 267.
[59] *DL*, p. 172; *DTS*, pp. 146–7.

in relation to the ' cult of the individual '.[60] The growth of the ' cult of the individual ' is only possible because of the secularisation of most sectors of social life. It contrasts with the traditional forms of *conscience collective* in that, while it consists of common beliefs and sentiments, these focus upon the worth and dignity of the individual rather than of the collectivity. The ' cult of the individual ' is the moral counterpart to the growth of the division of labour, but is quite distinct in content from the traditional forms of moral community, and cannot in itself provide the *sole* basis of solidarity in contemporary societies.

It is certainly what might be called a common faith; but, firstly, it is only made possible by the ruin of the others, and consequently cannot produce the same effects as this multitude of extinguished beliefs. Nothing compensates for that. Moreover, if it is common insofar as it is shared by the community, it is individual in its object.[61]

At this point, Durkheim's analysis runs into an obvious difficulty. If the growth of the division of labour is not inevitably associated with disruption in social cohesion, what explains the conflicts which are such an evident feature of the modern economic world? Durkheim recognises that burgeoning class conflict between capital and wage-labour has accompanied the expansion of the division of labour ensuing from industrialisation. It is, however, fallacious to suppose that this conflict results directly from the division of labour. It is, in reality, consequent upon the fact that the division of economic functions has temporarily outstripped the development of appropriate moral regulation. The division of labour does not everywhere produce cohesion because it is in an anomic state.[62] That is, the relationship between capital and wage-labour really *does* approximate to the condition considered ethically ideal in utilitarian theory – where there is little or no regulation upon the formation of contracts. What this leads to, however, is a chronic state of class conflict. In lieu of the requisite moral regulation, the formation of contractual relations tends to be determined by the imposition of coercive power. Durkheim calls this the ' forced division of labour ' (*la division du travail contrainte*). While the functioning of organic solidarity entails the existence of normative rules which regularise the relationships between different occupations, this cannot be achieved if these rules are unilaterally imposed by one class upon another. These conflicts can be obviated only if the division of labour is co-ordinated with the distribution of talents and capacities, and if the higher occupational positions are not monopolised by a privileged class. ' If one class of society is obliged, in order to live, to take any price for its services, while another can abstain from such action thanks to resources at its disposal which, however,

---

[60] *DL*, p. 172.

[61] *DL*, p. 172; *DTS*, p. 147.

[62] Durkheim seems to have adopted the term ' anomie ' from Guyau (see note 26, p. 70). Guyau, however, uses the term ' religious anomie ' in a sense close to Durkheim's ' cult of the individual '.

are not necessarily due to any social superiority, the second has an unjust advantage over the first at law.' [63]

The present situation, in which this does still pertain, is a transitional one. The progressive decline of inequality of opportunity (' external inequality ') is a definite historical tendency which accompanies the growth of the division of labour. According to Durkheim, it is easy to see why this should be so. In primitive society, where solidarity is based primarily upon community of belief and sentiment, there is neither the means nor the need for the equalisation of talent and opportunity. But the individualising effects of the division of labour mean that specific human faculties which previously remained latent increasingly become capable of actualisation, and thus create a pressure towards individual self-fulfilment:

we may thus say that the division of labour produces solidarity only if it is spontaneous and to the degree that it is spontaneous. But by spontaneity we must understand not simply the absence of express and overt violence, but of anything that might, even indirectly, shackle the free employment of the social force that each person carries in himself. This not only supposes that individuals are not relegated to particular functions by force, but also that no sort of obstacle whatsoever prevents them from occupying in the social framework the position which accords with their capacities.[64]

---

[63] *DL*, p. 384. For further discussion of Durkheim's views on this question, see below, pp. 229–31.
[64] *DL*, p. 377; *DTS*, p. 370.

6. Durkheim's conception of sociological method

The notions developed in *The Division of Labour* constitute the foundations of Durkheim's sociology, and the bulk of Durkheim's subsequent writings represent elaborations of the themes originally set out in that work. This is most obviously true of Durkheim's two major publications prior to the turn of the century: *The Rules of Sociological Method* (1895) and *Suicide* (1897). In *The Rules*, Durkheim explicates the methodological suppositions already applied in *The Division of Labour*. While the subject-matter of *Suicide* appears at first sight to be utterly different from *The Division of Labour*, the themes of the former actually mesh very closely with the latter, both within the context of Durkheim's own thought, and within the framework of nineteenth-century writing upon questions of social ethics more generally. Since the end of the eighteenth century, the study of suicide was used by a variety of writers as a specific problem in terms of which general moral issues could be analysed. Durkheim's analysis in *Suicide* is based upon the work of such authors, but also takes as its point of departure some of the general conclusions concerning the moral order of different forms of society established in *The Division of Labour*.

The problem of suicide

Durkheim's interest in suicide, and acquaintance with the large extant literature on the subject, was established some while prior to 1897. In 1888 he already writes: 'it is quite certain that a consistent increase in suicides always attests to a serious upheaval in the organic conditions of society'.[1] The attempt to document, through the precise analysis of a specific phenomenon, the nature of this moral *lacuna* in contemporary societies is perhaps the most basic of Durkheim's concerns in *Suicide*. But to this must be added a methodological objective: the application of sociological method to the explanation of what might *prima facie* appear to be a wholly 'individual' phenomenon.

A basic standpoint set out by numerous previous writers on suicide, and one which Durkheim adopts, is that a strict analytical separation must be drawn between the explanation of the distribution of suicide *rates*, and the actiology of individual cases of suicide. Nineteenth-century statisticians previously showed that the rate of suicide for a society typically shows a stable distribution from year to year, interspersed with specifically identifiable periodic fluctuations. The patterns of suicide rates, they concluded, must

[1] 'Suicide et natalité, étude de statistique morale', p. 447.

depend upon stably distributed phenomena of a geographical, biological, or social kind.[2] In *Suicide*, Durkheim discusses these first two in some detail, rejecting both as possible explanations for the distribution of suicide rates.[3] It is, therefore, to the third type of factor, the social, that we must look to explain the patterns of suicide rates.

The distribution of suicide in the countries of western Europe shows a close relationship between suicide rates and religious denomination: predominantly Catholic countries everywhere have lower suicide rates than those which are mainly Protestant. This consistent differential in suicide rates cannot be explained by reference to variation in the degree to which suicide is condemned in the *credo* of the two denominations; both prohibit suicide with equal stringency. Its explanation must be sought in differences rooted more generically in the social organisation of the two churches. The most obvious dissimilarity between the two, according to Durkheim, is that Protestantism is founded upon the promotion of a spirit of free enquiry. The Catholic church is formed around the traditional hierarchy of the priesthood, whose authority is binding in matters of religious dogma; but the Protestant is alone before God: 'like the worshippers, the priest has no other source but himself, and his conscience'.[4] Protestantism is, in Durkheim's phrase, a 'less strongly integrated' church than Catholicism.

The inference can be drawn from this that there is nothing specifically bound up with religion as such which needs to be invoked to explain the 'preservative effect' of Catholicism; in other words, that the degree of integration in other sectors of society is related to suicide rates in a comparable way. Durkheim finds that this is in fact so. Unmarried individuals generally show lower rates of suicide than married persons of comparable age, and there is an inverse relation between suicide and size of the conjugal unit – the greater the number of children in the family, the lower the suicide rate. This parallels the case of the relationship between suicide and religious denomination, supplying in this instance a measure of the relationship between suicide and degree of integration in family structure. A similar relationship between suicide rates and level of social integration can be demonstrated in another quite different institutional context. Suicide rates decline in times of national political crisis, and in times of war: in the latter case, not merely among those in the armed forces, but also among the civilian population of both sexes.[5] The reason is that political crises and wars, by

---

[2] Virtually all of the statistical relationships between suicide and social phenomena used by Durkheim in *Suicide* had been established by previous writers. See my article, 'The suicide problem in French sociology', *British Journal of Sociology*, vol. 16, 1965, pp. 3–18.   [3] *Su*, pp. 57–142.

[4] *Su*, pp. 160–1. Anglicanism, Durkheim admits, is a partial exception to this; but England has a lower rate than the other Protestant countries.

[5] In none of these cases, according to Durkheim, can the drop in suicide rates be attributed to less precise official documentation of suicide in war-time (*Su*, pp. 206–8).

stimulating an increased level of involvement within a definite set of events, ' at least for a time, bring about a stronger integration of society '.[6]

There is, consequently, a relationship between social integration and suicide which holds regardless of the particular institutional sector of society which is analysed: the proposition is established that ' suicide varies in inverse ratio to the degree of integration of the social groups of which the individual forms a part '.[7] Thus this type of suicide may be called ' egoistic ', and it is the resultant of a state where ' the individual self asserts itself to excess in the face of the social self and at its expense. . .'.[8] Egoistic suicide is particularly characteristic of contemporary societies; but it is not the only type of suicide found there. A second type of suicide springs from the phenomenon which Durkheim discusses at some length in *The Division of Labour*: the anomic state of moral deregulation characterising economic relationships. This is indexed by the correlation which can be demonstrated between suicide rates and the occupational structure. Suicide rates, Durkheim points out, are higher in occupations in industry and commerce than in agricultural occupations. Moreover, within non-agricultural occupations, suicide rates are inversely related to socio-economic level, being lowest among the chronically poor, and highest among the well-to-do and those in the liberal professions. This is because poverty is in itself a source of moral restraint: it is the occupations above the lowest levels which have become most freed from stable moral regulation. The relationship between anomie and suicide can also be demonstrated in reference to another phenomenon which Durkheim discusses in *The Division of Labour* as an outcome of the anomic state of industry: the occurrence of economic crises. In times of economic depression, suicide rates show a marked increase. This is not explicable simply in terms of the economic deprivation involved, since suicide rates increase to equivalent degree in times of marked economic prosperity. What both upward and downward fluctuations in the economic cycle share in common is that each has a disruptive effect upon accustomed modes of life. Those experiencing either a sudden downswing or uplift in their material circumstances are placed in a situation in which their habitual expectations come under strain. An anomic condition of moral deregulation results.

Anomie is thus, like egoism, ' a constant and specific factor in suicide in our modern societies; it is one of the sources upon which the annual contingent is nourished '.[9] Durkheim's discussion of the differences between egoistic and anomic suicide is not always unambiguous, and this has caused

---

[6] *Su*, p. 208; *LS*, p. 222.

[7] *Su*, p. 209; *LS*, p. 223.

[8] *Su*, p. 209; *LS*, p. 223.

[9] *Su*, p. 258; *LS*, p. 288. For a development of these ideas, considered in relation to psychological theory, see my ' A typology of suicide ', *Archives européennes de sociologie*, vol. 7, 1966, pp. 276–95.

some commentators to suppose that the two types in fact cannot, from the substance of Durkheim's analysis, be meaningfully distinguished.[10] Careful reading of Durkheim's account against the broader backdrop of *The Division of Labour*, however, makes this position difficult to maintain. Egoistic suicide is clearly linked by Durkheim to the growth of the 'cult of the individual' in contemporary societies. Protestantism is the religious forerunner and primary source of modern moral individualism, which has in other areas of social life become wholly secularised.[11] Egoistic suicide is thus an offshoot of the growth of the 'cult of the personality'. Where 'man is a God to man-kind', a certain growth in egoism is unavoidable: 'Individualism is un-doubtedly not necessarily egoism, but it comes close to it; the one cannot be stimulated without further spreading the other. Thus, egoistic suicide arises.'[12] Anomic suicide, on the other hand, derives from the lack of moral regulation particularly characteristic of major sectors of modern industry. In so far as anomie is, according to Durkheim, a 'pathological' phenomenon, then anomic suicide is also pathological, and therefore not an inevitable characteristic of contemporary societies.[13] Egoistic and anomic suicide are nevertheless closely related to one another, especially on the level of the individual suicide. 'It is, indeed, almost inevitable that the egoist should have some tendency to deregulation; for, since he is detached from society, it has not sufficient hold upon him to regulate him.'[14]

Suicide in traditional societies takes a different form to the egoistic and anomic types: this is directly traceable to the characteristics of social organi-sation, specified in *The Division of Labour*, whereby such societies differ from the modern form. In one category of suicides found in traditional societies, it is a duty for an individual, when placed in certain circumstances, to kill himself. A person kills himself because he has an obligation to do so. This is 'obligatory altruistic suicide'. There are other sorts of altruistic suicide which do not involve a definite obligation, but where suicide is associated with the furtherance of definite codes of honour and prestige ('optional' [*faculatif*] altruistic suicide). Both kinds of altruistic suicide, however, rest upon the existence of a strong *conscience collective*, which so dominates the actions of the individual that he will sacrifice his life in furtherance of a collective value.

---

[10] Barclay Johnson: 'Durkheim's one cause of suicide', *American Sociological Review*, vol. 30, 1965, pp. 875–86.

[11] Durkheim makes this point explicit in his neglected but important work *L'évolution pédagogique en France* (Paris, 1969).

[12] *Su*, p. 364; *LS*, p. 416.

[13] Durkheim holds that a certain minimal level of anomie is a necessary element in societies which are committed to progressive change. 'Every morality of improve-ment and progress thus presupposes a certain level of anomie.' *Su*, p. 364; *LS*, p. 417.

[14] *Su*, p. 288; *LS*, p. 325.

' Externality ' and ' constraint '

The ideas presented in *Suicide* constitute a particularly forceful testimony to the fruitfulness of Durkheim's conception of sociological method. Durkheim expresses the fundamental standpoint underlying *Suicide* as follows:

> At any given moment the moral constitution of society establishes the contingent of voluntary deaths. There is, therefore, for each people a collective force of a definite amount of energy, impelling men to self-destruction. The victim's acts which at first seem to express only his personal temperament are really the supplement and prolongation of a social condition which they express externally.[15]

This does not mean, Durkheim goes on to add, that psychology is irrelevant to the explanation of suicide: the proper contribution of the psychologist is to study the particular motives and circumstances which drive specific individuals, when placed in the relevant social circumstances (e.g., in a condition of anomie) to commit suicide. While Durkheim's methodological views are set out most systematically in *The Rules of Sociological Method*, he regards the approach documented in the work as stemming directly from the substantive studies represented by *The Division of Labour* and *Suicide*. ' The method which we have described is simply a summary of our practice.' [16]

A primary theme of *The Rules* is that the nature of the subject-matter of sociology must be clarified, and its field of investigation delimited. Durkheim repeatedly emphasises in his writings that sociology remains largely a ' philosophical ' discipline, consisting of a heterogeneous assortment of all-embracing generalisations which rest more upon logical derivation from *a priori* precepts than upon systematic empirical study. Sociology, Durkheim remarks in the beginning of *Suicide*, ' is still in the stage of system-building and philosophical syntheses. Instead of attempting to cast light upon a limited portion of the social field, it prefers brilliant generalities . . .' [17] The discipline is evidently in some way concerned with the study of man in society: but the category of the ' social ' is often employed in a very loose fashion. What are the specific characteristics of the class of phenomena which may be delimited as ' social ' and thereby separated from other categories such as the ' biological ' and ' psychological '? [18]

Durkheim's attempt to define the specificity of the social is based upon the use of the famous criteria of ' exteriority ' and ' constraint ' (*contrainte*). In spite of the variety of differing interpretations which have been placed upon Durkheim's argument at this point, the substance of Durkheim's position

---

[15] *Su*, p. 299.

[16] 'La sociologie en France au XIXe siècle ', *Revue bleue*, vol. 13, 1900, p. 649. Durkheim also says in *The Rules* that the method stated therein is ' of course, contained by implication in the book which we published recently on *The Division of Labour* '. *RSM*, p. ix.

[17] *Su*, p. 35.

[18] Parsons has pointed to an epistemological confusion involved in Durkheim's use of the phrase social ' fact ' as equivalent to social ' phenomenon ' (Parsons, pp. 41–2).

here can be elucidated without difficulty. There are two related senses in which social facts are ' external ' to the individual. Firstly, every man is born into an on-going society which already has a definite organisation or structure, and which conditions his own personality: ' the church-member finds the beliefs and practices of his religious life ready-made at birth; their existence prior to his own implies their existence outside of himself '.[19] Secondly, social facts are ' external ' to the individual in the sense that any one individual is only a single element within the totality of relationships which constitutes a society. These relationships are not the creation of any single individual, but are constituted of multiple interactions between individuals. ' The system of signs I use to express my thought, the system of currency I employ to pay my debts, the instruments of credit I utilise in my commercial relations, the practices followed in my profession, etc., function independently of my own use of them.' [20] It has often been pointed out that Durkheim uses the term ' individual ' here in more than one sense. At times the context makes it apparent that he is speaking of the (hypothetical) ' isolated individual ', the asocial being which forms the starting-point of utilitarian theory; at other times, Durkheim uses the word to refer to a given ' particular ' individual – a flesh-and-blood member of an empirical society.[21] But, in fact, for Durkheim's purposes, which are in part polemical, the distinctions which may be drawn between the various senses of the term ' individual ' are not important. The main burden of Durkheim's thesis is that *no* theory or analysis which begins from the ' individual ', either in the two senses mentioned above or in others, can successfully grasp the specific properties of *social* phenomena.

Durkheim's point here, in other words, is a conceptual one. It is true that this is to some extent obscured by Durkheim's insistence upon talking of social ' facts '; but it should be obvious that the criterion of ' exteriority ' is not an empirical one. If it were, it would lead directly to the ludicrous conclusion that society exists externally to *all* individuals: this is, Durkheim says, ' an obvious absurdity we might have been spared having attributed to us '.[22] Durkheim stresses many times that ' society is composed only of individuals '.[23] But a parallel statement can be made of the relationship between chemical elements and the substances which are composed of combinations of them:

What is so readily judged inadmissible in regard to social facts is freely admitted in the other realms of nature. Whenever any elements combine and thereby pro-

---

[19] *RSM*, p. 2.   [20] *RSM*, p. 2.

[21] cf. Harry Alpert: *Emile Durkheim and his Sociology* (New York, 1939), pp. 135–7; Parsons, pp. 367–8; Guy Aimard: *Durkheim et la science économique* (Paris, 1962), pp. 26–31.

[22] *Su*, p. 320.

[23] That is, individuals plus the artifacts which they construct; but physical objects only have social relevance when there are men in society who attribute some kind of significance to them. *RSM*, pp. 1ff.

duce, by the fact of their combination, new phenomena, it is plain that these new phenomena reside not in the original elements but in the totality formed by their union. The living cell contains nothing but mineral particles, as society contains nothing but individuals; and yet it is patently impossible for the phenomena characteristic of life to reside in the atoms of hydrogen, oxygen, carbon and nitrogen... Let us apply this principle to sociology. If, as we may say, this synthesis *sui generis* which every society constitutes, yields new phenomena, differing from those which take place in individual minds, we must, indeed, admit that these facts reside in the very society itself which produces them, and not in its parts, i.e., its members.[24]

The second criterion which Durkheim applies in specifying the nature of social facts *is an empirical one*: the presence of moral 'constraint'. Here it is best to proceed from an illustration which Durkheim himself offers, the case of 'fatherhood'. Paternity is in one sense a biological relation: a man 'fathers' a child through the act of procreation. But paternity is also a social phenomenon: a father is obliged, by convention and law, to act in various definite ways *vis-à-vis* his offspring (and, of course, other members of his family also). These modes of action are not created by the individual in question, but form part of a system of moral duties in which he is enmeshed with other men. While an individual might flout such obligations, in doing so he feels their force and thereby confirms their constraining character: 'Even when I free myself from these rules and violate them successfully, I am always compelled to struggle with them. When finally overcome, they make their constraining power sufficiently felt by the resistance they offer.'[25] This is, of course, most obvious in the case of legal obligations, which are sanctioned by a whole apparatus of coercive agencies: the police, the law courts, etc. But a large variety of other sanctions exist which reinforce adherence to obligations not expressed in law.

Durkheim frequently reiterates, however, that conformity to obligations rarely rests upon fear of the sanctions which are applied against contravention. In most circumstances individuals accept the legitimacy of the obligation, and thus do not consciously feel its constraining character: 'when I conform to them whole-heartedly, this constraint (*coercition*) is felt only slightly, if at all, since it is unnecessary. But it is, nonetheless, an intrinsic characteristic of these facts, the proof thereof being that it asserts itself as soon as I attempt to resist it.'[26] Durkheim's emphasis upon the importance of constraint is evidently directed primarily against utilitarianism. But moral obligation always has two aspects, the other being the acceptance of an ideal (however partial that acceptance may be) underlying it. Durkheim later remarked that he had consistently been misunderstood on this point:

---

[24] *RSM*, pp. xlvii–xlviii; *RMS*, pp. xvi–xvii.
[25] *RSM*, p. 3. In applying this criterion, Durkheim moves what Weber calls 'usage' – behaviour which is habitual, but not normatively condoned or condemned – to the borderline of sociology, thus actually reaching a rather similar conclusion to Weber. cf. below, pp. 153–4.   [26] *RSM*, p. 2; *RMS*, p. 4.

Since we have made constraint the *outward sign* by which social facts can be most easily recognised and distinguished from the facts of individual psychology, it has been assumed that according to our opinion, physical constraint is essential to social life. In reality, we have never seen in it any more than the material and evident expression of an internal and deep-rooted fact which is wholly ideal: this is *moral authority*.[27]

The logic of explanatory generalisation

In the preface to the second edition of *The Rules*, Durkheim takes up objections which were made to what became perhaps the most renowned proposition contained in the book: '*consider social facts as things*'.[28] This is obviously a methodological postulate rather than an ontological one, and has to be understood in terms of the conception of the mode of development of science which Durkheim takes over from Comte. All of the sciences, before they emerge as disciplines which are conceptually precise and empirically rigorous, are collections of crudely formed and highly generalised notions originally grounded in religion: '... thought and reflection are prior to science, which merely uses them methodically.' But these notions are never tested in any systematic fashion; ' facts intervene only secondarily as examples or confirmatory proofs '.[29] This prescientific stage is broken through by the introduction of empirical method, not by conceptual discussion alone. This is perhaps even more important in social than in natural science, since here the subject-matter relates to human activity itself, and consequently there is a strong tendency to treat social phenomena as either lacking in substantive reality (as creations of the individual will) or, on the contrary, as already wholly known: thus words such as ' democracy ', ' communism ', etc., are freely used as if they denoted precisely known facts, whereas the truth is that ' they awaken in us nothing but confused ideas, a tangle of vague impressions, prejudices and emotions '.[30] The proposition that social facts must be treated as ' things ' is advanced as a counter to these tendencies. Durkheim thus assimilates social facts to the world of natural reality only in that, like objects in nature, their properties cannot be immediately known by direct intuition, and they are not plastic to the individual human will. ' Indeed, the most important characteristic of a " thing " is the impossibility of its modification by a simple effort of the will. Not that the thing is refractory to all modification, but a mere act of the will is insufficient to produce a change in it ... We have already seen that social facts have this characteristic.' [31]

The maintenance of the principle of treating social facts as things, of object-ivity, demands rigorous detachment on the part of the investigator of social reality. This does not mean that he should approach a given field of study with a completely ' open mind ', but rather that he must adopt an

---

[27] *EF*, p. 239; *FE*, p. 298 (footnote). cf. Raymond Aron: *Main Currents in Sociological Thought* (London, 1967), vol. 2, pp. 63–4.

[28] *RSM*, p. 14. [29] *RSM*, pp. 14–15.

[30] *RSM*, p. 22. [31] *RSM*, pp. 28–9.

emotionally neutral attitude towards what he sets out to investigate.[32] This in turn depends upon the establishment of precisely formulated concepts which avoid the confused and shifting terminology of popular thought. It is evident, however, that at the outset of research we are likely to have little systematically derived knowledge of the phenomenon in question: thus we must proceed by conceptualising our subject-matter in terms of those properties which are 'external enough to be immediately perceived'.[33] In *The Division of Labour*, for example, Durkheim seeks to delimit what constitutes crime in terms of the 'external characteristic' of the existence of punitive sanctions; a crime is any action which evokes punishment. But this is a means of elaborating a more satisfactory concept of crime: that it is an act which contravenes collectively-held beliefs and sentiments.[34] This approach might be criticised as giving undue significance to the superficial attributes of a phenomenon at the expense of its more fundamental underlying traits. Durkheim counters this criticism by asserting that the definition based upon 'external' characteristics is only a preliminary usage, set up in order 'to establish contact with things'.[35] Such a concept provides an *entrée* into a field, by allowing research to begin from observable phenomena.

Durkheim's observations upon the logic of explanation and proof in sociology are closely tied-in to his analysis of the principal characteristics of social facts. There are two approaches which may be used in the explanation of social phenomena, the functional and the historical. The functional analysis of a social phenomenon involves establishing the 'correspondence between the fact under consideration and the general needs of the social organism, and in what this correspondence consists...'. 'Function' must be separated from psychological 'end' or 'purpose', 'because social phenomena do not generally exist for the useful results they produce'.[36] The motivations or sentiments which lead individuals to participate in social activities are not in most cases coterminous with the functions of those activities. Society is not simply an aggregate of individual motivations, but 'a specific reality which has its own characteristics': it therefore follows that social facts cannot be explained in terms of such motivations.

The identification of social function does not, according to Durkheim, provide an explanation as to 'why' the social phenomenon in question exists. The causes which produce a social fact are separable from the function which it has in society. Any attempt to assume an explanatory closure between function and cause, Durkheim points out, leads to a teleological explanation of social development in terms of final causes. 'Explanation' in terms of

---

[32] Durkheim warns that 'too great a detachment in relation to tested propositions has the serious drawback of preventing continuity in effort and thought'. 'Sur le totémisme', *AS*, vol. 5, 1900–1, p. 89.

[33] *RSM*, p. 35. See the penetrating analysis given in Roger Lacombe: *La méthode sociologique de Durkheim* (Paris, 1926), pp. 67ff.

[34] *RSM*, pp. 35–6.   [35] *RSM*, p. 42.   [36] *RSM*, p. 95.

final causes entails the sort of fallacious reasoning which Durkheim criticises in both *The Division of Labour* and *Suicide*:

Thus Comte traces the entire progressive force of the human species to this fundamental tendency 'which directly impels man constantly to ameliorate his condition, whatever it may be, under all circumstances'; and Spencer relates this force to the need for greater happiness... But this method confuses two very different questions... The need we have of things cannot give them existence, nor can it confer their specific nature upon them.[37]

The causes which give rise to a given social fact must therefore be identified separately from whatever social functions it may fulfil. It is appropriate methodological procedure, moreover, to establish causes prior to the attempt to specify functions. This is because knowledge of the causes which bring a phenomenon into being can, under certain circumstances, allow us to derive some insight into its possible functions. The separate character of cause and function, according to Durkheim, does not prevent the existence of a reciprocal relation between the two. 'The effect can doubtless not exist without its cause; but the latter, in turn, needs its effect. It is from the cause that the effect draws its energy; but it also restores it to the cause on occasion, and consequently it cannot disappear without the cause showing the effects of its disappearance.'[38] Thus, in the illustration which Durkheim gives from *The Division of Labour*, the existence of 'punishment' is causally contingent upon the prevalence of strongly held collective sentiments. The function of punishment consists in the maintenance of these sentiments at the same degree of intensity: if transgressions were not punished, the strength of sentiment necessary to social unity would not be preserved.

Normality and pathology

A substantial section of *The Rules* is devoted to an attempt to establish scientific criteria of social pathology. Durkheim's discussion here is a direct development of his concerns in his early articles, and is indeed of pivotal importance through the whole of his thought. Most social theorists, Durkheim points out, hold the view that there is an absolute logical gulf between scientific propositions (statements of fact) and statements of value. In this conception, scientific data can serve as a technical 'means' which can be applied in order to facilitate the attainment of objectives, but these objectives themselves cannot be validated through the use of scientific procedures. Durkheim rejects this Kantian dualism on the basis of denying that the division between 'means' and 'ends' which it presupposes can in fact be substantiated. For Durkheim, the abstract dichotomisation of means and ends involves similar errors in the sphere of general philosophy to those embodied in a more concrete way in the utilitarian model of society: namely, that both

[37] *RSM*, pp. 89–90.
[38] *RSM*, pp. 95–6.

the ' means ' *and* the ' ends ' which men follow are empirically an outcome of the form of society of which they are members.

Every means is from another point of view, itself an end ; for in order to put it into operation, it must be willed quite as much as the end whose realisation it prepares. There are always several routes that lead to a given goal ; a choice must therefore be made between them. Now, if science cannot aid us in the choice of the best goal, how can it inform us which is the best means to reach it? Why should it recommend the most rapid in preference to the most economical, the surest rather than the simplest, or vice versa? If science cannot guide us in the determination of ultimate ends (*fins supérieures*), it is equally powerless in the case of those secondary and subordinate ends which we call means.[39]

The dichotomy between means and ends can be bridged, in Durkheim's view, by application of similar principles to those which govern the separation of ' normality ' and ' pathology ' in biology. Durkheim admits that the identification of pathology in sociology poses peculiarly difficult problems. He therefore seeks to apply the methodological precept employed earlier: what is normal in the social realm can be identified by the ' external and perceptible characteristic ' of universality. Normality, in other words, can be determined, in a preliminary way, with reference to the prevalence of a social fact within societies of a given type. Where a social phenomenon is to be found within all, or within the majority, of societies of the same societal type, then it can be treated as ' normal ' for that type of society, except where more detailed investigation shows that the criterion of universality has been misapplied. A social fact, then, which is ' general ' to a given type of society is ' normal ' when this generality is shown to be founded in the conditions of functioning of that societal type. This may be illustrated by reference to the main thesis of *The Division of Labour*. Durkheim shows in that work that the existence of a strongly defined *conscience collective* is incompatible with the functioning of the type of society which has an advanced division of labour. The increasing preponderance of organic solidarity leads to a decline in the traditional forms of belief: but precisely because social solidarity becomes more dependent upon functional interdependence in the division of labour, the decline in collective beliefs is a normal characteristic of the modern type of society. In this particular case, however, the preliminary criterion of generality does not supply an applicable mode of determining normality. Modern societies are still in a period of transition; traditional beliefs continue to be important enough for some writers to claim that their decline is a pathological phenomenon. The persisting generality of these beliefs is not, in this instance therefore, an accurate index of what is normal and what is pathological. Thus in times of rapid social change, ' when the entire type is in process of evolution, without having yet become stabilised in

---

[39] *RSM*, p. 48; *RMS*, p. 48. As an implicit criticism of Weber's view on this matter, this is a similar point to that made by Strauss. Leo Strauss: *Natural Right and History* (Chicago, 1953), p. 41.

its new form ', elements of what is normal for the type which is becoming superseded still exist. It is necessary to analyse ' the conditions which determined this generality in the past and . . . then investigate whether these conditions are still given in the present '.[40] If these conditions do not pertain, the phenomenon in question, although ' general ', cannot be called ' normal '.

The calculation of criteria of normality in relation to specific societal types, according to Durkheim, allows us to steer a course in ethical theory between those who conceive history as a series of unique and unrepeated happenings, and those who attempt to formulate transhistorical ethical principles. In the first view, the possibility of any generalised ethics is excluded; in the second, ethical rules are formulated ' once and for all for the entire human species '. An example can be taken which Durkheim himself uses on many occasions. The sorts of moral ideas which pertained in the classical Greek *polis* were rooted in religious conceptions, and in a particular form of class structure based upon slavery: hence many of the ethical ideas of this period are now obsolete, and it is futile to try to resurrect them in the modern world. In Greece, for example, the ideal of the fully-rounded ' cultivated man ', educated in all branches of scientific and literary knowledge, was integral to the society. But it is an ideal which is out of accord with the demands of an order based upon a high degree of specialisation in the division of labour.

An evident criticism which might be made against Durkheim's position on this matter is that it induces compliance with the *status quo,* since it appears to identify the morally desirable with whatever state of affairs is at present in existence.[41] Durkheim denies that this is so; on the contrary, it is only through definite knowledge of the potentially emergent trends in social reality that active intervention to promote social change can have any success. ' The future is already written for him who knows how to read it. . . .' [42] The scientific study of morality allows us to distinguish those ideals which are in the process of becoming, but which are still largely hidden from the public consciousness. By showing that these ideals are not merely aberrations, and by analysing the changing social conditions that underlie them and which are serving to promote their growth, we are able to show which tendencies should be fostered and which need to be rejected as obsolete.[43] Of course, science will never be complete enough to allow us to escape altogether from the necessity of acting without its guidance. ' We must live, and we must often anticipate science. In such cases we must do as we can and make use of what scientific observations are at our disposal . . .' [44]

[40] *RSM*, p. 61.
[41] Critics were not slow to make this assertion. Durkheim replied to three of his early critics in the *AS*, vol. 10, 1905–6, pp. 352–69.
[42] *Ibid.* p. 368.
[43] ' The determination of moral facts ', in *Sociology and Philosophy* (London, 1965), pp. 60ff.
[44] *Ibid.* p. 67.

It is not the case, Durkheim argues, that the adoption of his standpoint renders all abstract ' philosophical ' attempts to create logically consistent ethics completely futile. While it is true that ' morality did not wait for the theories of the philosophers in order to be formed and to function ', this does not mean that, given empirical knowledge of the social framework within which moral rules exist, philosophical reflection cannot play a part in introducing changes in existing moral rules. Philosophers, in fact, have often played such a role in history – but usually without consciously being aware of it. Such men have sought to enunciate universal moral principles, but have in fact acted as the precursors and progenitors of changes immanent in their society.[45]

---

[45] *RSM*, p. 71. Marx makes a somewhat comparable point, discussing the innovatory character of criminal activity. *Theories of Surplus Value* (ed. Bonner & Burns), p. 376.

7. Individualism, socialism and the 'occupational groups'

The confrontation with socialism

The theory developed in *The Division of Labour*, and Durkheim's subsequent attempts to pursue themes originally set out therein, inevitably culminated in bringing about a direct confrontation with socialist doctrines. According to Mauss' testimony, while Durkheim was a student, he had already decided to devote himself to study of 'the relationship of individualism and socialism'.[1] Durkheim was familiar with the doctrines of Saint-Simon and Proudhon at this time, and had made an initial acquaintance with Marx's writings. But his knowledge of socialist theory was, at the time of the writing of *The Division of Labour*, fairly thin. The sort of socialism with which Durkheim was most closely concerned in the early part of his career was the reformist social democratic theory such as set out by Schäffle and the *Kathedersozialisten*.[2]

In both *The Division of Labour* and *Suicide*, and in numerous other writings, Durkheim makes reference to the crisis which is being experienced in contemporary societies. This is not, as *The Division of Labour* made clear, primarily a crisis which has economic roots, nor one which can be solved by economic measures. It follows from this that the sort of programmes offered by most socialists – involving mainly the redistribution of wealth through centralised control of the economy – in Durkheim's view fail to grasp the most significant problems which face the modern age. Socialism is an expression of the *malaise* of contemporary society, but it is not itself an adequate basis for the social reconstruction necessary to overcome it.

Durkheim's attitude towards socialism is founded upon the assumption that socialist doctrines themselves should be subjected to the sort of analysis which guides their own approach to other idea-systems: that is, socialist theories should be studied in relation to the social context from which they spring. In attempting such an analysis, Durkheim begins by drawing an elementary distinction between 'socialism' and 'communism'.[3] Whereas communist ideas, in Durkheim's sense of the term, have existed at many

---

[1] Marcel Mauss: 'Introduction' to the first edition of *Soc*, p. 32.
[2] Durkheim reviews Schäffle's *Der Sozialismus* in 'Le programme économique de M. Schäffle', *Revue d'économie politique*, vol. 2, 1888, pp. 3–7.
[3] Durkheim points out that there is some *prima facie* linguistic support for this distinction. The word 'socialism', unlike 'communism', is of recent origin, dating from the early part of the nineteenth century. *Soc*, p. 65. This was, of course, known to Marx, but he makes no consistent terminological distinction between them.

periods of history, socialism is uniquely a product of the very recent past. Communist writings typically take the form of fictional utopias: diverse examples are to be found in the works of Plato, Thomas More, and Campanella. The main notion supporting these utopian constructions is that private property is the ultimate source of all social evils. Consequently, communist writers regard material wealth as a moral danger which must be checked by the imposition of severe restrictions upon its accumulation. In communist theory, economic life is separated from the political sphere: in Plato's ideal community, for example, those who rule have no right to intervene in the productive activity of the labourers and artisans, nor do the latter groups have any right to influence the conduct of government.

The reason for this separation, according to Plato, is that wealth and all that relates to it is the primary source of public corruption. It is the thing that, stimulating individual egoisms, sets citizens to struggling and unleashes the internal conflicts which ruin states... It is necessary therefore to place it outside of public life, as far as possible from the state which it could only pervert.[4]

Socialism is a product of the social changes which transformed the European societies in the late eighteenth and nineteenth centuries. While communism is grounded in the notion that policy and economy must be separated, the very essence of socialism, in Durkheim's use of the term, is that it supposes that the two should be assimilated. The primary tenet of socialism is not merely that production should be centralised in the hands of the state, but that the role of the state should be a wholly economic one – in socialist society, the management or administration of the economy is to be the basic task of the state. While communism, which seeks to eschew wealth as far as possible, usually has an ascetic character, socialist doctrines are built upon the premise that modern industrial production offers the possibility of abundant wealth for all, and the attainment of universal abundance is their principal aim. Socialism advocates ' *the connection of all economic functions, or of certain of them, which are at the present time diffuse, to the directing and conscious centres of society* '.[5]

The aim of socialism, therefore, is the regulation and control of production in the interests of all members of society. But there is no socialist doctrine, in Durkheim's view, which considers that *consumption* should be regulated centrally: on the contrary, socialists hold that each individual should be free to use the fruits of production for his own individual fulfilment. In communism by contrast, ' it is consumption that is communal and production which remains private '. ' Without doubt ', Durkheim adds, ' – and this is deceiving – in both there is to be regulation (*réglementation*), but it must be noted that it operates in opposing ways. One aims to moralise industry by

---

[4] *Soc*, p. 68; *Le socialisme* (Paris, 1928), p. 44.

[5] *Soc*, pp. 54–5; *Le socialisme*, p. 25.

binding it to the State, the other, to moralise the State by excluding it from industry.' [6]

The connection of this analysis to that given in *The Division of Labour* now becomes apparent. Communism is a creed which is appropriate to, and which originally emerges from within, societies which have a low development of the division of labour. Communist theory retains the conception of each individual, or each family, as universal producer; since everyone produces from similar plots, and since their labour tasks are all similar, there is no sort of general co-operative dependence in production. This is the sort of society in which occupational specialisation has not advanced very far:

In Utopia each works in his own way, as he thinks proper, and is simply obliged not to be idle... As each one does the same thing – or almost the same – there is no co-operation to regulate. Only, what each has produced does not belong to him. He cannot dispose of it at will. He brings it to the community and consumes it only when society makes use of it collectively.[7]

Socialism, on the other hand, is a type of theory which could only have arisen in societies where the division of labour is highly developed. It is a response to the pathological condition of the division of labour in modern societies, and calls for the introduction of economic regulation which will reorganise the productive activity of the collectivity. We must understand, Durkheim stresses, that socialist theory does not advance the conception that the economy should be *subordinated* to the state; the economy and state are to be merged with one another, and this integration eliminates the specifically ' political ' character of the state.

In the doctrine of Marx, for example, the state such as it is – that is to say, insofar as it has a specific role, and represents interests which are superior, *sui generis*, to those of commerce and industry, historical traditions, common beliefs and a religious or other nature, etc. – would no longer exist. Purely political functions, which today are its special sphere, would no longer have a *raison d'être*, and there would only be economic functions.[8]

Class conflict, according to Durkheim, is not intrinsic to the fundamental doctrines of socialism. Durkheim recognises, of course, that most socialists – and especially Marx – consider the attainment of their objectives to be inseparably bound to the fate of the working class. But advocacy of the interests of the working class as opposed to those of the bourgeoisie, Durkheim states, is in fact secondary to the prime concern of socialism to realise the centralised regulation of production. According to socialists, the principal factor influencing the condition of the working class is that its productive activity is not harnessed to the needs of society as a whole, but to the interests of the capitalist class. It follows from this, in the view of the socialists, that the only way to overcome the exploitative character of capitalist society is through the abolition of classes altogether. But class conflict is simply the

---

[6] *Soc*, pp. 71 & 70; *Le socialisme*, pp. 48 & 47.
[7] *Soc*, p. 71.   [8] *Soc*, p. 57.

historical medium through which more basic goals are to be attained. 'The improvement of the workers' lot is thus not a special objective; it is but one of the consequences that the attachment of economic activities to the managing agents of society must necessarily produce.'[9]

In most respects, then, communism and socialism present a definite contrast. However, there is one important regard in which they are convergent: both are concerned to remedy situations in which the interests of the individual become preponderant over these of the collectivity. 'Both are impelled by this double feeling that the free play of egoism is not enough to automatically produce social order and that, on the other hand, collective needs must outweigh individual convenience.'[10] But even here the identity between the two is far from complete. Communism seeks to expunge egoism completely, while socialism 'considers dangerous only the individual appropriation of the large economic enterprises which are established at a specific moment in history'.[11] Historically, the upsurge of communist ideas in the eighteenth century presaged the subsequent development of socialist theories and became partially interwoven with them. 'Thus socialism was exposed to communism; it undertook to play a role in it at the same time as it pursued its own programme. In this sense it was actually the heir of communism, and, without being derived from it, absorbed it while remaining distinct.'[12] It is this confusion, Durkheim says, which causes socialists often to mistake 'the secondary for the essential'. That is, they 'respond only to the generous inclinations underlying communism', and devote most of their efforts to the attempt 'to lighten the burden of the workers, to compensate by liberality and legal favours what is depressed in their situation'. These are not, of course, completely undesirable endeavours; but they 'stray from the aim we should keep in sight...'.[13] The mode in which they pose the problem bypasses the true nature of the issues involved.[14] But socialism is a movement of primary significance in the modern world, in Durkheim's view, because not only are the socialists – or at least, the more sophisticated among them, such as Saint-Simon and Marx – conscious that contemporary society is distinctively different from the traditional types of social order, but they have formulated comprehensive programmes to effect the social reorganisation necessary to overcome the crisis which the transition from the old to the new has brought about. But the policies which have been suggested by the socialists are inadequate to remedy the situation which, in part, they have accurately diagnosed.

The role of the state

While Durkheim explicitly rejects the necessity of reorganising contemporary society on the basis of class revolution, he does foresee a definite trend

---

[9] *Soc*, p. 60; *Le socialisme*, p. 33.

[10] *Soc*, p. 75.

[11] *Soc*, p. 75.

[12] *Soc*, p. 91.

[13] *Soc*, p. 92.

[14] *Soc*, pp. 104–5.

towards the disappearance of class divisions.[15] The maintenance of rights of inheritance are a basic factor supporting a class division between the 'two main classes in society', labour and capital: the hereditary transmission of wealth allows the continuation of the concentration of capital in the hands of a few.[16] Durkheim also accepts the need for the extension of welfare programmes and other measures which alleviate the material conditions of life of the poor. All this is only possible, Durkheim concedes, on the basis of the regulation of the economy (which should not, however, in Durkheim's view be placed solely in the hands of the State).[17]

But economic reorganisation alone will exacerbate rather than resolve the crisis facing the modern world, since this is a crisis which is moral rather than economic. The increasing dominance of economic relationships, consequent upon the destruction of the traditional religious institutions which were the moral background of previous societal forms, is precisely the main source of anomie in contemporary society. In failing to understand this, socialism provides no more adequate solutions to the modern crisis than those offered by orthodox political economy. While being opposed on most issues, both the socialists and the economic theorists share certain characteristics in common: both take economic measures to be the avenue whereby modern society may overcome its present difficulties. Both believe it possible and desirable to reduce the role of government to a minimum. The economists propose that the free play of the market should be given full scope, so that government is limited to the enforcement of contracts; socialists wish to confine government to the ordering of the market via the centralised control of production. 'But both deny it the capacity to subordinate other social organs to itself and to make them converge upon an objective which surpasses them.'[18]

In Durkheim's conception, the state must play a moral as well as an economic role; and the alleviation of the *malaise* of the modern world must be sought in measures which are in general moral rather than economic. The dominant position of the authority of religion in former types of society provided all strata with a horizon for their aspirations, counselling the poor to accept their lot and instructing the rich in their duty to care for the less privileged. While this order was repressive, containing human actions and potentialities within narrow bounds, its nevertheless gave a firm moral unity to society. The characteristic problem facing the modern age is to reconcile the individual freedoms which have sprung from the dissolution of traditional society with the maintenance of the moral control upon which the very existence of society depends.

Durkheim's analysis of the state, and the nature of political participation in a democratic polity, is at the core of his conception of the probable trend

---

[15] See below, pp. 203–4.   [16] *PECM*, p. 213.
[17] 'La famille conjugale', *RP*, vol. 91, 1921, pp. 10ff.
[18] *Su*, p. 255; *LS*, p. 284.

of development of contemporary societies. The notion of the ' political ', Durkheim points out, presupposes a division between government and the governed, and is thus primarily characteristic of the more developed societies : in the simpler societies, specialised organs of administration barely exist. But the existence of authority as such cannot be taken as the only criterion for indicating the presence of political organisation. A kinship group, for instance, while it might have a definite individual or group in authority, such as a patriarch and a council of elders, is not thereby a political society. Durkheim also rejects the notion (to which Weber gives considerable prominence) that permanent occupation of a fixed territorial area is a necessary characteristic for the existence of a state. The development of fixed and clearly demarcated territories is a late occurrence in history : while it is characteristic of the advanced societies, it cannot be taken of essential importance in defining whether or not a society is a political society. This would be ' to deny any political character to the great nomad societies whose structure was sometimes very elaborate '.[19] Conversely, families have often possessed strictly demarcated territories of their own.

Some political thinkers have tried to establish size of population as an index of the existence of a political society. This is not acceptable, Durkheim states, but it does imply something which is a necessary characteristic of a political society : that the society in question is not just a single kinship unit, but is composed of an aggregate of families, or of secondary groups. ' We should then define the political society as one formed by the union of a greater or lesser number of secondary social groups, subject to the same one authority which is not itself subject to any other superior authority duly constituted.'[20] The term ' state ', Durkheim suggests, should not be made coterminous with political society as a whole, but should be reserved to designate the organisation of officials which is the instrument whereby governmental authority is focussed.

The three components of Durkheim's analysis are thus the existence of constituted authority, exercised within a society which has at least some degree of structural differentiation, and applied by a distinct group of officials. By reference to these characteristics, Durkheim attempts to separate his standpoint from the mainstreams of thought which he sees as offering contrasting theories of state and society : Hegelian idealism on the one hand, and utilitarianism and socialism on the other. The state is neither ' superior ' to society nor merely a parasitic encumbrance upon society if it regulates anything more than purely economic relationships. According to Durkheim, the state does, and must, fulfil moral functions (a conception he sees as distinct from both socialism and utilitarianism), but this does not entail, on the other hand, the subordination of the individual to the state, as (according to Durkheim) is posited by Hegel.

[19] *PECM*, p. 43.   [20] *PECM*, p. 45; *Leçons de sociologie* (Paris, 1950), p. 55.

Democracy and the occupational groups

As Durkheim shows in *The Division of Labour*, the main trend of development, as societies become more complex, is towards the progressive emancipation of the individual from subordination to the *conscience collective*. Associated with this process, is the emergence of moral ideals which stress the rights and dignity of the individual human being. This would at first sight appear to create an impossible opposition to the expansion of the activities of the state. It is plainly true, Durkheim says, that the state tends to grow in importance with the increasing differentiation of the division of labour: the growth of the state is a normal characteristic of societal development.[21] But this seeming antinomy is resolved through appreciation of the fact that, in modern societies, the state is the institution which is primarily responsible for the provision and protection of these individual rights. The expansion of the state is thus directly bound up with the progression of moral individualism and with the growth of the division of labour. However, no modern state acts solely as a guarantor and administrator of citizenship rights. The perpetuation of international rivalries has stimulated the development of common beliefs relating to the nation as a collectivity (patriotism, national pride). While nationalism is, in Durkheim's view, only of secondary importance in modern societies,[22] it nevertheless tends to generate conflict between affiliation to national ideals and the pan-humanism which is intrinsic to the notions of individual equality and freedom that have become so strongly rooted today. It is not inconceivable, on the other hand, that national pride will in the future become harnessed to the furtherance of the general ideals of humanity.[23]

Given this analysis, may it not be the case that the increasing expansion of the activities of the state will eventually reach a point where it becomes a bureaucratic tyranny? Durkheim admits this as a possibility. The state can become a repressive agency, isolated from the interests of the mass of individuals in civil society. This can occur if secondary groups which intervene between the individual and the state are not strongly developed: only if these are vigorous enough to form a counterbalance to the state can the rights of the individual be protected. It is this assertion of the need for pluralism which draws the connection between Durkheim's theory of the state and his

---

[21] As noted previously (p. 76, n. 49). Durkheim emphasises, however, that there is not a universal relationship between society and state: 'Kinds of society should not be confused with different types of state ... a change in a nation's system of government does not necessarily involve a change in the prevailing type of society.' This forms one element in Durkheim's critique of Montesquieu. See *Montesquieu and Rousseau* (Ann Arbor, 1965), p. 33 and *passim*.

[22] It may assume a pathological form, as in German militarism. cf. Durkheim's analysis of Treitschke's *Politik*, in '*L'Allemagne au-dessus de tout*' (Paris, 1915).

[23] *PECM*, pp. 73–5; cf. also *Moral Education* (New York, 1961), pp. 80–1, where Durkheim says that the nation may be 'conceived of as a partial embodiment of the idea of humanity'.

conception of democracy, and from thence with his call for the resurgence of occupational associations (*corporations*).

Durkheim rejects the traditional notion of democracy, in so far as this entails that the mass of the population participate directly in government.

Except for the least advanced small tribes, there are no societies where government is exercised directly by all in common: it is always in the hands of a minority chosen either by birth or by election; its scope may be large or small, according to circumstances, but it never comprises more than a limited circle of individuals.[24]

A society is more or less democratic, according to Durkheim's terminology, to the degree that there is a two-way process of communication between the state and other levels of society. According to Durkheim, there is an extremely significant consequence which flows from the existence of a democratic system, which is that the conduct of social life takes on a conscious and directed character. Many aspects of social life formerly ruled by unthinking custom or habit become the subject of intervention on the part of the state. The state is involved in economic life, and the administration of justice, in education, and even in the organisation of the arts and sciences.

The role of the state in democracy is thus not simply to summarise and express the views and sentiments held in a diffuse and unreflective way by the mass of the population. Durkheim calls the state the social ego (i.e., the 'consciousness'), while the *conscience collective* as a whole is the social 'mind' (i.e., includes many habitual, reflexive modes of thought). The state is thus often the origin of novel ideas, and leads society as much as being led by it. In those societies where the state does not assume this directive role, the result can be a stagnation almost as great as that in societies held in the yoke of tradition. In modern societies, where the influence of restraining traditions has been largely dispelled, there are many avenues open for the display of critical spirit, and changes of opinion and mood among the mass are frequent: if the government simply reflects these, the result is constant uncertainty and vacillation in the political sphere, which leads to no concrete change. Many superficial changes occur, but cancel each other out: 'Those societies that are so stormy on the surface are often bound to routine.'[25] It is in circumstances where there is a dearth of secondary groups mediating between the individual and the state that such a situation tends to pertain. This same condition which, given a strong state, can lead to a tyrannical despotism, can produce inconstant instability where the state is weak.

Even prior to the publication of *The Division of Labour*, Durkheim reached the conclusion that occupational associations should play a larger

---

[24] *PECM*, p. 85; *Leçons de sociologie*, p. 103.

[25] *PECM*, p. 94. Durkheim was not nearly as blind to the existence of social conflict as is often asserted; cf., for example, his criticism of Montesquieu, who fails to see that 'every society embodies conflicting factors, simply because it has gradually emerged from a past form and is tending towards a future one'. *Montesquieu and Rousseau*, p. 59.

part in contemporary societies than is the case at present.[26] While this theme is not developed at length in the book, it is not difficult to perceive the relationship between this and the analysis of the anomic division of labour formulated in the work.[27] Anomie is present in the occupational system in so far as moral integration is lacking at the 'nodal points' of the division of labour – the points of conjunction and exchange between different occupational strata. A primary function of the occupational associations would be to reinforce moral regulation at these points, and thereby promote organic solidarity. This is a task which cannot be accomplished by the family in modern societies, since the family is becoming increasingly restricted in its functions. The occupational group is the only one ' which is close enough to the individual for him to be able to rely directly upon it, and durable enough to be able to give him a perspective '.[28] It is evident, Durkheim admits, that the old kind of occupational guild, such as existed in mediaeval times, has completely disappeared. The trade unions which exist today are in general more loosely organised, and do not meet the necessary social needs, since they are in a state of permanent conflict with employers :

employers and workers are, in relation to one another, in the same situation as two autonomous states, but of unequal power. As nations do, through the mediation of their governments, they can form contracts between themselves. But these contracts only express the respective state of the economic power which they possess, in the same way as treaties concluded between two belligerents only express the respective state of their military power. They sanction a condition of fact, but they cannot make it a legal condition.[29]

Accordingly, it is necessary to re-establish occupational associations as legally constituted groups which ' play a social role instead of expressing only various combinations of particular interests '.

Durkheim refrains from offering a detailed exposition of how the occupational groups would be structured. They would not, however, simply be a revived form of mediaeval guild; while having a high degree of internal autonomy, they would be brought within the overall legal supervision of the state; they would have the authority to resolve conflicts both within their own membership and in relation to other occupational groups; and they would be the focus for a variety of educational and recreational activities.[30] They would also play an important role in the political system in a direct sense.

---

[26] Durkheim discusses the role of occupational associations in ' La famille conjugale ', originally a lecture given first in 1892. The lecture was not published until 1921 (*RP*, vol. 91, pp. 1–14).

[27] Durkheim planned a work, which he intended to write after *The Division of Labour*, specifically dealing with the significance of the occupational associations, but this project was never realised. cf. the Preface to the second edition of *The Division of Labour*, p. 1.

[28] ' La famille conjugale ', p. 18.

[29] *DL*, p. 6; *DTS*, pp. vii–viii.

[30] *PECM*, pp. 28ff. & 103–4; *Su*, pp. 378–82; *DL*, pp. 24–7.

One reason for the superficial volatility of some modern societies is to be traced to the prevalence of direct representation in the electoral system, which chains elected representatives closely to the whims of the electorate. This could be overcome by the establishment of a two-stage or multiple-level electoral system, in which the occupational groups would serve as the main intermediary electoral units.

These proposals, according to Durkheim, are not mere wishful thinking, but conform to his specification of the determination of ' normal ' social forms set out in *The Rules*. That is to say, the development of the occupational groups is an emergent principle of the complex division of labour.

The absence of all corporative institution creates, then, in the organisation of a people like ours, a void whose importance it is difficult to exaggerate. It is a whole system of organs necessary in the normal functioning of the common life which is wanting... Where the State is the only environment in which men can live communal lives, they inevitably lose contact, become detached, and thus society disintegrates. A nation can be maintained only if, between the State and the individual, there is intercalated a whole series of secondary groups near enough to the individuals to attract them strongly in their sphere of action and drag them, in this way, into the general torrent of social life. We have just shown how occupational groups are suited to fill this role, and that is their destiny.[31]

[31] *DL*, pp. 29 & 28. cf. Erik Allardt: ' Emile Durkheim: sein Beitrag zur politischen Soziologie ', *Kölner Zeitschrift für Soziologie und Sozialpsychologie*, vol. 20, 1968, pp. 1–16.

8. Religion and moral discipline

In his earliest writings Durkheim comments upon the importance of religion in society, recognising it to be the original source of all subsequently evolved moral, philosophical, scientific and juridical ideas. In *The Division of Labour*, he outlines the thesis that any belief which forms part of the *conscience collective* tends to assume a religious character, although in that work this is advanced only as a ' highly probable conjecture ' which needs further study.[1] But Durkheim's recognition of the probable significance of religion in relation to the influence of the *conscience collective* in society is counterbalanced by an awareness of the fact that very profound changes have occurred with the emergence of the modern societal type. Durkheim consistently supports the conclusion, reached at an early point in his intellectual career, that both the ' defenders of the old economic theories are mistaken in thinking that regulation is not necessary today ' and ' the apologists of the institution of religion are wrong in believing that yesterday's regulation can be useful today '.[2] The declining importance of religion in contemporary societies is a necessary consequence of the diminishing significance of mechanical solidarity:

the importance we thus attribute to the sociology of religion does not in the least imply that religion must play the same role in present-day societies that it has played at other times. In a sense, the contrary conclusion would be more sound. Precisely because religion is a primordial phenomenon, it must yield more and more to the new social forms which it has engendered.[3]

It was not until 1895, Durkheim admits, that he became fully aware of the importance of religion as a social phenomenon. According to his own testimony, this realisation of the significance of religion, which appears to have been in large degree the outcome of his reading of the works of the English anthropologists, caused him to reappraise his earlier writings in order to draw out the implications of these new insights.[4] The conventional interpretation of this is that Durkheim moved from the relatively ' materialistic ' position which he is presumed to have held in *The Division of Labour*, towards a standpoint much closer to ' idealism '. But this is misleading, if not wholly fallacious, and is a misinterpretation of Durkheim's views which stems in

---

[1] *DL*, p. 169.
[2] *DL*, p. 383.
[3] Preface to the *AS*, vol. 2, 1897–8, in Kurt H. Wolff: *Emile Durkheim et al., Essays on Sociology and Philosophy* (New York, 1964), pp. 352–3.
[4] Letter to the Editor of the *Revue néo-scolastique*, p. 613.

part from the frequent tendency of secondary writers to conflate Durkheim's functional and historical analysis in a way which is in fact foreign to Durkheim's thought.[5] Durkheim repeatedly stresses, almost as often as did Marx, the historical nature of man, and emphasises that the causal analysis of historical development is integral to sociology: 'history is not only the natural framework of human life; man is a product of history. If one separates men from history, if one tries to conceive of man outside time, fixed and immobile, one takes away his nature.'[6] The main underlying body of theory presented in *The Elementary Forms of the Religious Life* is functional in character; that is, it concerns the functional role of religion in society. But *The Elementary Forms* also has to be read genetically, in relation to the series of profound changes which have rendered modern societies very different in form from prior types. In criticising Tönnies at the outset of his career, Durkheim emphasises that there is not an absolute break between mechanical and organic solidarity: the latter type presupposes moral regulation as much as the first, although this regulation cannot be of the traditional sort. The importance of Durkheim's novel understanding of religion, as developed in *The Elementary Forms*, is that it leads to a clarification of the nature of this continuity between the traditional forms of society and the modern. 'In order to understand these new forms, one must connect them with their religious origins, but without thereby confusing them with religious phenomena, properly speaking.'[7]

That this allows Durkheim, at the same time, to elucidate certain themes in his analysis of modern societies in a direct sense cannot, of course, be doubted. One main element in this is that, in Durkheim's later writings, the emphasis upon the constraining character of social phenomena cedes place to a greater stress upon the significance of the specific character of the symbols which mediate 'positive' attachment to ideals. But this is not a sudden capitulation to idealism. The heavy emphasis upon constraint and obligation in Durkheim's early writings is in considerable degree an outcome of the form of critical attack in which these play a part; and throughout the whole

---

[5] Parsons treats all Durkheim's writings as a monolithic attack on the 'problem of order'; whereas the main trend of Durkheim's work is about the analysis of the *changing forms* of social solidarity over the course of societal development. Parsons, esp. pp. 306, 309 & 315–16. Moreover, Durkheim stresses that his work is not an attempt to 'treat sociology *in genere*', but is primarily confined to 'a clearly delimited order of facts', which are 'moral or judicial rules'. 'La sociologie en France au XIXe siècle', *Revue bleue*, vol. 13, 1900, part 2, p. 648.

[6] 'Introduction à la morale', *RP*, vol. 89, 1920, p. 89. For Durkheim's views on the relationship between history and sociology, see his review of three articles on the nature of history (two of which are by Croce and Sorel), *AS*, vol. 6, 1901–2, pp. 123–5. cf. also Robert Bellah: 'Durkheim and history', in Nisbet, *Emile Durkheim*, pp. 153–76. See also below, pp. 224–8.

[7] Preface to the *AS*, 1897–8, p. v. cf. the early study by Gehlke: Charles Elmer Gehlke: *Emile Durkheim's Contributions to Sociological Theory* (New York, 1915), pp. 48ff.

of his works Durkheim affirms that society is both the source and repository of human ideals.[8]

The character of the sacred

The Elementary Forms is based upon close scrutiny of what Durkheim calls 'the simplest and most primitive religion known today': Australian totemism.[9] In establishing a conceptualisation of religion, Durkheim follows Fustel de Coulanges' typification of the sacred and profane. It is fallacious, Durkheim states, to suppose that the existence of supernatural divinities is necessary to the existence of religion: there are systems of belief and practice which we should quite properly call 'religious', but where gods and spirits are either altogether absent, or are only of minor importance. What is a 'religious' belief cannot be defined with regard to the substantive content of ideas. The distinctive characteristic of religious beliefs is that ' they presuppose a classification of all things known to men, real and ideal, into two classes, two distinct kinds. . . '.[10] The character of religious thought is something which cannot be grasped except in terms of the notion of dichotomy *itself*: the world is separated into two entirely separate classes of objects and symbols, the 'sacred' and the 'profane': '*it is absolute*. In the history of human thought there exists no other example of two categories of things so profoundly differentiated or so radically opposed to one another.'[11]

The special character of the sacred is manifest in the fact that it is surrounded by ritual prescriptions and prohibitions which enforce this radical separation from the profane. A religion is never simply a set of beliefs: it always also involves prescribed ritual practices and a definite institutional form. There is no religion which does not have a church, although the form which this assumes varies widely. The concept of 'church', as Durkheim employs it, refers to the existence of a regularised ceremonial organisation pertaining to a definite group of worshippers; it does not imply that there is necessarily a specialised priesthood. Thus Durkheim reaches his famous definition of religion, as ' a unified (*solidaire*) system of beliefs and practices relative to sacred things . . . beliefs and practices which unite into a single moral community called a church, all those who adhere to them.'[12]

According to this definition, totemism is a form of religion, in spite of the fact that it has no personalised spirits or gods. It is certainly the most primitive type of religion which we know of today, and is probably the most primitive form which has ever existed.[13] Thus to isolate the factors underlying the origin of totemism is presumptively ' to discover at the same time the causes leading to the rise of the religious sentiment in humanity '.[14]

[8] cf. above, pp. 67–70.   [9] *EF*, p. 13; *FE*, p. 1.   [10] *EF*, p. 52; *FE*, p. 50.
[11] *EF*, p. 53; *FE*, p. 53.   [12] *EF*, p. 62; *FE*, p. 65.   [13] *EF*, p. 195.
[14] *EF*, p. 195. Durkheim rejects various theories which hold that totemism is itself derivative of a previous form of religion (pp. 195–214).

Totemism is integrally connected with the clan system of organisation which is characteristic of the Australian societies. A specific feature of the totemic clan is that the name which denotes the identity of the clan group is that of a material object – a totem – which is believed to have very special properties. No two clans within the same tribe have the same totem. Examination of the qualities which members of a clan believe to be possessed by their totem shows that the totem is the axis of the dichotomy between the sacred and the profane. The totem ' is the very prototype of sacred things '.[15] The sacred character of the totem is manifest in the ritual observances which separate it from ordinary objects which may be used to utilitarian ends. Various ritual prescriptions and prohibitions also surround the totemic emblem – the representation of the totem which is put on objects, or adorns the person; these are often even more stringently enforced than those relating to the totemic object itself.

In addition, however, the members of the clan themselves possess sacred qualities. While in more advanced religions the believer is a profane being, this is not the case in totemism. Every man bears the name of his totem, which signifies that he shares in the religiosity of the totem itself, and there are believed to be genealogical connections between the individual and his totem. Totemism thus recognises three sorts of objects as sacred: the totem, the totemic emblem, and the members of the clan themselves. These three classes of sacred object in turn form part of a general cosmology: ' For the Australian, things themselves, all the things which populate the universe, are part of the tribe; they are constituent elements of it and, so to speak, permanent members of it; just like men, they have a determined place in the organisation of society.' [16] Thus, for example, the clouds belong to one totem, the sun to another: the whole of nature is brought into an ordered classification based upon the totemic clan organisation. All objects classed in a given clan or phratry (a combination of a group of clans) are regarded as sharing qualities in common, and such objects are believed by the members of the clan to be affiliated to themselves – men ' call them their friends and think that they are made out of the same flesh as themselves '.[17] This shows that the scope of religion extends much further than might initially appear. ' It not only comprises the totemic animals and the human members of the clan, but since nothing exists that is not classified in a clan and under a totem, there is similarly nothing which does not receive, in varying degree, a certain quality of religiosity.' [18]

Thus no one of the three sorts of sacred objects previously distinguished derives its sacred character from either of the others, since they all share a

[15] *EF*, p. 140; *FE*, p. 167.
[16] *EF*, p. 166; *FE*, p. 201.
[17] *EF*, p. 174. For a detailed description of such systems of classification, cf. Durkheim and Mauss: *Primitive Classification* (London, 1963).
[18] *EF*, p. 179; *FE*, p. 219.

common religiosity. Their sacred character must therefore emanate from a source which embraces them all, a force which they all partially share in, but which is nonetheless separate from them. In Australian totemism, this sacred energy is not clearly differentiated as such from the objects which embody it. Elsewhere, however, it is; among, for example, the North American Indians and in Melanesia, where it is called *mana*.[19] The religious energy found in a diffuse and all-pervasive form in Australian totemism is the original source of all later more particularised incarnations of this general force which become manifest as gods, spirits and demons in more complex religions.

Hence in order to explain the existence of religion we must discover the basis of the general energy which is the fount of all that is sacred. It is clearly not the immediate sensations produced by the totems as physical objects which explains why they should be attributed with divine force. The totemic objects are often insignificant animals or small plants, which could not intrinsically evoke the powerful feelings of religiosity which are attributed to them. Moreover, the *representation* of the totem is usually regarded as more sacred than the totemic object itself. This proves that ' the totem is above all a symbol, a material expression of something else '. The totem thus symbolises both the sacred energy and the identity of the clan group. ' So ', Durkheim asks rhetorically, ' if it is at once the symbol of the god and of the society, is that not because god and the society are one? ' The totemic principle is the clan group itself, ' hypostatised and represented to the imagination in the perceptible forms of the vegetable or the animal which serves as totem '.[20] Society commands both obligation and respect, the twin characteristics of the sacred. Whether it exists as a diffuse impersonal force or whether it is personalised, the sacred object is conceived as a superior entity, which in fact symbolises the superiority of society over the individual.

In a general way, it cannot be doubted that a society has all that is necessary to awaken in human minds the sensation of the divine, simply by the influence which it exerts over them ; for to its members it is what a god is to his believers. A god, in fact, is first and foremost a being whom men think of as superior to themselves in certain ways, and upon whom they believe that they depend. Whether it be a conscious personality, such as Zeus or Jahveh, or merely abstract forces such as those in play in totemism, the believer, in both cases, believes himself held to certain manners of acting which are imposed upon him by the nature of the sacred principle with which he feels he is in communion... Now the modes of conduct to which society is strongly enough attached to impose them upon its members, are, by that very fact, marked with a distinctive sign which evokes respect.[21]

The equation which Durkheim draws here between ' society ' and ' the sacred ' must not be misunderstood. Durkheim does *not* argue that ' religion

[19] The development of an abstract conception of *mana* as a universal force, according to Durkheim, comes about only when the totemic clan system breaks down. *Mana* is discussed at some length in Henri Hubert and Marcel Mauss: ' Théorie générale de la magie ', *AS*, vol. 7, 1902–3, pp. 1–146.

[20] *EF*, p. 236; *FE*, p. 295.   [21] *EF*, pp. 236–8; *FE*, pp. 295–7.

creates society'; [22] it is just this misinterpretation which supports the notion that he adopts an ' idealist ' position in *The Elementary Forms*. What he proposes is, by contrast, that religion is the expression of the *self-creation*, the autonomous development, of human society. This is not idealist theory, but conforms to the methodological principle according to which social facts must be explained in terms of other social facts.[23]

Durkheim attempts to show in a concrete way how religious symbolism is created and re-created in ceremonial. The Australian societies pass through alternate cycles, in one of which each kinship group lives separately, giving over the whole of its activities to economic ends, and in the other of which members of the clans or phratries assemble together for a definite period (which may be as short as a few days or may last several months). This latter phase is an occasion for public ceremonial, which usually has a highly intense and emotional character. In these ceremonials, according to Durkheim, men feel overpowered by a force greater than themselves, which results from the collective effervescence of the occasion. The individual is conveyed into a world which appears to him to be utterly different to that of the everyday utilitarian activity to which the bulk of his life is devoted. Here we see, therefore, the notion of the sacred *in statu nascendi*. Awareness of the divine is born out of this collective ferment, and so is the conception of its separateness from, and its superiority to, the everyday world of the profane.

Ceremonial and ritual

But why should this religious force take the specific form of a totem? This is because the totem is the emblem of the clan: the sentiments aroused by the presence of the collectivity fix themselves upon the totem as the most easily identifiable symbol of the group. This explains why the representation of the totem is more sacred than the totemic object itself. This still leaves the question unresolved, of course, as to why the clan should have taken a totem to begin with. Durkheim suggests that the totemic objects are simply those things with which men are continually in contact, and that each clan group has as its totem the animal or plant most frequently found in the place of its ceremonial meeting. Beginning with the totemic object, the religious sentiments come to be attached to those substances which nourish it, which resemble and differ from it, and thereby produce a general classification of nature relative to the totem. Moreover, since the religious force emanates from the collective assembly, at the same time as it ' appears to be outside of the individuals and to be endowed with a sort of transcendence over them ', it ' can be realised only in and through them; in this sense, it is immanent in them and they neces-

---

[22] I have taken this phrase from H. Stuart Hughes: *Consciousness and Society* (New York, 1958), p. 285.

[23] *RSM*, p. 110.

sarily represent it as such '.[24] Thence derives the third feature of totemism, that the individual members of the collectivity share in the religiosity of the totem.

This explanation shows why it is futile to attempt to define religion in terms of the substantive content of beliefs. Whether or not a given object or symbol becomes sacred does not depend upon its intrinsic properties. The most common-place object may become sacred if it is infused with the religious force. ' In this way a rag achieves sanctity and a scrap of paper may become extremely precious.' [25] This also shows why a sacred object may be subdivided without losing its holy quality. A piece of Jesus's cloak is as sacred as the whole thing.

It remains to account for the second fundamental aspect of religion – the ritual practices which are found in all religions. Two closely intertwined sorts of ritual exist. Sacred phenomena are by definition separate from the profane. One set of rites function to maintain this separation: these are negative rites or taboos, which are prohibitions limiting contact between the sacred and the profane. Such interdictions cover verbal as well as behavioural relationships with sacred things. In the normal way, nothing from the profane world must enter the sphere of the sacred in unchanged form. Thus special sacred garments are put on for ceremonial occasions, and all the normal temporal occupations are suspended.[26] Negative rites have one positive aspect: the individual who submits to them has sanctified himself and has thereby prepared himself for entry into the realm of the sacred. Positive rites proper are those which affect fuller communion with the religious, and which constitute the core of the religious ceremonial itself. The function of both sets of rites is easily specified, and is a necessary adjunct to the explanation of the derivation of religious beliefs outlined previously. Negative rites serve to maintain the essential separation between the sacred and the profane that the very existence of the sacred depends upon; these rites ensure that the two spheres do not encroach upon one another. The function of positive rites is to renew the commitment to religious ideals which otherwise would decline in the purely utilitarian world.

At this point the relationship between this analysis and that established in *The Division of Labour* may be briefly re-stated. Small-scale, traditional societies depend for their unity upon the existence of a strong *conscience collective*. What makes such a society a ' society ' at all is the fact that its members adhere to common beliefs and sentiments. The ideals which are

[24] *EF*, p. 253. For a critical appraisal of Durkheim's analysis at this point, see P. M. Worsley: 'Emile Durkheim's theory of knowledge ', *Sociological Review*, vol. 4, 1956, pp. 47–62.

[25] *Sociology and Philosophy*, p. 94.

[26] There are undoubtedly close connections between religious ritual and play. Durkheim mentions that games originate in religious ceremonial. On this matter, cf. Roger Caillois: *Man, Play and Games* (London, 1962). Religious ceremonials are, of course, for Durkheim in a literal sense ' re-creation '.

expressed in religious beliefs are therefore the moral ideals upon which the unity of the society is founded. When individuals gather together in religious ceremonial they are hence re-affirming their faith in the moral order upon which mechanical solidarity depends. The positive rites entailed in religious ceremonial thus provide for the regular moral reconsolidation of the group, necessary because in the activities of day to day life in the profane world individuals pursue their own egoistic interests, and are consequently liable to become detached from the moral values upon which societal solidarity depends.

The only way of renewing the collective representations which relate to sacred things is to retemper them in the very source of religious life, that is to say, in assembled groups... Men are more confident because they feel themselves stronger; and they really are stronger, because forces which were languishing are now re-awakened in the consciousness.[27]

There exists yet another type of rite: the 'piacular' (expiatory) rite, the most important instance of which is that embodied in ceremonies of mourning. Just as religious sentiments of joy become raised to fever-point in the collective excitation produced by the ceremonial, so a 'panic of sorrow' is developed in mourning rituals.[28] The effect of this is to draw together the members of the group whose solidarity has been threatened by the loss of one of its members. 'Since they weep together, they hold to one another and the group is not weakened, in spite of the blow which has fallen upon it... the group feels its strength gradually returning to it; it begins to hope and to live again.'[29] This helps to explain the existence of malevolent religious spirits. There are everywhere two sorts of religious powers: benevolent influences on the one hand, and evil forces which bring sickness, death and destruction on the other. The collective activity involved in piacular rites provides a parallel situation to that which gives rise to the conception of beneficent forces, save that grief is the dominant emotion. 'This is the experience which a man interprets when he imagines that outside him there are evil beings whose hostility, whether constitutional or transitory, can only be placated by human suffering.'[30]

The categories of knowledge

In totemism the divine principle is much more all-pervasive than in more complex societal forms: we discover in the Australian societies religious ideas such as must have everywhere formed the original source of all subsequently differentiated systems of ideas. The totemic classification of nature provides the initial source of the logical categories or classes within which knowledge is ordered. The classification of objects and properties in nature

---

[27] *EF*, p. 387. The 'rhythm' of collective life is analysed in detail in Mauss's 'Essai sur les variations saisonnières des sociétés eskimos', *AS*, vol. 9, 1904–5, pp. 39–130.
[28] *EF*, p. 446.
[29] *EF*, pp. 447–8.   [30] *EF*, p. 459; p. 590.

is built upon the separation of society into totemic clan divisions. 'The unity of these first logical systems merely reproduces the unity of the society.'[31] This does not imply that society wholly structures the perception of nature. Durkheim does not declare that there are no biologically given perceptual discriminations, but points out, on the contrary, that the most rudimentary classification presupposes some recognition of sensory similarities and differences. The import of Durkheim's argument is that these native discriminations do not form the axis of the classificatory system, but constitute only a secondary principle of ordering: [32] 'The feeling of resemblances is one thing and the idea of class (*genre*) is another. The class is the external framework of which objects perceived to be similar form, in part, the contents.'

The existence of logical classes involves the formation of clear-cut dichotomies. However, nature itself manifests continuity in space and time, and the sensory information which we register from the world is not ordered in this discontinuous fashion, but is made up of 'indistinct and shifting images'.[33] Thus the notion of logical class itself, and the hierarchical distribution of relationships between categories, derive from the division of society into clans and phratries. But the mode in which objects are put into one category rather than another is directly influenced by sensory discriminations. For example, if the sun is in one category, the moon and stars will usually be placed in an opposed category; if the white cockatoo is in one category, the black cockatoo is put in the other.

Just as the axiomatic categories in terms of which abstract thought is ordered are derived from society, so too are the basic dimensions of force, space and time. The elemental religious force is the original model from which the concept of force was derived, and later incorporated into philosophy and natural science.[34] The same is true of the other of the Aristotelean categories: the notion of time finds its original prototype in the periodic character of social life, and space from the physical territory occupied by society. Time and space are not, as Kant held, inherent categories of the human mind. No doubt every individual is conscious of living in a present which is distinct from the past. But the *concept* of 'time' is not personalised; it involves an abstract category shared by all members of the group. 'It is not *my time* that is thus arranged; it is time in general...'[35] This must have originated from the experience of the collectivity: the temporal divisions of years, weeks and days stem from the periodic distribution of public ceremonials, rites and holy-

---

[31] *EF*, p. 170.
[32] This does introduce, however, difficulties of circularity in Durkheim's theory. cf. Parsons, p. 447.
[33] *EF*, pp. 171–2; *FE*, pp. 208–9.
[34] Durkheim notes that this has already been indicated by Comte. But Comte mistakenly inferred that the concept of force will eventually be eliminated from science, 'for owing to its mystic origins, he refused it all objective value'. *EF*, p. 234.
[35] *EF*, p. 23.

days. The notion of ' space ' similarly presupposes some original fixed point; there can be no ' north ' or ' south ', or ' right ' or ' left ' without some common standard whereby these can be judged. The territory occupied by the society provides this standard. This can be directly illustrated: in some of the Australian societies, space is conceived in the form of a circle, mirroring the circular shape of the camp, and the spatial circle is subdivided according to the position of each clan in the encampment.

Durkheim does not advance a simple form of ' mechanical materialism ' here, any more than, in other parts of *The Elementary Forms*, he relapses into the idealism for which the work is often criticised. He takes some pains, in fact, to emphasise that this standpoint takes as its premise the dynamic interplay between the ' substratum ' of society, and collectively-evolved ideas:

Certainly we consider it to be evident that social life depends upon its substratum and bear its mark, just as the mental life of the individual depends upon the nervous system and indeed the whole organism. But the *conscience collective* is something other than a mere epiphenomenon of its morphological basis, just as individual consciousness is something other than a simple efflorescence of the nervous system.[36]

As a theory of knowledge, the thesis advanced in *The Elementary Forms* is primarily genetic in character: it is not, as it is sometimes taken to be, a theory which postulates the existence of an unvarying set of connections between social organisation and collective ideas. Indeed, a basic aspect of Durkheim's general conception of the process of social development concerns the changing character of the content of the idea-systems which are found in contemporary societies, and the increasingly diversified nature of the social processes which underlie them. Of particular importance here is the relationship between modern rationalism and secularised morality. The importance of *The Elementary Forms*, in Durkheim's thought, is that it demonstrates conclusively that there can be no collective moral beliefs which do not possess a ' sacred ' character. Thus while both the content and the form of the moral order found in contemporary societies have changed radically, as compared to traditional societies, there is indeed no *solution de continuité* between the traditional and modern forms of solidarity.

The modern world is becoming increasingly penetrated by rationalism, which Durkheim calls the ' intellectual aspect ' of moral individualism. One consequence of this is the demand for a ' rational morality '. Now the maintenance of moral authority demands that moral ideas are ' as if surrounded by a mysterious barrier which keeps violators at arm's length, just as the religious domain is protected from the reach of the profane '.[37] This characteristic is easily preserved when religion and morality are one and the same, because the symbols and trappings of religion inspire attitudes of veneration. To seek to

---

[36] *EF*, p. 471; see below, pp. 218–19.
[37] *Moral Education*, p. 10.

expunge all traces of religion from morality, however, can lead to the result that all moral rules are rejected, because such rules can only survive if they are accorded respect and are regarded, within the conditions of their application, as being inviolable. This is why, even while they become detached from their original foundation in divine law, they are bound to retain a sacred character.[38]

Rationalism, ethics, and the ' cult of the individual '

This analysis can again be related back to the theory of the primitive inter-mingling of religion and morality. Man has everywhere in religious thought conceived himself to be two distinct beings, body and soul. The body is believed to reside in the material world, the soul in the discontinuous sphere of the sacred. A belief which is universal cannot be fortuitous, nor wholly illusory, and must rest upon some duality which is intrinsic to human life in society. This duality can be traced to the differentiation between sensation, on the one hand, and conceptual thought and moral beliefs on the other. These are in an important sense separate from one another. Sensation, and the sensory needs such as hunger and thirst, are ' necessarily egoistic ', in that they relate to the appetites of the individual organism, and have no implied reference to any other person.[39] Conceptual thought and moral rules are, by contrast, ' impersonal ' in the sense that they are universalised; they per-tain to no particular individual. Every man begins life as an egoistic being (although not, of course, an anomic one) who knows only sensation and whose actions are governed by sensory needs. But as the child becomes socialised, his egoistic nature becomes partly overlaid with what he learns from society. Each individual thus has an egoistic side to his personality, at the same time as he is a social being. The moral demands of life in society cannot be wholly compatible with egoistic inclinations: ' society cannot be formed or main-tained without our being required to make perpetual and costly sacrifices.' [40] Again, however, this has to be read within a historical dimension; while sen-sory needs are ' the type *par excellence* of egoistic tendencies ', there are a variety of egoistic desires which do not derive directly from sensory needs. ' Our very egoism is in large part a product of society.' [41]

Durkheim clarifies this elsewhere through historical analysis.[42] Christianity, and Protestantism more specifically, is the immediate source from which modern moral individualism is derived.

Since, for the Christian, virtue and piety do not consist in material procedures, but in interior states of the soul, he is compelled to exercise a perpetual watch

---

[38] *Ibid.* pp. 9–11. ' Moral life has not been, and never will be, able to shed all the characteristics that it holds in common with religion '. *Sociology and Philosophy*, p. 48.

[39] ' The dualism of human nature and its social conditions ', in Wolff, p. 327.

[40] *Ibid.* p. 338.

[41] *Su*, p. 360. [42] cf. *L'évolution pédagogique*, pp. 332–4 & 326–7.

over himself... Thus of the two possible poles of all thought, nature on the one hand, and man on the other, it is necessarily around the second that the thought of the Christian societies has come to gravitate...[43]

Christian ethics provided the moral principles upon which the ' cult of the individual ' is founded, but now Christianity is becoming surplanted by sacred symbols and objects of a new sort. This is most clearly exemplified, Durkheim says, in the events of the French Revolution, where freedom and reason were glorified, and where there was a high level of collective enthusiasm stimulated by public ' ceremonial '. But while this helped to give birth to the ideals which now dominate our life, the collective ardour of these times was ephemeral. The modern world is consequently in a moral hiatus :

In a word, the old gods are growing old or are dying, and others are not yet born. This is what made futile Comte's attempt to revive artificially the old historical memories: it is not a dead past, but life itself which can give rise to a living cult. But this state of uncertainty and bewildered turmoil cannot last forever. A day will come when our societies will again know those times of creative effervescence in which new ideas will spring up and new formulae will be discovered to serve for a while as a guide to humanity...[44]

The French Revolution gave the most decisive impetus to the growth of moral individualism in modern times. But the progression of individualism, while occurring irregularly in different periods of western history, is not the specific product of any definite epoch; its development takes place ' unceasingly throughout history '.[45] The sentiment of the supreme worth of the human individual is thus a product of society, and it is this which decisively separates it from egoism. The ' cult of the individual ' is based, not upon egoism, but upon the extension of quite contrary sentiments of sympathy for human suffering and the desire for social justice. While individualism cannot but produce an increase in egoism as compared with societies dominated by mechanical solidarity, it does not in any sense derive from egoism, and thus is not itself productive of a ' moral egoism which would make all solidarity impossible '.[46] This can be illustrated by the example of scientific activity. An intellectual branch of moral individualism is the spirit of free enquiry embodied in science : but far from entailing anarchy in the sphere of ideas, the pursuance of scientific enquiry can only be carried on within a framework of moral rules which enforce respect for the opinions of others, the publication of the results of investigations, and the exchange of information.

The trend towards increasing individualism is irreversible, since it is the outcome of the profound societal changes detailed in *The Division of Labour*. This is at the root of Durkheim's conception of freedom, and its relationship

---

[43] *Ibid.* p. 323.   [44] *EF*, p. 475; *FE*, pp. 610–11.
[45] *DL*, p. 171; *DTS*, p. 146.
[46] ' L'individualisme et les intellectuels ', pp. 7–13. ' Thus the individualist, who defends the rights of the individual, defends at the same time the vital interests of society...' (p. 12).

to the moral order. Freedom cannot be identified with liberation from all restraints: this is anomie, a state in which individuals are not free because they are chained to their own inexhaustible desires:

rights and liberties are not things inherent in man as such... Society has consecrated the individual and made him pre-eminently worthy of respect. His progressive emancipation does not imply a weakening but a transformation of the social bonds... The individual submits to society and this submission is the condition of his liberation. For man freedom consists in the deliverance from blind, unthinking physical forces; this he achieves by opposing against them the great and intelligent force which is society, under whose protection he shelters. By putting himself under the wing of society, he makes himself also, to a certain extent, dependent upon it. But this is a liberating dependence.[47]

Consequently it is a basic error to believe that moral authority and freedom are mutually exclusive opposites; since man only obtains whatever freedom he enjoys through his membership of society, he must be subject to the moral authority which the existence of society presupposes. For Durkheim there is no paradox in this, because ' to be free is not to do what one pleases; it is to be master of oneself...'.[48]

Discipline, in the sense of the inner control of impulse, is an essential component of all moral rules. But it follows from the position stated above that the view which equates discipline *inherently* with the limitation of human freedom and self-realisation is mistaken. There is no kind of life organisation, Durkheim points out, which does not function according to definite, regular principles; it is the same with social life. Society is an organisation of social relationships, and by this very fact entails the regulation of behaviour according to established principles, which in society can only be moral rules. It is only through acceptance of the moral regulation which makes social life possible that man is able to reap the benefits which society offers him. The failure to inject the historical element into Durkheim's analysis of this issue has led many critics to suppose that his views represent a thinly veiled rationale for an authoritarian political doctrine.[49] But it is, in fact, central to Durkheim's thesis that all forms of moral regulation are *not* identical. In other words, ' regulation ' (society, social constraint) cannot simply be juxtaposed in an abstract and universal sense with ' lack of regulation ' (anomie).[50] The notions of *both* egoism and anomie must be understood within the scope of the general conception of the development of society presented in *The Division of Labour*. Seen in this context, egoism and anomie are not simply functional problems

---

[47] *Sociology and Philosophy*, p. 72.
[48] *Education and Sociology* (Glencoe, 1956), p. 90.
[49] See, for example, John Horton: ' The de-humanisation of anomie and alienation ', *British Journal of Sociology*, vol. 15, 1964, pp. 283–300.
[50] Note Durkheim's statement on this point: ' it does not follow from a belief in the need for discipline that discipline must involve blind and slavish submission.' *Moral Education*, p. 52.

facing all types of society in equivalent degree: they are stimulated by the very moral individualism which is the outcome of social evolution. The dilemmas facing the modern form of society, Durkheim maintains, are not to be resolved through a reversion to the autocratic discipline found in traditional societies, but only through the moral consolidation of the differentiated division of labour, which demands quite different forms of authority from those characteristic of earlier types of society.

Part 3: Max Weber

9. Max Weber: Protestantism and capitalism

While Max Weber was an almost exact contemporary of Durkheim, the intellectual climate in which each lived was, in important respects, very different. The short period which Durkheim spent studying in Germany while a young man served to introduce him to some of the leading trends in German social thought, and he did not subsequently relinquish his interest in the works of German social scientists. Durkheim was certainly acquainted with Max Weber's writings, as well as with those of the latter's brother, Alfred. There are at least two sets of writings by German authors which connect Durkheim and Weber directly: those of Schmoller and the members of the *Verein für Sozialpolitik* on the one hand, and those of Georg Simmel on the other.[1] But even these fairly direct intellectual connections are of marginal significance. While Simmel's thought undoubtedly was of some importance in the shaping of Weber's views, Durkheim was highly critical of Simmel, and was not influenced by the latter's writing in any important respects; and while the writings of Schmoller and the *Kathedersozialisten* formed a point of departure for Durkheim's early works, those aspects of their views which Durkheim found most sympathetic were exactly the ones which Weber rejected, and indeed fought against.[2]

The apparent lack of any significant reciprocal influence between Durkheim and Weber has often occasioned surprise among subsequent writers.[3] But it is perhaps less remarkable than may appear at first sight, for the reasons stated above. The main intellectual influences in which Weber's work is steeped are as predominantly German as those which shaped Durkheim's writing are French. Moreover, Durkheim's early studies are rather abstract and philosophical in character – Durkheim wrote that ' having begun from philosophy, I tend to return to it, or rather I have been quite naturally

---

[1] Durkheim reviews Simmel's *Philosophie des Geldes* in *AS*, vol. 5, 1900–1, pp. 140–5, and two articles by Simmel in *AS*, vol. 7, 1902–3, pp. 646–9. Durkheim also discusses Simmel's formal sociology in ' Sociology and its scientific field ', in Wolff, pp. 354–75 (originally published in 1900).

[2] cf. above, pp. 66–9.

[3] e.g., Edward A. Tiryakian: ' A problem for the sociology of knowledge ', *Archives européennes de sociologie*, vol. 7, 1966, pp. 330–6. Tiryakian erroneously says that there is no mutual reference in the works of Durkheim and Weber. In fact, Durkheim mentions Weber in reporting upon the proceedings of the German Sociological Society (1911), *AS*, vol. 12, 1909–12, p. 26. (For Weber's contributions to the congress, see *GASS*, pp. 431–83.)

brought back to it by the nature of the questions I met with on my route '.[4]
Weber's first works, on the other hand, are detailed historical studies, and
it was from within the context of specific problems brought to light primarily
by the German historical school that Weber went on to expand the range of
his writings to embrace questions of a general theoretical nature. From the
flux of competing traditions in history, jurisprudence, economics, sociology,
and philosophy, Weber eventually fashioned a standpoint which borrowed
from many sources.

Early works

Weber's doctoral dissertation (1889) is a technical piece of work, dealing with
the legal provisions governing mediaeval trading enterprise.[5] In the thesis,
Weber gives particular attention to the Italian mercantile cities such as
Genoa and Pisa, showing that the commercial capitalism which developed
there entailed the formulation of principles of law regulating the mode in
which the distribution of risk and profit should be apportioned among the
collaborators in a business enterprise. At this time Weber was already concerned, although only from this limited aspect, with an issue which was later
to play an important role in his later writings: the impact of Roman law
upon the development of the juridical system of mediaeval and post-
mediaeval Europe. He found himself unable to deal with this matter satisfactorily, however, within the frame of reference which he had chosen for the
thesis.[6] Weber's second work, written under the aegis of Mommsen, and
which he finished some two years later, is expressly concerned with Rome
itself.[7] Again, the work is heavily technical in character, and is directed towards a current scholarly controversy of the day, providing a detailed analysis
of the evolution of Roman land-tenure, and connecting this with legal and
political changes.[8] In contrast to those who argued that the economic history
of Roman agriculture was unique in the specific form which it took, Weber
tries to show that it is amenable to treatment in terms of concepts derived
from other economic contexts.

These writings are perhaps rather less important for their substantive content than for what they indicate of the nascent line of Weber's intellectual

---

[4] The quotation is from a letter to Georges Davy, reported in the latter's ' Emile
  Durkheim ', *Revue française de sociologie*, vol. 1, 1960, p. 10.
[5] ' Zur Geschichte der Handelsgesellschaften im Mittelalter ', *Gesammelte Aufsätze
  zur Sozial- und Wirtschaftsgeschichte* (Tübingen, 1924), pp. 312–443. For the
  original title of the dissertation, see Johannes Winckelmann: ' Max Webers
  Dissertation ', in René König and Johannes Winckelmann: *Max Weber zum
  Gedächtnis* (Cologne and Opladen), 1963.
[6] *Jugendbriefe.* Tübingen, p. 274.
[7] *Die römische Agrargeschichte in ihrer Bedeutung für des Staats- und Privatrecht*
  (Stuttgart, 1891).
[8] For a brief discussion of the background to the work, cf. Günther Roth: ' Introduction ', *ES*, vol. 1, pp. xxxvi-xl.

development. They already manifest a concern with what was to be the principal focus of Weber's later work: the nature of capitalist enterprise, and the specific characteristics of western European capitalism. The early analysis of Roman agrarian history is only the first of several later writings, examining the social and economic structure of the ancient world.[9] As Marx did before him, Weber perceives in ancient Rome certain of the main elements which brooked large in the formation of modern capitalism. Like Marx, Weber considers that 'Ancient civilisation is distinct from the mediaeval in certain specifiable ways';[10] but that in its driving expansionism, in the formation of large-scale commercial interests, and in the development of a money economy, Rome reached a level of economic development comparable to that of early post-mediaeval Europe. His explanation of the decline of Rome in fact shares a good deal in common with the outline account which Marx had sketched in of these same events.[11]

Weber's early work on Roman history also shows an early awareness of the complicated nature of the relationship between economic structures and other aspects of social organisation, and more especially, a conviction that all forms of crude economic determinism must be rejected.[12] The continuity is clear between these initial historical writings and the studies which Weber published immediately after them, which deal with two different facets of the modern German economy: the first being an investigation of the condition of the peasantry to the east of the Elbe, the others being concerned with operations of financial capital in Germany. Both of these latter studies analyse aspects of the character and effects of modern commerce, and in the course of writing them Weber reached a number of conclusions which proved of lasting influence upon his work, and which lead directly into the themes explored in *The Protestant Ethic and the Spirit of Capitalism*.

Between 1894 and 1897 Weber wrote a number of articles concerned with the operations of the stock exchange and its relationship to capital financing.[13] Weber set out to counter a conception which, in his view, stems from a naive understanding of the characteristics of functioning of a modern economy, and which dismisses the stock exchange as nothing more than a 'conspiracy against society'.[14] The notion that the stock exchange is simply

---

[9] cf. 'Agrarverhältnisse im Altertum', *Gesammelte Aufsätze zur Sozial- und Wirtschaftsgeschichte*, pp. 1–288; and 'Die sozialen Gründe des Untergangs der antiken Kultur', *ibid.* pp. 289–311.

[10] 'Agrarverhältnisse im Altertum', p. 4.

[11] Key parts of Marx's account of the disintegration of the Roman Empire appear in *Grundrisse*, which was, of course, unavailable to Weber; cf. above, pp. 27–9, and my article 'Marx, Weber and the development of capitalism', *Sociology*, vol. 4, 1970, pp. 300–1.

[12] cf. also 'Zur Geschichte der Handelsgesellschaften', p. 322.

[13] The most general of these is 'Die Börse', in *GASS*, pp. 256–322. cf. Reinhard Bendix: *Max Weber, an Intellectual Portrait* (London, 1966), pp. 23–30.

[14] 'Die Börse', pp. 256–7.

a means of profit-making for a capitalist minority neglects altogether the mediating functions which the institution fulfils in the economy. The stock market provides a mechanism whereby a businessman, through the use of rational planning, can facilitate the progress of his enterprise. It is erroneous to identify the operations of the stock exchange solely with irresponsible speculation. The latter phenomenon does, of course, exist, but the main effect of the stock exchange is to promote the rational conduct of the market rather than to provide the opportunity for gambling coups. To show how this is so, Weber gives the example of credit deals. When a time bargain is made, such that a businessman is allowed to make an exchange in which he can consummate his side of the transaction at a specified time in the future, the result is an expansion of the range of trading operations which are possible. However, Weber makes note of the difficulties for the normative regulation of the stock market which the growth in scale and volume of transactions in the modern economy brings about. Thus the extension of commercial operations tends to neutralise the ethical controls which are necessary to the functioning of exchange transactions.

The effects of the spread of market relations are analysed in a different context in Weber's lengthy study of agricultural labour in eastern Germany, which appeared in 1892.[15] In the structure of agrarian enterprise in nineteenth century Germany, the river Elbe marked a major dividing-line. To the west of the river, most farmers were independent peasantry; but in the east the Junkers maintained large-scale estates, which in many respects preserved a semi-feudal organisation. Thus, to the east of the Elbe, agricultural workers consisted of two distinct types. On the one hand, there were those tied to their employers by annual contracts, and living within conditions similar to those of mediaeval times; and on the other, wage labourers, hired on a day-to-day basis, whose conditions of employment approximated to those of the industrial proletariat. In these circumstances, traditional and modern forms of labour relations became conjoined in a way which, as Weber notes in the work, is quite unstable. The day-labourers, he concludes, are certain to progressively replace the bonded workers (*Instleute*). This process, Weber shows, is transforming the overall structure of the estates; whereas the bonded workers are not merely tied to their employers by an economic relation, but are enmeshed in a whole set of ties of right and obligation, the day-labourers are hired on the basis of a wage-contract. The consequence is that the latter group has no organic connections with the social system within which the traditional workers live; therefore the interests of the day-labourers are almost completely bound up with the securing of as high a wage as possible. The increasing commercialisation of agriculture, which stimulates

---

[15] *Die Verhältnisse der Landarbeiter im ostelbischen Deutschland* (Leipzig, 1892). cf. also ' Capitalism and rural society in Germany ', in *FMW*, pp. 363–85.

the use of wage-labour, thus produces an accentuation of economic conflict between the workers and their employers.

In spite of this, the commercialisation of agriculture does not lead to an improvement in the living standards of the workers, but instead tends to depress them.[16] Weber describes in some detail conditions of life of the day-labourers, showing that the dearth of the range of secondary benefits open to the bonded worker frequently renders the overall economic position of the former group worse than that of the latter. In the short run, the wage of the day-labourer might be the higher, but in the long run this is reversed. Nevertheless, Weber points out, there is an obvious inclination among the bonded workers to attempt to escape from the position of dependence which their commitment to an annual contract entails. This search for independence can be seen in the proclivity of bonded workers to exchange their security for the uncertain existence of the day-labourer. According to Weber, this cannot be explained in sheerly economic terms, but is partly a result of a quest for personal ' freedom ' from the patriarchal ' relationship of personal dependence '.[17] Thus the worker who possesses his own small plot of land will endure the most extreme privations, and the most heavy indebtedness to usurers, in order to preserve his ' independence '.

The ' freedom ' which is thus obtained may be largely an illusion; but such illusions, Weber concludes, are basic to the understanding of human activity. It is not ' by bread alone ' that the actions of the farm workers may be understood. The ideas which guide the behaviour of the agricultural workers, while they are not simply the ' expression ' of economic interests, do not, however, spring from nothing. They in turn are related to the social and economic changes which have modified the mediaeval forms of community and labour. The nexus of relationships linking ideas and material interests is rarely specifiable in terms of a unilinear causal derivation from one ' level ' to the other. However, here Weber sets himself primarily against cultural history, which analyses historical development in terms of the content of ideas: it is always necessary to examine the possible bearing of deep-rooted social and economic changes upon the nature of the values held by the members of a given stratum or society.[18]

To suppose that these views developed in Weber's thought simply within the context of an encounter with Marxism would be to greatly oversimplify the intellectual milieu in which Weber wrote. When Weber wrote his first works, he took his point of departure from the contemporary problems which dominated the mainstream of German economic history and jurisprudence. Weber's early interest in Rome reflects the current debate over the causes of

---

[16] *Verhältnisse der Landarbeiter*, pp. 774ff.

[17] *Ibid.* pp. 797ff. Weber's account should be compared to Kautsky's views, as given in *Die Agrarfrage* (Stuttgart, 1899).

[18] cf. ' Sozialen Gründe des Untergangs der antiken Kultur ', pp. 291–6.

124 Part 3: Max Weber

the economic decline of Rome. His investigation of the east German agricultural workers is one part of a massive survey carried out by the members of the *Verein für Sozialpolitik*, and was generated by a concern with problems of practical political significance, which turned in large part upon the role of the Junker 'aristocracy' in German society.[19] Nonetheless, it is true to say that the conclusions which Weber reaches in these early studies increasingly channelled his concerns into avenues which brought him into direct relation with the areas in which Marxist thought was concentrated: in particular, the specific characteristics of modern capitalism and the conditions governing its emergence and development.

The origins of the capitalist ' spirit '

The Protestant Ethic and the Spirit of Capitalism, which Weber published in the form of two long articles in 1904 and 1905, marks his first attempt to confront certain of these issues on a general plane.[20] Some of the principal features of the ethos which occupies Weber's attention in the book are already indicated in his study of the agricultural labourers. The contrast between the conditions of life and the outlook of the bonded and the day-labourers is largely one between acceptance of traditional patterns of deference and patronage on the one hand, and an attitude of economic individualism on the other. This latter attitude is, however, clearly not merely an outcome of the economic circumstances of the day-labourers, but represents a part of an ethic which is itself helping to break down the old traditional structure of the landed estates.

Weber opens *The Protestant Ethic* by posing a statistical fact for explanation: the fact that in modern Europe ' business leaders and owners of capital, as well as the higher grades of skilled labour, and even more the higher technically and commercially trained personnel of modern enterprises, are overwhelmingly Protestant '.[21] This is not merely a contemporary, but also is an historical fact: tracing the association back, it can be shown that some of the early centres of capitalist development in the early part of the sixteenth century were strongly Protestant. A possible explanation for this is ready to hand: that the break with economic traditionalism which occurred

[19] cf. Dieter Lindenlaub: *Richtungskämpfe im Verein für Sozialpolitik* (Wiesbaden, 1967). See also below, pp. 190–1ff for a description of Weber's political assessment of Germany in 1895, as expressed in his Freiburg inaugural lecture.

[20] *The Protestant Ethic* first appeared in the *Archiv für Sozialwissenschaft und Sozialpolitik*, vols. 20 & 21, 1905, and is reprinted as the introductory part of *Gesammelte Aufsätze zur Religionssoziologie* (Tübingen, 1920–1). In this latter version, Weber makes some revisions, and adds comments on some of the criticisms given in the literature to which the first appearance of the work gave rise. cf. his ' Antikritisches Schlusswort zum " Geist des Kapitalismus " ', in the *Archiv*, vol. 31, 1910, pp. 554–99. A description of the debate with Rachfahl is given in J. A. Prades: *La sociologie de la religion chez Max Weber* (Louvain, 1969), pp. 87–95.

[21] *PE*, p. 35.

in these centres produced a sloughing off of tradition in general, and of religious institutions in their old form in particular. But this interpretation does not stand up to close scrutiny. It would be quite wrong to regard the Reformation as an escape from the controls of the church. In fact, the surveillance of the Catholic church over everyday life was loose : the movement to Protestantism involved acceptance of a very much higher degree of regulation of behaviour than that which was demanded by Catholicism. Protestantism adopts a resolutely stringent attitude towards relaxation and enjoyment – a phenomenon which is especially pronounced in Calvinism. The conclusion can be reached, therefore, that we must look to the specific character of Protestant beliefs if we are to account for the connection between Protestantism and economic rationality.

The novelty of Weber's interpretation, of course, did not lie in the suggestion that there is a connection between the Reformation and modern capitalism. Such a connection was assumed to exist by many writers before the appearance of Weber's work. Thus the characteristic Marxist explanation, deriving mainly from the writings of Engels, held that Protestantism is an ideological reflection of the economic changes which were incurred with the early development of capitalism.[22] In rejecting this as an adequate viewpoint, Weber's work begins from an apparent anomaly, the identification and explication of which constitutes the real originality of *The Protestant Ethic*. It is usually the case that those whose lives are bound up with economic activity and the pursuit of gain are either indifferent to religion, or positively hostile to it, since whereas their actions are directed towards the ' material ' world, religion is concerned with the ' immaterial '. But Protestantism, rather than relaxing the control of the church over day-to-day activities, demanded of its adherents a much *more* vigorous discipline than Catholicism, and thereby injected a religious factor into all spheres of the life of the believer. There is clearly a relationship between Protestantism and modern capitalism which cannot be wholly explained by seeing the former as a ' result ' of the latter; but the character of Protestant beliefs and codes of behaviour is quite different from that which might be expected, *prima facie*, to stimulate economic activity.

The elucidation of this anomaly demands not only an analysis of the content of Protestant beliefs and an assessment of their influence upon the actions of believers, but also the specification of the particular characteristics of modern western capitalism as a form of economic activity. Not only does Protestantism differ in certain important respects from the religious form which preceded it, but so also does modern capitalism display basic characteristics which separate it from prior sorts of capitalistic activity. The various other forms of capitalism which Weber distinguishes are all found within societies characterised by ' economic traditionalism '. The attitudes towards

[22] cf. below, pp. 189–90 & 210–11.

labour characteristic of traditionalism are illustrated graphically by the experience of modern capitalist employers who have attempted to introduce contemporary methods of production into communities where they have not previously been known. If the employer, interested in securing the highest degree of effort possible, introduces a piece-rate whereby workers can potentially increase their earnings well above those they are accustomed to receiving, the result is often that the amount of work done decreases rather than the reverse. The traditionalistic worker does not think in terms of maximising his daily wage, but rather considers only how much work he has to do in order to meet his usual needs. ' A man does not " by nature " wish to earn more and more money, but simply to live as he lives and as he is accustomed to live, and to earn as much as is required to do so.' [23]

Traditionalism is by no means incompatible with the greed for wealth. ' Absolute and conscious ruthlessness in acquisition has often stood in direct and close connection with the strictest conformity to tradition.' [24] Selfish avarice is found in all societies, and is in fact more characteristic of pre-capitalist than of capitalist society. Thus ' adventurers' capitalism ', for example, involving the pursuit of gain through military conquest or piracy, has existed at all periods of history. This is quite different, however, from modern capitalism, which is founded not upon the amoral pursuit of personal gain, but upon the disciplined obligation of work as a duty. Weber identifies the principal features of the ' spirit ' of modern capitalism as follows :

the acquisition of more and more money, combined with the strict avoidance of all spontaneous enjoyment . . . is thought of so purely as an end in itself, that vis-à-vis the happiness of, or utility to, the particular individual, it appears as quite transcendental and wholly irrational. Man is dominated by acquisition as the purpose of his life ; acquisition is no longer a means to the end of satisfying his material needs. This reversal of what we might call the ' natural ' situation, completely senseless from an unprejudiced standpoint, is evidently as definitely a leading principle of capitalism as it is foreign to all peoples not under capitalistic influence.[25]

The spirit of modern capitalism is thus characterised by a unique combination of devotion to the earning of wealth through legitimate economic activity, together with the avoidance of the use of this income for personal enjoyment. This is rooted in a belief in the value of efficient performance in a chosen vocation as a duty and a virtue.

A traditionalistic outlook, Weber stresses, is not wholly incompatible with modern forms of economic enterprise. Many small businesses, for instance, have been run according to traditionally fixed modes of procedure, traditional rates of exchange and profit, etc. ' Now at some time ', Weber says, ' this leisureliness was suddenly destroyed . . .'; [26] and this often happened without any technological change taking place within the enterprise. Where such

[23] *PE*, p. 60; *GAR*, vol. 1, p. 44.   [24] *PE*, p. 58; *GAR*, vol. 1, p. 43.
[25] *PE*, p. 53; *GAR*, vol. 1, p. 36.   [26] *PE*, p. 67.

enterprises have been restructured, what has occurred is a *rational reorganisation of production*, directed towards maximising productive efficiency. Such a change cannot be explained, in most cases, by a sudden influx of capital into the industry in question. It is the result, rather, of the introduction of a new spirit of entrepreneurial enterprise – the capitalist spirit. Hence the dominant characteristic which distinguishes the modern capitalist economy is that it

is rationalised on the basis of rigorous calculation, directed with foresight and caution towards the economic success which is sought in sharp contrast to the hand-to-mouth existence of the peasant, and to the privileged traditionalism of the guild craftsman and of the adventurers' capitalism, oriented to the exploitation of political opportunities and irrational speculation.[27]

The spirit of capitalism cannot simply be inferred from the growth of rationalism as a whole in western society. Such a way of analysing the problem tends to assume a progressive, unilinear development of rationalism : in fact, the rationalisation of different institutions in western societies shows an uneven distribution. Those countries, for example, in which rationalisation of the economy has proceeded further are, in respect of the degree of rationalism of law, retarded by comparison with some of the more economically backward states. (England is the most notable instance here.) Rationalisation is a complex phenomenon, which takes many concrete forms, and which develops variably in different areas of social life. *The Protestant Ethic* is concerned only with discovering ' whose intellectual child that particular concrete form of rational thought was, from which the idea of a calling and devotion to labour in the calling has derived. . .'.[28]

The concept of the ' calling ', Weber shows, only came into being at the time of the Reformation. It is not found, nor does any synonym for it exist, in Catholicism, nor in Antiquity. The significance of the notion of the calling, and the mode in which it is employed in Protestant beliefs, is that it serves to bring the mundane affairs of everyday life within an all-embracing religious influence. The calling of the individual is to fulfil his duty to God through the moral conduct of his day-to-day life. This impels the emphasis of Protestantism away from the Catholic ideal of monastic isolation, with its rejection of the temporal, into worldly pursuits.

The influence of ascetic Protestantism

But Lutheranism cannot be regarded as the main source of the capitalist spirit. The Reformation played an essential role in the introduction of the notion of the calling, and thereby in placing the dutiful pursuit of mundane activities at the centre of the stage. Luther's conception of the calling, how-

[27] *PE*, p. 76.
[28] *PE*, p. 78.

ever, remained in some respects quite traditionalistic.[29] The further elaboration of the conception of the calling was the work of the later Protestant sects which make up the various branches of what Weber calls ' ascetic Protestantism '.

Weber differentiates four main streams of ascetic Protestantism : Calvinism, Methodism, Pietism, and the Baptist sects. Of course, these were closely related to one another, and cannot always be clearly separated.[30] Weber's discussion of ascetic Protestantism is not concerned with an overall historical description of their dogma, but only with those elements in their doctrines which are most consequential in affecting the practical conduct of the individual in his economic activity. The most important part of the analysis is concentrated upon Calvinism : not, however, solely upon Calvin's doctrines as such, but rather upon those embodied in the teachings of Calvinists towards the end of the sixteenth century and in the seventeenth century.

Having made these qualifications, Weber proceeds to identfy three major tenets as most important in Calvinism. Firstly, the doctrine that the universe is created to further the greater glory of God, and only has meaning in relation to God's purposes. ' God does not exist for men, but men for the sake of God.'[31] Secondly, the principle that the motives of the Almighty are beyond human comprehension. Men can know only the small morsels of divine truth which God wishes to reveal to them. Thirdly, the belief in predestination : only a small number of men are chosen to achieve eternal grace. This is something which is irrevocably given from the first moment of creation; it is not affected by human actions, since to suppose that it were would be to conceive that the actions of men could influence divine judgement.

The consequence of this doctrine for the believer, Weber argues, must have been one of ' unprecedented inner loneliness '. ' In what was for the man of the age of the Reformation the most decisive concern of his life, his eternal salvation, he was forced to follow his path alone to meet a destiny which had been decreed for him from eternity.'[32] In this crucial respect, each man was alone; no one, priest or layman, existed who could intercede with God to produce his salvation. This eradication of the possibility of salvation through the church and the sacraments, according to Weber, is the most decisive difference which separated Calvinism from both Lutheranism and Catholicism. Calvinism thereby brought about a final conclusion to a great historical process which Weber discusses elsewhere in detail: the gradual process of the ' disenchantment ' (*Entzauberung*) of the world.[33]

---

[29] *PE*, p. 85. An important part of Weber's concern is to demonstrate the contrast between *Lutheranism* and Calvinism, rather than solely between Catholicism and Calvinism.

[30] Weber states that Methodism and Pietism were both derivative movements, while the Baptist sects represent an ' independent source of Protestant asceticism besides Calvinism ', *PE*, p. 144.

[31] *PE*, pp. 102–3.

[32] *PE*, p. 104; *GAR*, vol. 1, p. 94.

[33] See below, pp. 214–6.

There was not only no magical means of attaining the grace of God for those to whom God had decided to deny it, but no means whatsoever. Combined with the harsh doctrines of the absolute transcendentality of God and the corruption of everything pertaining to the flesh, this inner isolation of the individual contains ... the reason for the entirely negative attitude of Puritanism to all the sensuous and emotional elements in culture and in religion, because they are of no use toward salvation and promote sentimental illusions and idolatrous superstitions. Thus it provides a basis for a fundamental antagonism to sensuous culture of all kinds.[34]

The enormous strain to which this exposed the Calvinist is evident. The decisive question which every believer must eventually have felt compelled to ask himself – am I one of the chosen? – could not be answered. To Calvin himself, this presented no source of anxiety. Since he believed himself to be selected by God to carry out a divine mission, he was confident of his own salvation. But no such certainty was possible for his followers. Consequently Calvin's doctrine that there are no external differences between the elect and the damned quickly came under pressure on the level of pastoral care. Two related responses developed. Firstly, that the individual should consider it as obligatory to deem himself one of the chosen: any doubts as to the certainty of election are evidence of imperfect faith and therefore of lack of grace. Secondly, that 'intense worldly activity' is the most appropriate means to develop and maintain this necessary self-confidence. Thus the performance of 'good works' became regarded as a 'sign' of election – not in any way a method of *attaining* salvation, but rather of eliminating doubts of salvation.

Weber illustrates this by reference to the writings of the English puritan, Richard Baxter. Baxter warns against the temptations of wealth, but, according to Weber, this admonition is directed solely towards the use of wealth to support an idle, relaxed way of life. Idleness and time-wasting are the foremost sins. This doctrine 'does not yet hold, with Franklin: " time is money ", but the proposition holds to a certain degree in a spiritual sense. It is infinitely valuable because every hour lost is lost to labour for the glory of God.'[35] Calvinism demands of its believers a coherent and continuous life of discipline, thus eradicating the possibility of repentance and atonement for sin which the Catholic confessional makes possible. The latter effectively sanctions a haphazard attitude to life, since the believer can rely upon the knowledge that priestly intervention can provide release from the consequences of moral lapse.

Thus labour in the material world, for the Calvinist, becomes attributed with the highest positive ethical evaluation. The possession of riches does not provide a man with any sort of exemption from the divine command to labour devotedly in his calling. The Puritan conception of the calling, in contrast to the Lutheran, places a premium upon the duty of the individual to

[34] *PE*, p. 105.
[35] *PE*, p. 158; *GAR*, vol. 1, pp. 167–8.

approach his vocation in a methodical fashion as the instrument of God. The accumulation of wealth is morally condemned only to the degree that it forms an enticement to idle luxury; where material profit is acquired through the ascetic pursuit of duty in a calling, it is not only tolerated, but is in fact morally recommended. 'To wish to be poor was, it was often argued, the same as wishing to be unhealthy; it is objectionable as a glorification of works and derogatory to the glory of God.' [36]

It is crucial to Weber's analysis that these characteristics are not ' logical ', but ' psychological ' consequences of the original doctrine of predestination as formulated by Calvin. These subsequent developments in Puritan doctrine stem from the phenomenal isolation experienced by believers, and the anxieties to which this gave rise. The belief in predestination is not unique to Calvinism, and its consequences for human action vary according both to the other beliefs it is associated with, and the social context in which it occurs. The Islamic belief in predestination, for example, produced, not the worldly asceticism of Calvinism, but ' a complete obliviousness to self, in the interest of fulfilment of the religious commandment of a holy war for the conquest of the world '.[37]

The origins of the capitalist spirit thus have to be sought in that religious ethic which is most precisely developed in Calvinism. It is to this ethic that we may trace the unique qualities which distinguish the attitudes underlying modern capitalistic activity from the amoral character of most previous forms of capital acquisition. ' One of the integral characteristics of the modern capitalist spirit, and not only of this, but of modern culture: the rational conduct of life on the basis of the idea of the calling, was born – that is what this exposition has sought to show – from the spirit of Christian asceticism.' [38] The other varieties of Protestant asceticism, in general, have less of a rigorous discipline than Calvinism, which Weber speaks of as having an ' iron consistency '. Weber suggests, however, that there may be a historical relationship, in the origin of the capitalist spirit, between the forms of ascetic Protestantism and the social strata at different levels in the capitalist economy. Pietism, for example, which tended to induce, rather than the persistent energy of the Calvinist, an attitude of humility and renunciation, may have been most widespread among employees in the lower ranks of the industrial order, while Calvinism was probably more directly influential among entrepreneurs.[39]

What to the Puritan was compliance with divine guidance, increasingly, for the world of contemporary capitalism becomes a mechanical conformity to the economic and organisational exigencies of industrial production, at all levels of the hierarchy of the division of labour. Weber is careful to disclaim the suggestion that the Puritan ethos is a necessary component to the function-

---

[36] *PE*, p. 163.
[38] *PE*, p. 180; *GAR*, vol. 1, p. 202.

[37] *ES*, vol. 2, p. 573.
[39] *PE*, p. 139.

ing of modern capitalism, once it is established upon a broad scale. On the contrary, the specific conclusion of *The Protestant Ethic* is that, while the Puritan, because of his religious faith, deliberately chose to work in a calling, the specialised character of the capitalist division of labour forces modern man to do so.[40]

Since asceticism undertook to remodel the world and to work itself out in the world, the external goods of this world have gained an increasing and finally an inexorable power over the lives of men as at no previous period in history. Today its spirit – whether finally, who knows? – has escaped from the cage (*Gehäuse*). But, in any case, victorious capitalism, since it rests on mechanical foundations, needs this support no longer . . . the idea of duty in one's calling prowls about in our life like the ghost of dead religious beliefs.[41]

Weber intends *The Protestant Ethic* to be a programmatic work: it is a preliminary exploration of a complex set of issues, and his claims for the range of its application are modest and restricted. The main accomplishment of the work, according to Weber,[42] is that it shows that the moral instrumentality of the spirit of capitalism is an unintended offshoot of the religious ethic of Calvin, and more generally of the conception of the worldly calling whereby Protestantism broke with the monastic ideal of Catholicism. But ascetic Protestantism is nonetheless in part simply the culmination of tendencies which stretch far back into the history of Christianity as a whole. Catholic asceticism already had a rational character, and there is a direct line of development from the monastic life to the ideals of Puritanism. The main effect of the Reformation, and the subsequent history of the Protestant sects, was to transfer this from the monastery into the everyday world.

The Protestant Ethic demonstrates that there is an 'elective affinity' (*Wahlverwandtschaft*) between Calvinism, or more accurately, certain sorts of Calvinist beliefs, and the economic ethics of modern capitalist activity. The distinctive feature of the work is that it seeks to demonstrate that the rationalisation of economic life characteristic of modern capitalism connects with *irrational* value-commitments. This is a prefatory task to the assessment of causal relations, but is not in itself sufficient for the isolation of causes.[43] Weber explicitly states that, for this to be achieved, two broad tasks have to be undertaken: firstly, the analysis of the origins and spread of rationalism in other spheres besides that of the economic (e.g., in politics, law, science and art); and secondly, the investigation of in what ways Protestant asceticism was itself influenced by social and economic forces. None-

---

[40] 'Der Puritaner wollte Berufsmensch sein – wir müssen es sein' (*GAR*, vol. 1, p. 203). Weber stresses that the Puritan emphasis upon the importance of a fixed calling provided an initial moral validation of the specialised division of labour (*PE*, p. 163). cf. also Weber's discussion of the decline of 'church-mindedness' in American business, in 'The Protestant sects and the spirit of capitalism', in *FMW*, pp. 302–22.
[41] *PE*, pp. 181–2; *GAR*, vol. 1, pp. 203–4.
[42] cf. 'Antikritisches Schlusswort', pp. 556–7.
[43] *PE*, p. 54, pp. 90–91 & p. 183.

theless Weber is emphatic that the material analysed in *The Protestant Ethic* adequately disposes of ' the doctrine of naïve historical materialism ', according to which ideas such as those involved in Calvinist beliefs are regarded simply as ' reflections ' of economic conditions.[45] ' We must free ourselves ', Weber asserts, ' from the view that one can deduce the Reformation, as a historically necessary development, from economic changes.' [46] But Weber does not attempt to substitute any alternative ' theory ' for this conception of historical materialism which he rejects: indeed, as Weber seeks to show in his methodological essays, which were mostly written at the same period as *The Protestant Ethic*, such a theory is impossible to achieve.

[45] *PE*, p. 55; *GAR*, vol. 1, p. 37.
[46] *PE*, pp. 90–1; *GAR*, vol. 1, p. 83.

10. Weber's methodological essays

The Protestant Ethic concludes with a plea for the rejection of both materialistic and idealistic interpretations of history as overall theoretical schemes: 'each', Weber says, 'if it does not serve as the preparation, but as the conclusion of an investigation, accomplishes equally little in the interest of historical truth'.[1] Weber's methodological writings expound this position in considerable depth.[2]

The genealogy of Weber's methodological essays is complex, however, and they must also be placed within the framework of the then current controversy over the relationship between the natural and the 'human' or social sciences. Whereas Durkheim was steeped in a tradition of positivism which reached back to well before Comte, no directly comparable tradition existed in German social thought. The lengthy and complicated debate which arose in Germany over the status of the sciences of man thus explored issues which remained largely quiescent in French history and social philosophy. Weber, in common with most of his German contemporaries, bluntly rejects the Comtean notion that the sciences are ordered in the form of an empirical and logical hierarchy, in which each science depends upon the prior historical emergence of the one below it in the hierarchy. In this form of positivist orthodoxy, social science is treated as involving simply the extension of the presuppositions and methods of the natural science to the study of human beings. In repudiating this conception, Weber does not, however, wholly follow that of such authors as Rickert and Windelband in recognising two fundamentally different orders of sciences, the 'natural' and 'cultural', or the cross-cutting dichotomy of 'nomothetic' and 'ideographic'. While Weber adopts the distinction which these writers drew between the logic of statements of generalisation and the explanation of the unique, he applies it in a different way.

---

[1] *PE*, p. 183.
[2] For an exposition of the relevant background, especially with regard to idealism, cf. Alexander von Schelting: *Max Webers Wissenschaftslehre* (Tübingen, 1934), pp. 178–247. Weber's methodological essays represent only a partial treatment of problems which Weber intended to treat at greater length. See Marianne Weber: *Max Weber: ein Lebensbild* (Heidelberg, 1950), pp. 347–8. The 'partial' character of Weber's methodological essays is clearly demonstrated in F. Tenbruck: 'Die Genesis der Methodologie Max Webers', *Kölner Zeitschrift für Soziologie und Sozialpsychologie*, vol. 11, 1959, pp. 573–630.

Subjectivity and objectivity

Weber's critique of Roscher and Knies, the first of his methodological essays, makes the point that the supposed distinction between the natural and social sciences may be used to support a spurious intuitionism.[3] The writings of Roscher, for example, according to Weber, employ this distinction in such a way as to introduce an overriding component of semi-mystic idealism into the author's analysis.[3] The universe of human action is held to be one in which natural scientific methods do not apply, and consequently where inexact and intuitive procedures have to be employed. The human world is thus an 'irrational' one, which is epitomised by the *Volksgeist* or *Volksseele*, the 'spirit of the people'. It is impossible, Weber points out, to reconcile the use of such notions as this with the claim, which is advanced by this same author, that rigorous historical research is an end which should be striven for.

Weber concedes that the social sciences are necessarily concerned with 'spiritual' or 'ideal' phenomena, which are peculiarly human characteristics which do not exist in the subject-matter treated by the natural sciences. But this necessary differentiation of 'subject' and 'object' need not, and must not, involve the sacrifice of 'objectivity' in the social sciences, nor does it entail the substitution of intuition for replicable causal analysis. Weber's essay entitled ' " Objectivity " in social science and social policy' attempts to show how this is possible.[4]

The social sciences, Weber points out, originated in a concern with practical problems, and were stimulated by the concern of men to effect desired social changes. It was from within such a context that there emerged the impetus towards the establishment of disciplines interested in formulating 'objective' statements about human social and cultural reality. This development, however, was not accompanied by a clear understanding of the significance of the essential logical discontinuity between factual or analytic statements, on the one hand, and normative propositions concerning not what 'is', but what 'ought to be' on the other. Most forms of social thought have sought to establish a closure between factual and normative propositions, on the basis of one of two connected sorts of assumptions. The first is that the desirable can be identified with what is 'immutably existent': invariant laws governing the operation of social and economic institutions. The other is that the assimilation of the desirable and the real come to be located in general principles of evolutionary development: not in the immutably existent, but in the inevitably emergent.

Both of these conceptions must be rejected. It is logically impossible for

---

[3] *GAW*, pp. 9ff.

[4] *MSS*, pp. 50–112. Weber's essays also have to be understood against the views of Menger and his school of 'scientific' economics. cf. Marianne Weber, pp. 352–3; for a longer account, see Lindenlaub, pp. 96–141.

an empirical discipline to establish, scientifically, ideals which define what ' ought to be '. This constitutes a fundamental premise of the neo-Kantian epistemology which Weber adopts, and it is a position which informs the whole of his writing. But while value-judgements cannot be validated through scientific analysis, this most emphatically does not mean that they must be removed altogether from the sphere of scientific discussion. All judgements concerning whether or not a specified course of action ' ought to be taken ' can be separated into ' means ', which are employed to reach certain particular or general ' ends '. ' We desire something concretely either " for its own sake " or as a means of achieving something else which is more highly desired.' [5] Scientific analysis can allow us to determine the suitability of a given range of means for the attainment of a determinate end. But no amount of scientific knowledge can demonstrate logically that a man *should* accept a given end as a value. The social scientist is also able to show, if a given objective is sought, what advantages are to be gained by employing one means as compared to another, and thus also what costs are entailed. The costs entailed by the selection of a particular means to a given end can be of two sorts: (1) the partial rather than the complete realisation of a desired end, or (2) the bringing about of additional consequences which deleteriously affect other ends held by the individual. It is also possible, through empirical analysis, in a certain oblique sense, to evaluate the end itself, in terms of whether it is actually capable of realisation at all given the particular set of historical circumstances in which it is pursued.

Weber frequently illustrates these points by reference to the aspirations of revolutionary socialism, since the dilemmas posed by the striving to achieve the end of the establishment of a socialist society raise certain of these issues with especial poignancy. The realisation of a socialist society by revolutionary means involves the use of force to secure the desired social changes. But the application of force must necessarily involve political repression after the revolution, which will negate some of the freedoms which are embodied in the very ideal of socialism itself. Secondly, the construction of a socialised economy, particularly in a world where other countries remain capitalist, is likely to entail a range of economic difficulties which are neither previsaged nor desired by socialists.[6] Thirdly, *whatever* the means whereby a socialist society comes into being, the result will almost certainly contravene the objective which brought it into being, by creating a bureaucratic state.

There is still one additional sense in which scientific analysis can facilitate the pursuance of practical ends, but this is of a somewhat different order from those stated previously. This does not involve empirical study, but rather the assessment of the internal consistency of the relationship between the

[5] *MSS*, p. 52.
[6] On the latter point, see *ES*, vol. 1, pp. 65–8 & 100–7.

ideals which a person holds. It is very often the case that men are not clearly aware of the values implicated by the specific objectives which they strive for, and frequently they hold ends which are partially or even wholly incongruent with one another. If an individual has not ' thought through ' the ideals upon which his particular goals rest, we ' can assist him in becoming aware of the ultimate axioms which he unconsciously departs from, or which he must presuppose '.[7]

Further than this, however, we cannot go. The use of empirical science and logical analysis can show an individual what it is possible for him to accomplish, what the consequences of that accomplishment will be, and help to clarify the nature of his ideals; but science cannot, as such, show him what decision he should take.

No ethics in the world can dodge the fact that in numerous instances the attainment of ' good ' ends is bound to the fact that one must be willing to pay the price of using morally dubious means or at least dangerous ones – and facing the possibility or even the probability of evil ramifications. From no ethics in the world can it be concluded when and to what extent the ethically good purpose ' justifies ' the ethically dangerous means and ramifications.[8]

The logical consequence and the necessary support for this position which Weber adopts is that the human universe is characterised by the existence of *irreducibly competing ideals*. Since there is no single ideal or set of ideals which, at any point of history, can be shown by scientific analysis to be ' right ' or ' wrong ', there can be no universal ethics. This methodological standpoint finds its main empirical counterpart in Weber's writings in his sociology of religion, which traces the genesis of divergent ideals in history. But whereas ideals and meanings are created in religious and political struggles, they can never be derived from science itself:

The fate of an epoch which has eaten of the tree of knowledge is that it must know that we cannot learn the meaning of the world from the results of its analysis, be it ever so perfect; it must rather be in a position to create this meaning itself. It must recognise that general views of life and the universe can never be the products of increasing empirical knowledge, and that the highest ideals, which move us most forcefully, are always formed only in the struggle with other ideals which are just as sacred to others as ours are to us.[9]

Weber's analysis of politics, and of the logic of political motivation, is founded upon these considerations. Political conduct may be oriented within either an ' ethic of ultimate ends ' (*Gesinnungsethik*) or an ' ethic of responsibility ' (*Verantwortungsethik*).[10] The man who pursues an ethic of ultimate ends directs the whole of his political conduct towards the securing of an ideal, without regard to rational calculation of means:

You may demonstrate to a convinced syndicalist, believing in an ethic of ultimate ends, that his action will result in increasing the opportunities of reaction, in

---

[7] *MSS*, p. 54; *GAW*, p. 151.   [8] *FMW*, p. 121.
[9] *MSS*, p. 57; cf. also *FMW*, pp. 143–6.   [10] *FMW*, p. 120.

increasing the oppression of his class, and obstructing its ascent – and you will not make the slightest impression upon him. If an action of good intent leads to bad results, then, in the actor's eyes, not he but the world, or the stupidity of other men, or God's will who made them thus, is responsible for the evil.

Such conduct is finally ' religious ' in character, or at least shares with religious conduct its exemplary attributes: the individual whose action is directed towards an ethic of ultimate ends believes that his only duty is to ensure that the purity of his intentions is maintained: ' To rekindle the flame ever anew is the purpose of his quite irrational deeds. . .' [11]

The ethic of responsibility, on the other hand, involves consciousness of what Weber sometimes calls the ' paradox of consequences '. The actual consequences of an action on the part of an individual may often be quite different from, and sometimes even completely contrary to, his intentions in perpetrating that action. The political actor who is aware of this governs his actions not solely by the integrity of his motivation, but rather by the rational calculation of the probable consequences of his conduct for the goals which he wishes to obtain. The various uses of social science which have been specified above are thus of importance to the politics of responsibility, but are utterly irrelevant to the pursuit of an ethic of ultimate ends.[12] It is important to distinguish the pursuit of an ethic of responsibility from pragmatism, with which it has frequently been confused in secondary interpretations of Weber's thought. Pragmatism, as a philosophy, involves the identification of truth with what is practicable at any given moment. But Weber does not treat practicability as a criterion of ' truth '; the whole point of Weber's analysis is that there is an absolute logical gulf between factual and ethical truth, and that no amount of empirical knowledge can validate the pursuit of one ethic rather than the other.

It can, to be sure, be just as obligatory subjectively for the practical politician, in the individual case, to mediate between antagonistic points of view as to take sides with one of them. But this has nothing whatsoever to do with scientific ' objectivity '. *Scientifically the ' middle course ' is not truer even by a hair's breadth*, than the most extreme party ideals of the right or left.[13]

The substance of Weber's discussion of the nature of ' objectivity ' consists in the attempt to dispel the confusions which according to Weber, frequently obscure the logical relationships between scientific and value-judge-

---

[11] *FMW*, p. 121.

[12] Save in so far as logical analysis can assist in the clarification of ideals. But, as has been mentioned previously, this is not a result of empirical science *per se*.

[13] *MSS*, p. 57. It is worthwhile pointing out that each of the three figures treated in this book developed views which have at times been linked by critics to the philosophy of pragmatism. Durkheim felt the matter to be important enough to devote a whole course of lectures to the subject. cf. *Pragmatisme et sociologie* (Paris, 1955). To over-simplify somewhat, it could be said that all three would object to pragmatism for the same reason: that it denies the capacity of the acting subject to rationally effect change in the world.

ments. As has been mentioned before, for Weber this most definitely does not involve the elimination of ideals from scientific discussion. It is, in fact, incumbent upon the social scientist to attempt to be as clear as possible about his own ideals. If this obligation is rigorously observed, the result will not be a withdrawal of the values of the social scientist from relevance to his work: ' An *attitude of moral indifference (Gesinnungslosigkeit)* has no connection with *scientific* " objectivity ".' [14]

Judgements of fact and judgements of value

The absolute logical separation between factual and value-propositions – that is, that science cannot itself be a source of validated cultural ideals – must be distinguished from the sense in which the very existence of science pre-supposes the existence of values which define why scientific analysis is *itself* a ' desirable ' or a ' valuable ' activity. Science itself rests upon ideals which cannot, any more than any other values, be validated scientifically. Thus the principal objective of the social sciences, according to Weber, is ' the understanding of the characteristic uniqueness of the reality in which we move '. That is to say, the main goal of the social sciences is to comprehend why particular historical phenomena come to be as they are. But this presumes abstraction from the unending complexity of empirical reality. Weber accepts the neo-Kantianism of Rickert and Windelband in holding that there cannot conceivably be any complete scientific description of reality. Reality consists of an infinitely divisible profusion. Even if we should focus upon one particular element of reality, we find it partakes of this infinity. Any form of scientific analysis, any corpus of scientific knowledge whatsoever, whether in the natural or the social sciences, involves *selection* from the infinitude of reality.

Now, as has just been indicated, the social sciences are primarily interested in knowing ' on the one hand the relationships and the cultural significance of individual events in the contemporary manifestations and on the other the grounds of their being historically " so " and not " otherwise " '.[15] Since reality is extensively and intensively infinite, and since, therefore, some sort of selection of ' problems of interest ' to the social scientist is mandatory (whether or not this is consciously known to the individual concerned), we must ask what are the value-criteria which determine ' what we wish to know '. This question cannot be answered, according to Weber, simply by the assertion that what we should be searching for in the social sciences are regularly occurring relationships or ' laws ', such as exist in the natural sciences. The formulation of laws involves a special order of abstraction of the complexity of reality, such that every event which does not fall under those covered by the law is considered to be ' accidental ', and consequently

[14] *MSS*, p. 60; *GAW*, p. 157.
[15] *MSS*, p. 72; *GAW*, pp. 170–1.

scientifically unimportant. But this is plainly inadequate to comprehend the sorts of problems which occupy the centre of our interest in the social sciences. The main focus of Weber's own life's work can be quoted in illustration of this. The formation of western European capitalism, and the rationalism associated with it, is not of interest to us because (certain aspects of) these historical events can plausibly be subsumed under general, law-like principles; what makes these events of significance to us is their very uniqueness.

Moreover, it is mistaken to presume that the natural sciences are only interested in the discovery of laws. Astronomy, for example, is often concerned with particular sequences of development which are neither subsumable under laws, nor derive their interest from their relevance to the formulation of general relationships. Although Weber does not give this by way of illustration, a good instance of this is Rickert's example of the interest of astronomers in the detailed study of the origins of our solar system. In terms of generalisation about properties of the universe, our own solar system is utterly insignificant. Our own interest in its specific development derives from the fact that it is in this part of the heavens that the earth is situated.

This shows that the distinction between the natural and the social sciences is not an absolute one from the point of view of the differentiation between nomothetic and ideographic knowledge. While the main concentration of the natural sciences is upon the establishment of general principles, knowledge of the particular is also sometimes sought. Nor is it valid to consider that causal ' explanation ' is only possible through the classification of events under general laws. An event which is ' accidental ' from the point of view of a given law can equally well be traced back to its causal antecedents. But it must not be imagined that there is a single cause, or a definite restricted set of causes, which can yield a ' complete ' explanation of an historical individual. If it is the case that what is ' worth knowing ' only implicates certain aspects of reality, the same is true of causal explanation itself. The decision where to end an investigation, to pronounce that our understanding of a given phenomenon is adequate, is as much a matter of selection as the decision where to begin it:

the totality of all the conditions back to which the causal regression from the ' effect' leads had to ' act jointly ' in a definite way, and in no other for the concrete effect to be realised. In other words, the occurrence of the result is, for every causally working empirical science, determined not just from a certain moment but ' from eternity '.[16]

This does not mean, Weber stresses, that nomothetic propositions are not possible in the social sciences. But the formulation of general explanatory principles is not so much an end in itself as a means which may be used to facilitate the analysis of the particular phenomena which are to be explained:

[16] *MSS*, p. 187; *GAW*, p. 289.

' a *valid* imputation of any individual effect without the application of
" *nomological* " *knowledge* – i.e., the knowledge of recurrent causal
sequences – would in general be impossible '.[17] In other words, when the
researcher is attempting to impute causes, how far a given component is
designated as a cause will depend upon assumptions (which in cases of
doubt have to be justified) of valid relationships which pertain between
classes of events. How far the researcher can reach a valid causal imputation
' with his imagination sharpened by personal experience and trained in
analytic methods ', and how far he must seek the help of concretely established
generalisations, depends upon the particular case in question. But it is always
true that the more precise and certain our knowledge of relevant general
principles, the more certain the causal imputation we can make.[18]

But how, more concretely, do we establish the existence of a causal relationship? In his famous procedural illustration, Weber takes the example
of Eduard Meyer's treatment of the significance of the outcome of the battle
of Marathon for the subsequent development of western culture. The reason
why historians are interested in Marathon, which was in itself only quite a
small encounter, is precisely that its outcome had a decisive causal significance in the survival and independent development of Hellenic culture,
which later spread throughout Europe. In order, however, to show that the
battle of Marathon was causally significant in this way, we have to consider
two separate possible contingencies (Hellenism versus Persian theocratic influence over subsequent European cultural development). These are not, on-
tologically, ' real ' possibilities; only one set of events was ' possible ' – that
which really occurred. This procedure necessarily is one of abstraction by the
social scientist, involving the construction of a ' thought-experiment ', whereby he projects what would have happened if certain events either had not
taken place or had occurred in a different way.

The assessment of the causal significance of an historical fact will begin with the
posing of the following question: in the event of the exclusion of that fact from
the complex of factors which are taken into account as co-determinants, or in the
event of its modification in a certain direction, could the course of events, in ac-
cordance with general empirical rules (*Erfahrungsregeln*), have taken a direction
in any way different in any features which would be *decisive* for our interest? [19]

In the example of the importance of the battle of Marathon, this can be
shown: if a Persian victory is imagined, and its probable consequences
assessed, it is certainly the case that these would indeed have greatly influenced the subsequent development of Hellenic, and thence of European,
culture. Weber designates this as an example of ' adequate ' causation. We
can confidently state, in this case, that a different outcome of the battle of
Marathon would have been sufficient or ' adequate ' to produce changes in
subsequent European cultural development.

[17] *MSS*, p. 79.   [18] *MSS*, pp. 82ff.   [19] *MSS*, p. 180.

The fact that the selection and identification of the concerns of social science is necessarily 'subjective' – i.e., involves the selection of problems which are of interest because they have some definite cultural significance – does not, then, imply that objectively valid causal analysis cannot be made. On the contrary, causal explanation is verifiable by others, and is not 'valid' for any particular person only. But both the selection of issues for investigation, and the degree to which the researcher deems it necessary to penetrate into the infinite causal web, are governed by value suppositions. Given Weber's premise that the main focus of interest is in unique configurations, it follows that the subject-matter of the social sciences is ever in flux:

The stream of immeasurable events flows unendingly towards eternity. The cultural problems which move men form themselves ever anew and in different colours, and the boundaries of that area in the infinite stream of concrete events which acquires meaning and significance for us, i.e., which becomes an 'historical individual', are constantly subject to change.[20]

The formulation of ideal-type constructs

Weber's specification of the nature of 'ideal-type' concepts, and their usage in the social sciences, is logically rooted in this general epistemological standpoint. The concepts which are used in the social sciences cannot be derived directly from reality without the intrusion of value-presuppositions, since the very problems which define the objectives of interest are dependent upon such presuppositions. Thus the interpretation and explanation of an historical configuration demands the construction of concepts which are specifically delineated for that purpose and which, as in the case of the objectives of the analysis itself, do not reflect universally 'essential' properties of reality. In setting forth the formal characteristics of ideal-type concepts, Weber does not consider that he is establishing a new sort of conceptual method, but that he is making explicit what is already done in practice. However, since most researchers are not fully aware of the sort of concepts they are using, their formulations often tend to be ambiguous and imprecise. 'The language which the historian talks contains hundreds of words which are ambiguous constructs created to meet the unconsciously conceived need for adequate expression, and whose meaning is definitely felt, but not clearly thought out.'[21]

An ideal type is constructed by the abstraction and combination of an indefinite number of elements which, although found in reality, are rarely or never discovered in this specific form. Thus the characteristics of the 'Cal-

---

[20] *MSS*, p. 84. Weber frequently stresses the importance of distinguishing the two senses in which the social scientist may be interested in an 'historical individual': firstly, 'in acquiring the most comprehensive knowledge possible' of 'historically "great" and "unique" individuals', and, secondly, in analysing 'the significance to be attributed, in a concrete historical relationship, to the causal force of the actions of certain individuals – regardless of whether or not we would actually rate them as "significant" or "insignificant" individuals...', *GAW*, p. 47.

[21] *MSS*, pp. 92–3; *GAW*, p. 193.

vinist ethic' which Weber analyses in *The Protestant Ethic* are taken from
the writings of various historical figures, and involve those components of
Calvinist doctrines which Weber identifies as of particular importance in
relation to the formation of the capitalist spirit. Such an ideal type is
neither a ' description' of any definite aspect of reality, nor, according to
Weber, is it a hypothesis; but it can aid in both description and explanation.
An ideal type is not, of course, ideal in a normative sense : it does not carry
the connotation that its realisation is desirable. It is as legitimate to construct
an ideal type of murder or prostitution as of any other phenomenon. An ideal
type is a pure type in a logical and not an exemplary sense : ' In its conceptual
purity, this mental construct cannot be found empirically anywhere in
reality.' [22]

The creation of ideal types is in no sense an end in itself; the utility of a
given ideal type can be assessed only in relation to a concrete problem or
range of problems, and the only purpose of constructing it is to facilitate the
analysis of empirical questions. In formulating an ideal type of a phenomenon
such as of rational capitalism, then, the social scientist attempts to delineate,
through the empirical examination of specific forms of capitalism, the most
important respects (in relation to the concerns which he has set himself) in
which rational capitalism is distinctive. The ideal type is not formed out of a
nexus of purely conceptual thought, but is created, modified and sharpened
through the empirical analysis of concrete problems, and in turn increases the
precision of that analysis.

Ideal types are thus different in both scope and usage from descriptive concepts (*Gattungsbegriffe*). Descriptive types play an important and necessary
role in many branches of the social sciences. These simply summarise the
common features of groupings of empirical phenomena. Whereas an ideal
type involves ' the one-sided accentuation of one or more points of view ', the
descriptive type involves ' the abstract synthesis of those traits which are
common to numerous concrete phenomena '.[23] Weber gives the example of
the concepts of ' church ' and ' sect '. These may serve as the basis for a classificatory distinction; religious groups can be said to fall into one category or
the other. However, if we wish to apply the distinction in order to analyse the
importance of sectarian movements for the rationalisation of modern western
culture, we have to reformulate the concept of ' sect ' to emphasise the specific
components of sectarianism which have been influential in this particular
respect. The concept then becomes an ideal typical one. Any descriptive concept can be transformed into an ideal type through the abstraction and recom-
bination of certain elements : in practical terms, Weber says, this is what is
often done.

Weber concentrates his discussion upon the formulation of ideal types
which relate to the elucidation of specific historical configurations, since this

presents the clearest differentiation of descriptive and ideal types. But ideal type concepts are not solely limited to this objective, and there are various kinds of ideal types which, without being simple descriptive concepts, nevertheless are generic in character. The transition from descriptive to ideal types takes place when we move from descriptive classification of phenomena towards the explanatory or theoretical analysis of those phenomena. This can be illustrated by reference to the notion of 'exchange'. This is a descriptive concept in so far as we are simply content to observe that an indefinite number of human actions may be classified as exchange transactions. But if we attempt to make the notion an element in marginal utility theory in economics, we construct an ideal type of 'exchange' which is based upon a purely rational construct.[24]

The relationship between social science and value-judgements is central to Weber's discussion in the methodological essays published in 1904–5; this relationship is treated from a different aspect in Weber's essay on 'ethical neutrality' (*Wertfreiheit*), written a decade later.[25] In this latter essay, Weber deals with a question which, while of basic importance to the relationship between social science and social policy, concerns not the logical status of value-judgements, but the practical issue of whether the scientist should use his academic prestige or position to propagate ideals which he holds. This is itself a question which ultimately depends upon values, and consequently cannot be resolved by scientific demonstration. It is an issue which 'must in the last analysis, be decided only with reference to those tasks which the individual, according to his own value system, assigns to the universities'.[26] If the tasks of education be conceived in an extremely broad sense, so that it is the role of the educator to introduce his students to a wide spectrum of aesthetic and ethical culture, then it would be difficult for the teacher to remove his own ideals from the sphere of his instruction. The view which Weber expresses is that professional specialisation in education, especially in subjects which have some degree of scientific pretension, is the proper organisation of the modern university. In these circumstances, there is no warrant for allowing the teacher to express his own world-view; the problems of the social sciences, while they derive their interest as 'problems' from cultural values, cannot be solved except by technical analysis, and it is this latter which it is the sole responsibility of the teacher to disseminate from the lecture-platform.

However, what the student should, above all, learn from his teacher in the lecture-hall today is: (1) the capacity to fulfill a given task in a workmanlike fashion;

[24] For analyses of the logical status of 'individual' as opposed to 'generic' ideal types, cf. von Schelting, pp. 329ff; and Parsons, pp. 601ff.

[25] *MSS*, pp. 1–47. For an analysis of the political context against which Weber developed these views, cf. Wolfgang J. Mommsen: *Max Weber und die deutsche Politik, 1890–1920* (Tübingen, 1959).

[26] *MSS*, pp. 2–3.

(2) definitely to recognise facts, even those which may be personally uncomfortable, and to distinguish them from his own evaluations; (3) to subordinate himself to his task and to repress the impulse to make an unnecessary spectacle of personal tastes or other sentiments.[27]

The teacher in the university has all the opportunities which any other citizen has for the furtherance of his ideals through political action, and should not demand further privileges of his own. The professorial chair is not a 'specialised qualification for personal prophecy'. A professor who attempts to use his position in such a way is able to exploit his standing, moreover, in relation to an audience which is particularly receptive and lacking in mature self-confidence. In taking this position, Weber expresses a personal conviction. If the university were to be made a forum where values were discussed, this could only be on the basis of 'the most unrestrained freedom of discussion of fundamental questions from all value-positions'. But this does not at all pertain in the German universities, where basic political and ethical issues cannot be openly discussed; and as long as this is so, 'it seems to me to be only in accord with the dignity of a representative of science *to be silent* as well about such value-problems as he is allowed to treat'.[28] In saying this Weber does not, of course, mean that the university teacher should refuse to express political and moral judgements outside the sphere of the university itself. On the contrary, Weber scathingly dismisses the false invoking of 'ethical neutrality' outside the academic sphere. It is as illegitimate, in Weber's view, for a man to cloak his value-assertions in the field of politics with a spurious scientific 'neutrality', as it is for him to openly preach a partisan position within the university.

In any case it is essential to recognise, according to Weber, that the question of whether an individual should advance a specific value-position in his teaching should be recognised as separate from the logical relationship of factual and value-propositions in the social sciences. 'The problems of the empirical disciplines are, of course, to be solved " non-evaluatively ". They are not problems of evaluation. But the problems of the social sciences are selected by the value-relevance of the phenomena treated... In empirical investigation, no " practical evaluations " are legitimated by this strictly logical fact.'[29]

---

[27] *MSS*, p. 5; *GAW*, p. 493.
[28] *MSS*, p. 8.
[29] *MSS*, pp. 21–2.

11. Fundamental concepts of sociology

Interpretative sociology

Weber's methodological essays were mostly written within the context of the specific problems which occupied him in his early empirical works; they document a struggle to break out of the intellectual confines of the traditions of legal, economic and historical thought within which he was originally trained. In the methodological essays, sociology is treated as subordinate to history: the main problems of interest in the social sciences are deemed to be those concerned with questions possessing definite cultural significance. Weber rejects the view that generalisation is impossible in the social sciences, but treats the formulation of general principles mainly as a means to an end.

The very direction in which Weber's own empirical writings led, especially as manifest in the massive *Economy and Society*, caused a certain change in emphasis in this standpoint. Weber did not relinquish his fundamental stand upon the absolute logical disjunction between factual and value-judgements, nor the correlate thesis that the analysis of unique historical configurations cannot be carried through solely in terms of general principles, these latter being only of prefatory significance to such a task. In *Economy and Society*, however, the focus of Weber's interest moves more towards a direct concern with the establishment of uniformities of social and economic organisation: that is, towards sociology.

Sociology, Weber says, is concerned with the formulation of general principles and generic type concepts in relation to human social action; history, by contrast, ' is directed towards the causal analysis and explanation of particular, culturally significant, actions, structures, and personalities '.[1] This, of course, reiterates the basic position established in the methodological essays, and it may be said that in general the shift in Weber's concerns in the direction of sociology is a change of emphasis in his own personal interests rather than a modification of his basic methodological views. The degree to which *Economy and Society* represents a new departure in Weber's thinking has often been exaggerated in secondary accounts of Weber's thought. *Economy and Society* forms part of a large-scale collaborative work on different aspects of political economy: Weber intends his own contribution to provide a preface to the more specialised volumes written by his collaborating authors.[2]

---

[1] *ES*, vol. 1, p. 19; *WuG*, vol. 1, p. 9.
[2] The collection of volumes as a whole is entitled *Grundriss der Sozialökonomik*. Authors include Sombart, Michels, Alfred Weber, and Schumpeter. The first contributions were published in 1914, and others appeared up until 1930, when the

In describing his objectives in writing *Economy and Society* Weber indicates that the sociological analysis contained in it performs a task of ' very modest preparation ' which is necessary to the study of specific historical phenomena. ' It is then the concern of history to give a causal explanation of these particular characteristics.' [3]

In his essay on ' objectivity ', Weber emphasises that ' in the social sciences we are concerned with mental phenomena the empathic " understanding " of which is naturally a task of a specifically different type from those which the schemes of the exact natural sciences in general can or seek to solve '.[4] One of the main steps to the analysis of social phenomena, therefore, is that of ' rendering intelligible ' the subjective basis upon which it rests; a principal theme of the essay, of course, is that the possibility of the ' objective ' analysis of social and historical phenomena is not precluded by the fact that human activity has a ' subjective ' character. On the other hand, this subjectivity cannot simply be eschewed from consideration by conflating natural and social science. In outlining his conception of ' interpretative sociology ' in *Economy and Society*, Weber preserves this stress upon the significance of the subjective for sociological analysis.[5]

' In the sense in which this highly ambiguous word is used here ', Weber says, sociology ' shall be taken to refer to a science concerning itself with the interpretive understanding of social action and thereby with a causal explanation of its course and consequences '.[6] Social action or conduct (*soziales Handeln*) is that in which the subjective meaning involved relates to another individual or group. There are two senses in which the meaning of action may be analysed: either in reference to the concrete meaning which action has for a given individual actor, or in relation to an ideal type of subjective meaning on the part of a hypothetical actor.

There is no clear-cut separation in reality between action thus defined, and behaviour which is purely unthinking or automatic. Large sectors of human activity which are important for sociological purposes lie on the margins of meaningful action: this is especially true of behaviour of a traditional kind. Moreover, the same empirical activity may involve a fusion of understandable and non-understandable elements. This may be the case, for instance, in some forms of religious activity, which may involve mystical experiences which

---

collection was terminated. See Johannes Winckelmann: ' Max Webers Opus Post-humum ', *Zeitschrift für die gesamten Staatswissenschaften*, vol. 105, 1949, pp. 368–87.

[3] Letter to Georg von Below, June 1914, quoted in von Below: *Der deutsche Staat des Mittelalters* (Leipzig, 1925), p. xxiv.

[4] *MSS*, p. 74; *GAW*, p. 173.

[5] The account presented in the first volume of *ES* is a revised version of an earlier essay ' Über einige Kategorien der verstehenden Soziologie ', *GAW*, pp. 427–74 (originally published in 1913).

[6] *ES*, vol. 1, p. 4; *WuG*, vol. 1, p. 1. cf. Julien Freund: *The Sociology of Max Weber* (London, 1968), pp. 90–1.

are only partially understandable to a social scientist who has not experienced them. The full recapitulation of an experience is, of course, not necessary to this task of rendering it analytically intelligible: ' " one need not have been Caesar in order to understand Caesar " '.[7]

It is important to capture the main drift of Weber's argument here. While he accepts that subjective meaning is a basic component of much human conduct, Weber's point is that intuitionism is not the only doctrine which can offer the possibility of studying this; on the contrary, interpretative sociology can and must be based upon techniques of the interpretation of meaning which are replicable, and thus are verifiable according to the conventional canons of scientific method. This can be accomplished, according to Weber, either by rational understanding of logical relationships which form part of the subjective framework of the actor, or by understanding of a more emotive–sympathetic kind. Rational understanding is most complete and precise in the instance of the use by the actor of mathematical reasoning or formal logic. ' We have a perfectly clear understanding of what it means when somebody employs the proposition $2 \times 2 = 4$ or the Pythagorean theorem in reasoning or argument, or when someone correctly carries out a logical train of reasoning according to our accepted modes of thinking.' [8] But there is no absolutely clear line between the comprehension of propositions of logic in this strict sense, and the manner in which we understand the actions of a man who rationally selects and employs a given means to reach a practical end. While empathy is an important means of obtaining understanding of action which takes place in an emotive context, it is mistaken to identify empathy, and understanding: the latter demands not merely a sentiment of emotional sympathy on the part of the sociologist, but the grasping of the subjective intelligibility of action. In general, however, it is true that the more the ideals towards which human activity is directed are foreign to those which govern our own conduct, the harder it is to understand the meaning they have for those who hold them. We must accept, in these circumstances, that only partial comprehension is possible, and when even this cannot be attained, we have to be content to treat them as ' given data '.

Sociology, must of course, take account of objects and events which influence human activity, but which are devoid of subjective meaning. These phenomena (which include, for example, climatic, geographical and biological factors) are ' conditions ' of human behaviour, but do not necessarily have any relationship to any human purpose. But in so far as such phenomena do become involved with human subjective ends, they take on meaning, and become elements within social action. An artifact such as a machine ' can be understood only in terms of the meaning (*Sinn*) which its production and use have had or were intended to have. . .'.[9]

[7] *ES*, vol. 1, p. 5. Carlo Antoni: *From History to Sociology* (London, 1962), p. 170.
[8] *ES*, vol. 1, p. 5.   [9] *ES*, vol. 1, p. 7; *WuG*, vol. 1, p. 3.

The scientific analysis of social action, in so far as it proceeds beyond mere description, proceeds through the construction of ideal types: and, given the difficulties involved in the understanding of many forms of value-directed or emotively influenced action, it is normally useful to construct rational types. Having specified in the ideal type what constitutes rational action, deviation from it can be examined in terms of the influence of irrational elements. The main advantage of rational ideal types has already been demonstrated, Weber considers, in economics: they are precise in formulation and unambiguous in application. Weber emphasises this as a procedural point; it is a methodological device the use of which does not in any sense imply the existence of a 'rationalist bias'.

Weber distinguishes two basic kinds of interpretative grasp of meaning, each of which may be subdivided according to whether it involves the understanding of rational or of emotive actions. The first kind is 'direct understanding'. In this case, we understand the meaning of an action through direct observation: the rational subdivision of direct understanding can be illustrated by the example quoted previously, of the comprehension of a mathematical proposition. We understand the meaning of the sum $2 \times 2 = 4$ at once if we hear it spoken, or see it written. Direct understanding of irrational conduct, on the other hand, is shown, for example, where we 'understand an outbreak of anger as manifested by facial expression, exclamations or irrational emotional reactions'. The second kind of understanding, 'explanatory understanding' (*erklärendes Verstehen*) differs from this in that it involves the elucidation of an intervening motivational link between the observed activity and its meaning to the actor. Here there are similarly two subsidiary forms. The rational form consists in the understanding of action where an individual is engaged in an activity which involves the use of a given means to realise a particular purpose. Thus, in the example which Weber adduces, if an observer sees a man chopping wood, and knows that he wishes to get some fuel in to light his fire, he is able without difficulty to grasp the rational content of the other's action. The same sort of indirect process of motivational inference can be made in relation to irrational conduct. So, for instance, we are able to understand, in this sense, the response of a person who bursts into tears if we know that he has just suffered a bitter disappointment.

In explanatory understanding, the particular action concerned is 'placed in an understandable sequence of motivation, the understanding of which can be treated as an explanation of the actual course of behaviour. Thus for a science which is concerned with the subjective meaning of action, explanation requires a grasp of the complex of meaning (*Sinnzusammenhang*) in which an actual course of understandable action thus interpreted belongs.' [10] This is extremely important in Weber's conception of the application of interpretative

---

[10] *ES*, vol. 1, p. 9. For an analysis of the theoretical significance of this, see Parsons, pp. 635ff.

sociology to empirical analysis. The understanding of 'motivation' always involves relating the particular conduct concerned to a broader normative standard with reference to which the individual acts. In order to reach the level of causal explanation, a distinction has to be made between 'subjective' and 'causal' adequacy. The interpretation of a given course of action is subjectively adequate (adequate 'on the level of meaning') if the motivation which is attributed to it accords with recognised or habitual normative patterns. This entails showing, in other words, that the action concerned is meaningful in that it 'makes sense' in terms of accepted norms. But this is not enough, in itself, to provide a viable explanation of the particular action. Indeed, it is the basic fallacy of idealist philosophy to identify subjective adequacy with causal adequacy. The essential flaw in this view is that there is no direct and simple relationship between 'complexes of meaning', motives, and conduct. Similar actions on the part of several individuals may be the result of a diversity of motives and, conversely, similar motives can be linked to different concrete forms of behaviour. Weber does not attempt to deny the complex character of human motivation. Men often experience conflicts of motives; and those motives of which a man is consciously aware may be largely rationalisations of deeper motives of which he is unconscious. The sociologist must be cognisant of these possibilities, and ready to deal with them on an empirical level – although, of course, the more it is the case that an activity is the result of impulses that are not accessible to consciousness, the more this becomes a marginal phenomenon for the interpretation of meaning.

For these reasons, 'causal' adequacy demands that it should be possible 'to determine that there is a probability, which in the rare ideal case can be numerically stated, but is always in some sense calculable, that a given observable event (overt or subjective) will be followed or accompanied by another event '.[11] Thus, in order to demonstrate explanatory significance, there must be an established empirical generalisation which relates the subjective meaning of the act to a specified range of determinable consequences. It follows from the intrinsic suppositions of Weber's method, of course, that if any such generalisation, however precisely verified, lacks adequacy on the level of meaning, then it remains a statistical correlation outside the scope of interpretative sociology:

Only those statistical regularities are thus sociological generalisations which correspond to an understandable common meaning of a course of social action, and constitute understandable types of action, in the sense of the term used here. Only those rational formulations of subjectively understandable action which can at least with some degree of closeness be observed in reality, constitute socio-

---

[11] *ES*, vol. 1, pp. 11–12. Given this condition, as Weber makes clear in his critique of Roscher and Knies, 'The "interpretative" motive-research of the historian is causal attribution in exactly the same sense as the causal interpretation of any individual process in nature...'. *GAW*, p. 134.

logical types relating to real events. It is by no means the case that the actual likelihood of the occurrence of a given course of overt action is always proportional to the clarity of subjective interpretation.[12]

There are many sorts of statistical data which, while they may relate to phenomena which conceivably influence human behaviour, are not meaningful in Weber's sense of that term. But meaningful action is not refractory to statistical treatment: sociological statistics in this sense include, for example, crime rates or statistics of the distribution of occupations.

Weber does not limit the range of information which is of value in the study of human social conduct to that which can be analysed according to the method of interpretative sociology. There are many sorts of processes and influences which have causal relevance for social life which are not ' understandable ', but the importance of which Weber by no means discounts. It is essential to stress this, since it has become commonplace to suppose that, according to Weber, interpretative sociology is the sole basis of generalisation in relation to human social conduct. Weber is conscious that his own limitation of the term ' sociology ' to the analysis of subjectively meaningful action cross-cuts other conceptions of the range of the field which are often applied: ' sociology in our sense . . . is restricted to " interpretative sociology " (*verstehende Soziologie*) – a usage which no-one else should or can be compelled to follow.' [13]

Weber's specific reference to organicist sociology, such as represented by Schäffle's *Bau und Leben des Socialen Körpers* – which Weber calls a ' brilliant work ' – is of relevance here. Functionalism, Weber notes, has a definite utility in approaching the study of social life: as a means of ' practical illustration and for provisional orientation . . . it is not only useful but indispensable '.[14] Just as in the case of the study of organic systems, in the social sciences functional analysis allows us to identify which units within the ' whole ' [society] it is important to study. But at a certain point the analogy between society and organism breaks down, in that in the analysis of the former it is possible, and also necessary, to go beyond the establishment of functional uniformities. Rather than being a barrier to scientific knowledge, however, the achievement of interpretative understanding should be regarded as offering explanatory possibilities which are unavailable in the natural sciences. This does not come wholly without cost though: it is paid for by the lower level of precision and certainty of findings characteristic of the social sciences.

Where Weber does differ sharply with Schäffle is on the issue of the logical status of holistic concepts. Those sociologists who take their point of departure from the ' whole ' and from thence approach the analysis of individual

---

[12] *ES*, vol. 1, p. 12; *WuG*, vol. 1, p. 6.
[13] *ES*, vol. 1, pp. 12–13; *WuG*, vol. 1, p. 6.
[14] *ES*, vol. 1, p. 15.

behaviour are easily lured into the hypostatisation of concepts. Thus 'society', which is never more than the multitudinous interactions of individuals in particular milieux, takes on a reified identity of its own, as if it were an acting unit which has its own peculiar consciousness. Weber admits, of course, that it is necessary in the social sciences to use concepts which refer to collectivities, such as states, industrial firms, etc. But it must not be forgotten that these collectives are 'solely the resultants and modes of organisation of the specific acts of *individual* men, since these alone are for us the agents who carry out subjectively understandable action'.[15] There is another respect, however, in which such collective agencies are of vital importance in interpretative sociology: this is, that they form realities from the subjective standpoint of individual actors, and are frequently represented by them as autonomous unities. Such representations may play an important causal role in influencing social conduct.

Interpretative sociology, according to Weber, does not involve the connotation that social phenomena can be explained reductively in psychological terms.[16] The findings of psychology are certainly relevant to all the social sciences, but no more so than those of those of other borderline disciplines. The sociologist is not interested in the psychological make-up of the individual *per se*, but in the interpretative analysis of social action. Weber rejects unequivocally the notion that social institutions can be 'derived', in an explanatory sense, from psychological generalisations. Since human life is primarily shaped by socio-cultural influences, it is in fact more likely that sociology has more to contribute to psychology than *vice versa*:

the procedure does not begin with the analysis of psychological qualities, moving then to the analysis of social institutions... on the contrary, insight into the psychological preconditions and consequences of institutions presupposes a precise knowledge of the latter and the scientific analysis of their structure... We will not however deduce the institutions from psychological laws or explain them by elementary psychological phenomena.[17]

Social relationships and the orientation of social conduct

Social action covers any sort of human conduct which is meaningfully 'oriented to the past, present, or expected future behaviour of others'.[18] A social 'relationship' exists whenever there is reciprocity on the part of two or more individuals, each of whom relates his action to acts (or anticipated acts) of the other. This does *not* necessarily imply, however, that the meanings involved in the relationship are shared: in many cases, such as in a 'love' relationship which conforms to the proverb *il y a un qui aime et un qui se*

---

[15] *ES*, vol. 1, p. 13; *WuG*, vol. 1, p. 6. For an extensive critical consideration of this and other points in Weber's outline of interpretative sociology, see Alfred Schutz: *The Phenomenology of the Social World* (Evanston, 1967).

[16] *ES*, vol. 1, p. 19.

[17] *MSS*, pp. 88-9.

[18] *ES*, vol. 1, p. 22.

laisse aimer, the attitudes held by one party are not at all the same as those held by the other. Nevertheless in such relationships, if they are continued over time, there are mutually complementary meanings which define for each individual what is 'expected' of him. Following Simmel, Weber speaks of *Vergesellschaftung*, which carries the sense of the formation of relationships and means literally 'societalisation', rather than of *Gesellschaft* (society). Many of the relationships of which social life is compounded are of a transitory character, and are constantly in the process of formation and dissolution. Nor, of course, is it implied that the existence of a social relationship presupposes co-operation between those involved. As Weber is careful to point out, conflict is a characteristic of even the most permanent of relationships.

Not all types of contact between individuals constitute, in Weber's terms, a social relationship. If two men walking along the street collide with each other without having noticed the other prior to the collision, their interaction is not a case of social action: it would become so if they should subsequently argue over who was to blame for the mishap. Weber also mentions the case of interaction in crowds: if Le Bon is correct, membership of a crowd group can give rise to collective moods which are stimulated by subconscious influences over which the individual has little control. Here the behaviour of the individual is causally influenced by that of others, but this is not action which is oriented to others on the level of meaning, and hence is not 'social action' in Weber's terminology.

Weber distinguishes four types of orientation of social conduct. In 'purposively rational' conduct, the individual rationally assesses the probable results of a given act in terms of the calculation of means to an end. In securing a given objective, a number of alternative means of reaching that end usually exist. The individual faced with these alternatives weighs the relative effectiveness of each of the possible means of attaining the end, and the consequences of securing it for other goals which the individual holds. Here Weber applies the schema, already formulated with regard to the rational application of social scientific knowledge, to the paradigm of social action in general. 'Value rational' action, by contrast, is directed towards an overriding ideal, and takes no account of any other considerations as relevant. 'The Christian does rightly and leaves the results to the Lord.'[19] This is nonetheless rational action, because it involves the setting of coherent objectives to which the individual channels his activity. All actions which are solely directed to overriding ideals of duty, honour, or devotion to a 'cause', approximate to this type. A primary distinction between a value rational action and the third type, which is 'affective' action, is that, whereas the former presupposes that the individual holds a clearly defined ideal which dominates his activity, in the latter case this characteristic is absent. Affective

[19] *FMW*, p. 120.

action is that which is carried out under the sway of some sort of emotive state, and as such is on the borderline of meaningful and non-meaningful conduct. It shares with value rational action the characteristic that the meaning of the action is not located, as in purposively rational conduct, in the instrumentality of means to ends, but in carrying out the act for its own sake.

The fourth type of orientation of action, ' traditional ' action, also overlaps the margins of meaningful and non-meaningful conduct. Traditional action is carried out under the influence of custom and habit. This applies to the ' great bulk of all everyday action to which people have become habitually accustomed. . .'.[20] In this type, the meaning of action is derived from ideals or symbols which do not have the coherent, defined form of those which are pursued in value rationality. In so far as traditional values become rationalised, traditional action merges with value rational action.

This fourfold typology which Weber delineates underlies the empirical substance of *Economy and Society*, but it is not intended as an overall classification of social action; it is an ideal typical schema which provides a mode of applying Weber's stated dictum that the analysis of social action can best be pursued through the use of rational types against which irrational deviations can be measured. Thus a particular empirical instance of human conduct can be interpreted according to which of the four types of action it most closely approximates. But very few empirical cases will not in fact include, in varying combinations, a mixture of elements from more than one type.

In his discussion of the difficulties posed by the problem of verification in interpretative sociology, Weber stresses that causal adequacy always is a matter of degrees of probability. Those who have argued that human behaviour is ' unpredictable ' are demonstrably mistaken: ' the characteristic of " incalculability " . . . is the privilege of – the insane '.[21] But the uniformities which are found in human conduct are expressible only in terms of the probability that a particular act or circumstance will produce a given response from an actor. Every social relationship thus may be said to rest upon the ' probability ' (which must not be confused with ' chance ' in the sense of ' accident ') that an actor or plurality of actors will direct their action in a specified manner. To affirm the element of contingency in human conduct, in Weber's view, is not to deny its regularity and predictability; but it is to emphasise once again the contrast between meaningful conduct and the invariant response characteristic of, for example, a subconsciously mediated withdrawal reaction to a painful stimulus.

In setting out a conceptual taxonomy of the principal types of social relationship and more inclusive forms of social organisation, Weber thus couches his description in terms of probability. Every social relationship

---

[20] *ES*, vol. 1, p. 25.
[21] *MSS*, p. 124. See also *GAW*, pp. 65ff, where Weber discusses in detail the relationship between ' irrationality ', ' unpredictability ' and ' freedom of will '.

which is of a durable character presupposes uniformities of conduct which, at the most basic level, consist in what Weber calls 'usage' (*Brauch*) and 'custom' (*Sitte*). A uniformity in social action is a usage 'in so far as the probability of its existence within a group is based on nothing but actual practice'.[22] A custom is simply a usage which is long established. A usage or custom is any form of 'usual' conduct which, while it is neither expressly approved or disapproved of by others, is habitually followed by an individual or number of individuals. Conformity to it is not backed by any kind of sanctions, but is a matter of the voluntary accord of the actor. 'Today it is customary every morning to eat a breakfast which, within limits, conforms to a certain pattern. But there is no obligation to do so (except in the case of hotel guests); and it was not always a custom.'[23] The social importance of usage and custom must not be under-estimated. Consumption habits, for example, which are usually customary, have great economic significance. Uniformity of conduct founded upon usage or custom contrasts with that associated with the ideal type of rational action where individuals, subjectively pursue their own self-interest. The attitude of the capitalist entrepreneur in a free market is the prototypical case of this.[24] Where uniformity of conduct is adhered to from motives of self-interest – in other words, approximates to this type – a social relationship is usually much more unstable than one resting upon custom.

Legitimacy, domination, and authority

The most stable forms of social relationship are those in which the subjective attitudes of the participating individuals are directed towards the belief in a *legitimate order*. In order to illustrate the distinctions at issue here, Weber gives the following examples:

If furniture movers regularly advertise at the time many leases expire, this uniformity is determined by self-interest. If a salesman visits certain customers on particular days of the month or the week, it is either a case of customary behaviour or a product of self-interested orientation. However, when a civil servant appears in his office daily at a fixed time, he does not act only on the basis of custom or self-interest which he could disregard if he wanted to ; as a rule, his action is also determined by the validity of an order (viz., the civil service rules), which he fulfils partly because disobedience would be disadvantageous to him but also because its violation would be abhorrent to his sense of duty (of course, in varying degrees).[25]

Action may be guided by the belief in a legitimate order in other ways than through adherence to the tenets of that order. Such is the case with a criminal,

---

[22] *ES*, vol. 1, p. 29.   [23] *ES*, vol. 1, p. 29; *WuG*, vol. 1, p. 15.
[24] It might be pointed out that Weber here is speaking of empirical cases which approximate to purposively rational action. This is not, therefore, the equivalent of Durkheim's 'egoism', since in Weber's instance the subjective pursuit of self-interest is 'oriented towards identical expectations' (*ES*, vol. 1, pp. 29–30).
[25] *ES*, vol. 1, p. 31.

who, while violating laws, recognises and adapts his conduct to their existence by the very measures he takes to plan his criminal activity. In this instance, his actions are governed by the fact that violation of the legal order is punished, and he wishes to avoid the punishment. But his acceptance of the validity of the order purely as a ' fact ' is only at one extreme of many sorts of violations in which individuals make some attempt to claim legitimate justification for their acts. Moreover, it is extremely important to note that the same legitimate order may be interpreted in differing ways. This is something which can be readily illustrated from Weber's empirical analyses of the sociology of religion: thus the Protestantism of the Reformation was a radicalisation of the very same Christian order as was claimed by the Catholic church as the basis of its legitimacy.

There is no clear empirical line between usage and custom, and what Weber calls ' convention '. Conformity is not, in this case, a matter of the voluntary disposition of the individual. If, for example, a member of a high-ranking status group departs from the conventions governing appropriate standards of politeness, the probability is that he will be ridiculed or ostracised by the rest of the group. The mobilisation of such sanctions is often an extremely powerful mode of securing compliance to an established order. ' Law ' exists where a convention is backed, not simply by diffuse informal sanctions, but by an individual, or more usually a group, who has the legitimate capacity and duty to apply sanctions against transgressors.[26] The law-enforcement agency need not necessarily involve the sort of specialised professional body of judiciary and police found in modern societies; in the blood feud, for example, the clan group fulfils an equivalent task as a sanctioning agency. The empirical relationship between custom, convention and law is an intimate one. Even the hold of sheer usage may be very strong. Those who frame laws to cover conduct which was formerly merely ' usual ' frequently discover that very little additional conformity to the prescription in question is attained. However, usage and custom do in most cases provide the origin of rules which become laws. The reverse also occurs, although less frequently: the introduction of a new law may eventuate in new modes of habitual conduct. Such a consequence may be direct or indirect. Thus one indirect consequence of the laws which allow the free formation of contracts, for example, is that salesmen spend much of their time travelling to solicit and maintain orders from buyers; this is not enforced by the laws of contract, but nevertheless is conditional upon their existence.

Weber does not hold that we can only speak of the existence of ' law ' where the coercive apparatus involved is a political agency. A legal order

---

[26] Weber distinguishes at one point between ' guaranteed ' law and ' indirectly guaranteed ' law. The first type is backed directly by a coercive apparatus. The second type refers to the case of a norm the transgression of which is not legally punished, but has the consequence of infringing other norms which are guaranteed laws. But Weber normally uses ' law ' without qualification to denote guaranteed law.

exists in any circumstance in which a group – such as a kinship group or a religious body – assumes the task of applying sanctions to punish transgressions. In fact, the influence of religious groups upon the rationalisation of law is a main theme in Weber's empirical writings. In more general terms, the inter-relationships between the ' legal ', ' religious ' and ' political ' are of decisive significance to economic structures and economic development. Weber defines a ' political ' society as one whose ' existence and order is continuously safeguarded within a given territorial area by the threat and application of physical force on the part of the administrative staff '. This does not imply, of course, that political organisations exist only through the continual use of force, merely that the threat or actual employment of force is used as an ultimate sanction, which may be utilised when all else fails. A political organisation becomes a ' state ' where it is able successfully to exercise a legitimate monopoly over the organised use of force within a given territory.[27]

Weber defines ' power ' (*Macht*) as the probability that an actor will be able to realise his own objectives even against opposition from others with whom he is in a social relationship. This definition is very broad indeed: in this sense, every sort of social relationship is, to some degree and in certain circumstances, a power relationship. The concept of ' domination ' (*Herrschaft*) is more specific: it refers only to those cases of the exercise of power where an actor obeys a specific command issued by another.[28] Acceptance of domination may rest upon quite different motives, ranging from sheer habit to the cynical promotion of self-advantage. The possibility of obtaining material rewards and of securing social esteem, however, are two of the most pervasive forms of tie binding leader and follower.[29] But no stable system of domination is based purely upon either automatic habituation or upon the appeal to self-interest: the main prop is belief by subordinates in the legitimacy of their subordination.

Weber distinguishes three ideal types of legitimacy upon which a relationship of domination may rest: traditional, charismatic, and legal. Traditional authority is based upon the belief in the ' sanctity of age-old rules and powers '.[30] In the most elementary kinds of traditional domination, those who rule have no specialised administrative staff through which they exercise their authority. In many small rural communities, authority is held by the village elders: those who are oldest are considered to be most steeped in traditional wisdom and thereby qualified to hold authority. A second form of traditional

---

[27] Compare Durkheim's divergent conceptualisation, above, p. 100. Neither the possession of a fixed territory nor the capability of applying force appears in Durkheim's definition.

[28] For a summary of issues relevant to the terminological debate over whether *Herrschaft* should be translated as ' domination ' or ' authority ', see Roth's annotation in *ES*, vol. 1, pp. 61–2 (note 31). I have used the term ' domination ' as broader in denotation than ' authority ' (*legitime Herrschaft*).

[29] *FMW*, pp. 80–1.

[30] *ES*, vol. 1, p. 226.

domination, which in fact often exists in combination with gerontocracy, is patriarchalism. In this form, which is normally based upon a household unit, the head of the family possesses authority which is transmitted from generation to generation by definite rules of inheritance. Where an administrative staff exists, subordinated by ties of personal allegiance to a master, patrimonialism develops.

Patrimonialism is the characteristic form of domination in the traditional despotic governments of the Orient, as well as in the Near East and in mediaeval Europe. In contrast to the less complex patriarchal form, patrimonialism is marked by a clear distinction between ruler and 'subjects': in simple patriarchalism 'domination, even though it is an inherent traditional right of the master, must definitely be exercised as a joint right in the interest of all members and is thus not freely appropriated by the incumbent'.[31] Patrimonial authority is rooted in the household administration of the ruler; the intermingling of courtly life and governmental functions is its distinctive feature, and officials are first recruited from the personal retainers or servants of the ruler. Where patrimonial domination is exerted over large territories, however, a broader basis of recruitment is necessary, and frequently a tendency towards decentralisation of administration develops, providing a basis for a variety of tensions and conflicts between ruler and local patrimonial officials or ' notables '.

While in historical reality numerous mixtures of types are possible and have existed, the pure type of traditional organisation offers a contrast with the ideal type of rational bureaucracy, which is founded upon legal domination. In traditional organisations, the tasks of members are ambiguously defined, and privileges and duties are subject to modification according to the inclination of the ruler; recruitment is made on the basis of personal affiliation; and there is no rational process of ' law-making ': any innovations in administrative rules have to be made to appear to be rediscoveries of ' given ' truths.

Weber sets out the pure type of legal authority as follows.[32] In this type, an individual who holds authority does so in virtue of impersonal norms which are not the residue of tradition, but which have been consciously established within a context of either purposive or value rationality. Those who are subject to authority obey their superordinate, not because of any personal dependence on him, but because of their acceptance of the impersonal norms which define that authority; ' thus the typical person holding legal authority, the " superior ", is himself subject to an impersonal order, and orients his actions to it in his own dispositions and commands '.[33] Those subject to legal authority

---

[31] *ES*, vol. 1, p. 231. I have also used here Weber's earlier account of patrimonialism in *ES*, vol. 3, pp. 1006–10.
[32] Weber's alternative exposition is to be found in *ES*, vol. 3, pp. 956–1005; the later version is in vol. 1, pp. 217–26.
[33] *ES*, vol. 1, p. 217; *WuG*, vol. 1, p. 125.

owe no personal allegiance to a superordinate, and follow his commands only within the restricted sphere in which his jurisdiction is clearly specified.

The pure type of bureaucratic organisation shows the following characteristics. The activities of the administrative staff are carried out on a regular basis, and thus constitute well-defined official ' duties '. The spheres of competence of the officials are clearly demarcated, and levels of authority are delimited in the form of a hierarchy of offices. The rules governing conduct of the staff, their authority and responsibilities, are recorded in written form. Recruitment is based upon demonstration of specialised competence via competitive examinations or the possession of diplomas or degrees giving evidence of appropriate qualifications. Office property is not owned by the official, and a separation is maintained between the official and the office, such that under no conditions is the office ' owned ' by its incumbent. This type of organisation has distinct consequences for the position of the official:
1. The career of the official is governed by an abstract conception of duty; the performance of official tasks in a faithful manner is an end in itself rather than a means of obtaining personal material gain through rents, etc. 2. The official obtains his position through being appointed, on the basis of his technical qualifications, by a higher authority; he is not elected. 3. He normally holds a tenured position. 4. His remuneration takes the shape of a fixed and regular salary. 5. The occupational position of the official is such as to provide for ' career ' involving movement up the hierarchy of authority; the degree of progression achieved is determined either by manifest ability or seniority, or by a combination of the two.

It is only within modern capitalism that organisations are found which approximate to this ideal typical form. The main examples of developed bureaucracies, prior to the emergence of modern capitalism, were those of ancient Egypt, China, the later Roman principate, and the mediaeval Catholic church. These bureaucracies, particularly the first three, were essentially patrimonial, and were based largely upon the payment of officials in kind. This shows that the prior formation of a money economy is not an essential prerequisite to the emergence of bureaucratic organisation, although it has been of great importance in facilitating the growth of modern rational bureaucracy. The advance of bureaucratisation in the modern world is directly associated with the expansion of the division of labour in various spheres of social life. It is basic to Weber's sociology of modern capitalism that the phenomenon of specialisation of occupational function is by no means limited to the economic sphere. The separation of the labourer from control of his means of production which Marx singled out as the most distinctive feature of modern capitalism is not confined to industry, but extends throughout the polity, army, and other sectors of society in which large-scale organisations become prominent.[34] In post-mediaeval western Europe, the bureaucratisation

---

[34] cf. *GASS*, pp. 498ff. The importance of this point is amplified, in relation to Marx's position, see below, pp. 234–8.

of the state has preceded that in the economic sphere. The modern capitalist state is completely dependent upon bureaucratic organisation for its continued existence. ' The larger the state, or the more it becomes a great power state, the more unconditionally is this the case. . .' [35] While sheer size of the administrative unit is a major factor determining the spread of rational bureaucratic organisation – as in the case of the modern mass political party – there is not a unilateral relationship between size and bureaucratisation.[36] The necessity of specialisation to fulfil specific administrative tasks is as important as size in promoting bureaucratic specialisation. Thus in Egypt, the oldest bureaucratic state, the development of bureaucracy was primarily determined by the need for the regulation of irrigation by a centralised administration. In the modern capitalist economy, the formation of a supra-local market is a major condition stimulating the development of bureaucracy, since it demands the regular and co-ordinated distribution of goods and services.[37]

The efficiency of bureaucratic organisation in the performance of such routinised tasks is the main reason for its spread.

The fully developed bureaucratic apparatus compares with other organisations exactly as does the machine with the non-mechanical modes of production. Precision, speed, unambiguity, knowledge of the files, continuity, discretion, unity, strict subordination, reduction of friction and of material and personal costs – these are raised to the optimum point in the strictly bureaucratic organisation. . .[38]

These qualities are demanded above all by the capitalist economy, which requires that economic operations be discharged with speed and precision. Weber's position on this point has often been misunderstood. Weber was obviously aware of the view – common since the turn of the nineteenth century – that bureaucracy is associated with ' red tape ', and ' inefficiency '.[39] Nor was Weber ignorant of the importance in the substantive operation of bureaucratic organisations of the existence of informal contacts and patterns of relationship which overlap with the formally designated distribution of authority and responsibilities.[40] Bureaucratic organisation may produce ' definite impediments for the discharge of business in a manner best adapted to the individuality of each case '.[41] It is from this latter fact that the concern

---

[35] *ES*, vol. 3, p. 971; *WuG*, vol. 2, p. 568.

[36] Weber thus criticises Michels for exaggerating the ' iron ' character of the tendency towards the formation of oligarchy in bureaucracies. *ES*, vol. 3, pp. 1003–4.

[37] It is important to emphasise that the modern state and economy do not become totally bureaucratised. For those at ' the top ', specialised qualifications of a technical kind are not required. Ministerial and presidential positions are filled through some kind of electoral process, and the industrial entrepreneur is not appointed by the bureaucracy he heads. ' Thus at the top of a bureaucratic organisation, there is necessarily an element which is at least not purely bureaucratic.' *ES*, vol. 1, p. 222.

[38] *ES*, vol. 3, p. 973.

[39] cf. Martin Albrow: *Bureaucracy* (London, 1970), pp. 26–54.

[40] cf. Weber's contributions to the discussions of the *Verein für Sozialpolitik* in 1909, *GASS*, pp. 412–16.

[41] *ES*, vol. 3, pp. 974–5.

with ' red tape ' derives, and it is not wholly misplaced, because by its very nature as a rationalised structure, bureaucracy operates according to systematised rules of conduct. It is entirely conceivable, according to Weber, that prior forms of administrative organisation may be superior in terms of dealing with a given particular case. This can be illustrated by the instance of judicial decisions. In traditional legal practice, a patrimonial ruler intervenes at will in the dispensation of justice, and consequently may sometimes be able to render a verdict on the basis of his own personal knowledge of a defendant which is more ' just ' than a judgement returned in a similar case in a modern law-court, because in the latter instance ' only unambiguous general characteristics of the facts of the case are taken into account '.[42]

But this would certainly not happen in the majority of cases, and it is precisely the element of ' calculability ' involved in rational legal domination which makes bureaucratic administration quite distinct from prior types: indeed, it is the only form of organisation which is capable of coping with the immense tasks of co-ordination necessary to modern capitalism. Weber states the point as follows:

however many people may complain about the ' bureaucracy ', it would be an illusion to think for a moment that continuous administrative work can be carried out in any field except by means of officials working in offices. The whole pattern of everyday life is cut to fit this framework. If bureaucratic administration is, *ceteris paribus*, always the most rational type from a formal, technical point of view, the needs of mass administration (of people or of things) make it today completely indispensable.[43]

Charismatic domination, Weber's third type, is wholly distinct from the other two. Both traditional and legal domination are permanent systems of administration, concerned with the routine tasks of everyday life. The pure type of charismatic domination is, by definition, an extraordinary type. Charisma is defined by Weber as ' a certain quality of an individual personality by virtue of which he is considered extraordinary and treated as endowed with supernatural, superhuman, or at least specifically exceptional powers or qualities '.[44] A charismatic individual is, therefore, one whom others believe to possess strikingly unusual capacities, often thought to be of a supernatural kind, which set him apart from the ordinary. Whether a man " really " possesses any or all of the characteristics attributed to him by his followers is not at issue; what matters is that extraordinary qualities should be attributed to him by others. Charismatic domination can arise in the most varied social and historical contexts, and consequently charismatic figures range from political leaders and religious prophets whose actions have influenced the course of development of whole civilisations, through to many sorts of petty demagogue in all walks of life who have secured for themselves a temporary following. The claim to legitimacy in charismatic authority, in whatever con-

[42] *ES*, vol. 2, pp. 656–7.
[43] *ES*, vol. 1, p. 223; *WuG*, vol. 1, p. 128.   [44] *ES*, vol. 1, p. 241.

text it is found, is thus always founded upon the belief of both leader and followers in the authenticity of the leader's mission. The charismatic figure normally supplies ' proof ' of his genuineness through the performance of miracles or the issuing of divine revelations. While these are signs of the validity of his authority, however, they are not as such the basis upon which it rests, which ' lies rather in the conception that it is the duty of those subject to charismatic authority to recognise its genuineness and to act accordingly '.[45]

Membership of secondary authority positions in a charismatic movement is not based upon privileged selection through personal ties, nor upon the possession of technical qualifications. There is no fixed hierarchy of subordination, nor is there a ' career ' such as exists in bureaucratic organisations. The charismatic leader simply has an indeterminate number of intimates who share in his charisma or who possess charisma of their own. Unlike the permanent forms of organisation, a charismatic movement has no systematically organised means of economic support: its income is either received from donations of some kind or another, or is acquired by plunder. The charismatic movement is not organised around fixed juridical principles of a general kind, such as are found, with different content, in both traditional and legal domination; judgements are made in relation to each particular case, and are presented as divine revelations. ' The genuine prophet, like the genuine military leader and every true leader in this sense, preaches, creates, or demands *new* obligations. . .'[46]

This is symptomatic of the break with the accepted order which the emergence of charismatic domination represents. ' Within the sphere of its claims, charismatic authority rejects the past, and is in this sense specifically revolutionary.'[47] Charisma is a driving, creative force which surges through the established rules, whether traditional or legal, which govern an existing order. It is, according to Weber, a specifically irrational phenomenon. This is indeed essential to Weber's very definition of charisma, since the sole basis of charismatic authority is the recognition of the authenticity of the claims of the leader: the ideals of the charismatic movement are consequently in no way necessarily bound to those of the existing system of domination. Charisma is thus particularly important as a revolutionary force within traditional systems of domination, where authority is tied to precedents which have been handed down in a relatively unchanging form from the past. ' In prerationalistic periods, tradition and charisma between them have almost exhausted the whole of the orientation of action.'[48] With the advance of rationalisation, however, the rational implementation of social change (e.g., through the application of scientific knowledge to technological innovation) becomes increasingly significant.

---

[45] *ES*, vol. 1, p. 242.
[46] *ES*, vol. 1, p. 243. ' Kadi-justice ' is administered in this way, in principle; in practice, Weber says, it was actually closely bound to traditional precedent.
[47] *ES*, vol. 1, p. 244; *WuG*, vol. 1, p. 141.   [48] *ES*, vol. 1, p. 245.

Because of its antipathy to the routine and the everyday, charisma necessarily undergoes profound modification if it survives into anything like permanent existence. The ' routinisation ' (*Veralltäglichung*) of charisma hence
involves the devolution of charismatic authority in the direction of either
traditional or legal organisation. Since charismatic authority is focused upon
the extraordinary qualities of a particular individual, a difficult problem of
succession is posed when that person dies or is in some other way removed
from the scene. The type of authority relationship which emerges as a consequence of routinisation is determined in large degree by how the ' succession
problem ' is resolved. Weber distinguishes several possible avenues whereby
this may take place.

One historically important solution to the succession problem is where the
charismatic leader, or his disciples who share in his charisma, designates his
successor. The successor is not elected; he is shown to possess the appropriate
charismatic qualifications for authority. According to Weber, this was the
original significance of the coronation of monarchs and bishops in western
Europe.[49] Charisma may also be treated as a quality which is passed on
through heredity, and is consequently possessed by the closest relatives of
the original bearer. It is mainly in feudal Europe and Japan, however, that
this has become linked with the principle of primogeniture. When charismatic
domination is transmuted into a routine, traditional form, it becomes the
sacred source of legitimation for the position of those holding power; in this
way charisma forms a persisting element in social life. While this is ' alien to
its essence ', there is still justification, Weber says, for speaking of the persistence of ' charisma ', since as a sacred force it maintains its extraordinary
character. However, once charisma has in this way become an impersonal
force, it no longer is necessarily regarded as a quality which cannot be taught,
and the acquisition of charisma may come to depend partly upon a process
of education.

The routinisation of charisma demands that the activities of the administrative staff be placed upon a regular basis, which may be achieved through
either the formation of traditional norms or the establishment of legal rules.
If charisma becomes transmitted through heredity, the officialdom is likely
to become a traditional status group, with recruitment to positions itself being
based primarily upon inheritance. In other cases, criteria for admission to
office may become determined by tests of qualification, thus tending to the
rational legal type. Regardless of which of these lines of development is followed, routinisation always requires the setting up of a regular series of
economic arrangements which, if the trend is towards traditionalism, will be
benefices or fiefs, and if it is towards the legal type, will take the shape of
salaried positions.

The content of the ideals promoted by the emergence of a charismatic

---

[49] *ES*, vol. 1, pp. 247–8.

movement cannot be directly inferred from the pre-existing system of domination. This does not mean to say that the claims of the charismatic movement are not influenced by the symbols of the order in reaction to which it arises, nor that economic or ' material ' interests are not important in affecting the growth of a charismatic movement. It does mean, however, that the content of the charismatic ' mission ' is not to be explained away as an ideal ' reflection ' of material processes which are effecting social changes. The revolutionary dynamic, for Weber, is not to be pinned to any rational sequence of overall historical development. This preserves on a more empirical level the dismissal of developmental theories which Weber reaches according to purely theoretical considerations.

The influence of market relationships : classes and status groups

Weber's rejection of overall theories of historical development applies equally to Hegelianism and Marxism. But a further basic conceptual and empirical line of thought in Weber's work is particularly relevant to the claims of Marxism. If ' theories of history ' as a whole are impossible, it follows on the more specific level that any theory which attempts to tie historical development to the universal causal predominance of economic or class relationships is doomed to failure. Weber's discussion of ' class ', ' status ' and ' party ' thus establishes these as three ' dimensions ' of stratification, each of which is conceptually separate from the others, and specifies that, on an empirical level, each may causally influence each of the others.

Economy and Society contains two sections dealing with class and status groups.[50] Both sections, however, are short, and are incommensurate with the importance of the concepts in Weber's historical writings. Like Marx, Weber did not complete a detailed analytical account of the notion of class and its relationship to other bases of stratification in society. Weber's conception of class takes its point of departure from his more generalised analysis of economic action in a market. Economic action is defined by Weber as conduct which seeks, through peaceful means, to acquire control of desired utilities.[51] In Weber's usage, utilities include both goods and services. A market is distinguished from direct reciprocal exchange (barter) in so far as it involves speculative economic action oriented towards the securing of profit through competitive trading. ' Classes ' can only exist when such a market – which may take numerous concrete forms – has come into existence, and this in turn presupposes the formation of a money economy.[52] Money plays an extremely important part in this because it makes possible the estimation of the values exchanged in quantitative and fixed, rather than in subjective,

[50] The earlier rendition is in *ES*, vol. 2, pp. 926–40; the later analysis is to be found in *ES*, vol. 1, pp. 302–7.

[51] *ES*, vol. 1, p. 63. For an earlier formulation of the concept of the ' economic ', see *MSS*, p. 65.

[52] *ES*, vol. 1, pp. 80–2.

terms. Economic relationships thus free themselves from the particular ties and obligations of local community structure, and become fluidly determined by the material chances which individuals have of using property, goods or services which they possess for exchange on the competitive market. ' There-with ', Weber says, ' " class struggles " begin.' [53]

The ' market situation ' of any object of exchange is defined as ' all the opportunities of exchanging it for money which are known to the participants in exchange relationships and aid their orientation in the competitive price struggle.' [54] Those who own comparable objects of exchange (both goods and services) share ' in common a specific causal component of their life chances '.[55] That is to say, those who share the same market or ' class situation ' are all subject to similar economic exigencies, which causally influence both the material standards of their existence, and what sorts of personal life experiences they are able to enjoy. A ' class ' denotes an aggregate of individuals who thus share the same class situation. In these terms, those who are propertyless, and who can only offer services on the market, are divided according to the kinds of services they can offer, just as those who own property can be differentiated according to what they own and how they use it for economic ends.

Weber admits, with Marx, that ownership versus non-ownership of property is the most important basis of class division in a competitive market. He also follows Marx in distinguishing, among those who possess property, rentier classes and entrepreneurial classes, which Weber calls respectively ' owner-ship classes ' (*Besitzklassen*) and ' commercial classes ' (*Erwerbsklassen*). Ownership classes are those in which owners of property receive rents through their possession of land, mines, etc. These rentiers are ' positively advantaged ' ownership classes. ' Negatively advantaged ' ownership classes include all those without either property or skills to offer (for example, the *déclassé* Roman proletarians). Between the positively and the negatively advantaged groups fall a range of middle classes who either own small properties or who possess skills which can be offered as marketable services. These include such categories of persons as officials, artisans and peasants. Commercial classes are those where the positively advantaged groups are either entrepreneurs offering goods for sale on the market, or those who participate in the financing of such operations, such as bankers.[56] Wage-labourers constitute the negatively advantaged commercial classes. The middle classes include the petty bourgeoisie and administrative officials in government or in industry.

Most secondary discussions of Weber's conception of class have concentrated upon his earlier discussion (see below, note 59, p. 166), and have

[53] *ES*, vol. 2, p. 928.   [54] *ES*, vol. 1, p. 82.
[55] *ES*, vol. 2, p. 927.
[56] Positively advantaged commercial classes also sometimes include those who are able to control a monopoly of particular skills, such as professionals and craft workers. *ES*, vol. 1, p. 304.

neglected this second formulation. This is unfortunate, since it gives the impression that Weber's conception is less unified than in fact is the case. While in principle, according to the identification of class situation with market situation, there could be as many class divisions as there are minute gradations of economic position, in fact Weber regards only certain definite combinations, organised around the ownership and non-ownership of property, as historically significant. In his later exposition, besides differentiating ownership classes and commercial classes, Weber also distinguishes what he calls simply ' social ' classes. In so far as individuals may move freely within a common cluster of class situations (e.g., a man may move without difficulty from a clerical job in the civil service to one in a business firm), they form a definite social class. Compressing some of the divisions which compose the commercial classes, Weber describes the social class composition of capitalism as consisting of the following: 1. The manual working class. The existence of skill differentials – especially where they are controlled as monopolies – is a major factor threatening the unity of the working class. But the increasing mechanisation of industry is pushing a large proportion of workers into the semi-skilled category. 2. The petty bourgeoisie. 3. Propertyless white-collar workers, technicians and intelligentsia. 4. The dominant entrepreneurial and propertied groups, who also tend to share a privileged access to educational opportunities.[57]

The relationship between the existence of similar class interests, and the occurrence of manifest class conflict, is historically contingent. Groups of individuals may share a similar class situation without being aware of it, and without forming any organisation to further their common economic interests. It is not always the most marked inequalities in the distribution of property which lead to class struggles. Class conflict is likely to develop only where the unequal distribution of life-chances comes to be perceived as not an ' inevitable fact ': in many periods of history, the negatively advantaged classes accept their position of inferiority as legitimate. Class consciousness most readily becomes developed in circumstances where: 1. The class enemy is a group in visible and direct economic competition: in modern capitalism, for example, the working class can more readily be organised to fight against the industrial entrepreneur or manager, rather than against the more remote financier or shareholder. ' It is not the rentier, the shareholder, and the banker who suffer the ill will of the worker, but almost exclusively the manufacturer and the business executives who are the direct opponents of workers in wage conflicts.'[58] 2. There is a large number of people who share the same class situation. 3. Communication and assembly are simple to organise: as where,

---

[57] *ES*, vol. 1, p. 305. cf. Paul Mombert: ' Zum Wesen der sozialen Klasse ', in Melchior Palyi: *Erinnerungsgabe für Max Weber* (Munich and Leipzig, 1923), pp. 239–75.

[58] *ES*, vol. 2, p. 931. It is this fact, Weber points out, which has made possible the growth of patriarchal socialism. Similarly, in the army, the soldier resents the corporal rather than the higher echelons of command. *GASS*, p. 509.

for instance, in modern factory production, the workers are concentrated together in large-scale productive units. 4. The class in question is provided with leadership – such as from the intelligentsia – which supplies clear and comprehensible goals for their activity.

'Class' refers to the objective attributes of the market situation of numbers of individuals, and as such the influence of class upon social action operates independently of any valuations these individuals might make of themselves or others. Since Weber rejects the notion that economic phenomena directly determine the nature of human ideals, it follows that such valuations have to be conceptualised independently of class interests. Weber therefore distinguishes class situation from 'status situation' (*ständische Lage*). The status situation of an individual refers to the evaluations which others make of him or his social position, thus attributing to him some form of (positive or negative) social prestige or esteem. A status group is a number of individuals who share the same status situation. Status groups, unlike classes, are almost always conscious of their common position. 'In relation to classes, the status group comes closest to the "social" class and is most unlike the "commercial" class.'[59] However, there is no necessary or universal connection between status situation and any of the three types of class which Weber distinguishes. Property classes often, but by no means always, constitute definite status groups; commercial classes rarely do so.

Status groups normally manifest their distinctiveness through following a particular life-style, and through placing restrictions upon the manner in which others may interact with them. The enforcement of restrictions upon marriage, sometimes involving strict endogamy, is a particularly frequent way in which this may be achieved. Caste represents the most clear-cut example of this; here the distinctive character of the status group is held to rest upon ethnic factors, and is enforced by religious prescriptions as well as by legal and conventional sanctions. While it is only in traditional India that a whole society is organised according to strict caste principles, caste-like properties are also characteristic of the position of 'pariah' peoples. These are ethnic minorities, the most notable historical example of which is that of the Jews, whose economic activities are limited to a particular occupation or range of occupations, and whose contacts with the 'host' population are limited.

Stratification by status is not, for Weber, simply a 'complication' of class hierarchies: on the contrary, status groups, as differentiated from classes, are of vital significance in numerous phases of historical development. Moreover, status groups may act to influence in a direct way the operation of the market, and so may causally affect class relationships. One historically important way in which this has occurred is through the restriction of the

[59] *ES*, vol. 1, pp. 306–7; *WuG*, vol. 1, p. 180. For Marx's use of the term *Stand*, see above, p. 6, n. 22.

spheres of economic life which are permitted to become governed by the market:

For example, in many Hellenic cities during the ' status era ' and also originally in Rome, the inherited estate (as is shown by the old formula for placing spend-thrifts under a guardian) was monopolised, as were the estates of knights, pea-sants, priests, and especially the clientele of the craft and merchant guilds. The market is restricted, and the power of naked property *per se*, which gives its stamp to class formation, is pushed into the background.[60]

Many instances can be adduced in which men draw clear distinctions between economic possession and status privilege. The possession of material property is not by any means always a sufficient basis for entry into a dominant status group. The claims of *nouveaux riches* for entry to an estab-lished status group are not likely to be accepted by those within it, although the individual can ordinarily use his wealth to ensure that his offspring can acquire the necessary criteria for membership. Nevertheless, Weber does stress that, while status group membership ' normally stands in sharp opposi-tion to the pretensions of sheer property ', it is still the case that property is ' in the long run ' recognised ' with extraordinary regularity ' as a status qualification.[61] The degree to which status stratification is prevalent in any given social order is influenced by how far the society in question is subject to rapid economic transformation. Where marked economic changes are occurring, class stratification is a more pervasive determinant of action than in a situation where there is little change. In the latter case, status differentials come increasingly to the fore.

Both class and status group membership may be a basis of social power; but the formation of political parties is a further, analytically independent, influence upon the distribution of power. A ' party ' refers to any voluntary association which has the aim of securing directive control of an organisation in order to implement certain definite policies within that organisation. In this definition, parties can exist in any form of organisation in which the formation of freely recruited groupings is permitted: from a sports club up to the state.[62] The bases for the establishment of parties, even of modern political parties, are diverse. A common class or status situation may provide the sole source of recruitment to a political party but this is fairly rare. ' In any individual case, parties may represent interests determined through class situation or status situation.... But they need be neither purely class nor purely status parties; in fact, they are more likely to be mixed types, and sometimes they are neither.' [63]

The growth of the modern state has brought with it the development of mass political parties, and the emergence of professional politicians. A man whose occupation is concerned with the struggle for political power may

[60] *ES*, vol. 2, p. 937.
[61] *ES*, vol. 2, p. 932.
[62] *ES*, vol. 1, pp. 284–6.

[63] *ES*, vol. 2, p. 938.

either live 'for' politics or 'off' politics. An individual who relies upon his political activities to supply his main source of income lives 'off' politics; a man who engages in full-time political activities, but who does not receive his income from this source, lives 'for' politics. A political order in which recruitment to positions of power is filled by those who live 'for' politics is necessarily drawn from a propertied elite, who are usually rentiers rather than entrepreneurs. This does not imply that such politicians will pursue policies which are wholly directed towards favouring the interests of the class or status group from which they originate.[64]

[64] *FMW*, pp. 85–6.

12. Rationalisation, the 'world religions', and western capitalism

Weber collectively entitles his studies of Judaism and the religions of China and India, 'The economic ethics of the world religions'.[1] The title is indicative of the main thrust of Weber's interests, and manifests a line of immediate continuity with the themes of his earlier essay on Calvinism and the spirit of western capitalism. But in fact these subsequent studies embrace a much broader range of social and historical phenomena than is suggested by the relatively modest heading with which Weber prefaces them. The relationship between the content of religious beliefs and the forms of economic activity which characterise a given social order is often indirect, and is influenced by other institutions within that order.

Weber stresses that his studies of the world religions

do not in any way constitute a systematic 'typology' of religion. On the other hand, they do not constitute a purely historical work. They are 'typological' in the sense that they consider what is typically important in the historical realisations of religious ethics. This is important for the connection of religions with the great contrasts of *economic* mentalities. Other aspects will be neglected; these presentations do not claim to offer a well-rounded picture of world religions.[2]

More particularly, Weber states, the influence of religious ethics upon economic organisation is to be considered above all from one specific standpoint: in terms of their connections with the advance or retardation of rationalism such as has come to dominate economic life in the West.

In using the term 'economic ethic', Weber does not imply, then, that each of the sets of religious beliefs which he analyses contains an explicit and clearly formulated directive as to what sorts of economic activity are considered to be permissible or desirable. The degree of immediacy, as well as the nature, of the influence of religion upon economic life is variable. As in *The Protestant Ethic*, the focus of Weber's attention is directed not upon the internal 'logic' as such of a given religious ethic, but upon the psychological and social consequences for the actions of individuals. Weber continues to maintain his aloofness from either materialism or idealism as providing a viable general interpretation of either the sources or the effects of the religious phenomena: 'externally similar forms of economic organisation are compatible with very different economic ethics and, according to their particular character, may produce very different historical results. An economic ethic is not a simple " function " of a form of economic organisation; and just as

---

[1] *GAR*, vol. 1, p. 237.　　　　　　　　　　　　[2] *FMW*, p. 292.

little does the reverse hold.'[3] Of course, religious beliefs are only one among various sets of influences which may condition the formation of an economic ethic, and religion itself is heavily influenced by other social, political and economic phenomena.

Religion and magic

Weber's essays on the world religions should be placed against the background of the broad tenets of his sociology of religion as set out in *Economy and Society*.[4] In their participation in religion and magic, men typically distinguish between those objects and beings which have special qualities, and those which belong to the world of the ' ordinary '.[5] Only certain objects possess religious properties; only certain individuals are able to attain states of inspiration or grace which endow them with religious powers. These extraordinary powers are charismatic, and relatively undifferentiated forms such as *mana* are the original source of the charismatic qualities manifest in a more specific way in the persons of the great religious leaders whose lives led to the efflorescence of the major world religions. This is an important point to stress, since all too often the account presented in Weber's general discussion of charismatic domination has been quoted to reinforce the suggestion that he uses the concept of charisma to introduce a ' great man ' theory of history into his writings.[6] But, as should also be evident from Weber's analysis of the modes in which charismatic legitimation may be transmitted from generation to generation, charisma is not simply to be treated as wholly an ' individual ' property. Weber is in accord with Durkheim in accepting that, in the most primitive kinds of religion (which does not imply that they are the most elementary forms in the sense of being the evolutionary progenitors of more complex religions),[7] there are generalised spiritual agencies which are not personified as gods, but which nonetheless have volitional traits. When gods do emerge, they have only a precarious existence initially: a god may be considered as controlling only one specific event. Such *Augenblicksgötter* may have no personal *mana*, being referred to only by the name of the type of event they regulate. The conditions under which a god becomes a permanent and powerful deity are complicated and often historically obscure.

---

[3] *FMW*, pp. 267–8; *GAR*, vol. 1, p. 238.   [4] *ES*, vol. 2, pp. 399–634.
[5] But Weber does not stress, as Durkheim does, the radical nature of the dichotomy of the ' sacred ' and ' profane '. Weber holds that ' religious or magical behaviour or thinking must not be set apart from the range of everyday purposive conduct, particularly since even the ends of the religious and magical actions are predominantly economic '. *ES*, vol. 2, p. 400.
[6] cf., for example, Gerth and Mills: ' Introduction ' to *FMW*, pp. 53–5.
[7] Weber notes: ' The belief in the universality of totemism, and certainly the belief in the derivation of virtually all social groups and all religions from totemism, constitutes a tremendous exaggeration that has been rejected completely by now.' *ES*, vol. 2, p. 434.

Only Judaism and Islam, according to Weber, are monotheistic in the strict sense of the term. In Christianity, the supreme deity tends to be considered, in practice if not in theory, as one figure in the holy Trinity: this is particularly true of Catholicism. However, the beginning of trends towards monotheism can be discerned in all the religions of world-historical significance. The reasons why this has progressed further in some religions rather than others are various; but one factor of general importance has been the entrenched resistance of priestly strata who have vested interests in the maintenance of the cults of the particular gods whom they represent. A second factor is the need of the lay population in traditional societies for gods who are readily available and open to magical influence. The more all-powerful a god becomes, the more remote he becomes from the everyday needs of the mass of the population. Even where an omnipotent god has come to the fore, magical propitiation has usually persisted in the practical religious conduct of the lay believer.

Where men relate to divine entities through prayer, worship and supplication, we can speak of the existence of ' religion ', as distinct from the use of ' magic '. Magical forces are not worshipped, but are subordinated to human needs by the use of charms or formulae. The distinction between religion and magic corresponds to a status and power differentiation of considerable historical importance, between priests on the one hand, and magicians or sorcerers on the other. A priesthood consists of a permanent group of functionaries, who are in continuous charge of the operation of a cult. There is no priesthood which does not have a cult, although there may be cults which have no distinct priesthood.[8] The existence of a priestly stratum is of particular significance in the bearing which it has upon the degree of rationalisation of religious beliefs. In most cases of magical practice, or where a cult without priests exists, there is usually only a low degree of development of a consistent religious belief system.

In Weber's sociology of religion, the religious prophet is a figure of equal importance to the priest. A prophet is ' a purely individual bearer of charisma, who by virtue of his mission proclaims a religious doctrine or divine commandment '.[9] Although it is not only as a consequence of prophetic missions that new religious communities are formed – the activities of priestly reformers can achieve the same result – prophecy supplies for Weber the decisive historical source of doctrines which effect radical change in religious institutions. This is particularly true of the historical impulse towards the elimination of magic from the daily conduct of life: that process of the ' disenchantment ' of the world which reaches its culmination in rational capitalism.

In all times there has been but one means of breaking down the power of magic and establishing a rational conduct of life ; this means the great rational prophecy.

[8] *ES*, vol. 2, p. 426.   [9] *ES*, vol. 2, p. 439.

Not every prophecy by any means destroys the power of magic ; but it is possible for a prophet who furnishes credentials in the shape of miracles and otherwise, to break down the traditional sacred rules. Prophecies have released the world from magic and in doing so have created the basis for our modern science and technology, and for capitalism.[10]

Prophets only rarely emanate from a priesthood, and typically set themselves up in open opposition to a priestly stratum. An ' ethical ' prophet is one whose teaching is based upon the propagation of a divine mission, which may consist of a set of concrete ordinances or of more generalised ethical imperatives, and to which he requires compliance as a moral duty. An ' exemplary ' prophet is one who makes manifest the route to salvation by the example of his own personal life, but who puts forward no claim to be the mediator of a divine mission which others are obligated to accept. While exemplary prophecy is most common in India, and is also found in some instances in China, ethical prophecy is especially characteristic of the near East, a fact which is traceable to the omnipotent, transcendental god proclaimed as *Yahwe* in Judaism.

Both types of prophecy have the characteristic that they act to promote the revelation of a coherent world-view which stimulates a ' consciously integrated and meaningful attitude towards life '. The beliefs brought together as prophetic revelation may be, in a strictly logical sense, incompatible; what gives prophecy a unity is its typical consistency as a practical orientation to life. Prophecy ' always contains the important religious conception of the world as a cosmos which is challenged to produce somehow a " meaningful ", ordered totality. . .'.[11] The results of conflict between prophets and priests may vary, of course, leading either to the victory of the prophet and his following and the establishment of a new religious order, or to accommodation with the priesthood, or to the subjugation and elimination of the prophecy by the priests.

Indian and Chinese theodicy

The development of prophecy in traditional China was stultified at an early date. In India, by contrast, an important salvation religion did emerge, although since the Hindu (and Buddhist) prophets were exemplary, they did not see themselves as entrusted with a divine mission which must be actively disseminated. Hinduism differs in some important respects from each of the other world religions. Hinduism is an eclectic and tolerant religion : it is possible to be a devout Hindu and yet to accept ' highly important and most characteristic doctrines which every denominational Christian would consider exclusively his own '.[12] But there do exist certain beliefs which are shared by most Hindus, and which are ' dogmas ' in the sense that they con-

---

[10] *General Economic History* (New York, 1961), p. 265.
[11] *ES*, vol. 2, p. 451.
[12] *RI*, p. 21.

stitute truths the denial of which is considered to be heretical. The most important of these are those of transmigration of souls and compensation (*karma*). Both of these are directly bound up with the social ordering of the caste system. The doctrine of *karma* ' represents the most consistent theodicy ever produced by history '.[13] Because of it, Weber says, adopting a slogan from the *Communist Manifesto*, the Hindu of the very lowest caste can ' win the world ': he can realistically aspire, within the context of these beliefs, through successive incarnations, to reach the very highest levels, to reach paradise and obtain divinity. Through the doctrinal stipulation that the conduct of the individual in his present life has irremediable consequences in his next incarnation, and because this is directly tied into the caste system, Hindu orthodoxy places insuperable barriers in the face of any challenge to the existing social order.

Estranged castes might stand beside one another with bitter hatred – for the idea that everybody had ' deserved ' his own fate, did not make the good fortune of others more enjoyable to the socially underprivileged. For so long and insofar as the *Karma* doctrine remained unshaken, revolutionary ideas or the striving for ' progress ' were inconceivable.[14]

During the era in the early history of India in which Hinduism became firmly established, about four or five centuries before the birth of Christ, the development of manufacture and trade reached a peak. Merchant and craft guilds in the cities had an importance in urban economic organisation comparable to the guilds of mediaeval Europe. Moreover, rational science was highly developed in India, and numerous schools of philosophy flourished there at different periods. These existed in an atmosphere of tolerance which has been almost unrivalled elsewhere. Juridical systems were formed which were as mature as those of mediaeval Europe. But the emergence of the caste system, together with the ascendancy of the Brahmin priesthood, effectively prevented any further economic development in the direction of that taken in Europe.

The uniqueness of the development of India, however, lay in the fact that these beginnings of guild and corporate organisation in the cities led neither to the city autonomy of the Occidental type nor, after the coming into being of the great patrimonial states, to a social and economic organisation of the territories corresponding to the ' territorial economy ' of the Occident. Rather, the Hindu caste system, whose beginnings certainly preceded that era, became paramount. In part, this caste system entirely displaced the other organisations; in part, it crippled them; it prevented them from attaining any considerable importance.[15]

The main influence of caste upon economic activity has been to ritually stabilise the occupational structure, and thereby to act against the further advance of rationalisation of the economy. The emphasis of caste ritualism in labour is upon the dignity and value of traditional skills in the production

[13] *RI*, p. 21.
[14] *RI*, pp. 122–3; *GAR*, vol. 2, p. 122.   [15] *RI*, pp. 33–4; *GAR*, vol. 2, pp. 35–6.

of objects of beauty. Any attempt upon the part of an individual to break free of these vocational prescriptions damages his chances of a more favourable incarnation in his next life. It is for this reason that it is just the lowest-caste individual who is likely to adhere most rigorously to his caste obligations. The negative influence of the caste system upon economic development, however, is diffuse rather than specific. It would not be true to say, for example, that caste organisation is completely incompatible with the existence of large-scale productive enterprises with a complex division of labour, of the sort which are characteristic of modern industry in the West. This can be seen by the partial success of colonialist firms in India. Nevertheless, Weber concludes,

> it still must be considered extremely unlikely that the modern organisation of industrial capitalism would ever have *originated* on the basis of the caste system. A ritual law in which every change of occupation, every change in work technique, may result in ritual degradation is certainly not capable of giving birth to economic and technical revolutions from within itself...[16]

There were important similarities between the position of the Brahmins in India and that of the Confucian *literati* in traditional China. Both were status groups whose domination rested largely upon their access to classical scriptures written in a language separate from that of the laity, although, according to Weber, Hindu intellectualism was much less of a purely written culture than the Chinese. Both groups disclaimed any connection with magic even if this was not always successful in practice; both rejected every sort of Dionysian orgiasticism.[17]

However, there were equally important differences between the two groups. The Chinese *literati* were an officialdom, within a patrimonial bureaucracy; the Brahmins were originally a priesthood, but were also employed in a variety of occupations, as chaplains to princes, jurists, theological teachers and counsellors.[18] But among the Brahmins an official career was unusual. The unification of China under a single monarch allowed the linking of admission to official positions to literary qualification. Those having intellectual training became the source of recruitment to the bureaucratic officialdom. In India, on the other hand, the Brahmin priesthood became strongly established prior to the development of the early universal kingships. Thus the Brahmins were able to avoid incorporation within a hierarchy, and at the same time laid claim to a status position which was, in principle, superior to that of the kings.

In traditional China there were, at certain periods, a number of important developments which Weber distinguishes as conducive to the rationalisation of the economy. These include the emergence of cities and of guilds not

---

[16] *RI*, p. 112.

[17] In neither India nor China was magic eliminated from the activity of the bulk of the general population; magical cults often flourished in India and in China.

[18] *RI*, pp. 139–40.

unlike those of India; the formation of a monetary system; the development of law; and the achievement of political integration within a patrimonial state. But there were certain significant differences between the nature of some of these developments in China, and those which played a role in the rise of European capitalism. In spite of the relatively high degree of urbanisation achieved in China in ancient times, and of the volume of internal trade, the formation of money economy only reached a comparatively rudimentary level. Moreover, the Chinese city differed considerably from that characteristic of Europe. This was in part a result of the failure to develop a money economy beyond a certain point: 'In China, there were no cities like Florence which could have created a standard coin and guided the State in monetary policies.' [19] Equally important, the Chinese city did not acquire the political autonomy and legal independence which were possessed by the mediaeval European urban communities.

The citizen of the Chinese city tended to retain most of his primary kinship ties with his native village; the city remained embedded in the local agrarian economy, and did not set itself up against it, as happened in the West. No equivalent to the 'charter' of the English burgesses ever existed in China. Thus the potential importance of the guilds, which had a great deal of internal autonomy, was effectively curbed by the lack of political and legal independence of the urban administrations. The low level of political autonomy of the cities is partly to be attributed to the early development of the state bureaucracy. The bureaucrats played a major part in the promotion of urbanisation, but thereby were also able to regulate its subsequent development, a control which they never completely relinquished. This again contrasts with the West, where governmental bureaucracy was in large degree a product of the prior formation of the autonomous city states.[20]

One of the most important features of the social structure of traditional China was that the Emperor combined both religious and political supremacy. China lacked a powerful stratum of priests, and did not generate prophecy which offered a decisive challenge to the imperial order. While the charismatic component in the Emperorship became heavily overlain with traditional elements, even up to modern times the Emperor was expected to manifest his charisma in controlling rainfall and the rivers. If the rivers broke through the dykes, the Emperor had to perform public penitence, and in common with all the officials was subject to censorial reprimand.

The actual degree of effective administrative centralisation in traditional China, as in all large patrimonial states having poor communications, was low, as compared to the modern European nation state. But the centrifugal tendencies which might have permanently devolved into feudalism were effectively countered by the system of using educational qualifications as a

[19] *RC*, p. 13.
[20] *RC*, p. 16.

basis for appointment to bureaucratic positions: this had the consequence of binding the officialdom to the Emperor and to the state. The record of each official was reassessed every three years, and he was thus subject to the continuous supervision of the state educational authorities. The officials were salaried in theory, but in practice their salaries were not paid or only accounted for a fraction of their income. Their economic interests were highly conservative, because of the systematic use of official positions to obtain income from tax revenues:

Profit opportunities were not individually appropriated by the highest and dominant stratum of officialdom; rather, they were appropriated by the whole estate of removable officials. It was the latter who collectively opposed intervention and persecuted with deadly hatred any rational ideologist who called for 'reform'. Only violent revolution from above or below could have changed this.[21]

The lack of political autonomy of the urban communities in China must not be taken to imply the absence of local power. Much of Weber's analysis is in fact concerned with documenting the fluctuating tensions in the relationship between the central authority and the provinces. Particularly important in this connection were the powerful extended family units which provided a major focus of economic activity and co-operation. The kinship group (*tsung-tsu*) was either the direct basis or the model for virtually all forms of economic enterprise larger than the household. The *tsung-tsu* typically controlled food-processing, weaving, and other domestic handicraft industries, and also provided credit facilities for its members. In both rural and urban production, co-operative control by the kinship group was supreme, minimising individual entrepreneurial activity and free mobility of labour, both of which were essential characteristics of European capitalism. The power of the local elders provided a major counterweight to the rule of the *literati*. Irrespective of how qualified the official, in certain matters within the jurisdiction of the kinship group, he was subject to the authority of the most illiterate clan elder.

The Chinese educational system gave no training in calculation in spite of the fact that some forms of mathematics were already developed by the sixth century B.C. The methods of calculation which were used in commerce hence had to be learnt in practice, and were cut off from formal education. In content, education was wholly literary, and directed towards the intimate knowledge of classical writings. Because of their familiarity with these writings, the *literati* were believed to possess charismatic qualities. But they were not a hereditary priesthood like the Indian Brahmins, and Confucianism is very different from the mystic religiosity of the Hindus. Weber remarks that Chinese has no synonym for the English word 'religion'. The nearest approximations are terms meaning 'doctrine' and 'rite', which make no distinction between the sacred and the secular.

[21] *RC*, p. 60.

In Confucianism, the social order is regarded as a particular case of the cosmic order in general, the latter being considered to be eternal and inevitable.

The great spirits of the cosmic orders obviously desired only the happiness of the world and especially the happiness of man. The same applied to the orders of society. The 'happy' tranquillity of the Empire and the equilibrium of the soul should and could be attained only if man fitted himself into the internally harmonious cosmos.[22]

What is most valued in Confucianism is the 'cultivated man', who behaves with universal dignity and propriety, and who is in unison with himself and the outside world. Self-control, the regulation of emotion, is demanded by this ethic; since the harmony of the soul is the ultimate good, passion must not be allowed to disturb this balance. The notion of sin, and the corresponding concept of salvation, are absent. The Confucian emphasis upon self-control is most emphatically not wedded to an asceticism, such as is found in Hinduism, which seeks salvation from the toils of the world.

Weber concludes his study of China by drawing an explicit comparison between Confucianism and Puritanism. There are two primary, although interrelated, criteria in terms of which the degree of rationalisation of a religion may be determined: how far magic has been eliminated, and how far there has developed an internally consistent and universally applicable theodicy. With regard to the first, ascetic Protestantism has been more radical than any other religion; in terms of the second, however, Confucianism ranks with Puritanism as having attained a high level of formal rationality. But the content of Confucian rationalism and consequently its relationship to the imperfections or irrationalities of reality, was quite different from that of rational Puritanism. Whereas the Puritan ethic introduced a deep tension between religious ideals and the earthly world, that of Confucianism centred upon the harmonious adaptation of the individual to an inevitably given order.

For the Confucian ideal man, the gentleman, 'grace and dignity' were expressed in fulfilling traditional obligations. Hence, the cardinal virtue and goal in self-perfection meant ceremonial and ritualist propriety in all circumstances of life... The Confucian demanded no other kind of 'redemption' save that from the barbaric lack of education. As the reward of virtue he expected only long life, health, and wealth in this world and beyond death simply the maintenance of his good name. As for truly Hellenic man any sort of transcendental anchorage of ethics, any tension between obligations to a supra-mundane God and world of the flesh, any pursuance of a goal in the beyond, or conception of radical evil, was lacking... The relentlessly and religiously systematised utilitarianism peculiar to rational asceticism [i.e., ascetic Protestantism], to live 'in' the world and yet not be 'of' it, has helped to produce superior rational aptitudes and therewith the spirit of the specialised man [*Berufsmensch*] which, in the last analysis, was denied to Confucianism... The contrast can teach us that mere sobriety and thriftiness

[22] *RC*, p. 153.

combined with ' acquisitiveness ' and valuation of wealth, were far from representing and far from releasing the ' capitalist spirit ', in the sense that this is found in
the specialised economic man of the modern economy.[23]

Thus, in spite of the various factors which might have acted to promote its
rise, rational capitalism did not develop spontaneously in China. As in the
case of Japan, China would probably offer a fertile soil for the assimilation of
capitalist production introduced from the outside; but this is quite different
from providing the original impetus towards capitalist development.

It is important to specify the relationship between this conclusion and
Weber's analysis of the emergence of western European capitalism. In China,
Weber makes clear, the emergence of rational capitalism was inhibited ' by
the lack of a particular mentality ', due to the existence of normative prescriptions which were ' rooted in the Chinese " ethos " '.[24] In western Europe, this
' mentality ' did come into being, with the formation of ascetic Protestantism.
But it is misleading to regard Weber's studies of India and China as constituting, in any simple sense, an *ex post facto* ' experiment ' in which the relevant
material factors (i.e., those economic and political conditions conducive to
capitalism) are held constant, and the ' independent ' influence of the content
of ideas is analysed. While it is the case that in China, for example, there
existed, at particular periods, a number of ' material ' factors which can be
designated as necessary or favourable to the emergence of capitalism, these
were connected in a specific *combination*, different from that pertaining in
Europe. There were important differences, then, in both the ' material ' and
the ' ideal ' circumstances characterising the West as compared to the Orient.[25]

The spread of secular rationalism

Among the characteristics, in terms of which European development was
distinctive, were the specific form of the state and the existence of rational
law. Weber attaches great emphasis to the significance of the heritage of
Roman law for the subsequent social and economic development of Europe,
and in particular for the rise of the modern state. ' Without this juristic
rationalism, the rise of the absolute state is just as little imaginable as is the
[French] Revolution.' [26] The connection between this and the development
of rational capitalism, however, was not simple and clear-cut. Modern capi-

---

[23] *RC*, pp. 228 & 247; my parenthesis; *GAR*, vol. 1, pp. 514 & 534.

[24] *RC*, p. 104.

[25] Weber places some emphasis upon the special geographical position of Europe. In
India and China, the large continental land masses were formidable barriers to the
extensive development of commerce. In Europe, the Mediterranean, together with
many rivers providing easy transportation, offered a situation much more favourable to trading enterprises on an extensive scale. *General Economic History*, p. 260.
In addition, Weber analyses at length the special properties of the western city, and
the significance of the early dissolution of the solidarity of the extended kinship
group. *ES*, vol. 3, pp. 1212–372.

[26] *EMW*, p. 94, my parenthesis.

talism first took root in England, but that country was much less influenced by Roman law than other continental countries were. The prior existence of a system of rational law was only one influence in a complicated interplay of factors leading to the formation of the modern state. The trend towards the development of the modern state, characterised by the presence of a professional administration carried on by salaried officials, and based upon the concept of citizenship, was certainly not wholly an outcome of economic rationalisation, and in part preceded it. Nevertheless, it is true that the advance of the capitalist economic order and the growth of the state are intimately connected. The development of national and international markets, and the concomitant destruction of the influence of the local groups, such as kinship units, which formerly played a large part in regulating contracts, all promote ' the monopolisation and regulation of all " legitimate " coercive power by *one* universalist coercive institution. . .'.[27]

Essential to modern capitalistic enterprise, according to Weber, is the possibility of rational calculation of profits and losses in terms of money. Modern capitalism is inconceivable without the development of capital accounting. In Weber's view, rational book-keeping constitutes the most integral expression of what makes the modern type of capitalist production dissimilar to prior sorts of capitalistic activity such as usury or adventurers' capitalism.[28] The circumstances which Weber details as necessary to the existence of capital accounting in stable productive enterprises constitute those which Weber accepts as the basic prerequisites of modern capitalism, and include those factors upon which Marx placed most emphasis: 1. The existence of a large mass of wage-labourers, who are not only legally ' free ' to dispose of their labour power on the open market, but who are actually forced to do so to earn their livelihood. 2. An absence of restrictions upon economic exchange on the market: in particular, the removal of status monopolies on production and consumption (such as existed, in extreme form, in the Indian caste system). 3. The use of a technology, which is constructed and organised on the basis of rational principles: mechanisation is the clearest manifestation of this. 4. The detachment of the productive enterprise from the household. While the separation of home and workplace is found elsewhere, as in the bazaar, it is only in western Europe that this has proceeded very far.[29]

But these economic attributes could not exist without the rational legal administration of the modern state. This is as distinctive a characteristic of the contemporary capitalist order as is the class division between capital and labour in the economic sphere. In general terms, political organisations can be classified in the same way as economic enterprises, in relation to whether the ' means of administration ' are owned by the administrative staff or are separated from their ownership. As has been mentioned (in the previous chap-

---

[27] *ES*, vol. 1, p. 337.
[28] *ES*, vol. 1, pp. 164–6. [29] *General Economic History*, pp. 172–3; *PE*, p. 22.

ter), Weber here applies in a very broad sense Marx's conception of the ex-propriation of the worker from control of his means of production. Political organisations in traditional states are of an ' estate ' character, in which the means of administration are controlled by the officialdom. But such decen-tralised systems of political power typically exist in an uneasy balance with the centralised administration of an overlord or monarch. The monarch nor-mally attempts to consolidate his position by creating a staff which is materially dependent upon him, and by the formation of his own professional army. The greater the degree to which the ruler succeeds in surrounding him-self with a propertyless staff responsible only to him, the less he is challenged by nominally subordinate powers. This process is most complete in the modern bureaucratic state.

Everywhere the development of the modern state is initiated through the action of the prince. He paves the way for the expropriation of the autonomous and ' private ' bearers of administrative power who stand beside him, those who possess in their own right the means of administration, warfare, and financial organisation, as well as politically disposable goods of all sorts. The whole process is a complete parallel to the development of the capitalist enterprise through gradual expropriation of the independent producers. We perceive that, in the end, the modern state controls the total means of political organisation which actually come together under a single head.[30]

The growth of the bureaucratic state proceeds in close connection with the advance of political democratisation, because the demands made by demo-crats for political representation and for equality before the law necessitate complex administrative and juridical provisions to prevent the exercise of privilege. The fact that democracy and bureaucratisation are so closely related creates one of the most profound sources of tension in the modern capitalist order. For while the extension of democratic rights in the contemporary state cannot be achieved without the formulation of new bureaucratic regulations, there is a basic opposition between democracy and bureaucracy. This is, for Weber, one of the most poignant examples of the contradictions which can exist between the formal and the substantive rationality of social action: the growth of the abstract legal procedures which help to eliminate privilege them-selves reintroduce a new form of entrenched monopoly which is in some respects more ' arbitrary ' and autonomous than previously extant. Bureau-cratic organisation is promoted by the democratic requisite of impersonal selection for positions, from all strata of the population, according to the possession of educational qualifications. But this in itself creates strata of officials who, because of the separation of their position from the external influence of privileged individuals or groups, possess a more inclusive range of administrative power than before.

This does not mean – and this is where Weber differs from Michels and

[30] *FMW*, p. 82; *GPS*, pp. 498–9.

others [31] – that the modern democratic order is a mere sham in so far as it rests upon claims of the participation of the mass of the population in politics. The growth of democracy has had a definite ' levelling ' effect, which can be brought into sharp focus by comparing contemporary societies with previous historical examples of highly bureaucratised states. Such a comparison shows very clearly that, however close the connections between democracy and bureaucracy in modern times, it is entirely possible that, while the extension of democratic rights demands the expansion of bureaucracy, the reverse does not follow. The instances of ancient Egypt and Rome provide ample evidence of the total subordination of the population in a highly bureaucratised state.

In this respect, one has to remember that bureaucracy as such is a precision instrument which can put itself at the disposal of quite varied interests, purely political as well as purely economic ones, or any other sort. Therefore, the measure of its parallelism with democratisation must not be exaggerated, however typical it may be.[32]

In the modern democratic state it is obviously impossible for the mass of the population to govern, in the sense of participating continuously in the exercise of power. ' Direct ' democracy is only possible in small communities where the members of the group can gather together in a single spot. In the contemporary Western world, ' democracy ' can only refer to a situation in which, firstly, those who are governed can exert some influence, through the ballot box, over those who govern them; and secondly, where representational assemblies or parliaments can influence the decisions taken by executive leaders. The existence of large-scale parties is inevitable in the modern state; but if these parties are headed by political leaders who have a strong conviction of the significance of their vocation, bureaucratisation of the political structure can be partially checked. Democracy necessarily stimulates ' Caesarist ' tendencies in its major political figures, since under conditions of universal suffrage political leaders must possess the charismatic qualities required to attract a mass following. ' Caesarism ' itself presents a threat to democratic government, but may be controlled by the existence of a parliament in which political skills can be nurtured, and which provides a means of withdrawing the mandate of leaders who seek to depass the bounds of their legal authority. In the contemporary state, ' there is only the choice between leadership democracy with a " machine " and leaderless democracy, namely, the domination of professional politicians without a calling, without the inner charismatic qualities that make a leader '.[33]

Weber's attitude towards the likely consequences of the establishment of socialism derives from an extension of certain of these points. If the modern

---

[31] On Weber's relationship to Michels, cf. Günther Roth: *The Social Democrats in Imperial Germany* (Englewood Cliffs, 1963), pp. 249–57.

[32] *ES*, vol. 3, p. 990.

[33] *FMW*, p. 113; *GPS*, p. 532. For Marx's views on ' Caesarism ' as a concept applying to modern politics, see *SW*, vol. 1, pp. 244–5.

economy were organised on a socialist basis, and sought to attain a level of technical efficiency in the production and distribution of goods comparable to that of capitalism, this would necessitate ' a tremendous increase in the importance of professional bureaucrats '.[34] The specialised division of labour which is an integral characteristic of the modern economy demands the precise co-ordination of functions. This is a fact which has been at the root of the increase of bureaucratisation associated with the expansion of capitalism. But the formation of a socialist state would entail a considerably higher degree of bureaucratisation, since it would place a wider range of administrative tasks in the hands of the state.

Weber also foresees various economic problems which would be faced in a socialist society, especially in so far as it would be expected to operate using labour credits, rather than money, as a means of remuneration. Another source of difficulty in a socialist economy might be that of maintaining incentives to work, in so far as these are no longer reinforced by the possibility of losing a job because of inadequate performance. However, a socialist economy could potentially make use of a strong mass commitment to socialist ideals.[35] Any country which experiences a socialist revolution while those around it remain capitalist would face a variety of additional economic problems, particularly concerning the maintenance of foreign trade and credit.[36] But Weber's primary objections to socialism concern the bureaucratic ramifications which it would entail. This offers another example of the characteristic dilemma of modern times. Those who seek to set up a socialist society, whatever branch of socialism they adhere to, all act under the vision of the achievement of an order in which political participation and self realisation will go beyond the circumscribed form of party democracy found in capitalism. But the result of the impetus to realise this vision can only be in the direction of promoting the bureaucratisation of industry and the state, which will in fact further reduce the political autonomy of the mass of the population.

It is a singular feature of bureaucracy that once it has become established it is, in Weber's words, ' escape proof '. In those societies of the past where bureaucratisation has been highly developed, such as in Egypt, the bureaucratic officialdom has remained in uninterrupted control, and has only been undermined by the total disruption of the social order as a whole. Modern bureaucracy, characterised by a much higher level of rational specialisation than patrimonial organisations, is even more resistant to any attempt to prise society from its grip. ' Such an apparatus makes " revolution ", in the sense of the forceful creation of entirely new formations of authority, more and more impossible . . .' [37]

---

[34] *ES*, vol. 1, p. 224.
[35] *ES*, vol. 1, pp. 110–11.
[36] Weber regarded this as of critical importance in his evaluation of the likely success of a socialist revolution in Germany in 1918. See *GPS*, pp. 446ff.
[37] *ES*, vol. 3, p. 989.

The spread of bureaucracy in modern capitalism is both cause and consequence of the rationalisation of law, politics and industry. Bureaucratisation is the concrete, administrative manifestation of the rationalisation of action which has penetrated into all spheres of western culture, including art, music, and architecture. The overall trend towards rationalisation in the West is the result of the interplay of numerous factors, although the extension of the capitalist market has been the dominant impetus. But it must not, of course, be regarded as an ' inevitable ' evolutionary trend.

The concept of rationalisation enters into so many of Weber's historical writings that elucidation of the main spheres of its application is difficult. In a negative sense, the spread of rationalisation can be indexed by the progressive ' disenchantment of the world ' – the elimination of magical thought and practice. The great religious prophets, and the systematising activities of priests, are the main forces producing the rationalisation of religion which establishes coherent systems of meaning separate from the irregular magical forms of interpretation and propitiation. The rationalisation of religious thought, however, involves a number of related processes: the clarification of particular symbols (as occurs in the historical emergence, for instance, of the conception of a single omnipotent god in Judaism); the relating of such symbols to other symbols in a consistent fashion, according to general principles (as in the development of an internally coherent theodicy); and the extension of such principles to cover the whole of the cosmic order, so that there are no concrete events which cannot potentially be interpreted in terms of its religious meaning (thus, for example, Calvinism is a ' total ' ethic in this sense).

In assessing the significance of the growth of secular rationalisation in the West, it is important to bear in mind the distinction between formal and substantive rationality.[38] In Weber's view, this distinction is focal to sociological analysis, and application of it to the examination of the course of development of modern capitalism is critical in his interpretation of the dilemmas faced by contemporary man. The formal rationality of action refers to the degree to which conduct is organised according to rationally calculable principles. Thus the ideal type of bureaucracy is, in terms of formal rationality, the most rational type of organisation possible. In a broader way, it can be said that the formal rationality of western culture is evinced in its wholesale penetration by science. Science is not, of course, unique to the West, but nowhere else has it reached a comparable level of development. The fact that scientific principles underlie so much of modern social life does not entail that each individual knows what those principles are: ' Unless he is a physicist, one who rides on the streetcar has no idea how the car happened to get into motion. And he does not need to know... The savage knows incomparably more

---

[38] *ES*, vol. 1, pp. 85–6. cf. Friedmann's comments on Marcuse's paper ' Industrialisierung und Kapitalismus ', in the *Verhandlungen des 15. deutschen Soziologentages: Max Weber und die Soziologie heute* (Tübingen, 1965), pp. 201–5.

about his tools.' However, these principles are nevertheless 'known' in the sense of being available to the individual should he wish to ascertain them, and his conduct is governed by the belief that 'there are no mysterious incalculable forces that come into play, but rather that one can, in principle, master all things by calculation'.[39]

The relationship between the spread of formal rationality and the attainment of substantive rationality – that is, the application of rational calculation to the furtherance of definite goals or values – is problematic. Modern rational capitalism, measured in terms of substantive values of efficiency or productivity, is easily the most advanced economic system which man has developed. But the very rationalisation of social life which has made this possible has consequences which contravene some of the most distinctive values of western civilisation, such as those which emphasise the importance of individual creativity and autonomy of action. The rationalisation of modern life, especially as manifest in organisational form in bureaucracy, brings into being the 'cage' within which men are increasingly confined. This is the sense of Weber's concluding observations in *The Protestant Ethic*:

Limitation to specialised work, with a renunciation of the Faustian universality of men which it involves, is a condition of any valuable work in the modern world; hence deeds and renunciation inevitably condition each other today. This fundamentally ascetic trait of middle-class life, if it attempts to be a way of life at all, and not simply the absence of any, was what Goethe wanted to teach, at the height of his wisdom, in the *Wanderjahren*, and in the end which he gave to the life of his *Faust*. For him the realisation meant a renunciation, a departure from an age of full and beautiful humanity, which can no more be repeated in the course of our cultural development than can the flower of the Athenian culture of antiquity.[40]

In this sense, western society can be said to be founded upon an intrinsic antinomy between formal and substantive rationality which, according to Weber's analysis of modern capitalism, cannot be resolved.

39 *FMW*, p. 139.
40 *PE*, p. 181.

Part 4: Capitalism, socialism and social theory

13. Marx's influence

The intellectual relationship between the writings of Marx on the one hand, and those of Durkheim and Weber on the other, cannot be analysed satisfactorily without reference to the social and political changes which both conjoined and disconnected the works of the three writers. Durkheim and Weber were each critics of Marx, and consciously directed part of their work to the refutation or qualification of Marx's writings: indeed, the remark that the bulk of Weber's intellectual output represents a prolonged ' dialogue with the ghost of Marx ',[1] has often been reiterated in the secondary literature. But in both France and Germany, in the late nineteenth century, the influence of Marx's thought was far more than purely intellectual in character: in the shape of ' Marxism ', Marx's writings became the primary impetus within a vital and dynamic political movement. As such, Marxism, and ' revolutionary socialism ' more generally, formed a major element in the horizon of Durkheim and Weber, especially so in the case of the latter.[2]

Marx conceived his works to furnish a platform for the accomplishment of a definite *Praxis*, and not simply as academic studies of society. The same is true, although not of course in an exactly comparable manner, of both Durkheim and Weber; each directed his writings towards the prophylaxis of what they considered to be the most urgent social and political problems confronting contemporary man, and attempted to provide an alternative standpoint to that set out by Marx. It is worth remarking upon the fact that no British author of comparable status to Durkheim or Weber emerged in their generation. While the reasons for this are no doubt complex, it is unquestionably true that *one* factor responsible was the absence, in Britain, of a really significant revolutionary socialist movement.

Society and politics in Germany : Marx's standpoint [3]
At the turn of the nineteenth century, Germany consisted of thirty-nine competing principalities. The two leading German states, Prussia and Austria,

---

[1] See Albert Salomon: ' German sociology ', in Georges Gurvitch and Wilbert E. Moore: *Twentieth Century Sociology* (New York, 1945), p. 596.

[2] In the chapters which follow I shall adopt the procedure of calling those views which I attribute to Marx himself ' Marxian ' ideas, terming ' Marxist ' those propositions or actions adopted by professed followers of Marx. I shall use ' Marxism ' in a broad sense to refer generically to the latter group.

[3] In this chapter I have drawn upon material previously published in my article ' Marx, Weber, and the development of capitalism ', pp. 289–310. For a description

were both major European powers: their very rivalry was one factor hindering German unification. The hopes of German nationalists were also obstructed by the internal ethnic composition of Prussia and Austria. Austria, after 1815, had more non-Germans than Germans in her population; and Prussia incorporated large numbers of Poles within her territories to the east. Espousal of the nationalist doctrine could forcibly entail, for Prussia, the return of these lands to Polish dominion. The Austrian government was flatly opposed to any movement towards the formation of an integral German state.

But of greater weight than these factors in hindering the development of Germany were more basic characteristics of the social and economic structure of the country. Compared to the most advanced capitalist country, Britain, Germany was still almost in the Middle Ages, both in terms of the level of her economic development, and in terms of the low degree of political liberalisation within the various German states. In Prussia the Junker landowners, whose power sprung from their ownership of the large ex-Slavic estates to the east of the Elbe, maintained a dominant position within the economy and government. In the early part of the nineteenth century, as Landes has remarked, ' the further east one goes in Europe the more the bourgeoisie takes on the appearance of a foreign excrescence on manorial society, a group apart scorned by the nobility and feared or hated by (or unknown to) a peasantry still personally bound to the local *seigneur* '.[4]

But Germany could hardly remain isolated from the sweeping currents of change which had been set in motion in France by the events of 1789. Marx's early works were written in the anticipation of a German revolution. Indeed, it might be said that Marx's awareness of the very backwardness of Germany in its social and economic structure was at the root of his original conception of the role of the proletariat in history. In France, Marx writes in 1844, ' partial emancipation is a basis for complete emancipation '; but in Germany, so much less developed, a ' progressive emancipation ' is impossible: the only possibility of advancement is through radical revolution, which in turn can only be accomplished through a revolutionary proletariat. A proletariat at this time barely existed in Germany, and by 1847 Marx was clear that the imminent revolution in Germany would be a bourgeois one, and that ' the bourgeoisie in that country had just begun its contest with feudal absolutism '.[5] But the peculiar circumstances of the social structure of Germany, so it seemed to Marx, would make it possible for a bourgeois revolution to be closely followed by a proletarian one.[6]

---

of the influence of Marx's writings on sociology at the turn of the century, see Maximilien Rubel: ' Premiers contacts des sociologues du XIXe siècle avec la pensée de Marx ', *Cahiers internationaux de sociologie*, vol. 31, 1961, pp. 175–84.
[4] Landes, p. 129.   [5] *CM*, p. 167.
[6] cf. Engels' views on this matter, as set out in his ' Der Status Quo in Deutschland ', *We*, vol. 4, esp. pp. 43–6 and 49–51; and *Germany: Revolution and Counter-revolution* (London, 1933).

The failure of the 1848 revolutions, however, dispelled Marx's optimism about an immediate 'leap into the future' in Germany. The 1848 uprisings were also something of a salutary experience for the ruling circles in the German states, and especially in Prussia, but did not break their dominance. The failure of 1848 to produce any radical reforms served as a death-knell, not only to the hopes of the small groups of socialists, but also to those of the liberals. The maintenance of Junker economic power, of their dominance in the officer corps in the army, and in the civil service bureaucracy, led the bulk of the German liberals to acceptance of a series of compromise measures introducing nothing more than a semblance of parliamentary democracy, as well as fostering lasting divisions within their ranks.

The events of 1848 mark a line of direct historical connection between Marx and Weber. For Marx, the result was physical exile in England, and an intellectual recognition of the importance of showing in detail the 'laws of movement' of capitalism as an economic system. Within Germany, the failures of 1848 paved the way for the inept character of liberal politics which, as compared to the bold successes of Bismarck's hegemony, forms such an important background to the whole of Weber's thought.[7] Moreover, the persistence of the traditional social and political structure in Germany after 1848 drastically affected the role of the labour movement. It is not relevant in this context to analyse the complicated nature of Marx's relationship to Lassalle and to the movement which Lassalle founded, but certain aspects of this relationship are pertinent. There was from the beginning of the Social Democratic movement an inbuilt ambivalence towards Marx's doctrines which formed a permanent source of schism within the party. While on the one hand Lassalle was deeply indebted in his theoretical views to Marx's writings on the development of capitalism, in his practical leadership of the new movement he frequently acted in ways opposed to Marx's views on specific issues, and advocated policies difficult to reconcile with the theory he professed to accept. Thus, in contrast to Marx's opinion that the German working class should throw in its weight with the bourgeoisie in order to secure the bourgeois revolution which would subsequently provide the conditions for the assumption of power by the proletariat, Lassalle led the working class movement away from collaboration with the liberals. As Mehring remarked, Lassalle 'based his policy on the assumption that the Philistine movement of the progressive bourgeoisie would never lead to anything, "not even if we wait for centuries, for geological eras"....'.[8]

Lassalle died the same year that Weber was born. By this time the immediate future of Germany had already been set. The detachment of the labour

---

[7] In his copy of Simmel's book *Schopenhauer und Nietzsche*, where Simmel says: 'Society ultimately resides in what the individual *does*', Weber noted: 'Quite correct. cf. Bismarck'. Quoted in Eduard Baumgarten: *Max Weber: Werk und Person* (Tübingen, 1964), p. 614.

[8] Franz Mehring: *Karl Marx* (Ann Arbor, 1962), p. 313.

movement from the liberals, in conjunction with other factors, set the scene for Bismarck's unification of Germany, in which, as Bismarck said, ' Germany did not look to Prussia's liberalism, but to her power '.[9] In 1875, when Liebknecht and Bebel, Marx's leading advocates in Germany, accepted union with the Lassallean wing of the labour movement, Germany was in both political and economic terms a very different nation from that which Marx originally wrote about in the 1840s. Political integration had been achieved, not through the rise of a revolutionary bourgeoisie, but largely as a result of a policy of *Realpolitik* and nationalism founded essentially upon the bold use of political power ' from the top ' and occurring within a social system which – in spite of achieving some of the trappings of a ' welfare state ' – in large degree retained its traditional structure. The difficult phases of initial political unification, and the ' take off ' into industrialisation, were accomplished in quite a different fashion in Germany from the typical process of development in Britain. From the beginnings of his career, Marx remained conscious of the variations in historical development which have created social and economic differences between Germany, France and Britain. It is quite mistaken to suppose that, according to Marx's view, there is a unitary relationship between level of economic development and the internal character of the capitalist state (see below, p. 197). Nevertheless, Marx bases his writings upon the assertion that, in analytic terms, economic power is everywhere the foundation of political domination. Therefore, in *Capital*, Marx logically accepts Britain as providing the basic model for his theory of capitalist development, and in spite of his awareness of the complicated issues possessed by the peculiar character of the German social structure, he never abandoned the basic standpoint summed up in his use of the phrase ' *De te fabula narratur* ': ' It is of you that the story is told.' ' The country that is more developed industrially only shows, to the less developed, the image of its own future.' [10]

Thus neither the Marxist socialists nor the liberals in Germany of the late nineteenth century had an adequate historical model in terms of which they could satisfactorily comprehend the peculiarities of their position. Both

---

[9] Marianne Weber has testified to the strength of the emotional impact which the 1870 war had upon the household in which the young Weber was living. Marianne Weber, pp. 47–8. For a recent analysis of Weber's personality and psychological development (written, in part, in conscious attempt to revise aspects of Marianne Weber's biography), see Arthur Mitzman: *The Iron Cage: An Historical Interpretation of Max Weber* (New York, 1970).

[10] Preface to the first German edition of the first volume of *Capital*, *SW*, vol. 1, p. 449. Many economists and sociologists even today continue, explicitly or otherwise, to take the British experience as the model against which to analyse industrial/political development. But it is probably more appropriate, in some respects, to treat Britain as a ' deviant ' case. cf. on some relevant issues, Barrington Moore: *Social Origins of Dictatorship and Democracy* (London, 1969), pp. 413–32 and *passim*. A Marxist account of German social thought in relation to the ' backwardness ' of the country is given in Georg Lukács: *Die Zerstörung der Vernunft* (Berlin, 1955).

looked to theories developed in an earlier epoch, and based primarily upon the experience of Britain in the late eighteenth and early nineteenth centuries. In the Social Democratic Party, this situation forced out into the open the inherent tension between Marx's stress upon the revolutionary overthrow of capitalism, and the Lassallean emphasis upon the appropriation of the capitalist state through the achievement of a fully universal franchise. Bernstein's *Die Voraussetzungen des Sozialismus*, although itself based partly upon a British model, was the most concrete theoretical expression of the realisation that the relationship between the political and economic development of capitalism could not be adequately comprehended in terms of what most Marxists took to be the main theses of *Capital*: the progressive formation of a two-class society, the 'pauperisation' of the vast majority, and the immanent collapse of capitalism in a final catastrophic crisis. Bernstein's 'revisionism' was rejected by the SPD orthodoxy, but at the cost of strengthening the trend towards a mechanical materialism which effectively reverted to the 'passive' materialism which Marx had criticised and discarded in the early phases of his career. This trend was given a definite theoretical backing by the fact that 'Marxism' came to be identified, in the eyes both of its adherents and its liberal critics, with the systematic exposition set out by Engels in *Anti-Dühring*.[11] Today it is usual among western scholars to emphasise the fundamental discrepancies between the thought of Marx and Engels. The differences have undoubtedly been exaggerated.[12] Nevertheless, the implications of the position which Engels takes in this work are certainly at variance with the subject–object dialectic central to Marx's formulations. By transferring the dialectic to nature, Engels obscures the most essential element of Marx's conception, 'the dialectical relationship of subject and object in the historical process'.[13] In so doing Engels helped to stimulate the notion that ideas simply 'reflect' material reality in a passive sense.[14]

The partial disappearance of the principle upon which Marx's original writings were based – the creative dialectical interaction between subject and object – has two possible outcomes on the level of ethical theory, both of which

---

[11] *Anti-Dühring* (Moscow, 1954). See also the posthumously published *Dialectics of Nature* (Moscow, 1954).

[12] It is more accurate to say, in Laski's words, 'that the two men had, as it were, evolved in common a joint stock of ideas which they regarded as a kind of intellectual bank account upon which either could draw freely'. Harold J. Laski, Introduction to *CM*, p. 20.

[13] The phrase is Lukács', *Geschichte und Klassenbewusstein*, p. 22.

[14] Engels' own attempt to escape the theoretical impasse to which his views led is given in his statement that 'According to the materialist conception of history the determining element in history is *ultimately* the production and reproduction in real life. More than this neither Marx nor I have ever asserted.' Engels to Bloch, September 1890, *Selected Correspondence*, p. 475. Marx had earlier felt compelled to comment ironically that he 'was not a Marxist'. An interesting analysis, indicating the long-standing nature of Engels' sympathy to positivism, is given in H. Bollnow: 'Engels Auffassung von Revolution und Entwicklung in seinen "Grundsätzen des Kommunismus" (1847)', *Marxismusstudien*, vol. 1, pp. 77–144.

occurred in German Social Democracy. One outcome is to move in the direction of a philosophical materialism, which treats ideas as epiphenomena, and thereby is able to preserve the Marxian adherence to an immanent conception of ethics. The other path, taken by the revisionists, is to reintroduce the possibility of forming an ahistorical theoretical ethics on a par with traditional philosophy. This has the advantage of eliminating any embarrassment which might be felt in allowing ideas an ' independent ' role in conditioning social change, but introduces a voluntaristic standpoint which dislocates the presence of an ideal from the possibility of its attainment. This is the position adopted by Bernstein.

Weber's relation to Marxism and Marx

The import of Weber's many references to Marx and to Marxism can only be properly understood against this background, which has been sketched in an exceedingly brief fashion. An appreciation of the significance of ' political ', as distinct from ' economic ' power, such as wielded by Bismarck in successfully promoting the internal consolidation and the economic development of Germany (and, more specifically, the importance of the bureaucracy in this process), is a key dimension of Weber's approach to politics, and of his sociology more generally. Weber's commitment to nationalism, and his lifelong emphasis upon the primacy of the German state, also have to be understood in these terms. This determination to recognise the realities of the use of political power, however, is counterpointed in Weber's thought by an equally resolute adherence to the values of classical European liberalism. This is one main factor producing the pathos which is so strongly marked in much of Weber's writing; he finds himself compelled to recognise an expanding divergence between the typical line of development in modern society and the values which he recognises as representing the distinctive ethos of western culture. But this is in part an expression, albeit in a highly subtle and ratiocinated form, of the peculiar dilemmas of German liberalism as a whole.[15]

Weber's inaugural address at Freiburg in 1895 outlines his interpretation of the hopes of bourgeois liberalism in Germany in the fact of Romantic conservatism on the one side, and the Marxist party on the other. The lecture expresses a fervent advocacy of the ' imperialistic ' interests of the nation-state, and analyses the position of the various major classes in Germany in terms of the degree to which they are capable of generating the political leadership necessary to maintain German integrity in the face of international pressures. ' The object of our work in social policy ', Weber declares, ' is not to make the world happy, but to unify socially a nation surrounded by econo-

---

[15] For a lengthy description of Weber's political writings, see Mommsen. This work underplays, however, Weber's commitment to classical liberal values, towards what Weber calls ' man's personal autonomy ', ' the spiritual and moral values of mankind '. Quoted in Marianne Weber, p. 159. cf. Eduard Baumgarten, p. 607; and my *Politics and Sociology in the Thought of Max Weber*.

mic progress. . .' [16] Weber dissociates himself, however, from the 'mystical' conception of the state as advanced by conservative idealism, and condemns the Junkers as an economically declining class not capable of leading the nation. But the working class is also politically 'infinitely immature' and not able to provide the requisite source of political direction. Consequently, the main hope for leadership is to be found in the bourgeoisie; but this class has been stunted by its history of subordination to Bismarck's rule, and is itself not yet ready for the political tasks which it eventually must be called upon to assume. Weber derides the timidity of the bourgeoisie in the face of the 'red spectre':

The *threatening thing* in our situation, however, is that the bourgeois classes as the bearers of the *power* interests of the nation seem to wilt away, while there are as yet no signs that the workers are beginning to show the maturity to replace them. The danger . . . does *not* lie with the *masses*. It is not a question of the *economic* position of the *ruled*, but rather of the *political* qualifications of the ruling and ascending classes. . .[17]

It is wholly mistaken, according to Weber, to regard radical revolution as the only means for the political emancipation and economic advancement of the working class. In fact, the growth of the political power and the improvement in the economic circumstances of the working class are both possible within capitalism, and are actually in the interests of the bourgeoisie.

The strengthening of the liberal bourgeoisie, as Weber came to recognise with increasing clarity at later stages of his political career, entails developing a governmental system which would vest real political power in parliament, and create a reservoir of genuine political leaders. The result of Bismarck's rule, according to Weber, has left Germany without the parliamentary autonomy necessary to generate the political leadership which can take control of the bureaucratic machine of government bequeathed to the country from the past, and which threatens Germany with 'uncontrolled bureaucratic domination'.[18] Weber's attitude to the possibility of establishing socialism in Germany – including the transitory Eisner government – is directly bound up with these views upon the German social and political structure. Weber notes early on in his career that much of the revolutionary fervour of the leaders of the main body of the Social Democratic movement is quite divergent from the real trend of its development. As Weber expresses it, the German state will conquer the Social Democratic Party and not vice versa; the party will move

---

[16] ' Der Nationalstaat und die Volkswirtschaftspolitik ', *GPS*, p. 23. Compare Durkheim's account of Treitschke as the epitome of German conservative nationalism, in ' *L'Allemagne au-dessus de tout* ' (Paris, 1915). The significance of Weber's ' move to the left' in politics over the course of his career is often exaggerated (see, for example, Ralf Dahrendorf: *Society and Democracy in Germany* (London, 1968), pp. 41–61); Weber changed his evaluation of politics, rather than of fundamentals of political attitude. cf. Gustav Schmidt: *Deutscher Historismus und der Übergang zur parlamentarischen Demokratie* (Lübeck and Hamburg, 1964).

[17] *GPS*, p. 23.   [18] *ES*, vol. 3, p. 1453.

towards accommodation to the prevailing order rather than providing a realistically revolutionary alternative to it.[19] The SPD, Weber asserts, is itself already highly bureaucratised. The major political dilemma facing Germany is that of escaping from the toils of the arbitrary rule of bureaucracy: should a socialist government, and a planned economy, be set up, the result would be an extension of bureaucratic repression. Not only would there be no counterweight to the spread of bureaucracy in the political sphere, but this would be the case in the economic domain also. 'This would be socialism', in Weber's eyes, 'in about the same manner in which the ancient Egyptian "New Kingdom" was socialist.'[20]

Weber's views on the character of the SPD as a 'revolutionary' party remained fairly consistent over the course of his life. His evaluation of his own political position with regard to the policies of the party did change, however, with the changing nature of the German political structure, especially as a result of the Great War. Thus, towards the end of his life, having witnessed the occurrence of what he had previously foreseen – the increasing integration of the Social Democratic Party into the existing parliamentary order – Weber declared himself to be as close to the party as to find it difficult to separate himself from it.[21] But Weber's consistent view of 'Marxism' as represented by the SPD in Germany is that its professed objectives, the revolutionary overthrow of the state and the achievement of a classless society, are entirely divergent from the real role which it is destined to play in German politics.

The attitude which Weber took towards the theoretical and empirical writings of academic 'interpreters' of Marx cannot simply be deduced from his relationship to the Social Democratic Party, since the latter was determined in some degree by Weber's appreciation of the political realities of the German situation. Weber recognised, of course, that some of the leading Marxist authors of his time had made distinct and even brilliant contributions to economics, sociology, and jurisprudence, and he maintained a close contact with scholars influenced heavily by Marx.[22] It is important to recognise that the bulk of Weber's writing on capitalism and religion is not in a simple or

[19] *GASS*, p. 409.

[20] *ES*, vol. 3, p. 1453. For Weber's views on revolutionary Russia, in the early part of the nineteenth century, cf. *GPS*, pp. 192–210. Of the domination of Bolshevism, Weber observed in 1918, it 'is a pure military *dictatorship*, not simply that of generals, but of *corporals*' (*GPS*, p. 280).

[21] *GPS*, p. 472. Weber's views of the more radical attempts at socialist reconstruction were very severe: 'I am absolutely convinced that these experiments can and will only lead to the discrediting of socialism for 100 years' (letter to Lukács, quoted in Mommsen, p. 303); 'Liebknecht belongs in the lunatic asylum and Rosa Luxemburg in the zoological gardens' (quoted *ibid.* p. 300).

[22] On the relationship between Weber and Sombart, cf. Talcott Parsons: 'Capitalism in recent German literature: Sombart and Weber', *Journal of Political Economy*, vol. 36, 1928, pp. 641–61; on Weber and Michels, see Roth, pp. 249–57. On the reception of Marx's ideas by the *Kathedersozialisten*, see Lindenlaub, pp. 272–384.

direct way an intellectual response to Marx's works. Weber undoubtedly had a general acquaintance with Marx's writings at an early stage in his career; but other influences were far more important.[23] Most of Weber's interests, especially in the early part of his career, stemmed from orthodox problems of historical economics and law. Moreover, when Weber uses the term ' historical materialism ', the reference is often to the spate of scholarly works claiming Marxian ancestry which appeared in the 1890s. These sometimes represent what Weber takes to be a vulgarisation of Marx's ideas, or otherwise depart notably from what Weber considers to be the main tenets of Marx's position.[24] Thus *The Protestant Ethic* has a complicated genealogy. Weber was interested from his youth in religion as a social phenomenon.[25] While his studies of law and economics diverted him from following this interest directly in his first academic writings, the work is in some part an expression of which had remained in the forefront of his mind.

Weber's views upon the validity and usefulness of Marx's original work thus have to be partially disentangled from his assessment of ' vulgar ' Marxism. Nevertheless, the numerous scattered references to Marx contained in Weber's writings do furnish a clear exposition of the main sources of similarity and difference as Weber conceived them. Weber recognises, of course, that Marx had made fundamental contributions to historical and sociological analysis. But, according to Weber, Marx's developmental conceptions can never be regarded as anything other than sources of insight, or at most as ideal typical concepts, which might be applied to illuminate specific historical sequences. In Weber's eyes, Marx's attribution of overall rational ' direction ' to the course of history is, within the terms of the framework which Marx adopts, as illegitimate as that embodied in the Hegelian philosophy which helped to give it birth. While Weber admits, with strong reservations, the use of developmental ' stages ' as theoretical constructs which can be applied as a ' pragmatic means ' to aid historical research, he rejects completely the formulation of ' deterministic schemes ' based upon general theories of development.

[23] As Roth has pointed out, Weber's early writings embodied a preliminary critique of historical materialism, but this was by no means central to Weber's interests until later on. Günther Roth: ' Das historische Verhältnis der Weberschen Soziologie zum Marxismus ', *Kölner Zeitschrift für Soziologie und Sozialpsychologie*, vol. 20, 1968, pp. 433ff.

[24] See, for example, Weber's discussion of Stammler, in ' R. Stammlers " Uberwindung " der materialistischen Geschichtsauffassung ', *GAW*, pp. 219–383. The sarcastic reference which Weber makes to Bebel at the end of his thesis on Roman agrarian history is not untypical of various asides on contemporary Marxist theoreticians in Weber's writings. *Die römische Agrargeschichte*, p. 275.

[25] It is interesting to note that Weber was impressed at an early age by his reading of *Das Leben Jesu*, by David Strauss: the same work which played a prominent part in forming the views of the Young Hegelians. cf. Marianne Weber, pp. 117–20; *Jugendbriefe* (Tübingen, n.d.), pp. 205ff. In addition to the stimulus provided by the work of Sombart, Georg Jellinek's *Erklärung der Menschen- und Bürgerrechte* (1895) was probably important in influencing Weber's direction of interest.

It follows from this that there can be no more than contingent validity in the conception that economic relationships constitute the source of historical development. The specific importance of the ' economic ' is variable, and must be assessed by empirical study of particular circumstances. Weber accepts that ideas and values, while most definitely not being ' derivations ' of material interests in any simple sense, nevertheless must always be analysed in relation to such interests:

Liberated as we are from the antiquated notion that all cultural phenomena can be *deduced* as a product or function of the constellation of ' material ' interests, we believe nevertheless that the *analysis of social and cultural phenomena* with special reference to their *economic* conditioning and ramifications was a scientific principle of creative fruitfulness, and with careful application and freedom from dogmatic restrictions, will remain such for a very long time to come.[26]

But a theory which seeks to deny the independent historical significance of the content of ideas (which itself is variable) cannot be acceptable. The theory that economic factors in any sense ' finally ' explain the course of history, Weber asserts, ' as a scientific theorem, is utterly finished '.[27]

Weber recognises that Marx's writings vary in the degree of sophistication with which his materialist interpretation of history is presented. The *Communist Manifesto*, for example, sets out Marx's views ' with the crude elements of genius of the early form '.[28] But even in the more thorough formulation in *Capital*, Marx nowhere defines precisely how the ' economic ' is delimited from other spheres of society. Weber's distinctions between ' economics ', ' economically relevant ', and ' economically conditioned ' phenomena are aimed at clarifying this deficiency. There are many modes of human action, such as religious practices, which while they are not themselves ' economic ' in character, have relevance to economic action in so far as they influence the ways in which men strive to acquire or make use of utilities. These are economically relevant types of action. Actions which are economically relevant can in turn be separated from those which are economically conditioned: the latter are actions, which are again not ' economic ' but which are causally influenced by economic factors. As Weber points out, ' After what has been said, it is self-evident that: firstly, the boundary lines of " economic " phenomena are vague and not easily defined; secondly the " economic " aspect of a phenomenon is by no means *only* " economically conditioned " or *only* " economically relevant ". . .' [29]

Weber also points to another source of ambiguity in Marx's writings: that Marx fails to distinguish in a clear manner between the ' economic ' and the ' technological '. Where Marx slips into a more or less direct technological determinism, Weber shows, his work is sometimes manifestly inadequate. Marx's famous assertion that ' The hand-mill gives you society with the feudal

---

[26] *MSS*, p. 68; *GAW*, p. 166.   [27] *GASS*, p. 456.
[28] *MSS*, p. 68.   [29] *MSS*, p. 65.

lord; the steam-mill, society with the industrial capitalist ',[30] is according to Weber, 'a technological proposition, not an economic one, and it can be clearly proven that it is simply a false assertion. For the era of the hand-mill, which lasted up to modern times, showed the most varied kinds of cultural " super-structures " in different regions.' [31] A given form of technology may be associated with varying sorts of social organisation – a fact implicit in Marx's own views since, although it would involve essentially the same technological basis as capitalism, socialism would for Marx be a very different form of society.

Weber admits the significance of class conflicts in history, while denying that the role of class struggles is as important as is postulated by Marx. Although in some ways Weber's conceptions of class and class conflict are not so divergent from those of Marx as is often thought – Weber does heavily underscore the point that property versus lack of property constitutes the most important source of class divisions – it is true nonetheless that the historical significance of status monopolies is strongly emphasised by Weber. For Weber, status group conflicts, however, are no more important in history than conflicts between political associations and nation-states. In Weber's view, therefore, the concept of divergent sectional ' interests ' cannot be limited to economic interests, but must be extended to other spheres of social life. Thus political parties, for example, have interests which derive from their situation as aspirants to, or as wielders of, power, and such interests do not necessarily rest upon shared class situations.

But the most important respect in which Weber separates his views from those of Marx concerns the broad epistemological standpoint which underlies the whole of Weber's writings. The radical neo-Kantian position which Weber accepts takes as its premise the complete logical separation of factual and normative propositions. In Weber's work, the necessary corollary of this is the postulate of the irreducibility of competing values. It is this epistemological position which Weber takes as separating his perspective most decisively from that of Marx: Marx's work, whatever its undoubted merits, involves the commitment to the ' scientific ' ethic of ' ultimate ends ', and thus entails the acceptance of a ' total ' conception of history. The conception of charisma, and the role which it plays in Weber's work, manifests Weber's conviction that historical development cannot be interpreted in terms of a rational scheme which expresses what is normatively valid. For Weber, science cannot answer the question: ' " Which of the warring Gods should we serve? " ' [32]

---

[30] *Poverty of Philosophy*, p. 92. Weber does not, however, take account of the polemical context in which this statement is made. For Weber's own distinction between ' economy ' and ' technology ', see *ES*, vol. 1, pp. 65–7.

[31] *GASS*, p. 450.

[32] *FMW*, p. 153. cf. Weber's remark on socialist parties: 'I shall *not join these churches.*' Quoted in Baumgarten, p. 607.

France in the nineteenth century : Marx and the growth of Marxism

Marx and Marxism were parts of Max Weber's intellectual universe to a
degree which was not the case for Durkheim. Marx was a German, and wrote
most of his major works in that language; and no other country in the nineteenth century possessed as large or as politically significant a Marxist party as
the German Social Democratic Party. In spite of the fact that he spent a period
studying in Germany in the early part of his career, Durkheim's intellectual
perspective remained almost obstinately French. Nonetheless, the formative
social and political context in which Durkheim developed his sociology was
comparable in certain important respects with that which influenced Weber.
Like Weber, Durkheim lived and wrote in a situation in which two divergent
streams of political thought and activity threatened to submerge the liberal
principles bequeathed from the French Revolution: a conservative nationalism on the one hand, and a radical socialism on the other. In common with
Weber, Durkheim accepted some elements from each of these competing
systems of thought, and embodied them within his own political standpoint,
and within his social theory more broadly. The conclusions which each author
reached, however, are in some respects quite divergent, and this is in part to
be traced to the specific ways in which the overall development of France
contrasted with that of Germany in the latter part of the nineteenth century.

Marx's attitude towards France in the 1840s was, naturally enough, dominated by a consciousness of the relative superiority of the level of political
advancement of that country as compared to Germany. Whatever the strength
of the reaction which had set in against the Revolution in France, it was
obvious that the political sophistication of the French socialist thinkers was
rooted in a social structure which had already made its decisive break with its
feudal past. One of the principal criticisms which Marx directs against the
majority of German socialists was that they 'imported' ideas from France
without appreciating the depth of the disjunction between the material
differences between the two countries. As Marx writes in 1843:

If one were to begin with the *status quo* itself in Germany, even in the most
appropriate way, i.e. negatively, the result would still be an *anachronism*. Even
the negation of our political present is already a dusty fact in the historical lumber room of modern nations. I may negate powdered wigs, but I am still left
with unpowdered wigs. If I negate the German situation of 1843 I have, according to French chronology, hardly reached the year 1789, and still less the vital
centre of the present day.[33]

But the course of development taken after the Paris risings of 1848–9 made
it apparent that the degree to which the liberal bourgeoisie in France had
achieved a stable footing in the control of government prior to this date was
open to serious question. Engels documents at some length the reconsidera-
tions of previous views which were forced upon Marx and himself by the con-

[33] *EW*, pp. 44–5. See also *CM*, pp. 167–70.

sequences of the events of 1848 and 1849 in France. Although proletarian elements played a major role in the Paris rising of 1848, the results were really a victory for the *grande bourgeoisie*, who thereby consolidated the advances which had not been fully secured as a result of the counter-reaction of conservative forces subsequent to the 1789 Revolution. 'History has proved us, and all who thought like us, wrong', Engels writes. ' It has made it clear that the state of economic development at that time was not, by a long way, ripe for the elimination of capitalist production. . .' [34]

Marx discusses the situation in France at the mid-point of the nineteenth century in two lengthy analyses: *The Class Struggles in France* and *The Eighteenth Brumaire of Louis Bonaparte*.[35] It is an indication of the lack of a ' mechanistic ' conception of the relationship between economy and state in Marx's writings that, while treating Britain as the model for the economic theory of *Capital*, Marx nonetheless regards France as the purest example of advanced liberal bourgeois politics. The particular circumstances of British historical development, according to Marx, have created a state which is based upon an alliance between the bourgeoisie and the remnants of the old land-owning aristocracy.[36] In France, by contrast, such a ' compromise ' was not effected, and the political character of class conflicts is hence more clearly evinced. For Marx, the French bourgeoisie and proletariat are the ' politicians ' of Europe, as the Germans were the ' philosophers ', and the British the ' political economists '.[37]

Under Louis-Philippe, according to Marx, only one section of the bourgeoisie maintained control of political power: the financial capitalists, bankers and rentiers. The main group benefiting from the fall of Louis-Philippe are the large industrialists, who had little access previously to the reins of government. The result is a clarification of the class-struggle, bringing the division between working class and bourgeoisie into a sharper focus, and thus providing the source for a subsequent direct political confrontation between the two great industrial classes:

The French workers could not take a step forward, could not touch a hair of the bourgeois order, until the course of the revolution had aroused the mass of the nation, peasants and petty bourgeois, standing between the proletariat and the bourgeoisie, against this order, against the rule of capital, and had forced it to attach itself to the proletarians as their protagonists.[38]

Marx does not expect, however, that France will be immediately plunged into a new civil war in which the proletarians would emerge as victors; such hopes have to be postponed for an indefinite period. ' *A new revolution is possible only in consequence of a new crisis. It is, however, just as certain as this crisis.* ' [39] The crisis indeed did come, twenty years later, not, as Marx

---

[34] *SW*, vol. 1, p. 125.
[36] *We*, vol. 11, pp. 95–7.
[38] *SW*, vol. 1, p. 149.

[35] *SW*, vol. 1, pp. 139–344.
[37] *We*, vol. 1, p. 405.
[39] *SW*, vol. 1, p. 231.

expected, as a consequence of an economic depression in Britain, 'the demiurge of the bourgeois cosmos ', but as a result of the disastrous war which Louis Napoleon undertook against Germany in 1870.

The consequences of Bismarck's victory constitute the decisive axis which connects the thought of the three authors whose work is analysed in this book. In Germany, the military triumph was a major factor promoting Bismarck's programme of Prussian dominance in a unitary German state; for France, the results were calamitous, producing political disarray and lasting feelings of humiliation among large sections of the population. Marx's attitudes towards the Commune are notoriously complicated, and it is not possible to pursue this matter here. What is important is that the immediate effects of the brief life of the Commune, and of its savage repression, were to promulgate class hatreds which further accentuated the internal disunity of the French state. But the Commune was not to be, as Marx hoped, 'the glorious harbinger of a new society '.[40] Instead, it was succeeded by a period in which a resurgence of nationalism in France provided the most tangible ideological basis for the recovery of national unity, and in which the country to some extent came to terms with its own backwardness. For the bulk of provincial France had in many respects remained unchanged since the eighteenth century; strongly conservative elements remained powerful, in the form of the church, pro-pertied rentiers, and the peasantry. Even Marx's description in *The Class Struggles in France*, sober as it was compared to his earlier views, proved to be optimistic as an appraisal of the level of real political power attained by the progressive sectors of the industrial bourgeoisie.[41]

Under the Third Republic, however, considerable progress was made to-wards the emancipation of the country from the lingering hold of conservative elements. The Dreyfus affair brought to a head the conflict between republi-canism and the reactionary concerns of the church and the military, and eventuated in stimulating the separation of various administrative functions from hierocratic control: of basic importance here was the expansion of the secularisation of education. Much of this derived from the activities of the Radical Party. The history of Marxism in France in the late nineteenth cen-tury is a pale shadow of the powerful resurgence of the Social Democratic Party in Germany towards the end of the century. As in Germany, however, the seeds of Marxist thought which were implanted in France during the decades following the repression of the Commune became mixed with indi-genous socialist traditions with which Marxism existed in uneasy alliance. Given the much weaker position of the Marxist left in France, the result in this case was the evolution of a doctrine which, as Lichtheim has commented, 'was at best an approximation and at worst a caricature '.[42]

---

[40] *SW*, vol. 1, p. 542.
[41] See Marx's comments in 'The Eighteenth Brumaire of Louis Bonaparte ', *SW*, vol. 1, pp. 333–5 and *passim*.   [42] For footnote, see p. 199.

Durkheim's assessment of Marx

In these circumstances it is not difficult to appreciate why Marxism had little influence upon Durkheim in the early part of his career. Unlike Max Weber, Durkheim had little taste for active involvement in political action, and maintained an aloofness from the struggles and disputes of the ' *cuisine politique* '.[43] In general terms the main substance of Durkheim's political stance is clear enough, involving the repudiation of both conservatism and revolutionary socialism. As is the case with Weber, Durkheim's liberalism was heavily influenced by the specific social and political conditions of his native country. In Durkheim's case, the importance of national reconstruction following the catastrophes of 1870–1 is basic, and the influence of a general concern with moral consolidation is clearly imprinted upon the whole of Durkheim's writings. The leading theme, indeed, in Durkheim's work is the concern to reconcile the growth of secular individualism with the moral demands which are posed by the maintenance of unity in a modern differentiated society. Durkheim's contribution to the Dreyfus struggle, an article written in response to the expressed views of a leading Catholic conservative, delineates these issues very clearly.[44] The individualism of the *Dreyfusards*, Durkheim argues, is quite different from the amoral self-seeking with which it is identified by the partisans of church and army. The pursuit of egoistic ends which is the economists' model of man is not at all to be equated with rationalistic individualism. The economists reduce human conduct to a market exchange. This utilitarianism is now defunct; the emergent ethic of individualism is itself a moral, not an amoral, phenomenon: ' the human person ... is considered as sacred '.[45] There is thus no paradox in asserting that a modern society must be founded upon a collective moral unity, and that it must provide for the maximal expression of the rights and liberties of the individual. The issues which have to be faced cannot be solved by seeking to restrain individualism through the reimposition of the traditional forms of authority. On the contrary, the main problem is to extend the concrete opportunities of individuals to develop their potentialities, in conformity with the moral principles which today are basic to the social order.

Durkheim's proposals for the establishment of occupational associations intermediary between the individual and the state have their roots in the

---

42 George Lichtheim: *Marxism in Modern France* (New York, 1966), p. 9. cf. Althusser's remark that Marx's works first came to be known in France ' without the heritage and assistance of a national *theoretical* tradition '. Althusser: *For Marx*, p. 26.

43 Georges Davy: ' Emile Durkheim ', *Revue de métaphysique et de morale*, vol. 26, 1919, p. 189.

44 ' L'individualisme et les intellectuels.' The very occurrence of the Dreyfus case epitomises some of the main differences between France and Germany. In Germany, a Jew could not have attained the position achieved by Dreyfus; nor could such an affair have stimulated a comparable *crise de conscience* of national proportions.

45 *Ibid.* p. 8.

solidarisme of the Radical Socialists.[46] But, for Durkheim, these proposals rest upon strictly sociological premises, derived from the conclusions established in *The Division of Labour*. It would be misleading to suppose that Durkheim developed these notions in close conjunction with the political interests of the solidarists, in spite of the fact that his formulation undoubtedly did exert a significant influence upon a number of major political figures.[47] Durkheim is sympathetically inclined towards the solidarist programme for the provision of state-run welfare schemes covering unemployment, sickness and old age. But he insists that these should not be allowed to assume the dominant position, and that they must be integrated with a concern for the systematic moral regulation of industrial organisation.

The increasing spread of Marxism among various sectors of the French labour movement in the 1890s, and the growth of a scholarly interest in Marx's writings among intellectuals, eventually forced Durkheim to confront in a direct way the relationship between sociology and socialism. The diffusion of Marxist socialism in France at the turn of the century was manifest in the appearance of the translations of the works of, among others, Engels, Kautsky and Labriola, which thus replaced the crude Guesdist version of Marxism with a more comprehensive account of Marx's ideas. Durkheim's review of the French translation of Labriola's general exposition of Marx's thought contains the most explicit statement whereby Durkheim identifies his differences with Marx.[48] Durkheim's lectures on socialism, delivered in 1895–6, were apparently stimulated in part by the challenge posed by the conversion of some of his students to Marxism. While he devoted most of his attention to Saint-Simon, as the key figure whose writings form the most important single source of both socialism and sociology, he intended to proceed to a consideration of Proudhon, and thence to Lassalle and Marx. But the founding of the *Année sociologique* in 1896 meant that these plans had to be deferred, and Durkheim was never able to return to them at a later date. Durkheim lays some considerable stress in *Socialism* upon the closeness of the historical connections between socialism and sociology. In the period shortly after the opening of the nineteenth century, Durkheim points out, three sets of ideas came to the fore: ' 1. The idea of extending to social sciences the method of the positive sciences (out of which sociology has come) and the historical method (an indispensable auxiliary of sociology); 2. The idea of a religious regeneration; and, 3. The socialist idea.' [49] It is no accident,

---

[46] cf. Hayward. For Durkheim's views on revolutionary syndicalism, see the account of his discussion with Lagardelle, in *Libres entretiens*, 1905, pp. 425–34.

[47] Including leaders of the syndicalist movement. For Sorel's views on Durkheim's influence, see Georges Sorel: ' Les théories de M. Durkheim ', *Le devenir social*, vol. 1, 1895, pp. 1–26 & 148–80.

[48] Review of Antonio Labriola: *Essais sur la conception matérialiste de l'histoire*. *RP*, vol. 44, 1897, pp. 645–51. Labriola's work leans heavily on Engels; *Anti-Dühring* is called ' the unexcelled book in the literature of socialism '. Antonio Labriola: *Socialism and Philosophy* (Chicago, 1918), p. 53.   [49] *Soc*, p. 283.

Durkheim adds, that these three tendencies are again re-emerging strongly towards the end of the nineteenth century, in times which are as eventful and critical as the decades following the 1789 Revolution. At first sight, these appear to be three contrary currents of thought, which share little in common. The movement calling for a religious revival is conceived by its adherents to be hostile to rationalism and to science. The socialist movement, in general, is based upon the rejection of religion, and also upon the notion that sociological study must be subordinated to the normative demands of political action. But in fact these three streams of thought seem to be contradictory because each expresses only one side of social reality. Each expresses some of the needs which men feel when social change has radically upset accepted habits such that ' the unsettled collective organisation no longer functions with the authority of instinct '.[50]

The stimulus to sociology derives from the need to understand the causes of the changes which have called forth the exigency for far-reaching social reorganisation. But scientific study proceeds slowly and with caution. Durkheim often stresses in his writings that scientific activity is worthless if it does not in some way lead to practical results. Nevertheless, it is of the essence of science that its procedures and objectives be detached from immediately practical requirements; only by the maintenance of a ' disinterested ' attitude can scientific enquiry attain its maximal effectiveness. Science must not be made ' a sort of fetish or idol '; it allows us ' only a degree of knowledge, beyond which there is nothing else '.[51] The needs for solutions to urgent social problems, however, often go far beyond that which can be based upon scientifically established knowledge : hence the spur to the development of socialist doctrines, which present overall programmes for the necessary reorganisation of society. The reactionary call for a revival of religion similarly indicates the shortcomings of science. The moral hiatus which results from a situation in which old beliefs have come under question, but have not yet been replaced by new ones, produces a concern with the moral consolidation of society : hence the resurgence of religious ideals.

Durkheim does not except Marx from his overall judgement of socialism. Marx's writings offer a complete system of thought which is presented as a scientifically established body of propositions. But such a system in fact presupposes an enormous fund of knowledge, far and above that which is available at the present time. A great deal of research would be necessary to substantiate even some of the more limited generalisations contained in *Capital*. Thus, reviewing Gaston Richard's *Le socialisme et la science sociale*, Durkheim comments : ' of all the criticisms which Richard has directed at Marx, the strongest appears to us to be that which limits itself to setting in

---

[50] *Soc*, p. 284.
[51] ' L'enseignement philosophique et l'agrégation de philosophie ', *RP*, vol. 39, 1895, p. 146.

relief what a distance there is between the fundamental propositions of the system and the observations upon which it rests.'[52]

These views are amplified in Durkheim's discussion of Labriola's exposition of Marx's thought. Durkheim expresses his agreement with certain of the most important notions embodied in historical materialism. It is a fruitful conception, Durkheim states, which regards social life not merely from the point of view of the consciousness of the individuals involved, but which examines the influence of factors which escape consciousness and help to shape it. Moreover, it is also valid to hold, as Marx does, that these factors must be sought in the organisation of society. 'For in order for collective representations to be explicable, it is certainly necessary that they derive from something and, since they cannot form a circle closed upon itself, the source from which they derive must be located outside of themselves.'[53] It is quite correct to locate the source of ideas in a definite substratum; and what else, Durkheim asks rhetorically, can this substratum be composed of, if not the members of society organised into definite social relationships?

According to Durkheim, however, there is no reason to presume that this perspective commits whoever adopts it to the acceptance of the whole corpus of Marx's thought. Durkheim remarks that he himself arrived at this conception without accepting the rest of the principles upon which Marx's work is founded, and that his own formulations have in no way been influenced by Marx. One can, as follows from the general conclusions concerning the relationship between sociology and socialism stated above, study social organisation in this manner without accepting the additional premises entailed by Marxian socialism. The perspective which examines the interplay between ideas and their ' material ' substratum is simply the substance of sociological method, and is a necessary condition for studying society in a scientific manner. Just as Weber emphasises that socialism is not a conveyance which can be stopped at the wish of those who travel in it – socialist beliefs must themselves be made subject to the sort of analysis which socialists apply to other forms of belief – so Durkheim stresses that socialism itself must, from the point of view of the sociologist, be treated as a social fact like any other. Socialism is rooted in a definite state of society, but it does not necessarily express accurately the social conditions which gave rise to it.[54]

Moreover, the central thesis of historical materialism, which ties the origin of ideas directly to economic relationships, is ' contrary to facts which seem established '. It has been proved, Durkheim declares, that religion is the original source out of which all more differentiated systems of ideas have

---

[52] Review of Gaston Richard: *Le socialisme et la science sociale, RP*, vol. 44, 1897, p. 204. Durkheim expresses his approval of those socialists in Germany and Italy who were trying ' to renew and extend the formulae which they have been prisoner of for far too long ' – especially ' the doctrine of economic materialism, the Marxist theory of value, the iron law [of wages] . . . [and] the pre-eminent importance attributed to class conflict '. Review of Merlino: *Formes et essence du socialisme, RP*, vol. 48, 1889, p. 433.   [53] Review of Labriola, p. 648.   [54] *Soc*, pp. 40ff.

developed. But in the simplest forms of society, ' the economic factor is rudimentary, while religious life is, on the contrary, luxurious and enveloping '.[55] In this case, the economy is influenced much more by religious practice and symbolism than the other way around. It does not follow from this that, with the growth of organic solidarity and the consequent decline of the all-encompassing character of religion, the influence of economic relationships becomes predominant in determining the nature of the beliefs which occupy the primary place in the *conscience collective*. Once a set of beliefs are established, ' they are, in virtue of this, realities *sui generis*, autonomous, capable of being causes in their turn and of producing new phenomena '.[56] In primitive societies, which have a simple structure, all ideas are connected to a single system of religious representations, and are consequently closely tied in their content to the form of the organisation of the society. But with the growth of differentiation in the division of labour, and of the application of critical reason, producing the clash of divergent ideas, the relationship between beliefs and the substratum in which they are rooted becomes more complex.

In conjunction with this emphasis, Durkheim rejects the Marxian supposition that economic relationships – the class structure – are the major focus of political power in society. According to Durkheim, there is wide variability in the political organisation of societies which are otherwise structurally similar. It follows that the importance of classes, and of class conflict generally, in historical development, is minimised by Durkheim. It is significant, of course, that Durkheim does not use either the Saint-Simonian term ' industrial society ', or the economists' ' capitalism ' in his writings, but talks rather of ' modern society' or ' contemporary society '. Durkheim's model of development, while recognising the significance of definite ' stages ' of societal advancement, emphasises the importance of cumulative changes, rather than of revolutionary dynamism, in history. According to Durkheim, those societies in which political revolutions are most frequent are not those which manifest the greatest capacity for change. Indeed, the opposite is the case : these are societies in which the basic traditions remain the same. ' On the surface there is an uninterrupted stream of continually new events. But this superficial changeability hides the most monotonous uniformity. It is among the most revolutionary peoples that bureaucratic routine is often the most powerful.' [57] If the past development of society cannot be understood in terms of the primacy which Marx gave to class conflict, the same is true of the present. The prevalence of class conflicts in contemporary societies is symptomatic of the *malaise* of the modern world, but not its root cause. Class conflict derives from a disorder which has its origins elsewhere. ' From which it

---

[55] Review of Labriola, p. 650.   [56] *Ibid.* p. 651.
[57] *Moral Education*, p. 137; *L'Education morale* (Paris, 1925), p. 156. Marx's position on this matter should not be over-simplified. Marx makes a rather similar point, in relation to nineteenth-century France, in ' The Eighteenth Brumaire of Louis Bonaparte ', *SW*, vol. 1, pp. 249–50.

follows ', in Durkheim's view, ' that the economic transformations which
have been produced during the course of this century, the changeover from
small- to large-scale industry, do not necessitate an upheaval and radical
reorganisation (*renouvellement intégral*) of the social order. . .' [58]

Although Durkheim rejects the possibility of radically reorganising contemporary society on the basis of revolutionary change, he does foresee a
definite trend towards the disappearance of class divisions. The maintenance
of rights of inheritance is one main factor perpetuating class conflict between
labour and capital.[59] Inheritance is a survival of the old form of collective property, when property was owned in common by a kinship group, and will
eventually be abolished just as the hereditary transmission of status and legal
privileges has been abolished.[60] Of course, this does not, for Durkheim, entail
the collectivisation of property in the hands of the state. The moral individualism of contemporary societies demands that all barriers to the formation
of equitable contracts be removed, not that private property be abolished.

In Durkheim's view, however, economic reorganisation cannot provide
the main solution to the ' crisis ' in the modern world which has generated
socialism, because the causes of the crisis are not economic but moral. Elimination of the ' forced ' division of labour will not in and of itself put an end
to the ' anomic ' division of labour. This is the source of Durkheim's most
important conscious basis of divergence from Marx. Marx's programme for
the alleviation of the pathological state of capitalism rests upon economic
measures. Advocacy of the interests of the working class is directly bound up,
in Marx's writings, with the latter's views upon the ' contradictory ' nature
of the capitalist market economy. The ' anarchy of the market ' derives from
the class structure of capitalism, and will cede place to a system which regulates production in a centrally coordinated economy: ' In short, in Marxist
socialism, capital does not disappear; it is merely administered by society
and not by individuals.' [61] Marx's writings hence share a commitment to the
main principle which is the definitive characteristic of socialism according to
Durkheim's usage: the concentration of the productive capacity of society in
the hands of the state. But this in itself does nothing to alleviate the moral void
which results from the anomic condition of modern industry; rather, it accentuates the problem, because the result would be to further the domination of
society by ' economic ' relationships. Such a merging of the state with the
economy would have the same consequences as Saint-Simon's industrialism.
To Marx, as to Saint-Simon, ' it appears that the way to realise social peace
is to free economic appetites of all restraint on the one hand, and on the other
to satisfy them by fulfilling them. But such an undertaking is contradictory '.[62]

---

[58] Review of Labriola, p. 651.　　　　　　　　　　　　　　[59] *PECM*, p. 123.

[60] ' La famille conjugale ', *RP*, vol. 91, 1921, p. 10. Durkheim slightly qualifies this in
PECM, p. 217.

[61] *Soc*, p. 90. In fact, this is an exact description of what Marx regards as the *transitional*
stage between capitalism and communism.　　　　　　　[62] *Soc*, p. 241.

14. Religion, ideology and society

Marx's writings have their initial source in the critique of religion as formulated by David Strauss, Bruno Bauer and Feuerbach. Behind these looms the influence of Hegel, whose philosophy, as Feuerbach commented, 'negated theology in a theological manner'.[1] Hegel's philosophical system unites two basic elements which Marx later identified as characteristic of religion as a form of 'ideology': the transmuted representation of values which are in fact created by man in society, and the provision of principled support for an existing social and political order – in this case, that of the Prussian state. The influence of religion upon social life is also a leading concern of both Durkheim and Weber, and forms one most significant dimension along which some of the themes intrinsic to the writings of the latter two authors may be compared with those of Marx. There are two connected sets of problems in the analysis of the 'ideological' character of religion which are important here: the derivation of the content of religious symbolism, and the consequences of the 'secularisation' of modern life.

The first serves to focus some of the issues involved in the great, protracted debate over the nature of the 'materialistic' interpretation of history in the latter part of the nineteenth century. Both Durkheim and Weber, in common with all other liberal critics of Marx, reject what they take to be Marx's conception of the relationship between ideas and 'material interests'. In discussing this matter in this chapter, most attention is given to an examination of the relationship between Marx and Weber. The writings of Max Weber, as has been mentioned in the previous chapter, are much more directly aimed at the critical elucidation of historical materialism than are those of Durkheim. Moreover, the publication of *The Protestant Ethic* sparked off a controversy over the role of 'ideas' in historical development which has barely abated today.[2]

The second set of problems, to do with 'secularisation', relate not to the nature of the interplay between 'ideas' and 'material reality' as such, but to the implications of the *declining* influence of religion in the modern world. The consequences of the diminishing hold of religion upon social life concern each of the three writers discussed in this book, on both a practical and a theo-

---

[1] Feuerbach: *Sämmtliche Werke*, vol. 2, p. 275.
[2] Much of the debate over *The Protestant Ethic* has taken place in ignorance of Weber's published replies to his early critics. cf. his 'Antikritisches zum " Geist des Kapitalismus "', *Archiv für Sozialwissenschaft und Sozialpolitik*, vol. 30, 1910, pp. 176–202; and 'Antikritisches Schlusswort'.

retical level. All three attribute tremendous importance to the progressive displacement of religious thought and practice by the penetration of rationalism into all spheres of social life. Clarification of some of the main points of similarity and divergence on this issue provides another source of insight into some of the most significant contrasts between the works of Marx as compared to those of Durkheim and Weber.

Marx and Weber : the problem of religion as ' ideology '

In examining the relationship between Marx's views on religion and those of Weber, a major difficulty is presented, of course, by the fragmentary nature of Marx's writings on the subject. Most of Marx's statements about the influence of religious institutions are unequivocally hostile, but largely disinterested. Marx's concern, even in his early writings, is overwhelmingly with modern capitalism and its transcendence by socialism. He did not study religion in any detail after 1845, because in breaking with the Young Hegelians and with Feuerbach, and in perceiving the need to analyse sociologically the relationship between economics, politics, and ideology, he effectively overcame – in terms of his own objectives – the need to subject religion to a detailed analysis. The Young Hegelians, as is made clear in *The Holy Family*, continued to devote most of their efforts to the critique of religion, and thereby always remained imprisoned within a world-view which was, even if only negatively, a religious one.

Any attempt, therefore, to compare in detail the views of Marx and Weber on specific religious phenomena is doomed to failure. Thus Marx's account of oriental society is too skimpy to form the basis of detailed comparison with Weber's lengthy discussions of the religions of India and China. Even Marx's views upon the emergence and significance of Christianity in the development of the European societies have to be mainly inferred from various oblique statements in his critiques of Hegel and the Young Hegelians. These do indicate, however, both parallels and contrasts with Weber. As a close student of Hegel, Marx is obviously aware of the fundamental importance which historians and philosophers have attributed to Christianity in the West. Marx does not question the validity of this. What he does attack is the idealistic standpoint within which the influence of Christianity is analysed. Thus he objects to Stirner's treatment of the rise of early Christianity in that it is conducted wholly upon the level of ideas.[3] Christianity arose, Marx states, as a religion of wandering, uprooted vagrants, and the causes of its expansion have to be related to the internal decay of the Roman Empire : ' finally the Hellenic and Roman world perished, spiritually in Christianity and materially in the migration of the peoples '.[4] Weber, however, holds that Christianity has

---

[3] *GI*, pp. 143ff.
[4] *GI*, p. 151 (footnote).

always been primarily a religion of the urban artisanate.[5] But Marx does emphasise that the Christian ethical outlook formed a vital new current, contrasting with the moral decadence of Rome. Christianity substituted for Roman pantheism the conception of a single universal God, whose authority is founded upon uniquely Christian notions of sin and salvation. In the later evolution of Christianity in Europe, the Reformation provided a similar moral regeneration in relation to an internally disintegrating feudal society. ' Luther ... overcame bondage out of devotion by replacing it by bondage out of conviction. He shattered faith in authority because he restored the authority of faith... He freed man from outer religiosity because he made religiosity the inner man.' [6] Marx's hostile posture towards religion should not obscure the fact that, while religious ideology serves to content men with an existence of misery on this earth, it nevertheless provides a positive inspiration towards a better world: it constitutes ' a *protest* against real suffering '.[7]

But to proceed beyond the level of such relatively unsystematic comparisons, we have to revert to a more general plane of analysis. The questions raised by the interpretation of Marx's treatment of religion can only be satisfactorily dealt with, in relation to the issues posed by Weber's writings, in the context of Marx's overall conception of ' materialism '. In evaluating Marx's ' materialism ', two central points have to be borne in mind. Firstly, Marx was at no time concerned solely with the formulation of an academic theory. Marx's attitude is well conveyed in his famous epigram: ' The philosophers have only *interpreted* the world in various ways; the point is, to *change* it.' [8] In Marx's conception, the theories of the social thinker themselves form a part of the dialectic in terms of which social life both ' changes men ' and is ' changed by men '. Secondly, Marx's life's work encompasses no more than a fraction of the project which, in early adulthood, he determined to set himself. The bulk of Marx's theoretical writings consist, in effect, of successive drafts of *Capital*. Even this work remained unfinished in Marx's lifetime. But *Capital* itself was originally planned as the preliminary analysis of bourgeois economics which would establish in a precise fashion the class character of bourgeois society. It is misleading to treat *Capital*, compendious although it is in its four volumes,[9] as an overall study and critique of the structure of bourgeois society, although this is how the overwhelming majority of Marxists, and critics, have regarded the work. The same rider by which

---

[5] *ES*, vol. 2, pp. 481ff. For Kautsky's theory of the ' proletarian' character of Christianity – which Weber rejects – see his *Der Ursprung des Christentums* (Stuttgart, 1908).

[6] ' Contribution to the critique of Hegel's Philosophy of Right ', translation as per *On Religion* (Moscow, 1957), p. 51. Nonetheless, Marx is unequivocally hostile to Luther and Lutheranism; Luther ' freed the body from chains because he enchained the heart '.

[7] *EW*, p. 43.

[8] *WYM*, p. 402.

[9] The ' fourth volume ' of *Capital* is *Theorien über den Mehrwert*.

Marx qualifies the nature of his intentions in the 1844 *Manuscripts* could equally accurately be applied to *Capital*: ' in the present work, the relationships of political economy with the state, law, morals, civil life, etc., are touched upon only to the extent that political economy itself expressly deals with these subjects.' [10]

Marx did not, therefore, ever write a systematic exposition of his materialistic conception of history, even as applied to that societal form which occupied the prime focus of his attention, bourgeois society. Nevertheless, in the light of his early writings, it is no longer possible to doubt that Marx's conception of historical materialism does not represent a simple ' inversion ' of Hegelian idealistic philosophy. Feuerbach's writings, on the other hand, are founded upon such an inversion, and for this reason Feuerbach's philosophy of materialism remains confined to a transposed religious humanism. The consequence of Feuerbach's position is that religion is a symbolic ' representation ' of man, and that to eliminate human self-alienation religion has to be demystified, and placed upon a rational level. Marx's view is different. Feuerbach's errors, as Marx sees them, are to speak of ' man ' in the abstract, and thus to fail to understand that men only exist in the context of specific societies which change in the course of historical development; and, secondly, to treat ideas and ' consciousness ' as simply the ' reflection ' of human activities in the material world.

Feuerbach, in other words, preserves that philosophical connotation of the term ' materialism ', which Marx seeks to break away from. In Marx's words, ' The chief defect of all previous materialism (including Feuerbach's) is that the object, actuality, sensuousness, is conceived only in the form of the *object or perception*, but not as *sensuous human activity*, *Praxis*, not subjectively '.[11] It is just such a conception of materialism which stands behind the notion that ideas are mere ' epiphenomena ', and consequently that the analysis of the content of ideologies is irrelevant to the explanation of human action. It must be admitted that there is more than a trace of this conception in Marx's writings. Thus, in *The German Ideology*, Marx writes that ' in all ideology man and their circumstances seem to be standing on their heads, as in a *camera obscura. . .*'. But it is made clear that such statements are to be understood in a historical context. Human consciousness is, in the early stages of social development, ' the direct outcome ' of material activity; it is ' mere herd-consciousness '. With the expansion of social differentiation, however, ' consciousness is in a position to emancipate itself from the world and to proceed to the formation of " pure " theory, theology, philosophy, ethics, etc.'. (This ' emancipation ' is fallacious in the sense that ideas can never be wholly ' free ' of the social conditions which generate tthem.) This first be-

[10] *EW*, p. 63.
[11] *WYM*, p. 400; *We*, vol. 3, p. 5. For a recent discussion of Feuerbach, see Eugene Kamenka: *The Philosophy of Ludwig Feuerbach* (London, 1970).

comes possible with the appearance of a division of labour allowing the emergence of a stratum concerned with ' mental labour ', which occurs historically in the shape of the development of a priesthood.[12] The following paragraph expresses Marx's standpoint clearly:

This conception of history depends on our ability to expound the real process of production, starting out from the material production of life itself, and to comprehend the form of intercourse connected with this and created by this mode of production (i.e., civil society in its various stages), as the basis of all history ; and to show it in its action as state, to explain all the different theoretical products and forms of consciousness, religion, philosophy, ethics, etc., etc., and trace their origin and growth from that basis ; by which means, of course, the whole thing can be depicted in its totality (and therefore, too, the reciprocal action of these various sides on one another).[13]

Ideologies are thus ' rooted in the material conditions of life ', but this does not entail that there is a universal or unilateral relationship between the ' real foundation ' of society – the relations of production – and ' legal and political superstructures '. The specific conclusion which Marx reaches in criticising Feuerbach is that ideas are social products, which cannot be understood by the philosopher who stands outside history. The decisive characteristic of Marx's materialism is to be found in the links which are drawn between *class structure* and ideology. Simple and obvious although this appears, it is this which is fundamental to Marx's ' materialism ', rather than any notion of ideas as epiphenomena of material relationships. Where Marx generalises about the relationship between ideology and material ' substructure ', this is in terms of the specification that the class structure is the main mediating link between the two. The class structure of society exerts a determinate effect upon the ideas which assume prominence in that society; similarly, the emergence of ideas which can serve as an effective challenge to the dominant order depends upon the formation of class relationships which generate a structural base for the new ideology. Thus, while the ' idea of communism ' has been ' expressed a hundred times ' in history, the real possibility of a communist revolution ' presupposes the existence of a revolutionary class '.[14]

It may be pointed out that, even in Feuerbach's philosophy, religion is something more than a complete reflection of material reality: it is also the source of ideals towards which man should strive. God is man as he ought to

---

[12] *GI*, pp. 37 & 43; *We*, vol. 3, pp. 27 & 31. As Poulantzas says, according to this analysis ' the realm of the " sacred " would appear to be closer to the infrastructure than that of " law ", at least from the moment that we can speak of a juridical reality which begins to become distinct: it is the religious level which constitutes the most important medium whereby law can be understood in relation to the infrastructure '. Nicos Ar. Poulantzas: *Nature des choses et du droit* (Paris, 1965), p. 230.

[13] *GI*, p. 50.

[14] *GI*, pp. 51 & 62. Failure to grasp Marx's point on this matter is one element which has confused much of the recent discussion of so-called ' integration ' and ' coercion ' theory in sociology. cf. My article ' " Power " in the recent writings of Talcott Parsons ', *Sociology*, vol. 2, 1968, pp. 268–70.

be, and therefore the image of the deity holds out the hope of what man could *become*. Marx mates this conception with the dialectical view that it is the reciprocal interaction of such ideas with the social organisation of 'earthly men' which must form the core of an historical perspective. This reciprocity must be understood in terms of the empirical study of concrete forms of society, and cannot be grasped if we 'abstract from the historical process '.[15] The particular character of the relationship between class structure and ideology is thus itself historically variable. Capitalism, which strips away all the personalised ties of feudalism, substitutes for them the impersonal operations of the market; and by applying science to the construction of rational technology, cuts through the ideological embellishments of the traditional order – so much so, that the influence of religious beliefs upon the origins of the capitalist order tends to be forgotten:

Wholly absorbed in the production of wealth and in peaceful competitive struggle, it [bourgeois society] no longer comprehended that ghosts from the days of Rome had watched over its cradle. But unheroic as bourgeois society is, it nevertheless took heroism, sacrifice, terror, civil war and battles of peoples to bring it into being . . . Similarly, at another stage of development, a century earlier, Cromwell and the English people had borrowed speech, passions and illusions from the Old Testament for their bourgeois revolution. When the real aim had been achieved, when the bourgeois transformation of English society had been accomplished, Locke supplanted Habakkuk.[16]

Such considerations make clearly manifest that there is indeed a substantial order of truth in Schumpeter's assertion that 'The whole of Max Weber's facts and arguments (in his sociology of religion) fits perfectly into Marx's system '.[17] That is to say, given an understanding of the dialectic, as the active interplay between subject and object, it follows that ideology or 'consciousness' provides a necessary set of meanings whereby the individual acts upon the world at the same time as the world acts upon him. Reality is not merely 'external' to man, shaping his consciousness, but is adapted to human ends through the active application of consciousness and the modification of the pre-existing environment. In this approach, ideology is quite definitely not to be treated as an 'effect' which can be 'deduced' from material reality. The conception of Marx's thought adopted by Weber, on the other hand, is the characteristic 'interpretation' of Marx in the social thought of the late nineteenth century. Engels' later writings certainly played an important role in offering a basis for the legitimacy of such a transmutation of Marx. But, as had been indicated in the previous chapter, such an 'interpretation' was also generated by the practical exigencies of the position of the leading European Marxist party in the country of its origin. If the dialectic is deemed

---

[15] *WYM*, p. 40.

[16] *SW*, vol. 1, p. 248.

[17] Joseph A. Schumpeter: *Capitalism, Socialism and Democracy* (New York, 1962), p. 11.

to exist in nature, as in *Anti-Dühring*, the way is clearly laid open to a philosophical materialism which removes from the historical scene the role of ideas as the active source of social change: ideology is the 'effect', and material conditions are the 'cause'. This provokes the characteristic problem of philosophical materialism which Marx perceived early on in his career: if ideology is simply the passive 'reflection' of material circumstances, then there is no place for the active role of men as creators of social reality.[18]

Weber's writings on religion brilliantly refute the standpoint of 'reflective materialism' as a viable starting-point for sociological analysis. But in this respect, considered in relation to Marx, it might be said that Weber's writings almost bring the wheel full circle. Weber refused to wear the straitjacket of philosophical materialism which the followers of Marx sought to impose upon history in the name of historical materialism. From this regard, Weber's writings on the sociology of religion, beginning from the standpoint of subjective idealism, partially vindicate Marx against his own disciples. Weber treats as Marx's premise the contention that ideology can be rationally transposed to expose its 'real' content. But in fact, it is precisely this conception which Marx repudiates in breaking with the Young Hegelians. Thus Weber's use of the conception of 'elective affinity',[19] in analysing the relationships between idea-systems and social organisation, is perfectly compatible with Marx's treatment of ideology. Weber employs this conception to indicate the contingent nature of the connections between the symbolic content of beliefs which individuals 'elect' to follow, and the consequences which adherence to those beliefs entails for social action. Vice versa, the mode of life of a given social class or status group can generate an affinity to accept certain sorts of religious ethic, without 'determining' the nature of the beliefs involved. Thus urban artisans and traders, whose life is founded upon the use of practical calculation in economic enterprise, have an 'affinity' towards 'the attitude of active asceticism, of God-willed *action* nourished by the sentiment of being God's "tool", rather than the possession of the deity or the inward and contemplative surrender to God, which has appeared as the supreme value to religions influenced by strata of genteel intellectuals'.[20] Nevertheless, 'active asceticism' has not been limited to the religions of urban strata, nor have all urban groups by any means adhered to religious ethics of this type.

The phraseology in which Marx expresses his position is actually very similar to that often adopted by Weber. Thus, in Marx's words: 'Ideas cannot *carry anything out* at all. In order to carry out ideas men are needed who dispose of a certain practical force.'[21] Weber always stresses the contingent

---

[18] *WYM*, p. 401. The importance of this point is not fully brought out in the otherwise excellent discussion given in Norman Birnbaum: 'Conflicting interpretations of the rise of capitalism: Marx and Weber', *British Journal of Sociology*, vol. 4, 1953, pp. 125–41.   [19] cf. for example, *PE*, pp. 90–2.
[20] *FMW*, p. 285.   [21] *Holy Family*, p. 160.

nature of the relationship between the content of an ideology and the social position of the group who are its ' carriers ', but, like Marx, Weber frequently identifies instances where ideas express material interests in a very direct way. For both Marx and Weber, religious systems express the creation of human values, which are not ' given ' in the biological makeup of man, but are the outcome of the historical process. Both agree that stable religious orders characteristically legitimise relationships of domination; and also that, prior to the modern age, ' breakthroughs ' in the accomplishment of radical social change are achieved within a framework of religious symbolism. Moreover, Marx does not dispute the fact that, in pre-capitalist societies, religion provides a cosmology which makes existence intelligible to those who accept it.

The comparative analysis of these points, then, makes clear that the standard view that Weber's sociology of religion constitutes a ' refutation ' of Marx's historical materialism, by showing the role of ideology as an ' independent ' influence upon social change, is misconceived. Schumpeter's judgement, in this respect, must be considered apt. That this should not be allowed to overshadow the fundamental elements of difference between Marx and Weber which in fact – in the polemical context in which he wrote – made possible Weber's critique of philosophical materialism. For, according to Weber's premises, there can be no question of constructing the sort of rational scheme of historical development which Marx attempts to establish. In the sense that Weber denies the possibility of deriving objectively verifiable norms from the study of society and history, those who have stressed the similarity of his view to that of existentialism are perfectly correct. The moral faith of the individual, at least as regards acceptance of ultimate values, cannot be validated by science. On the other hand, the attribution of a discoverable rationality to history is an essential element in Marx's thought. As Marx says: ' My dialectic method is not only different from the Hegelian, but is its direct opposite.' [22] This does not entail that Marx's thought preserves Hegelian ideology in simply the ' reverse ' form of that found in Hegel's writings. In fact, Marx is at some pains to reject such a standpoint. It is, according to Marx, a ' speculative distortion ' which treats later history as ' the goal of earlier history ': ' what is designated with the words " destiny ", " goal ", " germ ", or " idea " of earlier history is nothing more than an abstraction formed from later history, from the active influence which earlier history exercises on later history '.[23] However Weber is obviously perfectly right in assuming that Marx's writings constitute a philosophy of history, insofar as this term is taken to refer to a theoretical position which asserts that there is a definite ' logic ' of development which can be derived from the empirical study of historical process.

On the more directly empirical level, these differences are expressed in

[22] *SW*, vol. 1, p. 456.
[23] *GI*, p. 60.

terms of the role of 'charisma' in Weber's writings, and that of 'class' in Marx's. Marx insists that class relationships form the basic axis upon which ideologies find general acceptance in a society. Thus ideology is, in an important sense 'illusory': not in the sense that the content of idea-systems is a mere 'reflection' of material life and therefore is irrelevant to the activity of the subject, but insofar as ideas which are thought to be of general or universal validity are in fact the expressions of sectional class interests.[24] According to Weber's position, however, ideology cannot be adjudged illusory in this sense, because this demands the assumption of a value-position which cannot rationally be said to be ethically superior to any other. The conception of charisma, as Weber uses it, connects closely with this. The point about charismatic innovation is that it is 'irrational' in relation to the pre-existing social order since, in its pure form, it depends solely upon belief in the extraordinary qualities of a leader. The relation of legitimacy in charismatic authority is hence the same regardless of the substantive interests which may be served by the existence of a charismatic organisation: the most ruthless terrorism may be 'charismatic' in exactly the same sense as the most bounteous goodness. This is focal in Weber's thought, and draws a tight logical connection between his conception of *verstehende Soziologie* on the one hand, and his neo-Kantian methodological position on the other. In this way, Weber seeks to document the fact that the understanding of 'complexes of meaning' is necessary, not only to the interpretation of social action which conforms to accepted cultural beliefs, but also to the explanation of revolutionary departures from the routine. Since such innovatory action is founded upon the irrational quality of charismatic attachment to a leader, it follows that the new norms which are created cannot be 'deduced' from the accompanying social or economic changes.[25] On the empirical level, this is the correlate of the logical impossibility of the deduction of value-judgements from factual knowledge, upon which Weber has laid so much stress as an abstract principle. Thus while Weber admits with Marx the importance of the connections between ideas and the sectional interests of groups, he does not accept the *normative* asymmetry of class interests and ideology. For Weber, adherence to any given set of ideals, whether they are religious, political, economic, or whatever, generates interests which can only be defined in terms of the content of those ideals themselves. In Marx's schema, on the other hand, the ascription of rationality to history is possible precisely because of his acceptance of the dichotomy between 'sectional' (class) interests and 'societal'

---

[24] *GI*, p. 52.

[25] It is important to recognise that, while the influence of Nietzsche on Weber is very profound, Weber rejects the Nietzschian view of the 'slave's revolt' as a reductionist theory of religion. But the significance which Weber gives to Nietzsche is indicated by the statement, made just before his death, that Marx and Nietzsche are the two most significant figures in the modern intellectual world.

interests which is progressively resolved, in favour of the latter, in the development from feudalism through capitalism to socialism.[26] On an empirical level, this divergence is manifest in Marx's assumption that class relationships constitute the source of political power. The assimilation of economic and political power is a key theorem in Marx's writings. For Weber, by contrast, both political and military power are historically as significant as economic power and do not necessarily derive from it.

Secularisation and the modern capitalist ethos

It is apposite at this point to turn to the question of 'secularisation'. Such a term, of course, hardly does justice to the manifold consequences which both Marx and Weber ascribe to the decline of religious belief with the advance of capitalism. For Weber, the progressive 'disenchantment' of the world is a process which is itself promoted by the rationalisation stimulated by religious prophecy. The elimination of magical ritual is completed with the advent of Calvinism, which in turn becomes increasingly irrelevant with the maturity of capitalist industrial production. It is dubious how far Marx would have acceded to the specific details of Weber's account of the affinity between the Protestant ethic and the 'spirit' of modern capitalist enterprise. But Marx accepts the historical importance of the connection, and strongly accentuates the 'ascetic rationality' of modern capitalism. According to Marx, this is manifest in the dominance of the market in human relationships, and in the pursuit of monetary gain as an end in itself. Money is the epitome of human self-alienation under capitalism, since it reduces all human qualities to quantitive values of exchange. Capitalism thus has a 'universalising' character, which breaks down the particularities of traditional cultures, and which generates its own 'money morality': 'capital develops irresistibly beyond national boundaries and prejudices ... it destroys the self-satisfaction confined within narrow limits and based upon a traditional mode of life and reproduction.'[27] Capitalism is 'ascetic' in that the actions of capitalists are based upon self-renunciation and the continued reinvestment of profits. This is manifest, Marx points out, in the theory of political economy: 'Political economy, the science of wealth, is, therefore, at the same time, the science of renunciation, of privation and saving... Its true ideal is the *ascetic* but *usurious* miser and the *ascetic* but *productive* slave.'[28] The pursuit of wealth for its own sake is a phenomenon which is, as general moral ethos, found only within modern capitalism. Marx is as specific on this point as Weber:

The passion for wealth as such is a distinctive development; that is to say, it is something other than the instinctive thirst for particular goods such as clothes, arms, jewelry, women, wine... The taste for possessions can exist without money;

[26] *Gru*, pp. 438–9.
[27] *Gru*, p. 313. Here Marx makes a point later elaborated in great detail by Weber in his studies of the 'rationalising' activities of priesthoods.
[28] *EW*, p. 171.

the thirst for self-enrichment is the product of a definite social development, it is not natural, but historical.[29]

Both Marx and Weber treat mature capitalism as a world in which religion is replaced by a social organisation in which technological rationality reigns supreme. Marx frequently underlines the secularising effects of the progression of capitalism, which ' has drowned the most heavenly ecstasies of religious fervour, of chivalrous enthusiasm, of philistine sentimentalism, in the icy water of egoistic calculation '. It is because of this that the theory of bourgeois society, political economy, can serve as the basis of a scientific explanation and critique of the development of capitalism; in bourgeois society, ' all that is holy is profaned, and man is at last compelled to face with sober senses his real conditions of life and his relations with his kind '.[30]

In Marx's conception, the decline of religion makes possible the real implementation of the beliefs which, in the traditional order, remained ' illusory ' – in the sense that the perfection of life in heaven is a mystical substitute for the possibility of a satisfying existence for all men here on earth. This is not, however, realisable within capitalism. The capitalist order serves to demystify and to sharpen the alienation of men, but in doing so creates the conditions which will allow the attainment of a new society in which the values expressed in religious form in Christianity will be capable of being actualised. ' The abolition of religion as the *illusory* happiness of men, is a demand for their *real* happiness.' [31] For Marx, this does not entail the ' disappearance ' of moral values, but rather the extirpation of value-commitments which, firstly, have the function of legitimating sectional class interests and, secondly, are not expressed in rational terms (' ideology ' has both of these characteristics). It is often said that the society of the future which Marx anticipated in his writings on the ' higher stage of communism ' constitutes merely another version of utilitarianism, and this would indeed be the case with a theory which rested solely on philosophical materialism. But given an understanding of Marx's view of consciousness which rests upon the subject–object dialectic, such a criticism cannot be sustained. Communism, in other words, generates its own intrinsic morality, which is certainly not definable in terms of an aggregation of individuals, each of whom follows his own egoistic interests.

The main source of disparity between Marx and Weber in relation to the consequences of the declining hold of religion upon social life does not lie where it is ordinarily sought – in the disappearance of ' ideals '. In fact the critical assessment of the characteristic mode of life stimulated in capitalism is quite remarkably similar in the writings of each author (the dominance of technological rationality). But for Weber the technical exigencies of the or-

---

[29] *Gru*, pp. 133–4. Marx's position here is close to that later formulated in detail by Simmel: Georg Simmel: *Philosophie des Geldes* (Leipzig, 1900). Weber remarks of Simmel's book: ' money economy and capitalism are too closely identified, to the detriment of his concrete analysis '. *PE*, p. 185.

[30] *CM*, p. 136.   [31] *EW*, p. 44.

ganisation of a 'secular' society are such that they necessarily involve the submergence or denial of some of the dominant values which stimulated the development of that society: there are no other possibilities open. In Marx's thought, on the other hand, the alienative characteristics of modern capitalism stem from its class character, and will be eliminated through the revolutionary restructuring of society. Weber's description of the effects of bureaucratic routine is almost identical to Marx's account of the consequences of alienation in capitalism:

Fully developed bureaucracy stands, in a specific meaning, under the principle *sine ira ac studio*. Its specific character, which is welcomed by capitalism, develops the more, completely the more the bureaucracy is 'dehumanised', the more completely it succeeds in eliminating from official business, love, hatred, and all purely personal, irrational and emotional elements which escape calculation.[32]

Weber thus perceives a primary irrationality within capitalism. The formal rationality of bureaucracy, while it makes possible the technical implementation of large-scale administrative tasks, substantively contravenes some of the most distinctive values of western civilisation, subordinating individuality and spontaneity. But there is no rational way of overcoming this: this is 'the fate of the times', to live in a society characterised by 'mechanised petrification'. Only the charismatic rebirth of new gods could conceivably offer an alternative.[33]

Integrity, however, compels us to state that for the many who today tarry for new prophets and saviours, the situation is the same as resounds in the beautiful Edomite watchman's song of the period of exile that has been included among Isaiah's oracles: 'He calleth to me out of Seir, Watchman, what of the night? The watchman said, The morning cometh, and also the night: if ye will enquire, enquire ye: return, come.' The people to whom this was said has enquired and tarried for more than two millenia...[34]

The most deeply rooted divergence between Marx and Weber, therefore, concerns how far the alienative characteristics which Marx attributes to capitalism as a specific form of class society in fact derive from a bureaucratic rationality which is a necessary concomitant of the modern form of society, whether it be 'capitalist' or 'socialist'.[35] This will be taken up in more detail in the next chapter.

Marx and Durkheim: religion and modern individualism

Durkheim's concerns in his sociology of religion, of course, differ in a number of specific respects from those of Weber. The attempt to formulate a general

---

[32] *ES*, vol. 3, p. 975; *WuG*, vol. 2, p. 571.
[33] *PE*, p. 182.
[34] *FMW*, p. 156.
[35] cf. E. Jürgen Kocka: 'Karl Marx und Max Weber. Ein methodologischer Vergleich', *Zeitschrift für die Gesamte Staatswissenschaft*, vol. 122, 1966, p. 328.

' theory ' of religion is foreign to the main thrust of Weber's writings. Nevertheless, it is easy to misconstrue the focus of Durkheim's attention in *The Elementary Forms*. It is generally agreed, and correctly so, that the conception of religion developed in that work is basic to Durkheim's thinking with regard to the structure of modern societies. But all too often secondary interpreters of Durkheim have failed to make the correlate inference: that the evolutionary dimension analysed in *The Division of Labour* has to be interpolated between the portrayal of the functions of religion in primitive society, and the relevance of this to the contemporary social order. It is one of Durkheim's principal emphases that the character of the ' sacred ' beliefs which exist in modern societies are distinctively *different* from those typical of traditional forms. It is evident that one main theme of *The Elementary Forms* is the identification of the functional significance of religion as the crucial basis of solidarity in traditional societies. It is this which has occupied the attention of the vast majority of anthropological and sociological studies which claim derivation from Durkheim. But there is a second *motif* which is equally important in Durkheim's work, and which is not expressed in the ' static ' tying of ideas to the categories of social structure in what is normally represented as Durkheim's ' sociology of knowledge '. This is that society, particularly as manifest in the collective enthusiasm generated in periodic ceremonial, is the source of *new* beliefs and representations. Religious ceremonial does not simply reinforce existing beliefs; it is a situation of both creation and re-creation.[36] ' Now this concentration brings about an exaltation of moral life which takes form in a group of ideal conceptions in which the new life thus awakened is portrayed; they correspond to this new set of psychical forces which is added to those which we have at our disposition for the daily tasks of existence.' [37]

There is no necessary contradiction between this conception and the apparently ' mechanical ' theory of social change advanced in *The Division of Labour*. In that work, Durkheim treats population change as the main factor leading to the expansion of the division of labour. But this effect is only produced because of the action of a mediating variable – ' dynamic density ' – which is both a social and a moral phenomenon. The moral character of the process at work here is indicated by the fact that Durkheim uses the terms ' moral density ' and ' dynamic density ' as synonymous. The breakdown of segmental social structure is associated with ' an exchange of movements between parts of the social mass which, until then, had no effect upon one another ... this moral consolidation can only produce its effect if the real distance between individuals has itself diminished in some way... It is

---

[36] *EF*, p. 464.

[37] *EF*, p. 476; *FE*, p. 603. Hence it is a notable misunderstanding to pose the question ' why, after all, is the worship of society any more readily explicable than the worship of gods? ' W. G. Runciman: ' The sociological explanation of " religious " beliefs ', *Archives européennes de sociologie*, vol. 10, 1969, p. 188.

useless to try to find out which has determined the other; suffice it to say that they are inseparable.'[38] The changes which lead to the differentiation of the division of labour are both social and moral, and each is dependent upon the other; moral individualism, the 'cult of the individual', is the normative counterpart of the emergence of a complex of division of labour: 'as individuals have differentiated themselves more and more and the value of an individual has increased, the corresponding cult has taken a relatively greater place in the totality of the religious life. . .'[39]

It is in emphasising the relativity of the connection between social organisation and systems of ideas that Durkheim seeks to separate his position from that of Marx:

Therefore it is necessary to avoid seeing in this theory of religion a simple resurrection of historical materialism: that would be a singular misunderstanding of our thought. In showing that religion is something essentially social, we do not at all mean to say that it confines itself to translating into another language the material forms of society and its immediate vital necessities.[40]

The historical implications of this are evident: Durkheim dissociates himself from a theory of knowledge which specifies a unilateral relationship between ideas and their social 'base'. This has to be placed in the forefront when considering how far Durkheim's thesis does in fact differ from that established in Marx's writings. *The Elementary Forms* is thus explicitly concerned with the simplest extant form of religion; the theory of knowledge set out in the work cannot be applied *en bloc* to more differentiated types of society. The main theoretical connection linking the simplest to the more complex societal types may be said to constitute a theoretical elaboration of the principle which Durkheim stated at the outset of his career: that, while there are very profound differences between traditional and modern societies, there is still, between mechanical and organic solidarity, a definite moral continuity.[41]

According to Durkheim's thesis in *The Elementary Forms*, the categories of thought in totemism are formed of representations of social facts: the notions of 'space', 'time', etc., are derived from 'social space', 'social time', and so on. As Durkheim says, this rests upon the general premise that content of religious beliefs 'cannot be purely illusory'.[42] Since Durkheim rejects the view that the elementary forms of religious belief are founded upon representations of natural phenomena, or upon categories innately 'given' in the human mind, it must be the case that they rest upon the only other 'reality', that factual order which is society. The effect of Durkheim's insistence upon a strict separation between 'nature' and 'society' is definitely to draw something of an opposition between the two. This is responsible for a

---

[38] *DL*, p. 257; *DTS*, pp. 237–8.
[39] *EF*, p. 472.
[40] *EF*, p. 471; *FE*, p. 605.
[41] Review of Tönnies, p. 421.
[42] *EF*, p. 464.

major difference of emphasis between Durkheim and Marx. Marx's view is not dissimilar to Durkheim's in recognising the relatively direct tie between social reality and ideas in simple societies. In such societies 'consciousness is ... merely consciousness concerning the *immediate* sensuous environment and consciousness of the limited connection with other persons and things outside the individual who is growing self-conscious '.[43] But, for Marx, this inevitably is built upon the interplay between man and nature in production. Primitive man is almost wholly alienated from nature; consequently, his comparatively feeble efforts to master the natural world are overshadowed by a sense of his own impotence in the face of cosmic forces which lie outside his own control. Nature appears as an ' all-powerful and unassailable force, with which men's relations are purely animal and by which they are overawed like beasts; it is thus a purely animal consciousness of nature (natural religion) '. Marx does not conceive of 'natural religion ', however, as the result of an unmediated confrontation between ' man ' and ' nature '; ' this natural religion ... is determined by the form of society and vice versa '.[44]

In common with Durkheim, Marx sees increase in population density as ' fundamental ' to advancement beyond this state of ' sheep-like or tribal consciousness '.[45] This leads to the development of the division of labour, which in turn, as has been shown previously, for Marx is the main precondition for the formation of systems of ideas which function to legitimate the existence of a class society. Durkheim's analysis, however, minimises the significance of the inter-relationship between economy and society, emphasising the specifically social character of the generation of religious beliefs in collective ceremonial. Durkheim admits the possible influence of economic activity upon the idea-systems of simple societies, but argues that it is most likely that economic relationships are, in the main, subordinate to religious conceptions.[46] This emphasis is also transferred to the portrayal of the morphology of more complex societies. In Durkheim's morphological scheme, the principal ordering principle is the degree of structural differentiation. Consequently, no special importance is given to the existence of economic classes: certainly class relationships do not constitute, for Durkheim, the major axis of the social structure of societies possessing a differentiated division of labour. Even the distribution of political power in Durkheim's typology of societies is regarded as of secondary importance to the basic morphological criterion of differentiation. The main source of divergence between Durkheim and Marx, then, concerns, not the degree to which ideas have ' independence ' from their social ' infrastructure ', but the *constituent character of that infrastructure*. The further development of this point can again be left to the next chapter.

The question of the ' illusory ' character of religious belief forms an appro-

---

[43] *GI*, p. 42.   [44] *GI*, p. 42.

[45] *GI*, p. 43.   [46] *EF*, p. 466 (footnote).

priate bridge between the theory of primitive religion, and the views of Durkheim and Marx upon the significance of religion in modern societies. In some measure, the differences between the two thinkers upon this issue, as in the case of Weber and Marx, stem from a discrepancy in their respective ethical standpoints. Durkheim rejects philosophical neo-Kantianism in favour of his own particular conception of ethical relativism, based upon the notion of social ' pathology '. According to this view, the ' valid ' morality for one type of society is not appropriate to a society of a different type; there are no moral ideals which can claim universal validity. Marx accepts, in large degree, a similar emphasis. But whereas for Durkheim the main criterion for the validity of a given set of moral ideals is their general ' correspondence to the needs of the social organism ', in Marx's conception this is linked to class relationships, so that morals express the asymmetry of the distribution of economic power in society. In Marx's writings, but not in those of Durkheim, this is in turn integrated with an underlying emphasis upon the historical resolution of the division between ' sectional ' and ' general ' interests (class structure / alienation).

For Marx, therefore, the ' illusory ' character of religion is measured against the historical development of alienation. Primitive man is alienated from nature, and this alienation is expressed in the form of ' natural religion '. With the expansion of the division of labour, yielding increased mastery of nature, religious beliefs become elaborated into more clearly ' rationalised ' systems of ideas (in Weber's sense) which express the *self*-alienation of man. Capitalism enormously advances man's mastery of nature: nature is increasingly ' humanised ' by human technical and scientific endeavour – but this is accomplished at the expense of a great increase in self-alienation, which is contingent upon the advance of the division of labour stimulated by capitalist production. The ' illusory ' character of religion here is to be found in the fact that it serves to legitimate the existing (alienated) social order, by transferring to a mythical universe the human capacities which are potential, but which are not actualised, in capitalism.

The immediate *sociological* content of Marx's (derogatory) statement that religion is the ' opium ' of the people,[47] since religious beliefs serve to legitimise the position of subordination of a dominated class, is the same as that of Durkheim's proposition that religion consoles the poor ' and teaches them contentment with their lot by informing them of the providential nature of the social order...'.[48] But, within the context of Marx's thesis of alienation, the hold of religion is nonetheless based upon an ' illusion ', since it disguises

---

[47] *EW*, p. 44.

[48] *Su*, p. 254. This is why it is misleading to take Durkheim's ' favourable ' and Marx's ' hostile ' attitudes towards religion at their ' face value ' in drawing a sociological comparison between them. For an example of this sort of *simpliste* viewpoint, see Robert A. Nisbet: *The Sociological Tradition* (London, 1967), pp. 225–6 and 243–51.

human capacities as those of super-human powers. For Durkheim, by contrast, religion cannot be illusory in this sense, except insofar as a given set of religious beliefs is no longer functionally compatible with the existence of a given type of society. This indeed is the case with traditional religion in modern society. Durkheim admits that Christianity, and more specifically, Protestantism, was the immediate source of the modern cult of the individual. The contrasts between the religious cults of Antiquity and the symbolic content of Christianity are given considerable stress by Durkheim: the religions of the ancient world were 'above all, systems of rites whose essential objective was to ensure the regular working of the universe'; their focus was thus 'turned towards the external world'. But Christianity places its emphasis upon the salvation of the individual soul:

Since, for the Christian, virtue, and piety does not consist in material rites, but in interior states of the soul, he is constrained to exercise a perpetual surveillance over himself... Thus, of the two possible poles of all thought, nature on the one hand and man on the other, it is necessarily around the second that the thinking of Christian societies came to gravitate...[49]

However, while moral individualism derives from this source, it is also expressive of the series of changes which have transformed modern societies from the end of the eighteenth century onwards, and which involve the penetration of rationalism into all aspects of social life. While these beliefs have a genuinely 'sacred' quality, they cannot be guaranteed by a reversion to the dominance which the church previously held; the state must increasingly assume the main responsibility for the overall maintenance of the contemporary moral order.

Durkheim's theoretical linkage between the religions of former times and the moral needs of the present should not be allowed to gloss over the equally significant divergences between traditional and contemporary society. Durkheim wholly rejects the conservative plea for a return to the traditional deism. It is because Durkheim defines 'religion' in a broad sense which identifies it with the sacred, and thence with moral regulation in his sense, that he is able to emphasise the continuity in symbols and values while at the same time stressing the important elements of discontinuity between past and present. The morality of the future, based on the 'cult of the personality' is nothing less than the transformation of religion into secular humanism. What makes this conception distinct from that of Marx (and of Feuerbach) is not the notion that traditional religion must be replaced by a humanist ethic, a standpoint common to both French and German social thought from the early part of the nineteenth century, but the nature of the relationship between this ethic and the concrete social structure (i.e., the division of labour). At this point, a methodological issue must be briefly touched upon.

In interpreting the relationship between Durkheim's conception of social

[49] *L'évolution pédagogique*, p. 323.

facts as 'external' to and exerting 'constraint' over the individual, and Marx's emphasis that one must 'above all avoid postulating " society " once more as an abstraction confronting the individual', it is important to bear in mind Marx's distinction between alienation and objectification. For Marx, social 'facts' – in bourgeois society – are 'external' to the individual in two senses. Firstly, in common with the material artifacts created by men, social relationships are objectified in that they are 'realities': thus Marx's consistent criticism of utopian socialism (and idealism generally) is that it assumes away the reality of social life by treating society as the creation of the intellect. In this sense, every man is both a product and producer of the social relationships of which he forms a part; this holds, of course, for every sort of society, including socialism. But in bourgeois society, social facts also have an 'external' and constraining character which is historically relative, and which derives from the structure of alienated relationships. Thus, in this sense, the individual worker is compelled to enter into relationships which are 'external' to him in the various ways which Marx specifies in his analysis of alienation; but this duality between the individual and society will be dissolved with the transcendence of capitalism. Hence, while in Durkheim's methodology, externality and constraint are necessarily closely independent, in Marx's thinking externality/constraint, in the sense of *alienation*, are not universal characteristics of social phenomena. In socialist society, the character of moral authority will not demand the maintenance of the Kantian element of obligation or duty, insofar as this is linked with the necessity of adhering to moral norms which the individual finds antipathetic.

These theoretical considerations underlie the differential treatment of the consequences of secularisation in the writings of Marx and Durkheim. According to Marx, religion is always a form of alienation, because religious beliefs involve the attribution to mystical entities of capabilities or powers that are in fact possessed by man. The *Aufhebung* of religion does not, according to this standpoint, simply entail the replacement of religious symbolism by rational, scientific knowledge, but the conscious recovery of those human capacities or modalities previously expressed in mystical form. The transcendence of religion is possible because the resolution of the dichotomy and opposition between the individual and society is possible. From Durkheim's position, this is sheerly utopian, as regards the organisation of contemporary societies. There is a sense in which Durkheim is in accord with Marx that a form of society can exist in which there is no dichotomy between the individual and society – in the case of mechanical solidarity. Mechanical solidarity 'binds the individual directly to society without any intermediary'.[50] But this societal form has ceded place to organic solidarity, and cannot be recovered; and even if it were possible, the type of society envis-

[50] *DL*, p. 129.

aged by Marx would only be conceivable given a reimposition of a pervasive *conscience collective*, which would necessarily entail a vast re-extension of the realm of the sacred.

The contrast between Durkheim and Marx concerning the consequences of secularisation in modern societies becomes most significant in relation to their respective diagnoses of the primary trends of development which are *emergent* in those societies. This leads into one major theme in the writings of Marx, Durkheim and Weber which both unites and expresses some of the main points of difference in their works: that which concerns their various interpretations of the effects of the social differentiation entailed by the growth in complexity of the division of labour.

15. Social differentiation and the division of labour

The writings of Marx, Weber and Durkheim, in their varying ways, fuse together an analysis and a moral critique of modern society. Weber's insistence upon the absolute logical dichotomy between empirical or scientific knowledge, and value-directed action, should not be allowed to obscure his equally emphatic affirmation of the relevance of historical and sociological analysis to active involvement in politics and social criticism. Both Marx and Durkheim reject Kant's ethical dualism, and attempt more directly to integrate a factual and a moral assessment of the characteristic features of the contemporary social order. Durkheim maintained a lifelong commitment to the formulation of a scientific foundation for the diagnostic interpretation of the 'pathological' features of the advanced societies. Marx's work and political actions are predicated upon the argument that 'Man must prove the truth, that is, the actuality and power, the this-sidedness of his thinking, in *Praxis*'.[1]

In the works of the latter two writers, the concepts of 'alienation' and 'anomie' respectively provide the focal point of their critical interpretation of modern society. The conception of alienation is the main prop of Marx's critique of capitalism, and therefore of his thesis that the bourgeois order can be transcended by a new kind of society. It does not merely represent an early utopian position which Marx later abandoned, nor does it become reduced to the relatively minor place which Marx's discussion of the 'fetishism of commodities' occupies in *Capital*. The same is true of Durkheim's notion of anomie: it is integral to his whole analysis of the modern 'crisis' and the mode in which it can be resolved.

Alienation, anomie, and the 'state of nature'

It might appear obvious that the primary differences between the concepts of alienation and anomie, as employed by Marx and Durkheim respectively, rest upon divergent implicit views of man in a 'state of nature'. It is conventionally asserted that Marx's concept of alienation is founded upon the premise that man is 'naturally' good, but has been corrupted by society; and that the notion of anomie, by contrast, stems from the assumption that man is 'naturally' a refractory being, whose egoism must be rigidly restrained by society. The first view is assumed to be close to that of Rousseau, the second

[1] *WYM*, p. 401; *We*, vol. 3, p. 5.

to that of Hobbes.[2] But this considerably over-simplifies the relevant issues. To measure alienation and anomie primarily against a hypothetical state of nature is to neglect what is the most essential dimension of both Marx's and Durkheim's writings: the *historical* nature of man. As Durkheim expresses it: 'The present opposes itself to the past, yet derives from and perpetuates it.'[3] Both thinkers explicitly and decisively separate their position from that of abstract philosophy, which stands outside of history. Durkheim specifically criticises both Rousseau and Hobbes from this standpoint. Both, according to Durkheim, begin from the assumption of a 'break in continuity between the individual and society', and hold that 'Man is thus naturally refractory to the common life; he can only resign himself to it when forced'. Durkheim emphasises here that the meaning which he gives to the term 'constraint' is quite different to that of Hobbes.[4]

It is true that Durkheim anchors egoistic needs in the biological (i.e., 'pre-social') structure of the individual organism; but he nevertheless makes it clear that egoism is also in large part a product of society – the impulse to economic self-advancement, for instance, is as much a creation of modern society for Durkheim as it is for Marx.[5] In modern societies, where individuality is highly developed, egoism presents a concomitantly greater threat to social unity. Individualism is very emphatically not the same as egoism, but its growth nevertheless expands the range of egoistic inclinations. The condition of anomie which prevails in certain sectors of modern societies reflects the very advance in the range of motives and sensibilities of individual men which is the outcome of a long process of social development. Modern man, in other words, when experiencing a situation of anomie, is a quite different being from a (hypothetical) savage in the pre-social state of nature. The latter would not be in an anomic position. Similarly, a human infant, when newly born, is an egoistic being, but not an anomic one, since his needs are tied to defined biological limits. As the child becomes a socialised being, the range of his egoistic impulses expand, and so do the possibilities of his becoming placed in a state of anomie. 'Let all social life disappear, and moral life will disappear with it, since it would no longer have any objective. The state of nature of the philosophers of the eighteenth century, if not immoral, is at least *amoral*.'[6]

This general standpoint is not nearly so different from that of Marx as is usually assumed. Marx is as aware as Durkheim that the eighteenth-century

---

[2] See for example, John Horton: 'The de-humanisation of anomie and alienation', pp. 283–300; Sheldon S. Wolin: *Politics and Vision* (Boston, 1960), pp. 399–407; a more sophisticated discussion is offered in Steven Lukes: 'Alienation and anomie', in Peter Laslett and W. G. Runciman: *Philosophy, Politics and Society* (Oxford, 1967), pp. 134–56.

[3] *L'évolution pédagogique*, p. 21.   [4] *RSM*, pp. 121 & 124.

[5] *Su*, p. 360; cf. also *DL*, vol. 11, 272–4 & 403–4.

[6] *DL*, p. 399. 'Although a child is naturally an egoist . . . the civilised adult . . . has many ideas, feelings and practices unrelated to organic needs.' *Su*, p. 211.

rationalists endowed man in a state of nature with faculties which are in reality derived from society. The early forms of human society, which are dominated by the relatively uncontrolled vagaries of nature, are accompanied by a restricted range of human qualities and capacities. It is precisely the social character of man which, for Marx, makes him ' human ': that is, distinguishes man from the animals. All the senses and biological urges of the human being are capable of this transformation. Sexual activity, or eating and drinking, for instance, are not for human beings the simple satisfaction of biological drives, but have become transformed, during the course of the development of society, into actions which provide manifold satisfactions. As Marx writes: ' Our desires and pleasures spring from society; we measure them, therefore, by society and not by the objects which serve for their satisfaction. Because they are of a social nature, they are of a relative nature.' [7]

In this sense, then, there is a much closer similarity between the ' constants ' lying behind the concepts of alienation and anomie than might appear from superficial comparison.[8] Both Marx and Durkheim emphasise the fact that human qualities, needs and motives are in large part the product of social development. Both perceive a primary flaw in the theory of political economy, which treats egoism as the foundation of a theory of social order. As Marx comments: ' The *division of labour* and *exchange* are the two phenomena which lead the economist to vaunt the social character of his science, while in the same breath he unconsciously expresses the contradictory nature of his science – the establishment of society through unsocial, particular interests.' [9] Similarly, Durkheim criticises Tönnies because the latter's conception of *Gesellschaft* treats society in the manner of utilitarian theory, as an aggregate of independent, individual ' atoms ', which only constitutes a unity insofar as it is cohered by the ' external ' influence of the state. According to Durkheim, this is completely inadequate: the activity of individuals in forming contracts expresses a broad network of social ties in the division of labour; and this is in fact the foundation of the state. Marx makes almost exactly the same point in a different polemical context. The individual in civil society is not comparable to an atom, because an atom ' *has no needs* ' and ' is *self-sufficient* '. The fallacy of the conception of the atomic individual, adopted by the economists, is that the member of civil society is bound to others by relationships of interdependence. It is these unacknowledged relationships which are the real foundation of the state: in reality it is the

---

[7] *SW*, vol. 1, p. 94.

[8] The over-facile comparisons often made between Freud and Durkheim also neglect the latter's emphasis upon the historical and social character of human needs. How far Durkheim's position is comparable to Hobbes' in the relevant respects depends upon how far the latter did, in fact, assume a state of nature. See C. B. Macpherson: *The Political Theory of Possessive Individualism* (London, 1962), pp. 19ff.

[9] p. 187; cf. also the criticism of Stirner's philosophy of egoism, *GI*, pp. 486–95.

state which ' is held together by civil life '.[10] The *integrative* character of the growth of the division of labour in bourgeois society is in fact one pole of Marx's critique of political economy: the expansion of capitalism destroys the autonomous local community, and brings men within the framework of an interdependence which is enormously more inclusive – although, according to Marx, this occurs only at the expense of a ramification of alienation.

Moreover, Marx's conception of ' freedom ' is in fact quite close to the notion of autonomous self-control taken by Durkheim, and is definitely not to be identified with the utilitarian view. The words ' free ' and ' rational ' are as closely associated in Marx's writing as they are in that of Hegel. Hegel dismissed the notion, implicit in utilitarianism, that a man is free to the degree that he can do whatever his inclinations lead him to desire. ' The man in the street thinks he is free if it is open to him to act as he pleases, but his very arbitrariness implies that he is not free.' [11] Freedom is not the exercise of egoism, but is in fact opposed to it. A course of action is ' arbitrary ' rather than ' free ' if it simply involves irrational choice among alternative courses of action with which the individual is confronted. An animal which chooses, in a situation of adversity, to fight rather than to run from an enemy, does not thereby act ' freely '. To be free is to be autonomous, and thus not impelled by either external or internal forces beyond rational control; this is why freedom is a human prerogative, because only man, through his membership of society, is able to control, not only the form, but also the content of volition. In Hegel's view, this is possible given the identification of the individual with the rational ideal. For Marx, it presupposes concrete social reorganisation, the setting up of a communist society. The position of the individual in society will be analogous to that characteristic, for instance of the scientists within the scientific community. (This is an example Durkheim also uses in a similar context.) A scientist who accepts the norms which define scientific activity is not less free than one who deliberately rejects them; on the contrary, by being a member of the scientific community, he is able to participate in a collective enterprise which allows him to enlarge, and to creatively employ, his own individual capacities. In this way, acceptance of moral requisites is not the acceptance of alien constraint, but is the recognition of the rational.

This is not to say, of course, that there are no important differences in the respective standpoints of Marx and Durkheim which can be regarded as of ' ahistorical ' significance. Durkheim is emphatic that the individual personality is overwhelmingly influenced by the characteristics of the form of society in which he exists and into which he is socialised. But he does not

---

[10] *Holy Family*, p. 163. Marx also makes the point that the ' atomic ' position of the individual in civil society is legitimised by norms of contract and property. As contrasted with feudalism, ' *Right* has here taken the place of privilege ' (p. 157).

[11] *Philosophy of Right*, ed. Knox (London, 1967), p. 230. For Weber's conception of ' freedom ', see his discussion of Roscher and Knies, in *GAW*.

accept a complete historical relativism in this respect: every man, no matter whether 'primitive' or 'civilised', is a *homo duplex*, in the sense that there is an opposition in every individual between egoistic impulses and those which have a 'moral' connotation. Marx does not adopt such a psychological model; in Marx's conception, there is no asocial basis for such an implicit antagonism between the individual and society. For Marx, 'The individual *is* is the *social being* . . . Individual human life and species-life are not different things.' [12] The egoistic opposition between the individual and society which is found in a particularly marked form in bourgeois society is an outcome of the development of the division of labour. Durkheim's identification of the duality of human personality, on the other hand, is founded upon the supposition that the egoism of the infant, deriving from the biological drives with which he is born, can never be reversed or eradicated completely by the subsequent moral development of the child.

This can again be connected to the discrepant role of productive activity in the model of society employed by Durkheim and Marx respectively. For Durkheim, the emphasis upon the causal specificity of the 'social' – the autonomy of sociological explanation – leads to a general neglect of the interrelationships between society and nature. In a specific way, this is manifest in the proposition that those needs connected with physical survival in the material world are not assimilated to those impulses which are rooted in *social* commitments. Marx, by comparison, makes the interplay between society and the natural world the focus of his analysis, and thereby emphasises the socialised character of the 'sensuous needs' which mediate between the individual organism and his adaptation to the physical environment. But this must not be exaggerated: as has been shown above, both Marx and Durkheim stress the historical dimension in the conditioning of human needs. For Durkheim, egoism becomes a threat to social unity only within the context of a form of society in which human sensibilities have become greatly expanded: 'all evidence compels us to expect our effort in the struggle between the two beings within us to increase with the growth of civilisation.' [13]

The future of the division of labour

In Marx's analysis of bourgeois society, there are two directly related but partially separable sources of alienation rooted in the capitalist mode of production. The first of these is alienation in the labour-process, in the productive activity of the worker. The second is the alienation of the worker from his product, that is, from control of the *result* of the labour-process. I shall refer to these, for the sake of convenience, as 'technological alienation' and 'market alienation' respectively. [14] Both of these derive from the division of

[12] *EW*, p. 158.   [13] 'The dualism of human nature', p. 339.
[14] This does not exactly correspond to the various senses of alienation which Marx distinguishes, but provides a basic distinction for the purposes of this chapter.

labour involved in capitalist production. The latter expresses the fact that the organisation of productive relationships constitutes a class system resting upon an exploitative dominance of one class by another; the former identifies occupational specialisation as the source of the fragmentation of work into routine and undemanding tasks.

For Marx, both types of alienation are integral to the expansion of the division of labour: the emergence of class societies in history is dependent upon the growth of the specialisation of tasks made possible by the existence of surplus production. The formation of a classless society will thus lead to the abolition of the division of labour as it is known under capitalism. In Marx's conception both market and technological alienation are thus inseparable from the division of labour: ' the *division of labour* is nothing but the *alienated* form of human activity...' [15] The overcoming of market alienation through the revolutionary reorganisation of society will lead to the reversal of the fragmenting effects of specialisation which, by channelling the activities of the individual within the confines of a limited task, provides no opportunity for him to realise the full range of his talents and capacities in his labour.

Durkheim's theory of the division of labour leads him in quite a different direction. For Durkheim, the growth of the division of labour is portrayed in terms of the integrating consequences of specialisation rather than in terms of the formation of class systems. Consequently, Durkheim treats class conflict, not as providing a basis for the revolutionary restructuring of society, but as symptomatic of deficiencies in the moral co-ordination of different occupational groups within the division of labour. In Durkheim's thesis, the ' forced ' division of labour is largely separate from the ' anomic ' division of labour, and the mitigation of the first will not in itself cope with the problems posed by the second. According to him, the socialism of Marx is wholly concerned with the alienation of the forced division of labour, which is to be accomplished through the regulation of the market – the socialisation of production. But, in Durkheim's stated view, which he opposes to this, the increasing dominance of economic relationships, consequent upon the destruction of the traditional institutions which were the moral backbone of prior forms of society, is precisely the main cause of the modern ' crisis '.

In fact, Durkheim is mistaken in supposing that the regulation of the market (the elimination of market alienation) is the sole focus of Marx's interest. Marx is from the outset concerned more fundamentally with just the same issue as Durkheim: the *amoral* domination of modern society by economic relationships, and conceives the socialisation of production as a means to the elimination of the conditions of labour (technological alienation) which, by subordinating man to economic production, ' dehumanise ' him. Durkheim himself certainly recognises the alienative character of the modern labour process, whereby the worker ' repeats the same move-

---

[15] *EW*, p. 181; *We, Ergd*, p. 557.

ments with monotonous regularity, but without being interested in them, and
without understanding them ', and he agrees that this is ' a debasement of
human nature '.[16] But whereas Durkheim's proposals for the reduction or
eradication of this dehumanisation of the worker are based upon the moral
consolidation of specialisation in the division of labour, Marx's hope and
expectation is that this division of labour will itself be radically changed.
This is really the crux of the most significant differences between Marx's use
of the conception of alienation and Durkheim's employment of the notion of
anomie. For Durkheim, the dehumanisation of productive activity is a phenomenon which derives, not from the fragmenting consequences of the division
of labour itself, but from the anomic moral position of the worker. In other
words, the dehumanisation of the labour process has occurred because the
individual worker has no clear conception of a unity of purpose which binds
his work activity together with the collective productive endeavour of society.
This situation can therefore be remedied by providing the individual with a
moral awareness of the social importance of his particular role in the division
of labour. He is then no longer an alienated automaton, but is a useful part
of an organic whole: ' from that time, as special and uniform as his activity
may be, it is that of an intelligent being, for it has direction, and he is aware
of it.' [17] This is entirely consistent with Durkheim's general account of the
growth of the division of labour, and its relationship to human freedom. It
is only through moral acceptance in his particular role in the division of
labour that the individual is able to achieve a high degree of autonomy as a
self-conscious being, and can escape both the tyranny of the rigid moral conformity demanded in undifferentiated societies on the one hand, and the
tyranny of unrealisable desires on the other.

Not the moral integration of the individual within a differentiated division
of labour, but the effective *dissolution* of the division of labour as an organising principle of human social intercourse, is the premise of Marx's conception. Marx nowhere specifies in detail how this future society would be
organised socially, but, at any rate, this perspective differs decisively from
that of Durkheim. The vision of a highly differentiated division of labour,
integrated upon the basis of moral norms of individual obligation and corporate solidarity, is quite at variance with Marx's anticipation of the future
form of society.[18]

According to Durkheim's standpoint, the criteria underlying Marx's hopes
for the elimination of technological alienation represent a reversion to moral
principles which are no longer appropriate to the modern form of society.
This is exactly the problem which Durkheim poses at the opening of *The*

---

[16] *DL*, p. 371.
[17] *DL*, p. 373; *DTS*, p. 365. For a critique of Durkheim's position, see Georges
Friedmann: *The Anatomy of Work* (London, 1961), pp. 72–81 and *passim*.
[18] The views set out by Engels, however, are much closer to Durkheim's position. cf.
Engels, ' On authority ', *SW*, vol. 1, pp. 636–9.

Division of Labour: ' Is it our duty to seek to become a thorough and complete human being, one quite sufficient unto himself; or, on the contrary, to be only a part of a whole, the organ of an organism? ' [19] The analysis contained in the work, in Durkheim's view, demonstrates conclusively that organic solidarity is the ' normal ' type in modern societies, and consequently that the era of the ' universal man ' is finished. The latter ideal, which predominated up to the seventeenth and eighteenth centuries in western Europe, is incompatible with the diversity of the contemporary order.[20] In preserving this ideal, by contrast, Marx argues the obverse: that the tendencies which are leading to the destruction of capitalism are themselves capable of effecting a recovery of the ' universal ' properties of man, which are shared by every individual:

the abolition of division of labour is conditional upon the development of intercourse and productive forces to such a degree of universality that private property and division of labour become fetters on them ... private property can be abolished only on condition of an all-round development of individuals... Within communist society, the only society in which the original and free development of individuals is not a mere phrase, this development is determined precisely by the interrelationship of individuals, an interrelationship which consists partly in the economic prerequisites and partly in the necessary solidarity of the free development of all, and, finally, in the universal character of the activity of individuals on the basis of the existing productive forces.[21]

Contrary to what is often held, this conception does not entail any commitment to a metaphysical ' perfectibility ' of man. The imputation of such a view to Marx rests upon a confusion of alienation and objectification – which is precisely the charge which Marx levels at utilitarianism. If the overcoming of alienation is read to mean the complete disappearance of any barriers to the activity of the subject-man – then this would indeed suppose a utopian world in which human self-determination reigns supreme, and all human potentialities are finally realised. But the transcendence of alienation does not involve the end of objectification; society (and the material environment) will continue to be ' external ' to the individual. They will not, however, as in a condition of alienation, represent worlds which are opposed to or cut off from conscious *Praxis*, but will be recognised to be integrated with it. In all previous eras, according to Marx, the ideal of the universal man has been either achieved only at the expense of the alienation of man from nature – as in primitive societies – or has remained exclusive to minority classes. Through

---

[19] *DL*, p. 41; *DTS*, p. 4.

[20] *L'évolution pédagogique*, pp. 374ff. Durkheim says elsewhere: ' We evaluate, in *The Division of Labour*, the old ideal of humanist morality, the moral ideal of the cultivated man: we show how it can today be regarded as increasingly anachronistic, how a new ideal is forming and developing as the result of the increasing specialisation of social functions.' *AS*, vol. 10, 1907, p. 355.

[21] *GI*, p. 495. The influence of Hegel and, through Hegel, Schiller, is evident here. cf. Schiller's *On the Aesthetic Education of Man* (1795) (Oxford, 1967), pp. 31–43 (6th letter).

the abolition of the division of labour with the overthrow of capitalism, every man will be released from the occupational categorisation which makes a specialised work task the principal social quality of the individual (a man ' is ' a teacher, or ' is ' a wage-labourer). Since each individual will then contain within himself the universal properties of humanity, the alienation of man from his ' species-being ' is thereby dissolved.[22]

It is in such a context that the more general divergence between the respective standpoints of Marx and Durkheim must be set. For Durkheim, the social structure of modern society exacerbates the opposition between egoism and the moral demands which membership in the collectivity places upon the individual. There is no possibility of this dichotomy being resolved, because the very organisation of contemporary society, which makes possible the development of individuality and self-consciousness, necessarily heightens the egoistic inclinations of the individual. Moreover, since Durkheim's theory of the division of labour involves the contention that organic solidarity – functional interdependence in the division of labour – is the ' normal ' modern type, it follows that the problem of moral integration (anomie) must be given overriding prominence. The problem of ' restraining one's horizons ', or conversely of the opening-out of desires which cannot be satiated, is particularly acute in a social order which has the organisational requisite of maintaining the existence of specialised and restricted tasks in the division of labour, and which is not dominated by a strong ethic subordinating the individual to the collectivity. Durkheim foresees the existence of a society with multiple occupational positions, in which access to the leading strata will depend, not upon transmitted privilege, but upon competitive selection of the talented through the medium of the educational system. Such a society, which places a premium upon individual attainment through the public manifestation of ability, clearly exerts a pressure towards the expansion of incompatible egoisms. In such a society, the ' war of all against all ' is a ready threat, which must be contained by the balancing of egoism with altruism; these are destined to be in perpetual conflict.

The problem of bureaucracy

In Marx's analysis of the extension of the division of labour underlying the formation of capitalist enterprise, the expropriation of the worker from his means of production is given pride of place. In Marx's view, this is the most essential condition for the emergence of bourgeois society, and identifies, along an historical dimension, the formation of the class relationship between capital and labour which is implicit in the capitalist mode of production. It is the intrinsic nature of the connection between the division of labour and the class structure which makes it possible for Marx to proceed to the

---

[22] cf. Thilo Ramm: ' Die künftige Gesellschaftsordnung nach der Theorie von Marx und Engels ', *Marxismusstudien*, vol. 2, 1957, pp. 77–179.

conclusion that the transcendence of alienation is possible through the abolition of capitalism. Neither Durkheim nor Weber denies the possibility of the formation of socialist societies: but both assert that the transition to socialism will not radically change the existing form of society. However, the substance of Durkheim's position here diverges sharply from that of Weber, and it may be said that Weber's conception of the development of the division of labour in the occidental societies constitutes a third alternative to that offered both by Marx and by Durkheim.

Weber's epistemology separates his general perspective upon social development from that assumed by the other two authors who, whatever their differences, share a commitment to a definite overall pattern in the 'stages' of development of society, from primitive society to modern times. It has often been remarked that, in Weber's writings, 'the general drift of secular rationalisation' [23] is the counterpart to the schemes of development offered by other writers. But it should not be forgotten that, from Weber's standpoint, the analysis of the growth of rationalisation does not equal the 'only' or the 'correct' representation of history, but simply knowledge from one culturally given 'point of view'. With this important qualification in mind, however, it is possible to essay a comparison of Weber's analysis of the typical process of capitalist development with that given by Marx.

An important part of Weber's writings consists in delineating the factors promoting rationalisation 'on the level of meaning', in the sphere of religious belief. However, Weber always insists upon tracing the nexus of social relationships which both influence, and are influenced by, the growth in rationalisation. In this sense, the most important questions concern, not only the 'degree' of rationalisation, but the mode in which its effects promote a particular conjunction of social relationships and institutions. Thus not only the degree, but the 'direction' assumed by rationalisation in the West, and more specifically, in capitalism, differs from that of the other major civilisations. In modern western capitalism, there are various spheres in which rationalisation has proceeded in a direction, as well as to an extent, unknown elsewhere. The first is in the spread of science, a phenomenon of basic significance: not only does it complete the process of 'disenchantment', but it makes possible the progressive implementation of rational technology in production. Moreover, 'Scientific work is chained to the course of progress... Every scientific "fulfilment" raises new "questions"; it *asks* to be "surpassed" and outdated.' [24] Thus the institutionalisation of science weds modern life to an implicit dynamic of innovation and change which cannot, in itself, confer 'meaning' (except to the professional practitioners of science, to whose activity scientific enquiry serves as an organising norm). The application of scientific innovation to technology is combined, in the

[23] Gerth and Mills: 'Introduction: the man and his work', *FMW*, p. 51.
[24] *FMW*, p. 138.

modern economy, with the introduction of methods of rational calculation, exemplified in book-keeping, which promote that methodical conduct of entrepreneurial activity which is so distinctive of contemporary capitalism. The conduct of rational capitalism in turn entails unavoidable consequences in the sphere of social organisation, and inevitably fosters the spread of bureaucracy.

Weber does not, of course, deny that modern capitalism entails the formation of a class system based upon capital and wage-labour, and he recognises the importance of the historical expropriation of the peasantry upon which Marx places so much stress. But this is not in itself, according to Weber's standpoint, the main structural axis in the differentiated division of labour which characterises capitalism. By emphasising the significance of the rationalisation of activity as characteristic of modern capitalist production, and by stressing its partial independence of class relationships, Weber separates (but in a different manner from Durkheim) the class system of capitalism from differentiation in the division of labour as such. In other words, bureaucratic specialisation of tasks is treated by Weber as the most integral feature of capitalism. This is reinforced upon a more empirical level by Weber's analysis of the partly separable processes of bureaucratisation in the economy and the polity. The growth of the rational state, which has its corpus of bureaucratic officials, is not wholly derivative of economic rationalisation, but has to some extent preceded the development of capitalism – and indeed, has created conditions which promoted its rise.

Thus Weber expressly denies that the expropriation of the worker from his means of production has been confined to the immediate sphere of industry, and instead applies the conception to other institutional contexts. In Weber's thesis, any form of organisation which has a hierarchy of authority can become subject to a process of 'expropriation': for the Marxian notion of the 'means of production' Weber substitutes the 'means of administration'. Oversimplifying somewhat, it might be said that Weber gives to the organisation of relationships of domination and subordination the prominence which Marx attributes to relationships of production. Any political association, according to Weber, may be organised in an 'estate' form, in which the officials themselves own their means of administration. Thus in the Middle Ages, vassals were in direct control of the financing of their administrative districts, and were responsible for providing their own soldiery and military equipment. The formation of the modern state apparatus was promoted by the actions of the monarch in gathering the means of administration into his own hands:

No single official personally owns the money he pays out, or the buildings, stores, tools, and war machines he controls. In the contemporary 'state' – and this is essential for the concept of state – the 'separation' of the administrative staff, of the administrative officials, and of the workers from the material means of administrative organisation is completed.[25]

These developments were the most important factors promoting the emergence of the modern state in which ' expert officialdom, based on the division of labour '[26] is wholly separated from ownership of its means of administration. In general, the advance of the division of labour progresses in step with the centralisation of the means of administration, and the concomitant ' expropriation ' of officials. This can be documented, Weber points out, in military organisations. In feudal armies, each soldier supplies his own weaponry: this is the case with militia of all types. But in states where there is a need for a permanent army at the disposal of the monarch, such as in ancient Egypt, a bureaucratised structure develops, in which the king owns and supplies the arms and military equipment. In western capitalism, under the twin influences of centralisation of administration and the rational calculation of tasks, the process of expropriation from the means of administration penetrates into many spheres, including not only that of the military, but also into other organisations in which there is a specialised division of labour – universities, hospitals, and so on. The spread of bureaucratic specialisation is mainly promoted by its technical superiority over other types of organisation in co-ordinating administrative tasks. This in turn is partly dependent upon the filling of bureaucratic positions according to the possession of specialised educational qualifications. ' Only the modern development of full bureaucratisation brings the system of rational, specialised examinations irresistibly to the fore.'[27] The expansion of bureaucratisation hence necessarily leads to the demand for specialist education, and increasingly fragments the humanist culture which, in previous times, made possible the ' universal man ', the ' thorough and complete human being ' whom Durkheim speaks of. Weber expresses an essentially similar point in holding that the ' cultivated man ' of earlier ages is now displaced by the trained specialist. Since the trend towards bureaucratisation is irreversible in capitalism, it follows that the growth of functional specialisation is a necessary concomitant of the modern social order.

According to Weber, ' the further advance of bureaucratic mechanisation ' is ' inevitable ' in the modern world.[28] But, as has been pointed out in a previous chapter, in Weber's eyes the progression of bureaucratisation increasingly reveals a tension between the demand for technical efficiency of administration on the one hand, and the human values of spontaneity and autonomy on the other. The bureaucratic division of labour constitutes the ' cage ' in which modern *Berufsmenschen* are compelled to live: ' The Puritan

---

[25] *FMW*, p. 82.
[26] *FMW*, p. 88.
[27] *ES*, vol. 3, p. 999; *WuG*, vol. 2, p. 585; cf. also *GASS*, pp. 500–1.
[28] *GASS*, p. 413.

wanted to work in a calling; we are forced to do so.' [29] The Faustian ' universal man ' has to be renounced in favour of the specialisation of labour which is the condition of the efficiency of modern production – ' specialists without spirit, sensualists without heart '. The main normative issue, in Weber's view, is not how the process of bureaucratisation can become reversed, because that is impossible in a society which requires calculative precision in the administration of its various institutions: ' the great question thus is . . . what we can set against this mechanisation to preserve a certain section of humanity from this fragmentation of the soul, this complete ascendancy of the bureaucratic ideal of life? '.[30]

It should be clear that, in Weber's terms, there can be no possibility of the transformation of the bureaucratisation of social life through the occurrence of socialist revolution. Precisely the opposite is the case. In the capitalist economy, a considerable number of operations are left to the play of market forces; but in a socialised economy, these would be taken over by the state, and would then become subject to bureaucratic administration. A socialist society would hence inevitably be more imprisoned within the toils of bureaucratic control than is already the case in capitalism: the elimination of private property in the means of production would not enable this process to be reversed, but would further hasten its advancement. Marx's view of bureaucracy is quite different, and again the difference lies primarily in the connection which Marx establishes between market alienation and technological alienation – that is, between the class structure and bureaucratic specialisation. The substance of Marx's thinking on the question of bureaucracy is set out in his early critique of Hegel's writings on the same question.

In Hegel's treatment of the matter, the state bureaucracy is represented as the ' universal class ' which is responsible for implementing what is in the general interest of society, and which hence cuts across the egoistic *bellum omnia contra omnes* which exists in civil society. According to Hegel, the ' division of labour in governmental affairs ', the civil service bureaucracy, forms the organisational mediation between the particular, individual interests of men in civil society, and the universal qualities of the state. The hierarchical character of bureaucracy is explained in terms of the necessity of establishing levels of co-ordination between the ' concrete ' interests of individuals in civil society and the ' abstract ' character of state policy. Appointment of officials on the basis of examinations, and the separation into salaried offices, together with the conception of impersonal moral ' duty ', ensures that the member of the ' universal class ' renunciates the ' capricious satisfaction of subjective purposes . . . So far as public business is concerned,

[29] *PE*, p. 181. The individual worker today is ' a small wheel ' in the bureaucratic machine, and ' asks himself only whether or not he can progress from this small wheel to being a bigger one '. *GPS*, p. 413.
[30] *GASS*, p. 414.

here lies the link between universal and particular interests, constituting the concept of the state and its inner stability.' [31] In Marx's terms, however, Hegel's discussion of bureaucracy merely exemplifies in a particularly direct way the general errors contained in the Hegelian concept of the state. Bureaucracy does not represent the common interest, but a particular interest; bureaucratic authority rests upon an illusory universality which in fact cloaks a specific class interest. The state bureaucracy is thus the administrative organ through which the sectional power of the dominant class is institutionalised. The formal hierarchy of authority which is embodied in bureaucratic organisation hence does not create the link between civil society and the state which Hegel specifies, but instead acts to concentrate political power and to *separate* it from the control of those in civil society: the bureaucratic state is ' an organ superimposed upon society '.[32] Moreover, because of its tightly integrated character, bureaucracy is an especially irresponsible form of political administration: ' Bureaucracy is a circle no-one can leave ... Bureaucracy possesses the state's essence, the spiritual essence of society, as its *private property*. The universal spirit of bureaucracy is the *secret*, the mystery sustained within bureaucracy itself by hierarchy and maintained on the outside as a closed corporation.' [33]

For Marx, then, the state bureaucracy is the archetype of bureaucratic organisation, and the possibility of its eradication is given as one consequence of the revolutionary transition to socialism. According to Marx, the countries which are marked by the existence of a highly developed bureaucratic state – both France and Germany fall into this category – are those in which the struggle of the bourgeoisie against the land-owning aristocracy for political power has been particularly severe. Thus the French bureaucratic machine originated in the days of the absolute monarchy, and was given a mighty thrust forward by the Revolution of 1789. As regards its historical content, Marx's analysis of bureaucracy hence shares certain central points with that of Weber. Marx agrees that the bureaucratic state in Europe arose as an instrument serving the monarchy in its attempts to reduce the feudal dispersal of powers: the centralisation of the state in the hands of the monarch was a major condition allowing the rise of bourgeois interests, which then appropriated power to themselves.[34] But in Marx's view this is not, as it is for Weber, one part of an irreversible general trend towards bureaucratic specialisation of the division of labour in all spheres of social life. To Marx, bureaucratic centralisation is rather one particular manifestation of the bourgeois state, and consequently is as transitory a social form as is capitalism itself.

Some indication of how Marx envisages the elimination of bureaucracy in socialist society is given in his remarks upon the bureaucratisation of the

---

[31] Hegel, quoted by Marx, *WYM*, p. 181.
[32] *SW*, vol. 2, p. 32.
[33] *WYM*, pp. 185–6. cf. Iring Fetscher: *Karl Marx und der Marxismus* (Munich, 1967), pp. 164–73.   [34] *SW*, vol. 1, p. 516.

French state. In France, this ' parasitic body' has acquired ' a ubiquity, an omniscience ' which surpasses even that in Germany. Marx specifically comments upon the persistent growth which has characterised the French bureaucracy since the late eighteenth century: ' All revolutions perfected this machine instead of smashing it.' [35] But the existence of such an independent bureaucratic order is not intrinsically necessary to the maintenance of a centralised economy; socialism will make it possible to ' simplify the administration of the state ', and to ' let civil society and public opinion create organs of their own, independent of the governmental power '.[36] Such a programme of change, as Marx makes clear in discussing the Commune in *The Civil War in France*, is equivalent to the abolition of the bourgeois state altogether. The Commune was to be composed of officials who were ' chosen by universal suffrage ... and revocable at short terms '. The judiciary and police were also to be ' turned into the responsible and at all times revocable ' agents of the Commune. In such conditions, the bureaucratic state, as an agency of political power independent of civil society, has ceased to be: ' Public functions ceased to be the private property of the tool of the central government.' [37]

The differences between this standpoint and that adopted by Weber are evident. Weber generalises the influence of bureaucratisation on the basis of linking the advance of bureaucracy to the administrative requisites of rational authority. Consequently, for Weber, the analysis of the growth of the bureaucratic state provides a paradigm for the explanation of the progression of bureaucratisation in all spheres. For Marx, on the other hand, the ' systematic and hierarchical division of labour ' [38] in the administration of the state represents a concentration of political power which will be *aufgehoben* when the bourgeois state itself is transcended. The problem of bureaucratisation in the sphere of industry is not discussed by Marx in relation to the question of the bureaucratic state, but is nevertheless handled in comparable terms. The authority system of the modern factory, according to Marx, is intrinsically linked to the necessities engendered by the capitalist economy. But the various forms of co-operative factory which have been set up show that a quite different type of authority structure can be created, which will break down the bureaucratic hierarchy. In the co-operative factories, there is no longer a unilateral distribution of authority.[39]

[35] *SW*, vol. 1, p. 333.

[36] *SW*, vol. 1, p. 284.

[37] *SW*, vol. 1, p. 519. cf. Marx's comments in the first draft of *The Civil War in France*, *We*, vol. 17, pp. 538–49. The Commune, Marx says, was ' the political form of social emancipation ' (*ibid*. p. 545).

[38] *SW*, vol. 1, p. 516. Marx's representation of the political system of bourgeois society, in relation to the bureaucratisation of the governmental machine, closely parallels Weber's view. Thus, discussing nineteenth-century France, Marx says, ' The segments and parties of the ruling class, which alternately struggle to power, regarded the possession and leadership of this enormous government machinery as the highest fruit of victory '. *We*, vol. 17, p. 539.   [39] *Cap*, vol. 3, p. 431.

Conclusion

The object of this concluding chapter has been to emphasise that the socio-logical perspectives of Marx, Durkheim and Weber are rooted in divergent conceptions of the basic structure and trend of development of the modern form of society. Marx's analysis of capitalism is wholly predicated upon the postulated connection between the expansion of the division of labour (and thus the ramification of the forms of alienation) on the one hand, and the emergence of a polarised class structure on the other. For Marx, a primary factor underlying the early origins of capitalism in western Europe is the historical process of the expropriation of producers from control of their means of production. Capitalism is thus, in its very essence, a class society; the existence of a bourgeois class *presupposes* a subordinate class of property-less workers, *and* vice versa. However, the class system of capitalism differs decisively from that of the form of society which preceded it in Europe. In feudalism, domination is certainly founded upon differential access to con-trol of the means of production, i.e., landed property. But the feudal class structure, expressed in the differentiation between the *Stände*, does not wholly separate the individual from participation in communal relationships; the 'social' and the 'economic' are not clearly separated. The emergence of capitalism transforms the ties of civil society into pure ties of the market: the individual functions as a member of a 'community' only in the abstract sense in which he has rights as a citizen in a separate 'political' sphere. The modern social order thus 'separates the *subjective* essence of man' from human control, and transforms man's own capacities into forms in which they are 'externalised'.[40] The material expropriation of the worker from his means of production – which, historically speaking, is the same thing as the formation of the class system of bourgeois society – thus proceeds hand-in-hand with his alienation from his 'species-being', from the exercise of the capacities and faculties which his participation in society could *potentially* offer him. Capitalism, in other words, vastly increases the productive powers of society, but only at the expense of maximising alienation. In bourgeois society, the rational explication of the world through science has largely dis-pelled the religious world-view, according to which reality is ultimately governed and controlled by gods or spirits. But it has replaced this form of human alienation by one in which men are controlled by the economic forces of the market. The 'rule of the gods' is replaced by the 'rule of the market': human goals and objectives thus appear as conditional upon the external play of economic forces. On a concrete level, this is manifest in the helpless-ness of the *Fachmensch*, who is subordinated to the division of labour.

Expressing this in the economic terms of *Capital*, capitalism is a system of commodity production, in which the driving impulse is the search to maxi-mise exchange-value. Exchange-value, not use-value, is integral to the logic

[40] *We*, vol. 1, p. 285.

of capitalist production, and this applies even to human labour itself: labour has value only as labour-*power*, as the abstract expenditure of energy. The basic ' contradictions ' inherent in the capitalist economy derive directly from its character as a system based upon production for exchange-value. The need to maintain, or to expand, the rate of profit, is in opposition to the tendential law of declining profits; the separation of the producer and consumer (i.e., the necessity of capitalism to maximise exchange-value rather than to produce for known needs) is the main factor lying behind the crises to which capitalism is recurrently subject; and the operation of the capitalist market entails both that labour-power cannot be sold above its exchange-value (thus condemning the majority of the working-class to continued economic deprivation), and that there comes into being a large ' reserve army ' destined to live in pauperism. The economic transformations generated by the ' laws of movement ' of capitalist production both transform the system from within, and at the same time, prepare it for its dialectical supersession by a new social order. The transcendence of the class system of bourgeois society, according to Marx, allows for the development of a society in which the existing division of labour is radically transformed.

For Durkheim and Weber, on the other hand, the class structure is not integral to the progressive differentiation in the division of labour. Both authors accept that the modern form of society is a class society: but each repudiates the notion that these class divisions express its underlying nature. In Durkheim's conception, the ' forced ' division of labour is an ' abnormal form ', but it is not a necessary consequence of the extension of social differentiation in itself. Class struggles, in contemporary society, are an outcome of the fact that ' the institution of classes ... does not correspond, or no longer corresponds, to the distribution of natural talents '.[41] In other words, it is primarily the use of economic power to enforce unjust contracts which explains the occurrence of class conflict. What distinguishes the modern form of society from the traditional types is not its specific class character, but the prevalence of organic solidarity. The basic organising principle of modern society is to be found, not in its ' capitalist ' character, as a class system of propertied and propertyless, but in the ' organic ' specialisation of co-operative occupational divisions.

From Durkheim's standpoint, Marx's linking of class structure and the alienation of the individual in the division of labour rests upon a confusion between ' egoism ' and ' individualism '. The ' individualism ' of the modern social order is not to be confused with the ' egoism ' of the political economists and utilitarian philosophers: individualism – the moral sanctioning of specialisation in the division of labour – is an inevitable concomitant of the development of modern society. The characteristic factor underlying the ' pathology ' of the modern order is precisely the *lack* of moral validation of

41 *DL*, p. 375; *DTS*, p. 368.

the division of labour. Such moral validation cannot be secured from the traditional source – religion; in a rationalised world, the old symbols and the old forms of moral domination have become obsolete. Hence the state and the occupational associations must become the principal sources of moral support for the ' cult of the individual'. There can be no possibility of a movement forward into a society in which the existing division of labour is radically transformed, and, correspondingly, in which the state, as a separate political sphere, disappears. On the contrary, the separation of the state from society is a necessary condition for the reduction of anomie. For Durkheim, the state is certainly not to be a merely ' political' agency; but it fulfils its moral role only insofar as it remains a unity connected with, but distinct from, civil society.[42]

Weber, in contrast to Durkheim, uses the term 'capitalism',[43] but his identification of the basic character of the modern form of society is similarly divergent from that of Marx. In Weber's conception, rational calculation is the primary element in modern capitalistic enterprise, and the rationalisation of social life generally is the most distinctive attribute of modern western culture. The class relation which Marx takes to be the pivot of capitalism is in fact only one element in a much more pervasive rationalisation, which extends the process of the 'expropriation of the worker from his means of production' into most of the institutions in contemporary society. The economic gains which the transition from 'capitalism' to 'socialism' could possibly help to bring about for the working class are only attainable given a further growth of bureaucratisation. The ' parcelling-out' of humanity brought about by the bureaucratised division of labour is a necessary concomitant of this rationalisation of human conduct. The 'disenchantment' of the world which is both prerequisite to, and completed by, the advent of rational capitalism, transforms what previously was only a ' means ' (rational pursuit of gain in a specialised vocation) into the ' end ' of human activity.[44]

In a social world which is organised on the basis of a routinised division of labour, the avenues for the expression of individual autonomy and spontaneity become limited to the interstices of social institutions.[45] Anything else is a flight from the irrational dominance of rationality in the contemporary world. An individual ' who cannot bear the fate of the times ' can seek refuge in established religion, or in new forms of mysticism; but these are nothing more than an escape from the demands of the modern social

---

[42] *PECM*, pp. 55–69.
[43] cf. Parsons: ' Capitalism in recent German literature '.
[44] See Karl Löwith: ' Max Weber und Karl Marx ', *Archiv für Sozialwissenschaft und Sozialpolitik*, vol. 67, 1932, part 1, p. 85.
[45] Thus Weber notes: ' It is not accidental that our greatest art is intimate and not monumental, nor is it accidental that today only within the smallest and most intimate circles, in personal human situations, in *pianissimo*, that something is pulsating that corresponds to the prophetic *pneuma*, which in former times swept through the great communities like a firebrand, welding them together.' *FMW*, p. 155.

order. Weber's own methodological requirements for social science mesh closely with this analysis: the man who faces ' the fate of the times ' is one who possesses ' the trained relentlessness in viewing the realities of life, and the ability to face such realities and to measure up to them inwardly '.[46]

The existence, therefore, of ' contradictions ' within capitalism generates no historical necessity for such contradictions to be resolved. On the contrary, the advance of rationalisation, which certainly creates a hitherto unknown material abundance,[47] inevitably stimulates a further separation between the distinctive values of western civilisation (freedom, creativity, spontaneity) and the realities of the ' iron cage ' in which modern man is confined.

---

[46] *FMW*, pp. 126–7. cf. Löwith: ' The ideal-typical " construction " has as its basis a specifically " disillusioned " humanity . . .', Löwith, part 1, p. 75.

[47] ' Quite correctly did the *Communist Manifesto* emphasise the economic – not the political – *revolutionary* character of the work of the bourgeois capitalist entrepreneur.' *GPS*, p. 448.

Postscript: Marx and modern sociology

There are two polar sorts of orthodoxy in terms of which the relationship between Marx's writings and those of the other two authors discussed at length in this book, is usually presented. The first, adopted by many western sociologists, holds that Marx's works belong to the 'pre-history' of social thought; and that the history of sociology proper only begins with the generation of writers to which Durkheim and Weber belonged.[1] The second is that usually expressed by Marxists, and holds that the works of this subsequent generation of social thinkers represent nothing more than a bourgeois response to Marx – and that, consequently, most of what passes for 'sociology' can be dismissed as simply a latter-day expression of liberal bourgeois ideology. Each of these orthodoxies contains more than a substance of truth; and each is dangerously misleading.

The first standpoint rests upon straightforward acceptance of the stated views of the writers of the generation of Durkheim and Weber, that their own work was 'scientific' in its formulation, and thereby different substantially from the grandiose, 'speculative' constructions of earlier nineteenth-century writers. Those who have accepted this view, by and large, have defined as irrelevant the social and political circumstances in which Durkheim, Weber, and their contemporaries developed their ideas, and have consequently largely ignored the broader *Weltanschauung* which, in each case, was intrinsically bound up with the academic writings of the thinker in question. Latterday Marxists, by contrast, in mounting their critiques of sociology, have concentrated upon the identification of the social context in which Durkheim and Weber wrote, and the political interests which their writings are presumed to mask.[2] The content of their works is thus defined, in the cruder versions of such attacks, as 'fallacious', since they represent a more or less direct partisan defence of liberal bourgeois society in the face of the Marxist challenge.

This latter view is not even consistent with Marx's own epistemology, which avoids such a naïve relativism. Marx accepts, for example, a great deal of bourgeois economic theory as valid for the explanation of capitalist development, while recognising its truth to be only partial and, in some ways, distorted. In Marxist terms, both Durkheim and Weber are committed to a 'bourgeois' political position, but this is hardly an adequate basis for dismis-

---

[1] See Talcott Parsons: 'Some comments on the sociology of Karl Marx', in *Sociological Theory and Modern Society* (New York, 1967), pp. 102–35.

[2] cf. Herbert Marcuse: 'Industrialisierung und Kapitalismus', pp. 161–80.

243

sing the content of their writings as false and thus to be discounted. The fact of the matter is that Weber's own critique of Marxism, departing from premises of neo-Kantian idealism, reaches conclusions which are in some respects closer to the original Marxian dialectic than are the deterministic doctrines of some of Marx's declared followers. It is no accident that the political views of both Durkheim and Weber are difficult to categorise in terms of the traditional division between liberalism and socialism. Weber's methodological position is more ' individualistic ' than that of Durkheim, but both reject – as Marx did before them – the theoretical solipsism of the utilitarians, and with it certain of the suppositions of nineteenth-century political liberalism. As I have tried to show in the foregoing chapters, the social and political background to this can be understood in terms of the development of Britain, France and Germany in the latter part of the century. This stands at the back both of the critique of Marx contained in the works of Durkheim and Weber, as well as of the main differences between the latter two authors, which I have not analysed in this book.

The writings of both Durkheim and Weber have their origin in an attempt to defend – or rather to re-interpret – the claims of political liberalism within the twin pressures of Romantic hypernationalistic conservatism on the one side, and revolutionary socialism on the other. Marx's writings, on the other hand, constitute an analysis and critique of early capitalism. As the source of a political mass movement, however, Marx's work achieved prominence during the period of the consolidation of capitalism in the latter part of the nineteenth century. This occurred within a context which transmitted Marx's original conception into one which appeared much more as the direct *expression* of the main intellectual trends of the nineteenth century than as a critical analysis and an attempt to supersede them. The result is that the Marx's writings share a good deal more in common with those of Durkheim and Weber than was apparent to either of the latter two authors: in perceptible measure, the polemical foils of the three writers were the same, since Marx's works, like those of the two later writers, constitute an attempt to transform and supersede both Romantic conservatism (in German philosophy) and utilitarianism as manifest in classical economics.

This having been said, it must, of course, be recognised that there are irreconcilable differences of theoretical perspective and empirical interpretation between Marx and the other two authors. I have attempted to show that some of the most basic differences centre upon divergent explanations of the consequences of the growth of the division of labour – understood not in sheerly economic terms, but as social differentiation – in modern society. For those, however, who recognise the significance of Marx's contribution to sociology, but who are able to treat Marx not as ' a dead saint ' but rather as a ' living thinker ',[3] there are many significant problems which can be

---

[3] Erich Fromm: ' Foreword ', *EW*, p. i; cf. Iring Fetscher, pp. 9ff.

conveniently posed through the comparative analysis of Marx's writings and those of other social thinkers, considered in terms of their intellectual content.

It is no exaggeration to say that a major process of theoretical re-thinking is taking place today within both Marxism and in academic sociology.[4] In large degree, this has been stimulated by the same circumstance: the apparent 'convergence' in the social structure of capitalist and socialist societies. At the time at which Durkheim and Weber wrote the bulk of their works, there was no extant society which either called itself 'socialist' or claimed to derive its primary inspiration from Marx. However, large-scale working class movements, of a self-professed revolutionary character, existed in both France and Germany, and the occurrence of a socialist revolution was by no means beyond the bounds of possibility. But the October Revolution in Russia took place in a country which was one of the least advanced, in economic terms, in Europe. It was not the clarion call for the revolutionary overthrow of western European capitalism which Marx anticipated when, late in his career, he accepted the possibility that the communal organisation of the *mir* could allow Russia to move directly to socialism. Instead, it was a stimulus to revolutionary change only to countries of comparable or of a lower level of economic development than Russia itself.

If the advanced capitalist countries have changed, it has not been by means of revolution, but by the gradual accumulation of change from within themselves. Today it is no longer possible to deny the profound nature of some of these internal modifications in such things as the increasing intervention of the state in the economy, the growth in the white-collar sector, and the partial replacement of the old propertied upper class by a more amorphous pluralism of elites. But just as the western capitalist countries have changed in considerable degree over the past three or four decades, so have Russia and the European countries which followed it in experiencing socialist revolutions. In these countries, Marx's anticipations of an order in which class domination would be replaced by a rational order 'in which the free development of each is the condition for the free development of all'[5] appears as far from attainment as in the western liberal democracies. Rather, an epistemologically distorted form of Marxism has been employed to legitimate a commitment to industrialisation, in which the 'overtaking' of the economic level of the western countries has become the primary goal.

As a consequence, at least until quite recently, Marxist social thought has utterly failed to come to grips with the problems posed by the trends of development in both capitalist and socialist societies over the past few decades. The Hobson–Lenin theory of 'imperialism' has been used to bolster

---

[4] cf. Norman Birnbaum: 'The crisis in Marxist sociology', in Hans Peter Dreitzel: *Recent Sociology No. 1* (London, 1969), pp. 12–42. See also Jürgen Habermas: *Theorie und Praxis* (Neuwied and Berlin, 1967), pp. 261–335.

[5] *CH*, p. 162.

the assumption that these trends are not to be explained in terms of any important *intrinsic* modifications in the structure of these societies, but derive from the exploitative relationship between them and the ' underdeveloped ' countries. Any theoretical reassessment of the development of the socialist societies themselves has been precluded by the ideological dogma which Marxism has itself become in these countries. The ironical outcome of this is that ' sociology ' in these countries has come to be understood as a peculiarly narrow descriptive discipline. But neither have western sociologists yet come to grips with these problems. In general, those writings which have attempted to comprehend the changes that have occurred in the capitalist societies, have been simply extrapolations of views given in the writings of the generation of social thinkers to which Durkheim and Weber belonged. The most important emphasis, however, has been placed upon the attempt to formulate a body of ahistorical ' general theory ', a concern which consciously directs attention away from problems of social change or development.[6] Until recently, as in Marxist social thought, where the study of development has been undertaken, interest has been concentrated upon the non-industrial countries.

The impact of western technology and culture upon the non-industrialised countries is obviously an area of theory and research which is of enormous significance for sociology. But the framework within which this is approached normally betrays an implicit assumption that the main characteristics of the ' developed societies ' are *known*, and that the question is simply how far the societies of the ' third world ' will successfully match this model at some time in the future. The way in which the term ' industrial society ', or more recently ' post-industrial society ', has slipped into almost universal usage in sociology to denote both societies which are nominally ' capitalist ' and those which are socialist ', signifies the assumptions which underlie this standpoint. But the various debates which have recently arisen concerning the question of the ' convergence ' of capitalist and socialist societies,[7] and of the supposed dissolution of class relationships in the form in which these are traditionally conceived,[8] are symptomatic of a resurgence of interest in the analysis of the trends of development within the ' advanced ' societies.

In important respects, this represents a return to the issues which were of over-riding significance in the writings of the three authors discussed in this book. Their works must still form the main point of departure if this is to effect an important reorientation of social theory. It may be granted that Marx's model of capitalism, in its entirety, ' is inappropriate to the post-

---

[6] See, above all, Talcott Parsons: *The Social System* (London, 1951).

[7] See John H. Goldthorpe: ' Social stratification in industrial society ', in Paul Halmos: *The Development of Industrial Society*, Sociological Review Monograph, no. 8, 1964, pp. 97–122.

[8] Ralf Dahrendorf: *Class and Class Conflict in Industrial Society*; Norman Birnbaum: *The Crisis of Industrial Society* (New York, 1969).

bourgeois industrial society in which we live. . . '.[9] It does not follow from this that some of the major elements of Marx's analysis of bourgeois society are not of considerable significance today. This does not imply the reiteration of the familiar theme that Marx accurately ' predicted ' some of the important characteristics of contemporary societies, or that others of his supposed ' predictions ' have subsequently been falsified. It is to hold that Marx's analysis poses issues which must still be regarded as *problematic* for modern sociology: exactly the same is true of the writings of Durkheim and Weber. To argue that it must be one of the main tasks of modern sociology to revert to some of the concerns which occupied its founders is not to propose a step which is wholly regressive: paradoxically, in taking up again the problems with which they were primarily concerned, we may hope ultimately to liberate ourselves from our present heavy dependence on the ideas which they formulated.

---

[9] George Lichtheim: ' On the interpretation of Marx's thought ', in Lobkowicz, p. 4.

Bibliography of works cited in text

Marx and Engels : original works

Marx and Engels: *Werke*. Vols. 1–41, plus supplementary volumes. Berlin, 1956–67.

Marx and Engels: *Historische-kritische Gesamtausgabe*. Vols. 1–11. Frankfurt–Berlin, 1929–31.

Marx: *Grundrisse der Kritik der politischen Ökonomie*, Berlin, 1953.

T. B. Bottomore: *Karl Marx, Early Writings*. New York, 1964.

Loyd D. Easton and Kurt H. Guddat: *Writings of the Young Marx on Philosophy and Society*. New York, 1967.

Marx and Engels: *Selected Works*. Vols. 1–2. Moscow, 1958.

    Capital. Vols. 1–3. Vol. 1, London, 1970 ; vol. 2, Moscow, 1957 ; vol. 3, Moscow, 1962.

    The German Ideology. London, 1965.

    The Communist Manifesto. New York, 1967 (Laski's edition).

    The Holy Family, or Critique of Critical Critique. Moscow, 1956.

    Selected Correspondence. London, 1934.

    On Religion. Moscow, 1957.

T. B. Bottomore and Maximilien Rubel: Karl Marx: *Selected Writings in Sociology and Social Philosophy*. London, 1963.

Marx: *Pre-Capitalist Economic Formations*. London, 1964.

Marx: *The American Journalism of Marx and Engels*. New York, 1966.

Marx: *Articles on India*. Bombay, 1951.

Marx: *Marx on China, 1853–60*. London, 1951.

Marx: *A Contribution to the Critique of Political Economy*. Chicago, 1904.

Marx: *The Poverty of Philosophy*. London, n.d.

Marx: *Theories of Surplus Value* (ed. G. A. Bonner and E. Burns). London, 1951.

Marx: *Theories of Surplus Value*. Vols. 1–2. London, 1964 & 1969.

Engels: *Anti-Dühring*. Moscow, 1954.

Engels: *The Dialectics of Nature*. Moscow, 1954.

Engels: *The Condition of the Working Class in England in 1844*. Oxford, 1968.

Engels: *Germany : Revolution and Counterrevolution*. London, 1933.

Durkheim : original works

The Division of Labour in Society. London, 1964.

De la division de la travail social. Paris, 1960.

The Elementary Forms of the Religious Life. New York, 1965.

Les formes élémentaires de la vie religieuse. Paris, 1960.

Professional Ethics and Civic Morals. London, 1957.

Leçons de sociologie. Paris, 1950.

The Rules of Sociological Method. London, 1964.

Les règles de la méthode sociologique. Paris, 1950.

Socialism. New York, 1962.

Le socialisme. Paris, 1928.

Suicide, a Study in Sociology. London, 1952.

Le suicide, étude de sociologie. Paris, 1960.

(with E. Denis): *Qui a voulu la guerre ?* Paris, 1915.
' *L'Allemagne au-dessus de tout* '. Paris, 1915.
L'évolution pédagogique en France. Paris, 1969.
Sociology and Philosophy. London, 1965.
(with M. Mauss): *Primitive Classification.* London, 1963.
Montesquieu and Rousseau. Ann Arbor, 1965.
Moral Education. London, New York, 1961.
L'éducation morale. Paris, 1925.
Education and Sociology. Glencoe, 1956.
Pragmatisme et sociologie. Paris, 1955.
Journal Sociologique. Paris, 1969.
Review of Schäffle: *Bau und Leben des socialen Körpers, Revue philosophique,*
vol. 19, 1885, pp. 84–101.
Review of Gumplowicz: *Grundriss der Soziologie, Revue philosophique,* vol. 20,
1885, pp. 627–34.
' Les études de science sociale ', *Revue philosophique,* vol. 22, 1886, pp. 61–80.
Review of Guyau: *L'irréligion de l'avenir, Revue philosophique,* vol. 23, 1887,
pp. 299–311.
' La science positive de la morale en Allemagne ', *Revue philosophique,* vol. 24,
1887, pp. 33–58 ; 113–42 ; and 275–84.
' Le programme économique de M. Schäffle ', *Revue d'économie politique,* vol. 2,
1888, pp. 3–7.
' Suicide et natalité, étude de statistique morale ', *Revue philosophique,* vol. 26,
1888, pp. 446–63.
Review of Tönnies: *Gemeinschaft und Gesellschaft, Revue philosophique,* vol.
27, 1889, pp. 416–22.
'L'enseignement philosophique et l'agrégation de philosophie ', *Revue philoso-
phique,* vol. 39, 1895, pp. 121–47.
Review of Labriola: *Essais sur la conception matérialiste de l'histoire, Revue
philosophique,* vol. 44, 1897, pp. 645–51.
Review of Richard: *Le socialisme et la science sociale, Revue philosophique,* vol.
44, 1897, pp. 200–5.
' L'individualisme et les intellectuels ', *Revue bleue,* vol. 10, 1898, pp. 7–13.
' Deux lois de l'évolution pénale ', *Année sociologique,* vol. 4, 1899–1900, pp.
65–95.
' La sociologie en France au XIXe siècle ', *Revue bleue,* vol. 13, 1900, part 1,
pp. 609–13, part 2, pp. 647–52.
' Sur le totémisme ', *Année sociologique,* vol. 5, 1900–1, pp. 82–121.
Review of Merlino: *Formes et essence du socialisme. Revue philosophique,* vol.
48, 1889, pp. 433–9.
Debate with Lagardelle, *Libres entretiens,* 1905, pp. 425–34.
Review of works by Fouillé, Belot and Landry, *Année sociologique,* vol. 10,
1905–6, pp. 352–69.
Review of Deploige: *Le conflit de la morale et de la sociologie, Année Socio-
logique,* vol. 12, 1909–12, pp. 326–8.
' La famille conjugale ', *Revue philosophique,* vol. 91, 1921, pp. 1–14.

Weber : original works
Economy and Society. New York, 1968.
Wirtschaft und Gesellschaft. Tübingen, 1956.
H. H. Gerth and C. Wright Mills: *From Max Weber : Essays in Sociology.* New
York, 1958.

Gesammelte Aufsätze zur Religionssoziologie. Vols. 1–3, Tübingen, 1920-1.
Gesammelte Aufsätze zur Soziologie und Sozialpolitik. Tübingen, 1924.
Gesammelte Aufsätze zur Wissenschaftslehre. Tübingen, 1968.
Gesammelte politische Schriften. Tübingen, 1958.
The Methodology of the Social Sciences. Glencoe, 1949.
The Protestant Ethic and the Spirit of Capitalism. New York, 1958.
The Religion of China. London, 1964.
The Religion of India. Glencoe, 1958.
Gesammelte Aufsätze zur Sozial – und Wirtschaftsgeschichte. Tübingen, 1924.
Jugendbriefe. Tübingen, n.d.
Die römische Agrargeschichte in ihrer Bedeutung für des Staats – und Privatrecht. Stuttgart, 1891.
Die Verhältnisse der Landarbeiter im ostelbischen Deutschland. Leipzig, 1892.
General Economic History. New York, 1961.
' Antikritisches zum " Geist des Kapitalismus " ', *Archiv für Sozialwissenschaft und Sozialpolitik,* vol. 30, 1910, pp. 176–202.
' Antikritisches Schlusswort zum " Geist des Kapitalismus " ', *Archiv für Sozialwissenschaft und Sozialpolitik,* vol. 31, 1910, pp. 554–99.

Secondary works

H. B. Acton: *The Illusion of the Epoch.* London, 1955.
Lord Acton: *Lectures on Modern History.* London, 1960.
Guy Aimard: *Durkheim et la science économique.* Paris, 1962.
Martin Albrow: *Bureaucracy.* London, 1970.
Erik Allardt: ' Emile Durkheim: sein Beitrag zur politischen Soziologie ', *Kölner Zeitschrift für Soziologie und Sozialpsychologie,* vol. 20, 1968, pp. 1–16.
Harry Alpert: *Emile Durkheim and his Sociology.* New York, 1939.
Louis Althusser: *For Marx.* London, 1969.
Louis Althusser *et al.: Lire le Capital.* Paris, 1967.
Carlo Antoni: *From History to Sociology.* London, 1962.
Raymond Aron: *Main Currents in Sociological Thought.* Vols. 1 & 2. London, 1968 & 1967.
Shlomo Avineri: *The Social and Political Thought of Karl Marx.* Cambridge, 1968.
J. A. Barnes: ' Durkheim's *Division of Labour in Society* ', *Man* (New series), vol. 1, 1966, pp. 158–75.
Eduard Baumgarten: *Max Weber: Werk und Person.* Tübingen, 1964.
Georg von Below: *Der deutsche Staat des Mittelalters.* Leipzig, 1925.
Reinhard Bendix: *Max Weber, an Intellectual Portrait.* London, 1966.
' Social stratification and the political community ', *Archives européennes de sociologie,* vol. 1, 1960, pp. 181–210.
Norman Birnbaum: *The Crisis of Industrial Society.* New York, 1969.
' Conflicting interpretations of the rise of capitalism: Marx and Weber ', *British Journal of Sociology,* vol. 4, 1953, pp. 125–41.
H. Bollnow: ' Engels Auffassung von Revolution und Entwicklung in seinen " Grundsätzen des Kommunismus " (1847) ', *Marxismusstudien,* vol. 1, 1954, pp. 77–144.
Roger Caillois: *Man, Play and Games.* London, 1962.
A. Cornu: *Karl Marx et Friedrich Engels.* Vols. 1–3. Paris, 1955.
Ralf Dahrendorf: *Class and Class Conflict in Industrial Society.* Stanford, 1965.
Society and Democracy in Germany. London, 1968.

Georges Davy: 'Emile Durkheim', *Revue française de sociologie*, vol. 1, 1960, pp. 3–24.
'Emile Durkheim', *Revue de métaphysique et de morale*, vol. 26, 1919, pp. 181–98.

Phyllis Deane and W. A. Cole: *British Economic Growth*. Cambridge, 1969.

Simon Deploige: *The Conflict between Ethics and Sociology*. St Louis, 1938.

Maurice Dobb: *Studies in the Development of Capitalism*. London, 1963.

Hans Peter Dreitzel: *Recent Sociology No. 1*. London, 1969.

Jean Duvignaud: *Durkheim, sa vie, son oeuvre*. Paris, 1965.

Iring Fetscher: *Karl Marx und der Marxismus*. Munich, 1967.

Louis Feuer: 'What is alienation? The career of a concept'. *New Politics*, 1962, pp. 116–34.

Ludwig Feuerbach: *The Essence of Christianity*. New York, 1957.
Sämmtliche Werke. Vols. 1–10, 1903–11.

Julien Freund: *The Sociology of Max Weber*. London, 1968.

Georges Friedmann: *The Anatomy of Work*. London, 1961.

Walter Gagel: *Die Wahlrechtsfrage in der Geschichte der deutschen liberalen Parteien*. Düsseldorf, 1958.

Charles Elmer Gehlke: *Emile Durkheim's Contributions to Sociological Theory*. New York, 1915.

Anthony Giddens: 'A typology of suicide', *Archives européennes de sociologie*, vol. 7, 1966, pp. 276–95.
' " Power " in the recent writings of Talcott Parsons', *Sociology*, vol. 2, 1968, pp. 268–70.
'Durkheim as a review critic', *Sociological Review*, vol. 18, 1970, pp. 171–96.
'Marx, Weber, and the development of capitalism', *Sociology*, vol. 4, 1970, pp. 289–310.
Politics and sociology in the thought of Max Weber. (Forthcoming).
'The suicide problem in French sociology', *British Journal of Sociology*, vol. 16, 1965, pp. 3–18.

John H. Goldthorpe: 'Social stratification in industrial society', Paul Halmos: *The Development of Industrial Society*. Sociological Review Monograph, No. 8, 1964, pp. 97–122.

Fred M. Gottheil: *Marx's Economic Predictions*. Evanston, 1966.

Georges Gurvitch: *La vocation actuelle de la sociologie*. Paris, 1950.

Georges Gurvitch and Wilbert E. Moore: *Twentieth Century Sociology*. New York, 1945.

Jürgen Habermas: *Theorie und Praxis*. Neuwied and Berlin, 1967.

R. M. Hartwell: *The Causes of the Industrial Revolution in England*. London, 1967.

J. E. S. Hayward: 'Solidarist syndicalism: Durkheim and Duguit', *Sociological Review*, vol. 8, 1960, parts 1 & 2, pp. 17–36 & 185–202.

G. W. F. Hegel: *Philosophy of Right*. London, 1967.

Donald Hodges: 'The "intermediate classes" in Marxian theory', *Social Research*, vol. 28, 1961, pp. 241–52.

John Horton: 'The de-humanisation of anomie and alienation', *British Journal of Sociology*, vol. 15, 1964, pp. 283–300.

Henri Hubert and Marcel Mauss: 'Théorie générale de la magie', *Année Sociologique*, vol. 7, 1902–3, pp. 1–146.

H. Stuart Hughes: *Consciousness and Society*. New York, 1958.

Jean Hyppolite: *Etudes sur Marx et Hegel*. Paris, 1955.

Barclay Johnson: ' Durkheim's one cause of suicide', *American Sociological Review*, vol. 30, 1965, pp. 875–86.

Z. A. Jordan: *The Evolution of Dialectical Materialism*. London, 1967.

Eugene Kamenka: *The Philosophy of Ludwig Feuerbach*. London, 1970.

Karl Kautsky: *Die Agrarfrage*. Stuttgart, 1899.
Der Ursprung des Christentums. Stuttgart, 1908.

Helmut Klages: *Technischer Humanismus*. Stuttgart, 1964.

E. Jürgen Kocka: ' Karl Marx und Max Weber. Ein methodologischer Vergleich', *Zeitschrift für die gesamte Staatswissenschaft*, vol. 122, 1966, pp. 328–57.

René König and Johannes Winckelmann: *Max Weber zum Gedächtnis*. Cologne and Opladen, 1963.

Karl Korsch: *Marxismus und Philosophie*. Leipzig, 1930.

Leopold Labedz: *Revisionism*. London, 1963.

Antonio Labriola: *Socialism and Philosophy*. Chicago, 1918.

Roger Lacombe: *La méthode sociologique de Durkheim*. Paris, 1926.

David S. Landes: *The Unbound Prometheus*. Cambridge, 1969.

V. I. Lenin: *Selected Works*. London, 1969.

George Lichtheim: ' Marx and the " Asiatic mode of production " ', *St Antony's Papers*, No. 14, 1963, pp. 86–112.
Marxism, an Historical and Critical Study. London, 1964.
Marxism in Modern France. New York, 1966.

Dieter Lindenlaub: *Richtungskämpfe im Verein für Sozialpolitik*. Wiesbaden, 1967.

Nicholas Lobkowicz: *Marx and the Western World*. Notre Dame, 1967.

Karl Löwith: ' Max Weber und Karl Marx ', *Archiv für Sozialwissenschaft und Sozialpolitik*. Vol. 67, 1932, part 1, pp. 53–99 and part 2, pp. 175–214.

Georg Lukács: *Der junge Hegel*. Zurich and Vienna, 1948.
Geschichte und Klassenbewusstein. Berlin, 1932.
Die Zerstörung der Vernunft. Berlin, 1955.

Steven Lukes: ' Alienation and anomie ', in Peter Laslett and W. G. Runciman: *Philosophy, Politics and Society*. Oxford, 1967, pp. 134–56.

Ernest Mandel: *Marxist Economic Theory*. Vols. 1 & 2. London, 1968.

Marcel Mauss: ' Essai sur les variations saisonnières des sociétés eskimos ', *Année sociologique*, vol. 9, 1904–5, pp. 39–130.

David McLellan: *Marx Before Marxism*. London, 1970.
The Young Hegelians and Karl Marx. London, 1969.

C. B. Macpherson: *The Political Theory of Possessive Individualism*. London, 1962.

Ronald Meek: *Studies in the Labour Theory of Value*. London, 1956.

Franz Mehring: *Karl Marx*, Ann Arbor, 1962.

István Mészáros: *Marx's Theory of Alienation*. London, 1970.

Alfred G. Meyer: *Marxism, the Unity of Theory and Practice*. Ann Arbor, 1963.

Arthur Mitzman: *The Iron Cage : An Historical Interpretation of Max Weber*. New York, 1970.

Wolfgang J. Mommsen: *Max Weber und die deutsche Politik, 1890–1920*. Tübingen, 1959.

Barrington Moore: *Social Origins of Dictatorship and Democracy*. London, 1969.

Robert A. Nisbet: *Emile Durkheim*. Englewood Cliffs, 1965.
The Sociological Tradition. London, 1967.

Stanislaw Ossowski: *Class and Class Structure in the Social Consciousness*. London, 1963.

Melchior Palyi: *Erinnerungsgabe für Max Weber.* Munich and Leipzig, 1923.

Talcott Parsons: 'Capitalism in recent German literature: Sombart and Weber ', *Journal of Political Economy*, vol. 36, 1928, pp. 641–61.

Sociological Theory and Modern Society. New York, 1967.

The Social System. London, 1951.

The Structure of Social Action. Glencoe, 1949.

Alessandro Pizzorno: 'Lecture actuelle de Durkheim ', *Archives européennes de sociologie*, vol. 4, 1963, pp. 1–36.

John Plamenatz: *Man and Society.* Vols. 1 & 2. London, 1968.

Heinrich Popitz: *Der entfremdete Mensch.* Frankfurt, 1967.

Nicos Ar. Poulantzas: *Nature des choses et du droit.* Paris, 1965.

J. A. Prades: *La sociologie de la religion chez Max Weber.* Louvain, 1969.

Thilo Ramm: 'Die künftige Gesellschaftsordnung nach der Theorie von Marx und Engels ', *Marxismusstudien*, vol. 2, 1957, pp. 77–179.

Hanns Günther Reissner: *Eduard Gans.* Tübingen, 1965.

Reminiscences of Marx and Engels. Moscow, n.d.

Joan Robinson: *An Essay on Marxian Economics.* London, 1966.

Günther Roth: *The Social Democrats in Imperial Germany.* Englewood Cliffs, 1963.

'Das historische Verhältnis der Weberschen Soziologie zum Marxismus ', *Kölner Zeitschrift für Soziologie und Sozialpsychologie*, Vol. 20, 1968, pp. 429–447.

Maximilien Rubel: 'Premiers contacts des sociologues du XIXe siècle avec la pensée de Marx ', *Cahiers internationaux de sociologie*, vol. 31, 1961, pp. 175–84.

W. G. Runciman: 'The sociological explanation of " religious " beliefs ', *Archives européennes de sociologie*, vol. 10, 1969, pp. 149–191.

Alexander von Schelting: *Max Webers Wissenschaftslehre.* Tübingen, 1934.

F. von Schiller: *On the Aesthetic Education of Man.* Oxford, 1967.

Alfred Schmidt: *Der Begriff der Natur in der Lehre von Marx.* Frankfurt, 1962.

Gustav Schmidt: *Deutscher Historismus und der Übergang zur parlamentarischen Demokratie.* Lübeck and Hamburg, 1964.

Joseph A. Schumpeter: *Capitalism, Socialism and Democracy.* New York, 1962.

Alfred Schutz: *The Phenomenology of the Social World.* Evanston, 1967.

Georg Simmel: *Philosophie des Geldes.* Leipzig, 1900.

Georges Sorel: 'Les théories de M. Durkheim ', *Le devenir social*, vol. 1, pp. 1–26 & 148–80.

Leo Strauss: *Natural Right and History*, Chicago, 1953.

Paul Sweezy: *The Transition from Feudalism to Capitalism.* London, 1954.

The Theory of Capitalist Development. New York, 1954.

Böhm-Bawerk's Criticism of Marx. New York, 1949.

F. Tenbruck: 'Die Genesis der Methodologie Max Webers ', *Kölner Zeitschrift für Soziologie und Sozialpsychologie*, vol. 11, 1959, pp. 573–630.

Edward A. Tiryakian: 'A problem for the sociology of knowledge ', *Archives européennes de sociologie*, vol. 7, 1966, pp. 330–6.

Robert C. Tucker: *Philosophy and Myth in Karl Marx.* Cambridge, 1965.

Verhandlungen des 15. deutschen Soziologentages: Max Weber und die Soziologie heute, Tübingen, 1965.

Marianne Weber: *Max Weber: ein Lebensbild.* Heidelberg, 1950.

Johannes Winckelmann: 'Max Webers Opus Posthumum ', *Zeitschrift für die gesamten Staatswissenschaften*, vol. 105, 1949, pp. 368–97.

Karl A. Wittfogel: *Oriental Despotism*. New Haven, 1957.

Kurt H. Wolff: *Emile Durkheim et al., Essays on Sociology and Philosophy*. New York, 1964.

Murray Wolfson: *A Reappraisal of Marxian Economics*. New York, 1964.

Sheldon S. Wolin: *Politics and Vision*. Boston, 1960.

P. M. Worsley: ' Emile Durkheim's theory of knowledge ', *Sociological Review*, vol. 4, 1956, pp. 47–62.

Index